Sylvia Scribner's research and theory have been monumental in forming the emergent field of cultural psychology. Her studies of reasoning and thinking in their cultural and activity contexts added new concepts, methods, and findings to what many are now viewing as a distinctive branch of psychological studies. She was among the first to combine ethnographic studies with experimental studies in order to determine relationships among indigenous literacy and logical activities and their cognitive outcomes.

Mind and Social Practice brings together published and unpublished work from Sylvia Scribner's productive and wide-ranging career. The book is arranged chronologically and includes five section introductions by the editors, placing Scribner's work in the context of her life, her commitments, and the political and intellectual events of the times. Her later, more theoretically rich writing is enhanced by an appreciation of her earlier work.

D1707094

Mind and social practice

Mind and social practice

Selected writings of Sylvia Scribner

Edited by

ETHEL TOBACH
American Museum of Natural History

RACHEL JOFFE FALMAGNE
Clark University

MARY B. PARLEE
Massachusetts Institute of Technology

LAURA M. W. MARTIN
Arizona Museum of Science and Technology

AGGIE SCRIBNER KAPELMAN
National Labor Relations Board

CAMBRIDGE
UNIVERSITY PRESS

PUBLISHED BY THE PRESS SYNDICATE OF THE UNIVERSITY OF CAMBRIDGE
The Pitt Building, Trumpington Street, Cambridge CB2 1RP, United Kingdom

CAMBRIGE UNIVERSITY PRESS
The Edinburgh Building, Cambridge CB2 2RU, United Kingdom
40 West 20th Street, New York, NY 10011-3211, USA
10 Stamford Road, Oakleigh, Melbourne 3166, Australia

First published 1997

Printed in the United States of America

Typeset in Ehrhardt

*A catalog record for this book is available from
the British Library*

Library of Congress Cataloguing-in-Publication Data
Scribner, Sylvia, 1925–
Mind and social practice : selected writings of Sylvia Scribner /
edited by Ethel Tobach . . . [et al.].
p.   cm. — (Learning in doing)
Includes bibliographical references and indexes
ISBN 0 521 46203 7 hardback
ISBN 0 521 46767 5 paperback
1. Cognition and culture.   2. Thought and thinking—Social
aspects.   I. Tobach, Ethel, 1921–   .   II. Title.   III. Series.
BF109.S29A25   1996
150—DC20   96-12328
                                                   CIP

ISBN 0 521 46203 7 hardback
ISBN 0 521 46767 5 paperback

Contents

Contents

Series foreword

This series for Cambridge University Press is becoming widely known as an international forum for studies of situated learning and cognition.

Innovative contributions are being made by anthropology, by cognitive, developmental, and cultural psychology, by computer science, by education, and by social theory. These contributions are providing the basis for new ways of understanding the social, historical, and contextual nature of the learning, thinking, and practice emerging from human activity. The empirical settings of these research inquiries range from the classroom, to the workplace, to the high technology office, to learning in the streets and in other communities of practice.

The situated nature of learning and remembering through activity is a central fact. It may appear obvious that human minds develop in social situations, and that they come to appropriate the tools that culture provides to support and extend their sphere of activity and communicative competencies. But cognitive theories of knowledge representation and learning alone have not provided sufficient insight into these relationships.

This series was born of the conviction that new and exciting interdisciplinary syntheses are under way, as scholars and practitioners from diverse fields seek to develop theory and empirical investigations adequate for characterizing the complex relations of social and mental life, and for understanding successful learning wherever it occurs. The series invites contributions that advance our understanding of these seminal issues.

Roy Pea
John Seely Brown

Preface

When Sylvia Scribner died in July 1991, suddenly and much too soon, we began almost immediately to plan a volume of her collected papers. We wanted her work, in her own voice, to be readily accessible to students and colleagues, and we wanted the volume as a whole to reflect the broad range of her interests. Papers written by colleagues in tribute to Sylvia Scribner and her work were published last year by Cambridge University Press in a volume entitled *Socio-cultural Psychology: The Practice of Doing and Knowing* and edited by L. W. Martin, Katherine Nelson, and Ethel Tobach.

Because of the richness of Sylvia Scribner's thinking and the breadth of her concerns, a collection of her papers could have been selected and organized in a number of ways. We decided to present her scientific writings in the context of her life, the time in which she lived, and her political and moral commitments. These elements are of course intertwined for all scientists. Unlike most of us, however, and from the beginning of her work as a psychologist, Sylvia theorized these connections explicitly as part of doing her science, and she enacted her societal concerns concretely, daily. We hope this volume will convey the unity of Sylvia Scribner's life and work as a scientist, teacher, colleague, union employee, poet, activist for justice and peace, spouse, mother, friend — a woman with a sense of humor and an appreciation for beautiful things.

The papers are arranged chronologically within sections organized around certain themes. The sections themselves are arranged roughly in chronological order of the emergence of these themes as a major focus in Sylvia's work, though we hope their continuity and development throughout Sylvia's life will be evident. In our brief introductions to the sections we identify the thematic focus and say something of its relationship to Sylvia's work and life during that period. Sylvia's style was to work collaboratively with students and colleagues. At the end of each section we acknowledge this aspect of her productivity by listing selected coauthored works relevant to the theme of the section. An extensive bibliography of Sylvia's writings is given at the end of this volume.

In the general introduction we convey how Sylvia's work, politics, and family were interconnected throughout her life. The editors were each part of Sylvia Scribner's scientific, political, and personal worlds (a unique blend in each case) at different phases of her adult life. In the course of editing this collection we all contributed our knowledge of and perspective on Sylvia's life and work and collaborated on the editorial essays. Mary Parlee had final responsibility for the general introduction, Rachel Joffe Falmagne and Ethel Tobach for the introductions to Parts 1–4, and Rachel Falmagne, Laura Martin, and Ethel Tobach for the introduction to Part 5. Aggie Scribner Kapelman, Sylvia and David Scribner's daughter, researched and wrote the biography that expands and enriches the general introduction by telling Sylvia's life story from a different perspective with different emphases.

Julia Hough of Cambridge University Press supported this project enthusiastically from the beginning. Barbara Rogoff kindly agreed to contribute the foreword. The cataloguing of Sylvia Scribner's papers, correspondence, and library was begun by Emily Filardo and continued by Malka Grinkorn. Malka Grinkorn also helped us assemble Sylvia's published and unpublished papers, and made it possible in many ways for this volume to be produced and for the materials to be prepared for archival use. Sylvia Scribner's published and unpublished papers will be deposited in the Archives of the History of American Psychology at the University of Akron, Akron, Ohio.

Foreword

Barbara Rogoff

Watch the WRIGGLE
Of my toes
In the air.

My head is on the ground
And I don't care.
Some people think it neat
To always have their feet

Planted firma
on the terra
where it is

A dull biz.

If pie is in the sky
Treading dirt
Won't bring it nigh.

Sylvia Scribner

Sylvia Scribner was a practical theorist, with her theoretical contributions well grounded and her practical aspirations sky high. Her work across the decades provides a continuing legacy of inspiration. This volume provides a collection of her ideas in written form that gives those of us who knew and worked with Sylvia a chance to revisit her ideas and those who never knew her to explore her line of thought. It provides us with a chance to examine the development of Sylvia's ideas historically, with access to her older and newer classic work (much of it never published before), in Sylvia's words and in the words of her editors and biographers.

In this volume, we see Sylvia as an individual – a poet, a scholar, a woman, a colleague, and a mother, committed to connecting broad ideas with practical social action – and as a participant in and contributor to societal institutions. Institutional forces that shaped her life include the constraints on the roles of women in academia and factories and the societal issues of her times, including civil rights, the interpretation of intelligence tests, and the role of schooling in the social order; she contributed to shaping institutions through her social action, institutional leadership, and clear-minded analyses of the relation of individual and society.

In the sociohistorical approach in which Sylvia has been a key pioneer, it is clear that our work, the institutions and times in which we work, and the goals toward which we work all fit together. Comprising the grand enterprise that connects and extends beyond particular individuals is the rich detail of the dynamics and feeling of personal relationships as well as the enduring value of individual contributions. The relations of individual and society, of particulars and universals, were central to Sylvia's work, and in this volume we have the opportunity to learn from her ideas as well as to learn about how Sylvia as a person contributed to and was shaped by the institutions and societies in which she participated.

I am honored to have the opportunity to provide the foreword to this collection, both because of my gratitude to Sylvia as a person and because of the importance of her ideas and their contextualization by the editors in this volume. Sylvia's editors provide an extremely valuable account of the background and events surrounding Sylvia's written work, including biographical information far more complete than that with which I was familiar. My contact with Sylvia began two decades ago; I had a partial understanding of the course of her ideas and work before that time, and was glad to have the chance in reading preliminary sections of this volume to learn about the larger trajectory. My contact with Sylvia, though she died in 1991, continues in the present, as her ideas continue to provide me with inspiration.

I met Sylvia about 1975, on a visit to her and Mike Cole at Rockefeller. I was a doctoral student at Harvard, working on a dissertation that was greatly influenced by their work in the book *Culture and Thought* (Cole & Scribner, 1974) and in the *Science* article on formal and informal education (Scribner & Cole, 1973). During my first visit and subsequent correspondence, Sylvia became an informal but essential dissertation advisor. She provided me with a depth of understanding of important concepts of activity theory and compatible research methods, as well as with her warmth and character as a person. Sylvia did not mince words in giving suggestions for my research, and important suggestions they were, offered straightforwardly and generously. In subsequent years, I have continued to gain from Sylvia's intellectual acumen, both in reading her written work and in formal and informal discussion. I have learned from her clarity of thought, her commitment to social action, and her wit. My work continued to be inspired by her example and her ideas.

Sylvia's work on cross-cultural use of logic, classification, and memory was influential in bringing attention to the practical direction of thinking, especially in her work distinguishing empiric and theoretic uses of logic. In everyday circumstances, she noted the hypothetical reasoning of nonliterate Liberian people who declined to consider the hypothetical connections between premises in logical syllogisms. Regarding logical syllogisms, Sylvia wrote:

> This will be a miracle if it works.
> It works.
> It is a miracle.
>
> It is also a syllogism
> proving syllogisms
> are miracles.

The cross-cultural work on cognition was transformed with the collaborative translation of Vygotsky's *Mind in Society* in 1978. The groundbreaking research on the role of literacy in cognition (Scribner & Cole, 1981) has reoriented the views of the field on how particular practices (such as Vai letter-writing, Q'uranic literacy, and school-based literate tasks) relate to the development of specific cognitive skills – a major shift from the field's earlier assumption that literacy would provide a general transformation in thinking.

Sylvia's subsequent work involved a continued, close examination of the relation between individual thinking and its use in institutions such as the workplace and the school. She focused on locating mathematical activities in work and cognitive tests as particular formats of knowledge and thought embedded in their respective institutional histories. In explicating activity theory and social practice and in articulating concepts of development and history in sociocultural thinking, Sylvia exemplified the advances possible in taking a transdisciplinary perspective.

Sylvia developed the notion of the mutually constituting processes of societal institutions and individual action, developing over historical and personal time. Her research showed a commitment to using methods as a tool carefully designed to address specific questions in order to elucidate individual and institutional/cultural change. Her studies employed ethnographic analyses of naturally existing cognitive activity as people engaged in social practices, combined with experimental cognitive tasks designed according to analyses of the social practices.

She emphasized a functional approach to the study of cognition as people engaged in social practices in the institutions of their culture. She drew attention to the notion that people's cognitive strategies are purposive, flexible, and minimize the effort needed to accomplish a task, examining this idea in her observations of dairy workers as they assembled orders. Sylvia integrated the work of the head and of the hands in the cognitive processes of purposive activities. Her work reveals a deep understanding and respect for the complex mental processes for action that workers carry out, which may or may not be facilitated by the formalisms taught in school or by those introduced by management to order the workers' process. Sylvia's colleagues and students extend her ideas and work in her absence.

The commitment of Sylvia's colleagues and students to the continuation of this line of thinking and work was made concrete by the establishment of the Sylvia Scribner Award from the American Educational Research Association. I was deeply honored to receive the first Scribner Award; Jean Lave received the second.

Sylvia's work is both classic and ahead of our times. In the years preceding her death, I urged Sylvia to put her ideas together in a book to make them more accessible. Some of her most important ideas were in unpublished and difficult-to-access papers; she was the sort of author who did not repeat her ideas in several outlets. Unfortunately, Sylvia's own life span did not allow her to pull the work together in a book herself. So it is fortunate for all of us that her colleagues and daughter have taken on the job.

Shortly before Sylvia died, she asked me if I would think about illustrating some of her poems. (She knew that I was in the midst of illustrating a children's book written by Sheila Cole, Mike's wife.) A sheaf of poems came to me in the mail about the time that Sylvia died. I have quoted several of them directly, in this foreword.

In preparing my contribution, I have struggled to find a way to characterize Sylvia as a person, a scholar, and a colleague. I have listened to her other colleagues for their efforts to do the same, and have noted that for each of us there is a somewhat (or even quite) different characterization. My attempt to sum it up in a few words was clarified by referring to the poems she sent. In reading them I was struck by how they are whimsical with a punch. I think that characterization applies to other aspects of Sylvia's life and work as well. Consider Sylvia's poem on the human cognitive process of writing and responding to poetry.

Please Try AI

Put it in your APPLE
See what it can do.
Will it know
The rhyme I want
Is through
Or blue?
(Not gu-ru
Ne-ver new)
Will it read the metre
Carry on the beat?
Scan a set
of standing lines
Into running feet?

Will it glimpse
The image
Be-neath the metaphor?
And seeing
Fall to weeping
As it
Never wept
Before?

When I tried to think about how I might illustrate Sylvia's poems, I was stumped, because they are cerebral wit and commentary more than visual story lines. Accompanying the words of her poems, as I read them, is Sylvia's laughter framing her strength of commitment. The best illustration I can think of for Sylvia's poetry, as well as her scholarly wit and wisdom, is this view of Sylvia herself.

A daughter's perspective

Aggie Scribner Kapelman

I'm feeling awe
  for Ma and Paw.

How nice they were
To have a Her
They knew a She
Was what to be.

Something good
Through womanhood.

How truly noble
Great and wise
That they saw life
Through my clear eyes.[1]

Sylvia Scribner's soul was a political and philosophical blend. She uniquely understood how seemingly minute actions of human behavior could become critical components of the whole. This was evident throughout her professional life as union organizer, researcher, and scientist.

Sylvia Cohen was born in New Bedford, Massachusetts, in 1923 and she was unique from the start. In a town that was steeped in the American legends of sea captains and whaling expeditions, she was a first-generation American. In a town with few Jews, Sylvia's grandmother had been killed in a European pogrom.

Sylvia's relatives were immigrants. Her maternal grandfather, Mates Kranzler, had sailed from Austria, passed through Ellis Island, and settled in New Bedford in the early 1900s. Having to support five children from his first marriage and eventually six from his second marriage, Mates opened up a small junk shop. Sylvia's mother, Gussie, was the youngest of five children born in Austria and it was Gussie who had the primary responsibility of raising the younger children. Gussie was not, however, only a caregiver but an employee and part-time manager of her brother's flower shop. Sylvia's paternal grandfather brought her father Harry and his siblings to the United States from Russia. When still a child, Harry sold pencils on the street and went to work in a circus. He later became an itinerant peddler in the South and eventually opened a junk store in New Bedford.

Gussie and Harry married and had two children, Shirley and Sylvia. Education was valued in their household. Although they had little formal education, Gussie and Harry were well read and self-educated. Sylvia often mentioned how proud her mother had been when a college professor had once assumed Gussie had been formally educated, when in fact she had only gone to school through fourth grade. Harry was known in town as an "independent cuss" and "socialist" because of his independence of spirit and strong sense of justice. Sylvia evidently acquired some of his traits. As a child, she was labeled a "firebrand" and she took nothing for granted. One cousin fondly remembers that her brother was called "Manny." Sylvia, at seven years old, logically asked why her cousin could not be called "Womanny." Even then she constantly challenged her world.

At a young age Sylvia became enamored with the written word, a theme threaded throughout her life, and she started writing poetry when she was seven. By the time she was nine years old her poetry was published in the *New Bedford Standard Times*. At age ten she won a Blue Ribbon for a poem entitled "Be a Man." During these early years several of her poems were published in the paper.

Active in high school, Sylvia was a debater and worked on the school newspaper. When she graduated, she was class valedictorian. That summer, she worked on an assembly line at Nonquitt Mills, Inc., in New Bedford. Years later she would recall the work as laborious. It was clear, however, that her experience at a relatively young age must have given her an appreciation for the importance and tremendous strength of workers.

Sylvia went to Smith College on a full scholarship on the basis of her poetry, which she had continued to write throughout high school, as well as her academic achievements. Throughout her life she appreciated the education she received at Smith and spoke highly of women being educated together, in the absence of men. She spoke not only of the camaraderie of being among other women but of the importance of having women as mentors.

During her years at Smith she was an academic achiever. As a freshman she was a William Allan Nielson scholar and in October 1941, as a sophomore, she was awarded the Arthur Ellis Hamm Scholarship Prize on the basis of her academic achievements during her freshman year. In the fall of her sophomore year, she held the position of vice president of the American Student Union (ASU).

The ASU was an outcome of the growth in student movements on college campuses in the early 1930s.[2] At that time, students became active in the antiwar movements and revolted against the increasing call for suppression of their civil liberties. In 1935 the ASU held its first session. Created by the merger of two student groups, the National Student League and the Student League for Industrial Democracy, its agenda included racial equality, equal educational opportunity and economic security, and support for the labor movement. By the mid-1930s leaders of the student movement "saw the working class as the primary agent of social change"[3] and some of the former leaders joined the labor movement. By 1941 its national platform included promoting labor's right to organize and bargain collectively and advocating full civil liberties and academic freedom. That summer, Sylvia attended the ASU's summer camp in Delaware, where she participated in seminars that provided formal training in political thinking and activity.

Sylvia soon became involved in the politics on campus. Among other activities, in May 1942 Sylvia became a member of the Interrace Commission, which was started by the Interfaith Commission on the Smith campus. The Interrace Commission was formed to delve into existing racial problems. It became an affiliate of the NAACP and held suppers and discussions on issues involving racial inequities. During this period of time Sylvia attended the Group Prejudice and Interfaith Commission of the NE Student Christian Movement conference in Boston on issues concerning minority groups. Issues raised concerned prejudice directed toward African Americans, Japanese Americans, and Jews. By October 1942 Sylvia became chair of the Interrace Commission. Although World War II was foremost in people's minds, racial equality was never far away in hers. Linking the two, Sylvia stated: "Just as the outcome of effort to extend full democracy to minorities is dependent upon the outcome of the war, so does victory require an immediate halt to all discriminatory practices."[4] With Sylvia as its chair, the commission organized a course on the role of African Americans in American history and formed a poll tax committee. While on the committee Sylvia went to Washington and spoke with legislators to oppose the poll tax.

At Smith, Sylvia became a labor economics major and eventually met her mentor, Dr. Dorothy W. Douglas, assistant professor of economics. In retrospect, it appears that Dr. Douglas's work influenced Sylvia's. Dr. Douglas wrote about the workers in society generally and about women more specifically. She was on the executive committee of the American Association for Labor Legislation, studied trade unions in the USSR and was a visiting professor of economics at the University of East Africa in Kenya at age seventy-four. From unions to Africa the similarity in interest and study, as will be seen, appears uncanny.

After her graduation from Smith in December 1943, as valedictorian and Phi

Beta Kappa, Sylvia was employed by the United Electrical, Radio and Machine Workers of America (UE). During the time that she worked for the UE, she was involved with numerous issues: minority issues, women in industry, equal pay for equal work, improved working conditions, and politics – themes that resonated throughout her life.

Beginning her career as the UE research director and an organizer, she was limitless as to her capabilities. She immersed herself in issues involving women and minorities.[5] Over the years, she used her burgeoning knowledge to organize outlines for courses on minorities and economics. She had significant knowledge as to the numbers of women in the industry and their rates of pay. Sylvia administered educational programs for the union and helped develop the union's first health plan by doing a comparative study of other countries. She was, however, particularly interested in the issue of women in industry.

Scribner's work on behalf of women impacted thousands of workers and set new standards in the industry. She focused on preventing the layoffs of women employees. In the process of breaking down the various jobs and their pay, she became acutely aware that women had lower-paying jobs than men. Several women's jobs were upgraded because she argued successfully that women had greater dexterity and therefore should be recognized for that fact with increased pay. Sylvia was also a liaison between the union and women employees, informing them of the union's interest in their working conditions and what the union was trying to do to help improve their situation. In addition, according to one union representative, she helped the union staff members themselves see how and why women were being discriminated against in industry.

Over the years, one particular organizational victory remained "dramatic and vivid" to her.[6] Scribner led the union's negotiations with a large electrical manufacturing plant in New Jersey. The plant had several thousand workers, approximately 35 percent of whom were women. The plant determined job scales according to an evaluation plan for jobs and wages. This plan maintained wage differentials for women workers, the majority of whom were on the production line. The employer justified its wage differential for women by making the distinction that their work required fine eye–hand coordination and not heavy manual labor. Scribner researched fatigue and found studies that established that repetitive movement could result in greater fatigue than occasional heavy manual labor. Scribner focused and organized the women's discontent into a fight for comparable worth. Regular meetings were conducted and women were encouraged to develop leadership capabilities. Women wore buttons to work and leaflets were distributed. Sylvia also was able to garner the support of the male employees who had initially been afraid to upset the social structure. They came to realize that the issue was important to all employees and was not a fight between the sexes. The organizing efforts were successful and the plant removed its pay differential for women. Thereafter, UE became the first international union to organize a conference concerning the elimination of discrimination against women workers and on developing leadership among women.[7]

Scribner's work with the UE seems to be the forerunner of her later work in the field of psychology. She became fascinated with the process of learning and adapting one's environment to both increase individual knowledge and gain advantage. In this vein, Scribner's union activity gave her access to industrial plants and thousands of employees where she gained insight into the ingenious ways the workers manipulated their environment to improve their working conditions. One such example was at a Singer plant in New Jersey where, in or around 1950 or 1951, the UE organized a strike that lasted for six months. The strike was prompted by the employer's position that it was going to change the incentive plan formula by which employees were paid. In reality, the employer's formula did not work to the employees' advantage. Employees who increased their production levels in fact received only minimal increases in pay. To allow for a more equitable system, the workers had devised their own system wherein they would vary the production level of each worker. In order to sustain this system the workers had to discipline themselves to either reduce or increase their productivity levels and back up their production levels with work records. Therefore, the employees did not want the employer to change a system that they had elaborately manipulated to work for them rather than against them. The union was unable to dissuade the employer from dismantling its payment system, however, and eventually the plant moved to the South, a notoriously low-wage district.

With the onslaught of the McCarthy period, the UE, branded a communist organization, took on the fight. During this period of time, Sylvia was involved in a myriad of issues, writing policy papers on the effect of the Taft–Hartley Act, obtaining dossiers on congressmen who were going to be interviewing union representatives before the House Un-American Activities Committee, and trying to determine who, if anyone, involved with the union might turn informer. More and more shops dropped out of the union and the membership eventually declined from five hundred thousand to sixty thousand or fifty thousand.

While working for the UE, Sylvia met David Scribner, general counsel for the union from approximately 1937. In David she met an individual whose social and political goals merged – justice and social change for the working class. In 1953 they married. Their son, Oliver, was born in 1954 and in 1958 a daughter, Aggie, was born. David also had three daughters by an earlier marriage, Toni, Wendy, and Nancy, with whom she was close. Although her sister had died in 1969, Sylvia was also close to her sister's daughter, Barbara. In later years, she had much joy with all of their children.

In 1958 Sylvia became the assistant to the director and operational research analyst at the Jewish Board of Guardians. Subsequently, as her interests expanded to include mental health and psychology, she held several positions in the mental health field while she was going to school for her master's in psychology. By 1967 she was assistant clinical professor of psychiatry (psychology) at the Albert Einstein College of Medicine.

Sylvia was a working mother in a generation that was not yet familiar with the term. Working and going to school at night, she received her Ph.D when she was forty-five years old. Yet despite her academic achievement and accolades she worried that she would be unable to obtain a job because of what she perceived was her advanced age and because she was a woman. Shortly thereafter, however, she obtained a position at Rockefeller University.

In 1972, while at Rockefeller, she conducted her first cross-cultural research in Liberia, West Africa, among the Kpelle people. I joined my mother and together we spent five months in Sinyea, a small village on the edge of the bush, approximately three hundred miles from the capital of Monrovia. Without indoor plumbing and electricity, and with a leaky tin roof in the rainy season, Sylvia worked and assimilated. Within three days of our arrival, the two of us hiked sixteen or so miles into the bush to see the coming out of the Sande society – girls who had lived in the bush for three years, without their parents, learning about traditional life. Sylvia danced to the drums, like everyone else. She had a way of enjoying people that transcended any cultural boundaries. At times she would sit on a small wooden table next to the general store in Sinyea, playing whist with some of the men in town. Other times she might join in a sip of palm wine or listen not only intently, but enthralled, to a storyteller in town although none of the words were in English. She refused to use mosquito netting over her bed because it was too "Western"; amusingly enough, in Sinyea she was called "Kwita" – Kpelle for Western town. At the time of her departure three chiefs of nearby villages gave her a going-away party – quite a tribute for someone from a Western town. Although she never returned to Sinyea, she went back to Liberia several times to conduct research among the Vai.

In 1978, Sylvia left Rockefeller and became an associate director at the National Institute of Education in Washington, D.C., and thereafter a scientist at the Center for Applied Linguistics.

Sylvia became a professor in the Developmental Psychology Program at the City University of New York, Graduate School and University Center in 1981, where she stayed until her death. In 1982 she founded the Laboratory for the Cognitive Study of Work, where all her interests seemed to come together. She continued to work at the Graduate Center until shortly before her death in July 1991.

Politics was essential to Sylvia. She was vocal with her opinions and believed in action. In 1953 she was arrested and spent the night in jail after demonstrating against the execution of Julius and Ethel Rosenberg. She marched on Washington and in New York. Civil rights, opposition to the war in Vietnam, women's rights, workers' rights – all were supported and discussed. She believed in clear, precise thinking and in taking a stand on the issues. These discussions were not confined to the adults in her life but included her children. She was interested in their opinions, engaging them and challenging them to probe further. Her children went with her on peace marches and learned about activism. Most important, they learned that a professional life did not have to be, and should not be, devoid of politics and social consciousness.

Although clearly engaged with her work and her family, Sylvia had many other passions. She continued to write poetry throughout every stage of her life. She also enjoyed the theater, music (both jazz and classical), and cool hours at the ballet with David. For those close to her, there are many memories of her dancing with David in their living room. Nothing better than a few close friends and music for an evening. In fact, their dancing started in the late 1940s at the jazz clubs in Harlem. It has been said that at one club in particular, they were the only people allowed to dance because they were just so good. Sylvia also had a wonderful sense of humor, appreciating, and participating in, both silly farce and sophisticated double entendres.

Sylvia's life was not simple. She juggled many things and overcame many stereotypes. No matter what the situation, however, her intellect and strength of ideas could not be ignored. As in her poetry, Sylvia could capture an idea and run with it to a new dimension as she put words and thoughts into a framework that was unique. She was able to convey her ideas so clearly that people often commented what a pleasure it was to discuss something with her or to read her books and articles.

Although she had several different fields during her lifetime there was a natural progression. From the labor movement to psychology her primary interest and devotion lay in the nature of people and their work. It was the foundation of her life.

It seems impossible that time has passed without her. At least we have her words.

Notes

1. "A Daughter's Praise," by Sylvia Scribner, December 19, 1980.
2. The information set forth regarding the history of the American Student Union was obtained from Robert Cohen, *When the Old Left Was Young: Student Radicals and America's First Mass Student Movement 1929–1941* (New York: Oxford University Press, 1993).
3. Ibid., 196.
4. *The Smith College Associated News,* October 6, 1942.
5. Much of the information regarding Sylvia's UE work was obtained from an interview of union representative Walter Barry by Emily Filardo in 1992.
6. "Comparable Worth in the Forties: Reflections by Sylvia Scribner," interview by June Duffy, *Women's Rights Law Reporter,* Rutgers, 8, nos. 1–2 (Winter 1984): 107.
7. Ibid., 105–107.

Introduction

Sylvia Cohen Scribner's Life and Work

Sylvia Scribner's life and work as a psychologist did not fit neatly into conventional categories and narratives. Her scientific writings were addressed at different times to academic psychologists, anthropologists, community psychologists, labor union officials, mental health professionals, politically concerned social scientists, and educational policy analysts. Her topics included reasoning, memory, IQ research, social class and psychiatric diagnoses, textbooks, thinking at work, formal schooling, literacy, developmental theory, and culture and thinking. Her methods of data collection and analysis were drawn and adapted from several academic disciplines.

Yet through all the diversity of intellectual traditions, audiences, aims, forms of knowing, and forms of persuasion – indeed, *using* this diversity – Scribner consistently focused on certain key themes in her work and activities. In some sense she was always, in all ways, concerned with the interweaving of theory and practice, of doing and knowing – and with the moral responsibility and accountability this entails for researchers. In this collection we sketch some of the personal and sociohistorical circumstances surrounding Sylvia Scribner's work at different periods in her life and let her writings themselves provide both examples and, reflexively, analyses of how she integrated knowing and doing in her life and work.

Born in 1923 and raised in New Bedford, Massachusetts, Sylvia Cohen wrote poetry and talked politics from an early age – activities she continued throughout her life. As a student at Smith College she studied economics and was active in the American Student Union. Graduating summa cum laude in 1944, Cohen found work as activities director for Local 415 of the United Electrical, Radio and Machine Workers of America (UE). There she met activist civil rights lawyer and UE general counsel David Scribner, whom she later married. Their son Oliver was born in 1954; daughter Aggie, in 1958. (The biography of Aggie Scribner Kapleman preceding this introduction describes Sylvia Scribner's life in greater detail.)

1

By the early 1960s the UE's policies had changed, and Sylvia and David Scribner decided to seek employment elsewhere. Sylvia Scribner's commitment to working people led her in 1963 to become Associate Director of the Mental Health Program of the National Institute of Labor Education in New York City. There, according to a curriculum vitae she later prepared, Scribner participated in developing national policy for public and private programs to meet the special mental health needs of labor, and worked with the Director and National Advisory Committee to organize multidisciplinary research teams at various universities, helping them design and implement research proposals.

In 1964 Scribner became Research Director of the Mental Health Program of the Sidney Hillman Health Center in New York City. She designed and conducted research to evaluate the effectiveness of a National Institute of Mental Health-funded demonstration program introducing new techniques for identifying and treating mental illness among blue-collar workers. Part of this research was a home interview study of the treatment histories of workers disabled by mental illness prior to the inception of the demonstration program.

Through these activities Scribner became interested in the roles psychologists played or could play in working people's lives. She began to take psychology courses at New York University and then enrolled as a graduate student in psychology at the New School for Social Research. In 1966 Scribner received an M.A. in social psychology, being awarded the Dorothy Kelgor Prize in Psychology from the New School's Graduate Faculty of Political and Social Science. During this period she, Ethel Tobach, Eleanor Leacock, and Howard Gruber engaged in philosophical study and discussions.

Scribner's interests in how people think about their social conditions led her to find employment in 1967 at the Albert Einstein College of Medicine, where she worked and became friends with, among others, Hannah Levin, Frank Riessman, and Jane Knitzer. As an Assistant Clinical Professor of Psychiatry (psychology), Scribner developed material for postdoctoral training in community psychology, conducted research on concepts of mental disorders in various cultures, and designed a research program on the cognitive consequences of literacy.

Then in her mid-forties and working full-time, she was mother of two young children and had an extended family that included three grown children from her husband's previous marriage. Scribner also enrolled in the Ph.D. program of the New School, where she took evening courses in cognitive psychology with Mary Henle and lectured in courses on memory and thinking.

It was the late 1960s: public debates about and activities surrounding the Vietnam War and civil rights were reaching their height; the beginnings of second-wave feminism were in the air. At the New School Scribner worked with Howard Gruber to organize brown bag lunches where students and faculty could discuss the social responsibility of psychologists and actions they might collectively undertake, such as demonstrations and teach-ins. She was active in antinuclear activities in New York, working with Ethel Tobach and Eleanor Leacock among others, and in Psychologists for Social Action (PSA) with Howard Gruber and Doris K. Miller.

Scribner wrote for the PSA Newsletter and worked with others for the election of Kenneth Clark as President of the American Psychological Association. According to PSA's statement of purpose at the time, the Association had come into being because "We psychologists feel a deep sense of social responsibility. This responsibility calls for action beyond talk and study. We seek ways of applying our knowledge and experience toward the resolution of the urgent social problems of our time."

During these years David Scribner continued his work as a civil rights lawyer, participating among other cases in highly publicized trials involving the Black Panthers, prisoners in New York's Attica State Prison, and students at Kent State University. Oliver and Aggie accompanied their parents on marches and demonstrations, and political talk filled the household.

During the late 1960s, and early 1970s the field of psychology was undergoing changes as well. The "cognitive revolution" had refocused many psychologists' attention away from behaviorism and toward language, thinking, reasoning, remembering, and other aspects of higher mental function. Psychologists, along with scientists of other disciplines, were reconsidering the social relevance of their laboratory research, and Kurt Lewin's decades-old tradition of action research was again in the wind. These changes provided both organizational venues for Scribner's activities and scientific resources for her developing psychological analyses. The discussions within psychology of scientists' objectivity and social relevance offered openings for her analyses of psychologists' roles as both scientists and citizens.

In 1970 Sylvia Scribner was awarded a Ph.D. in psychology, having completed a dissertation ("A Cross-Cultural Study of Perceptions of Mental Disorder") under the sponsorship of Mary Henle, Solomon Miller, and Bernard Weitzman. She was forty-seven years old, and, from a narrowly academic perspective, was about to begin her work as researcher and teacher.

The papers reprinted in Part 1 reflect Sylvia Scribner's early and continuing commitment to promoting human welfare and justice through psychological research. She argued (with exquisite tact and unmistakable critique) that psychologists need to take responsibility for the values, aims, and interests embedded in their research practices and what they produce. To this end she articulated connections among the goals, priorities, and assumptions of the organizations and institutions with which psychologists work, the research questions they ask, and the theoretical concepts and methods they use. And she simultaneously worked to change the institutions.

In these papers and elsewhere Scribner did more than critique supposedly "neutral" science and professional practices, though she did so at a time when such analyses were rare outside radical science circles. She simultaneously theorized psychology as practice, as activities with social and human effects, and she clarified some of the roles psychological researchers can play (including advocacy) in addressing societal problems. In the parlance of the times, though she would have eschewed the trite expression, Scribner repeatedly challenged herself and other psychologists to consider whether they were part of the problem or part of the solution (and from whose point of view) – and to act accordingly.

Scribner's 1968 manuscript, "The Cognitive Consequences of Literacy," is both a crystallization of her psychological thinking at the time she was at Albert Einstein and the New School and a preview of directions her work took in the future. (It is included here in Part 3.) When she recognized similarities between her analysis of thinking as embedded in cultural systems and the work Michael Cole was carrying out at Rockefeller University, she contacted him for dialogue. As she put it in a 1970 letter to Cole, "From my speculative route and your empirical one, we seem to have arrived at similar constructs. We agree that on the "input" side we are dealing with cultural systems and technologies – not mentalities and capacities – and on the "output" side we are dealing with certain specific mental skills, such as the intentional structuring of cognitive tasks – not "intelligence.' " Cole responded generously, obtaining funds to offer Scribner an appointment as Senior Research Associate at Rockefeller, and in 1970 they began a fruitful collaboration.

Cole's laboratory at Rockefeller was an active part of a rich and varied intellectual environment for behavioral scientists. Cole's independently functioning laboratory (which later became the Laboratory of Comparative Human Cognition) was institutionally located in William Estes' Mathematical Psychology Laboratory, and members interacted extensively with each other and also with George Miller's Psycholinguistics Laboratory.

Scribner participated in seminars, working groups, and conversations with visitors on a wide range of topics and issues, including mathematical models of memory, children's narratives, logical thinking, and intelligence tests. During these years, in addition to Michael Cole, Scribner also developed several other significant and lasting collegial, intellectual, and personal friends, including William Estes, Kay Estes, Rachel Joffe Falmagne, Elsa Bartlett, Steve Reder, Sue Sugerman, William Hall, Anderson J. Franklin, Ray McDermott, George Miller, Tom Sibarowski, and Dalton Miller-Jones.

Relatively few of the women scientists at Rockefeller in the early 1970s held faculty appointments (as was typical of elite institutions at the time), and Scribner therefore sought opportunities elsewhere to obtain a faculty position. In 1974, while still at Rockefeller, she also held an appointment as Visiting Professor in the Ferkauf Graduate School of Arts and Sciences of Yeshiva University.

Given Scribner's continuing and deepening concern with the societal roots and effects of psychologists' research practices, some of her work during the Rockefeller years involved detailed critical analyses of widely accepted concepts and methods in psychology. In particular she focused on research practices in the study of race and intelligence, of class and psychiatric diagnoses, arguing they embodied assumptions about individuals, capacities, and abilities that enabled (as she put it in an earlier paper) the "continued avoidance by psychology of the significant dimensions of social life." She knew and cared that this "avoidance . . . of the significant dimensions of social life" carried profound consequences for poor and minority children in schools, for people in psychiatric hospitals, and for others. Her earlier papers had provided analyses of psychologists' roles in more direct and overtly political and moral language, but now her rhetoric changed as her critiques were directed toward scientific audiences.

With remarkable clarity, and tailored persuasively to the concerns and language of those she addressed, this critical work keeps probing for an analysis of scientific concepts and methods that will enable researchers to understand other people's thinking in a way that does not impose, without reflection, the powerful analytic categories embodied in traditional psychological research practices. (Some of these writings are included in Parts 1 and 2.)

Some of Scribner's poems from this period may be related to her feelings about expressing deep scientific and political convictions within academic psychology's conventional logic and styles of writing.

It Doesn't Mean A Thing

The words I use
and mis-abuse
have nothing in common
with my views.
not what they mean
but what they say
is how I deal them
every day
and if you think
that something keen
gets lost between

the line?

Fine.

Lexical Lament

Pull them out
From those dark places
Exil – ees
Return!

Lovely we's
and I's
Dot spaces
Actives take
Your turn.

No mercy to
Usurpers who
Parade as Things.
Data, Research, Study
Go!
None of you
Can ever "show"

Author, author
From the wings
Show us, please
How science sings.

As part of Michael Cole's ongoing research program on culture and cognition, Scribner spent several extended periods between 1970 and 1978 carrying out research in Liberia, West Africa. For five months in 1972 her daughter Aggie was with her; her biography of her mother describes memories of Scribner's concrete daily life in Liberia, her relationship with people there, and the regard in which they held her. Other information about the trips and the circumstances of the work in Africa is contained in the two books coauthored by Scribner and Cole. More than a decade later, when Scribner was living in Manhattan and commuting daily to work by subway through Times Square, she recalled to a colleague the pleasure she had felt in Liberia – and her respect for such sensible living – when she could simply sweep the floor, go out the door, and work.

On her first trip to Liberia Scribner lived in a small village in the bush, working closely with Kpelle collaborators to investigate how Kpelle people reason, remember, and carry out other cognitive activities. Cole and Scribner's book reporting this research, *Culture and Thought: A Psychological Introduction*, was published in 1974. It was well received, as was Scribner and Cole's 1973 *Science* paper on cognitive consequences of formal and informal education (which was reprinted in several anthologies on culture and education).

In 1973 Scribner and Cole undertook research among the Vai people in Liberia. The Vai were of particular interest: they have an original written script transmitted from one generation of men to the next, and a large segment of the population is not formally educated in schools. Thus, literacy in this group is not confounded with schooling. It was possible to examine specifically how each is related to thinking, remembering, and other cognitive activities.

Scribner and Cole's report of the Vai research, *The Psychology of Literacy*, appeared in 1981, receiving the African Studies Association's Melville J. Herskovitz Award the following year. This book builds on methodological and theoretical analyses of the earlier one, and presents a clear shift away from the approach current in cross-cultural work at that time.

During the Rockefeller years, Michael Cole, Vera John-Steiner, Sylvia Scribner, and Ellen Souberman were also editing *L. S. Vygotsky: Mind in Society*, the volume of Vygotsky's work that would appear in 1978. Scribner had earlier made a thorough study of Vygotsky's writings and those of other Russian cultural-historical psychologists and had incorporated them in her thinking. According to Cole's account of this period in the *LCHC Newsletter* (1992),[1] Scribner played an important role in promoting deeper understanding of this work among LCHC's members, an influence now evident in the widespread discussions among psychologists and others of the cultural-historical approach. Her classic paper, "Modes of Thinking and Ways of Speaking: Culture and Logic Reconsidered" (1978), was written during this time, merging her interest in logical thinking from graduate school days with her societal perspective on thinking. (It is reprinted in Part 2.)

Emerging out of direct engagement with societal and scientific issues, Scribner's theoretical understanding of thinking and learning had clear implications for real-world education policies. In 1978 she was recruited by National Institute of Education Director Patricia Albjerg Graham to become Associate Director and head of its Teaching and Learning Program. Scribner's interest in shaping research-based educational policy, the Laboratory of Comparative Human Cognition's move to California, and her lack of independent institutional status at Rockefeller converged to make the invitation attractive.

Both the NIE and the Teaching and Learning Program have since been dissolved, but at that time NIE's program was a major site of educational planning and a source of funding for research aimed at improving educational opportunities for all Americans. In addition to Pat Graham, Scribner's colleagues during this period included Lois Ellin-Datta, Ned Chalker, Susan Chipman, Judith Orasanu, Judith Siegel, Lauren Resnick, Michale Timpane, and Ramsay Selden – several of whom became lifelong friends.

At NIE Scribner sought to institute broader conceptions of learning, education, and literacy to include learning in sites other than schools – in the workplace, for example – and to focus on learning in adults as well as children and adolescents. She promoted an NIE program (jointly with the American Psychological Association) for minority researchers, and initiated discussions of technology and learning. She also launched a program of cognitive science applications to education.

In 1980 Scribner traveled to China as part of an NIE-funded Educational Research Delegation to the People's Republic of China to study literacy education programs in that country. A report of this trip is included in Part 3, together with other papers on literacy that show the range of audiences Scribner addressed and the scope and coherence of the questions and research methods with which she was concerned.

Colleagues describe the work she did at NIE as having a "cascading effect," although she was there for only a year. Her passionate commitment to quality in research, together with her personal contacts in many fields, enabled her to enlist as reviewers and advisors first-rate scientists who had not been involved in education research. For the NIE staff, the review process came to resemble seminars. One colleague recalled how Scribner would sit with twinkling eyes, playing with a twinkling gold necklace, "taking us all on a wild intellectual ride."

David Scribner had moved with Sylvia to Washington D.C. (Their children were then grown and in graduate school or working.) He had curtailed his activities because of heart problems, but continued to do civil rights work and train lawyers in labor law, and he represented the student body of his daughter's law school in a lawsuit against the university. Sylvia Scribner continued to be an avid and informed theatergoer, as she had been in New York, and made frequent lunchtime visits to the Smithsonian's Museum of Modern Art.

While at NIE Scribner began to establish connections with the Center for Applied Linguistics in Washington, and she was appointed Senior Scientist there in 1979, joining Ed Fahrmeier, Evelyn Jacob, and others. She left her administrative position at NIE soon thereafter and began a highly productive period of scientific work.

Scribner's previous labor union work and personal manner gave her the credibility necessary to establish relations of trust with union members and officials and with management at a dairy distribution plant in nearby Baltimore. There she developed a research program on thinking at work that brought together themes woven throughout all her scientific and political life.

In Scribner's own words,

[My research] has three objectives. On the most ambitious level, I would like it to serve as a vehicle for elaborating the very general constructs of activity theory. I want to develop and test a method that integrates observational studies of naturally occurring phenomena with experimentation on model tasks. And most concretely, I want to discover something about the characteristics of practical thinking in everyday life.

What activities might be suitable for investigating practical thinking? I chose to study work activities for reasons of both significance and strategy. Significance is apparent. In all societies, work is basic to human existence; in most it consumes the greater part of waking time, and, in many – certainly our own – it is a principal source of self-definition. Although we are not wholly defined through our participation in productive activities, the circumstances under which we work and what we do when we work have deep implications for intellectual and personal development.[2]

In 1981 Sylvia and David Scribner returned to New York City when she was recruited by Katherine Nelson to a professorship in Developmental Psychology at the Graduate School and University Center of the City University of New York. There she joined Katherine Nelson, Joseph Glick, and Harry Beilin on the Developmental Psychology faculty, which later added Dalton Miller-Jones, Mary Parlee, and David Bearison as well.

Scribner's CUNY appointment as Professor of Psychology at the age of fifty-nine was her first and only "real" faculty job. Her lifelong political and moral commitments had led her to work for much of her life outside the university. Her clarity and persistence as a scientist had enabled her to respond creatively to some of the personal and historical circumstances that often keep women and politically active psychologists at the margins of the academy and major research enterprises. She would continue to produce the psychological research and theory for which she is recognized internationally. There is no simple narrative of an academic career here; it is the life of an intellectual activist.

At CUNY Scribner taught graduate seminars on memory, mind and society, Vygotsky, and research methods, and attracted and trained a group of highly talented graduate students and postdoctoral fellows. These included King Beach, Pat Sachs, Lia DiBello, Michael Cohen, and others, contributions from many of whom are reflected in their joint publications with Scribner. Scribner also had a lasting influence on students who did not work directly with her in research but took seminars with her. One of them remembers most clearly Scribner's "passion for clarity, her interest in having us speak very clearly on an issue and listen to each other and say what we meant – and she provided a wonderful model of how to do it."

While at CUNY Scribner worked consistently to strengthen the research training offered in psychology by increasing the diversity of the faculty and student body. This is a connection she had been making in theory and practice since she entered the field: if ways of knowing and the resulting knowledge depend on who asks the research questions, why, how, and on whose behalf, then diversity of perspectives is more likely to be scientifically fruitful than monocular vision. Working with other faculty members and with Graduate Center President Harold Proshansky she was successful in bringing Dalton Miller-Jones, whom she had known at Rockefeller, onto the developmental psychology faculty, enriching the growing interest and depth within the program in a sociocultural approach to psychological questions. She consistently promoted the work of minority scholars at CUNY and nationwide and supported, financially and otherwise, a diverse group of students in her laboratory.

Scribner's commitment to diversity and antiracism were not limited to psychology, and she worked as well with other faculty at CUNY concerned with these issues (Del Jones, Leith Mullings, Bill Kornblum, Frank Riessman) until the end of her life. She continued to be an activist in non-academic arenas well. Among other efforts she worked to organize a demonstration against a proposed berthing of nuclear submarines near Staten

Island – publicity being generated by Graduate Center faculty in full academic regalia marching along 42nd Street behind a saxophonist's "When the Saints Come Marching In."

In the late 1980s Scribner's research program was gaining momentum. With funding from the Spencer Foundation, the Office of Educational Research and Improvement, the National Center for Education and the Economy, and the National Center for Research in Education, she founded the Laboratory for Cognitive Studies of Work, developing it into an intellectual center for students, colleagues, and visitors and a site for planning and analysis of field and laboratory research. Laura Martin and Patricia Sachs collaborated with Scribner as Project Directors on some of the grants. Some of the research was coordinated through the National Center for Education and Employment at Teacher's College, Columbia University, where Susan Berryman and Ray McDermott were colleagues and friends.

Scribner's work, long known to researchers at the forefront of several disciplines, was beginning to generate excitement among more mainstream psychologists as well. When Scribner and some of her students presented their "thinking at work" research at the Eastern Psychological Association meeting in Boston in 1985, the large room was filled to overflowing – there was a sense in the air that something significant was happening. There were frequent invitations to address national and international meetings. Scribner maintained an active correspondence with colleagues in Germany, Japan, Russia, Norway, Finland, Sweden, and France.

By the late 1980s Sylvia and David Scribner were grandparents, and Sylvia took special pleasure – her face would light up when she talked about him – in being with her daughter Aggie's son Alex, who lived nearby. David Scribner's illness had worsened, however, and he died in April 1991. Sylvia Scribner's "sciatica" – which did not keep her from protesting against the Gulf War or from her research and teaching – was diagnosed as cancer in the spring of 1991, four months before her death. Her second grandchild, Aggie's son Scott, was born shortly before she was hospitalized.

When Sylvia Scribner died, friends and colleagues from around the world joined together through electronic mail to express their sense of loss and love, to share memories. In February 1992 a memorial symposium, "Sylvia at Work," was held at the CUNY Graduate Center to celebrate her life and work. The auditorium was filled with Sylvia's family, friends, and colleagues from different phases of her life. Sylvia Scribner, union employee, professor, protester, scientist, mentor, and friend, was remembered as the unique and remarkable person she was.

This is a collection of her work, in her own voice, speaking of things she cared about with her indomitable, passionate intelligence. Sylvia Scribner at work, Sylvia Scribner working, Sylvia Scribner's work – the dancer and the dance are one.

Notes

1. Michael Cole, Introduction, Sylvia Scribner memorial issue of *The Quarterly Newsletter of the Laboratory of Comparative Human Cognition* 14, no. 4 (1992).
2. S. Scribner, "Head and Hand: An Action Approach to Thinking." Eastern Psychological Association, Arlington, Va., April 1987. [Reprinted by the National Center on Education and Employment, Teachers College, Columbia University.]

Kaleidoscope

In small lights
darting off a prism
or a glass
of low proportions
the world comes back to me.
Its yellow far from red
and green from blue.
Shining only when
in shards
it gives a partial view.

Sylvia Scribner

PART 1

Psychology as social practice

Introduction

For Sylvia Scribner, the purpose of understanding either psychological or societal processes was to promote human dignity. The formulation of theoretical statements was but one component of the activity of solving human problems. Scribner was committed to a dialectical-materialist approach, viewing human behavior and societal processes as mutually transformative; hence, understanding either psychological or societal processes could only be achieved through an analysis and a method that reflected their dialectic integration.

This concern is exemplified in the first talk on the subject found in her files, "Issues in the Development of a Labor Mental Health Program," and in two other papers on mental health as societal process included in this section. While at the National Institute of Labor Education, Scribner spoke on the need for a labor mental health program at the American Orthopsychiatric Association meeting in March 1963. After analyzing inequities of mental health policies in the treatment of workers, she develops a proposal for social action based on two principles that would guide her throughout: that those groups affected by the research be an integral part of the research activity, and that they act to make concrete changes in their lives. She proposes collective bargaining, the problem-solving procedure traditionally used by labor, as the activity of choice in the development of a mental health program, and sees the program as involving, in addition to care components, research on prevention and education, which she views as inseparable from research and service. She describes the partnership between labor and mental health representatives as "hold[ing] a dual promise of progress in both the social and scientific spheres." In this paper, she characteristically stresses that research is accountable to society at large and must extend its frame of reference and its standard procedures accordingly.

Scribner's experience at the Labor Education Institute provided the bridge between her practice in the labor movement and her return to academic scholarship at the New School for Social Research. The next two papers were written and delivered while Scribner was in graduate school, during a period of heightened political activity in the country at large. Critical concerns of the day had to do with the Vietnam policies of the United States, with mental health needs of the people, and with issues of educational and racial inequities.

In "Advocacy: Strategy or Solution?" she urges professionals to recognize the societal and political impact of their work, an impact they may not have intended: "professional 'neutrality' often masks support of dominant interest groups" (p. 28). She stresses an activist construal of professionals' roles, on behalf of the poor and unrepresented, but points to the limitations of advocacy within institutions and professional channels. She urges professionals and advocates to select thoughtfully the appropriate arena of struggle for a particular social problem and to consider the concrete societal and political context in which advocacy takes place.

15

During that period, she worked at the Albert Einstein Mental Health facility, continuing her analysis of mental health as a societal issue. In "What Is Community Psychology Made Of?" she discusses what she saw as the fundamental problem in the relationship between psychology and society: the need for psychologists to take social responsibility for the theory and practice of their work. She defines four kinds of community psychologists differing in terms of their frame of analysis and intervention, alternatively systemic or individual, and in terms of their broader commitments. Each group is seen in its limitations but also in its potential "for theory development . . . on the level of practice." All share a common need to "build a new database which will make it possible for all psychologists – in the community or the laboratory – to progress toward a more complete theory of human development and functioning" (p. 38).

Written a few years later while Scribner was at Rockefeller, "Social Class and Mental Illness" offers a critical appraisal of Hollingshead and Redlich's (1958) book by the same title. She recognizes the importance of the book's impact in stimulating a broader societal approach to psychiatric practice and theory, and praises their contribution for yielding useful investigations of social class and mental illness in "functional linkage to sociocultural . . . variables" (p. 41), but she emphasizes problematic consequences of their specific analysis. Based on a careful reexamination of their data, she explicates how these researchers' methods and their formulation of the research question – in particular, their definition of mental illness and other descriptive categories – result in interpretations that counter their original intentions, thus stressing again the need for method to be grounded in knowledge of societal processes.

Her concern about the role of psychologists in the problems of the day was brought to the fore by a significant event in the history of psychology. In 1968, in response to the police assault on demonstrators against the Vietnam War during the Democratic Party Convention in Chicago, a group of psychologists attending the annual meeting of the American Psychological Association (APA) formed an Ad Hoc Committee of Psychologists for Social Responsibility (later to formally become American Psychologists for Social Action, or PSA), and called on the APA to cancel plans to hold the next annual meeting in Chicago – a request the APA honored. When Scribner joined PSA soon thereafter, she proposed requesting the APA to organize its 1969 annual convention on the theme of psychologists' social responsibility. The APA redefined the proposed convention theme as "Psychology and the Problems of Society" and formally organized sessions on that theme; members of PSA organized independent sessions as well, some listed in the official program and some not.

The next paper in this section, "Research as a Social Process," was presented by Scribner at the Symposium on Community Psychology organized by PSA, and was not included in the official convention proceedings. Scribner's dialectical view of the relationship of science and society is clear. "Whatever the topic of investigation, research is always embedded in larger social and political processes which influence its course and outcome. In turn, the research process has an impact upon the larger social processes through the new knowledge it produces and the methodologies it adopts." She criticizes the widely held idea that social sciences are homogeneous and offers as illustration a comparison of the NASA and HUD research programs, each shaped by their societal locations; psychologists must set research priorities and practices in collaboration with the community affected by the research. As is the case of labor and mental health, bringing the researcher and the population together produces a "tension between the two [that] will have the most advantageous yield for both."

In recognition of Scribner's role in initiating the theme of the APA convention, the PSA newsletter invited her to analyze *Psychology and the Problems of Society* (1970), a selection of papers from the convention. In her review of the book, she finds that the volume reveals "the limitations of efforts to relate psychology to specific social problems without an analysis of the basic social forces" (p. 70). She continues by calling for an integration of theory and practice. "To act responsibly on . . . aroused social consciousness, however, requires not only a scientific knowledge of psychology but a scientific understanding of society and the dynamic forces operating within it" (p. 70).

Shortly thereafter, psychologists were embroiled in debate about another societal implication of their activities, the writings of Jensen on IQ, race, and class. In "Psychologists, Process, and Performance," Scribner stresses that societal responsibilities are inescapably involved in asking "scientific research questions" and explains how sensitivity or insensitivity to those responsibilities affects research outcomes. She calls into question seemingly understood terms such as "culture" and the practice of "marking off populations": the marked-off populations are defined, not by accident, in terms of the presence or absence of specific kinds of privileges. She states: "this comparative psychological enterprise . . . interprets the problem of education . . . in terms of competencies or incompetencies of people, not inadequacies or adequacies of societal institutions" (p. 73). Specific in her critique of logical and factual inadequacies in Jensen's interpretations, she stresses that the deployment of skills is always situated and elicited by particular tasks, and urges her audience to participate with her in elucidating how the development of particular skills is shaped by specific cultural activities.

The early years in the transition of Sylvia Scribner from the world of labor and its special needs and instruments to that of the scientist in a world of active practice produced a body of work that continues to speak to how we understand the relations between the individual and society. The themes and commitments expressed here would continue to guide her research and writings throughout her life.

Selected coauthored works

Scribner, S.; Reiff, R. (1964): Issues in the new national mental health programs relating to labor and low income groups. In: *Mental health of the poor* (Ed.: Riessman, F.). The Free Press, New York, 443–56.
Scribner, S.; Riessman, F. (1965): Underutilization of mental health services by workers and low income groups: causes and cures. *American Journal of Psychiatry* 121, 798–801.

1 Issues in the development of a labor mental health program

For the past four years, the National Institute of Labor Education – an independent organization of universities and trade unions whose purpose is the development of workers' education – has been conducting a study to conceptualize and organize a mental health program in labor organizations.

As a statement of purpose, this sounds relatively simple and clear-cut; and since I am here principally to acquaint you with the nature of our work in this area, I might assume that the *objective* of organizing a labor mental health program is a self-evident one. But to do so would be to skip over some very fundamental questions.

It isn't customary, after all, to characterize a particular endeavor in the mental health field in terms of its sponsorship and the consumer group to which it is addressed rather than in terms of its specific content. Moreover, considering the fact that the labor movement has been a powerful force on the American scene for several decades and that the organized mental health movement has been flourishing for at least the same period of time, it should give pause for thought that no lasting liaison has yet been effected between the two and that it is still necessary in 1963 to describe our purpose on such a primitive level as *conceptualization* and *organization* of a labor mental health program. As a matter of fact, the coupling of "unions" and "mental health activities" is so new and unstable that even in the planning of this panel, the title slipped – almost of its own accord – into the traditional one of "Mental Health Activities in Industrial Settings" rather than the intended and more accurate heading which the program now carries of "Mental Health Activities in Union Settings."

Granted that the approach is new, the question still remains, is it valid? What do we mean by a labor mental health program? Is it meant to imply that union

This paper was originally presented at an American Orthopsychiatric Association meeting, March 8, 1963.

19

members as such have problems which are different from those of other workers? What can be accomplished by mental health activities within labor organizations that cannot be handled through existing private and public professional and lay resources?

NILE does not stress the necessity of a labor mental health program because it believes union members have unique psychological problems which set them apart from other working-class people who may not happen to belong to unions. NILE does believe, however, and feels it has been amply demonstrated in the last decade that working people as a group have certain special mental health needs and that these needs are less adequately met than those of other groups in our society. NILE believes that the labor movement is in an exceptional position to take affirmative and effective action around these unmet needs and that in so doing it can strengthen the whole national effort for improved psychiatric programs of prevention and care for all.

In other papers we have reviewed the extensive evidence which has been accumulated about the inadequacies of psychiatric programs for working people. Our own surveys and interviews with union members throughout the country have corroborated the findings of Hollingshead and Redlich in New Haven, of Srole, Rennie, Langner *et al.* in the Midtown Study that there are striking differences in the kinds of diagnosis, care, and treatment given members of the lower socioeconomic or working class groups as compared to those of the middle classes (1,2). Blue collar workers, even when apparently suffering from the same illness as their white collar counterparts, are more often institutionalized and treated by physical-chemical rather than psychological techniques.

Let me cite just two of the most recent studies confirming these facts. Group Health Insurance of New York, reporting on its investigation into the feasibility of short-term psychiatric insurance, found that the great majority of its patients were treated by means of individual psychotherapy in the psychiatrist's office – with this exception: "...... the older, less educated blue-collar patients were treated with drugs more often than not." (3) In the extensive study conducted in Maryland of the population served by outpatient psychiatric clinics, two important differences were found to be associated with economic status: patients from lower economic areas did not stay as long in the clinic as those from higher economic areas and their improvement rates were lower. (4)

The very consistency of the findings, regardless of the particular community or treatment facility under study, dramatizes the scope of the problem and the magnitude of the program needed to solve it. Here is truly a challenge for the mental health professionals, yet the problem cannot be conceived as a professional one alone. Inadequate psychiatric programs for the many millions who comprise the industrial working class population in this country is a major social problem. The solution of social problems requires informed social action, and the trade union movement is one of the most effective instrumentalities for such action. Through its collective bargaining position, its participation in community affairs, and state and national legislative activities it can substantially raise the standards of care for its members with mental health problems just as it has in respect to their physical health problems.

Moving from concern with and action around its own special interests, the labor movement can develop into a powerful new resource in the national mental health effort. Trade unions have the organization, leadership, and strength of numbers to enlist significant sections of society – up till now unreached by the mental health movement or apathetic or unsympathetic to its aims – in the fight against mental illness. From a public health point of view the importance of such a development can hardly be overstated.

As we see it then:

The *purpose* of a labor mental health program is to enlist the strength of the labor movement in the social action required to solve what is generally acknowledged to be our leading public health problem.

The *basis* for enlisting labor's participation is the fact that working men and women have unique mental health problems arising from their position in society and that these problems are inadequately met. Labor is in an advantageous position to undertake education and action programs to meet these special needs and to support those within the mental health professions who are seeking to develop both theory and techniques applicable to working people.

This view clearly differs from the basic concepts underlying most other efforts in the field. For one thing, it sees labor as more than simply another "audience" to which prevailing mental health concepts are to be brought. Nor does it look upon labor as merely a production force whose emotional health is to be maximized for the sake of maximized output. The content of a labor mental health program that is geared toward meeting the full range of needs of labor membership quite clearly cannot be taken over from the existing mental hygiene and industrial psychology fields. It has to be developed through creative effort centered around the concrete problems facing workers as a group, and taking into account the traditions, goals and organized structure of the labor movement. The knowledge and skills of many professional disciplines are needed for this task.

We should like now to give a brief review of some of the specific issues around which we feel labor can develop an action program, indicating as we do so what kinds of educational and research efforts are needed to make these possible, the various forms in which professional–labor collaboration can take place and some of the projects we have already developed in these areas.

Collective bargaining

Let us deal first with the unions in their traditional role of collective bargaining agents.

We have singled out the issue of adequate psychiatric diagnosis and treatment for working people as a central one facing labor and the country. One of the ways in which unions can help improve the situation is to use their collective bargaining powers to remove some of the financial obstacles which stand in the way of workers receiving the benefits of modern psychiatry. Medical insurance discriminates against mental illness in two main ways: by its failure to provide coverage for psychiatric services and by withholding from workers suffering from mental illness the weekly cash benefits which are paid to offset the loss of wages due to physical illness. The pilot program conducted by Group Health Insurance would seem to indicate the feasibility of at least short-term psychiatric insurance coverage. The labor movement, which negotiates the provisions of group insurance plans covering hundreds of thousands, is in a position to help break down existing barriers and to make this possibility a reality. As a negotiating guide, however, labor needs specific information on comparative costs and benefits, as well as a thorough analysis of experience under insurance plans to date.

Another way in which unions can help to make improved psychiatric services available is to explore the provision of fuller services through their own or jointly run labor–management health centers. We have heard a report today on the pioneering efforts of one trade union to provide psychiatric treatment under its own auspices with employer-contributed funds.

There are many questions about the extent to which and manner in which unions should attempt to meet the mental health needs of their membership through such self-service programs; whether these would be better limited to diagnostic, referral and follow-up services; what therapeutic techniques should be employed if treatment services are included; what relationships should be established between union and community psychiatric care programs. It seems clear that a number of pilot projects are needed to demonstrate for different groups of workers in different localities what are the components of a model psychiatric care program and what role union health settings can play within this program. The Labor Education Department of Roosevelt University, four union health centers and city and lay mental health groups in Chicago have drawn up a project affiliated with NILE which is addressed to some of these questions and for which funds are presently being sought.

In addition to negotiating agreements, unions play an important role in handling day-to-day problems arising in the plant. Here one of the crucial problems is recognition of emotional disturbance as an illness. Certain types of emotional disturbances lead to situations in the plant where the disturbed workers become the center of intense and protracted grievance procedures. Very often both the company and the union fail to recognize the problem as an emotional disturbance and the situation is handled and sometimes settled in a way disadvantageous to all the parties concerned.

A team of psychiatrists, mental health educators and trade unionists has been organized at Wayne State University in Detroit under NILE auspices to collect a number of actual cases in which a mental health problem was the focus of the grievance, discuss these cases and formulate a policy as to how to handle them in a way most helpful to the disturbed employee. The goal of this project is to produce a casebook of grievances involving mental health problems which can serve as a guide to contractual agreements and at the same time be used as an instruction manual for shop stewards and committeemen.

We cannot cover the numerous other areas in which unions can utilize their collective bargaining position to secure increased protection and more satisfactory conditions for workers with mental health problems but we should like to draw attention to the constructive role which union leaders can play to facilitate the rehabilitation of workers returning to the shop from mental institutions. The interdisciplinary Research Center and the Institute of Management and Labor Relations of Rutgers University in collaboration with five major New Jersey unions, has planned a study to identify some of the problems encountered by union members in their readjustment to the work and community situations and to formulate a program for union intervention to help meet these problems.

Just as research and demonstration are vitally needed to fill the gap created by limited experience and to lay the basis for sound collective bargaining there is an equally urgent need for widespread union education. At the present time there is little awareness within the labor movement of the discriminatory situation prevailing in psychiatry. Facts concerning the need for more adequate psychiatric treatment services must be culled from the professional journals and widely disseminated among union staff, local union leadership and rank-and-file in order to build up informed support for a collective bargaining program dealing with these issues. We have given the preparation of such materials high priority.

Community action

Unions perform a representative function not only in the plant but in the community as well. Their participation in community affairs is carried out through a staff of over 100 full-time community service representatives and through the volunteer activities of thousands of local union leaders. As a result of labor's growing interest in community affairs and its increased prestige, it has become more and more common for community organizations to appoint at least one labor representative to their committees or boards. The mental health movement has been no exception. Unfortunately, because they are not yet well informed about their own or the community's mental health needs, labor representatives have often contributed little to such undertakings and have tended to limit their activities to the conventional ones of fund-raising and sponsorship of social and recreational programs for institutionalized patients. There is no reason, however, why an informed labor movement cannot play a similar role on mental health problems that it has on other economic and social problems where it has often been the decisive factor in compelling the community to face critical issues and take constructive action.

If labor is to fulfill the function of prodding the development of community programs to better serve working-class needs, a close and continuing collaboration is required between its representatives and trained professional personnel. It will be essential for labor not only to react to proposals, but to take responsibility for pointing out the gaps and deficiencies that exist and mobilizing support for the new programs that are required. To be effective, labor must be able to answer such questions as: What standards should be established? Under whose auspices should new services be organized? How can the totality of services be integrated for maximum value? What forms of cooperation can labor evolve with other community groups to achieve some of these goals?

Merely listing these questions gives some picture of the far-reaching effect which meaningful labor participation can have in the future development of community mental health services. We have previously pointed out that one of the main weaknesses in the mental health movement as a whole has been labor's failure to develop a mental health program of its own. At this particular historical juncture, however, this drawback may have its virtues. The labor movement does not yet have a fixed philosophy of mental health. Because of this, its support is not wedded to any one theoretical school nor to any one therapeutic technique. It has no hard and fast position on such controversies as the respective roles of hospital-based versus community clinic-based programs, or of state-versus city-supported facilities, or the optimum relationship among them all. It is not even necessarily committed to the traditional community pattern of shared public and philanthropic responsibility or to the manner in which these responsibilities are presently parcelled out or accounted for.

An informed labor movement committed only to the search for answers and improved programs can find common ground with all those within the social sciences and mental health professions who are dedicated to the same objectives. Thus, while we can expect that one outcome of greater labor participation in community mental health affairs will be pressure for *more* facilities and services, we cannot reckon the total impact in numbers alone without taking into account the catalytic role which labor might play in bringing about a fundamental reshaping and restructuring of mental health services.

Legislative and political action

Legislative and political action on both a state and national basis is another form in which the labor movement seeks to advance its objectives. There are a host of mental health issues determined in these arenas and on a number of them labor can play a decisive role.

Let us take, for example, the pressing need to strengthen state labor statutes so that they will provide the job and income protection which mentally ill no less than physically disabled workers vitally require. Over the years labor has devoted considerable attention to changes required in Workmen's Compensation laws so that they might keep pace with changing industrial conditions and greater knowledge of physical diseases and disabilities. But little has been done to systematically investigate and put forward proposals for coverage of psychological disabilities related to or aggravated by work conditions.

Some states also enacted temporary disability insurance laws whose purpose is to protect the worker against the effects of loss of wages because of illnesses which are not job connected. These laws require that employers provide a minimum schedule of weekly cash benefits either through the State Insurance Fund or privately negotiated plans. Here is an important vehicle for mitigating the catastrophic effects on workers' families of protracted periods of unemployment due to mental illness, but it exists in only a handful of states. Both labor and public health representatives have an important piece of unfinished business in trying to secure the enactment of such legislation throughout the country.

In addition to their legislative function, state governments play a decisive role in shaping mental health programs through executive action by setting priorities for services, establishing and enforcing standards, and operating key facilities. Here, too, a working partnership between professional and labor groups would make it possible for labor to add its voice to the demand for bolder and more extensive state mental health programs and for higher standards of service.

When we turn to the Washington scene and consider the role which the national labor movement has played in such fields as housing, social security, medical care for the aged and the like we become immediately aware of the contribution it could make in helping to determine the goals of public mental health policy and securing their implementation through political action.

Research

Consideration of what labor might do to help mold public policy on mental health and illness confronts us with the fact that we do not yet have a sufficient body of knowledge on which to base realistic programs of prevention and care for working people.

The need for developing and testing new therapeutic theories and techniques has already been emphasized, and it has been pointed out that the establishment of psychiatric programs in union settings offers a splendid opportunity for carrying out such treatment-oriented research. It is equally true, however, that we know far too little about how the circumstances of life of blue-collar workers affect their psychological well-being and shape their psychological disabilities to formulate scientifically sound preventative programs. This is well illustrated by our very limited understanding of the psychological meaning of work and the interconnections between various kinds of working conditions and the workers' psychological and social adjustment.

Our lack of knowledge is all the more serious because we are living in a period when drastic changes are taking place in the work environment through the rapid spread of automation. As technological innovations are introduced into one industry after another, literally millions of workers will be required to work under physical and social conditions radically different from those to which they have become accustomed, and hundreds of thousands of others may find that they are displaced persons in an economy which has rendered their skills obsolete and their labor superfluous.

In NILE's opinion, the importance of investigating the mental health consequences as well as the economic consequences of automation cannot be over-emphasized, and we are encouraging the efforts of a number of unions and universities to develop basic research projects in this area.

Many other problems requiring basic research could be mentioned. The main point we should like to make, however, is that in the course of developing a mental health program for labor organizations new opportunities will be opened up for studying some of the most challenging questions posed by social psychiatry. In the past such research opportunities have been circumscribed by the narrow objectives of industrial psychology and its identification with man-agement's goal of cutting costs and increasing output. Union interest in and sponsorship of research in industrial settings can restore these problems to the broad public health and social science domains where they rightfully belong.

Education

In what we have said thus far it has become obvious that a comprehensive and diversified program of mental health education is needed for all levels within the labor movement. We have highlighted some of the components of such a program and have suggested that it will require the development of both new materials and new techniques. Unlike traditional mental hygiene approaches, education within the labor movement will be effective only if it is oriented toward group action rather than focused on individual attitude change as such.

Another basic principle is the indivisibility of education, service and research activities. We have already seen that support will not be forthcoming for new service programs unless union leadership and membership are convinced of their importance. Even when new services are established, there is no guarantee that they will be utilized by those in need. In short, labor and professional personnel have the problem not only of making psychiatric services more *available* and financially *possible* for workers, but of making them *acceptable* as well.

Conversely, it is hard to conceive of an educational program divorced entirely from service considerations. Opening up the subject in any union forum immediately calls forth a flood of requests for individual help. Under these circumstances, local union leadership, already harassed by the mounting number of such requests and frustrated by the absence of adequate referral facilities, is not likely to "stir up any further trouble" unless some practical relief is in sight.

This has by no means been a complete round-up of the content of a labor mental health program. We were interested mainly in conveying the "flavor": indicating the areas for action, the approaches needed, the gains which might be achieved. None of it can be realized, however, nor even the beginning steps taken without the interest, enthusiasm and participation of the professional community – the educators, writers, therapists, consultants, mental health planners and administrators.

To facilitate such participation and because we in NILE are in a position to know many of the openings and possibilities that exist, we are setting up a professional roster of those who are interested in working on these problems in cooperation with labor.

In the beginning of this paper we stressed the importance of developing active labor participation in the mental health movement as a means of strengthening the social forces needed to cope with the social aspects of mental illness. What emerges from our review is the clear indication that the basing of mental health research, educational and service programs in labor settings can open the door to broad new advances in the body of knowledge about mental health and illness. This country has not yet seen the development of a working partnership between mental health professionals and labor representatives although NILE has made some progress toward this new and difficult objective.

The building of such a partnership holds the dual promise of progress in both the social and scientific spheres. We find the promise and the opportunity exciting and hope that many of you will share this view.

Notes

1. National Institute of Labor Education Mental Health Project *Bibliography*. (Mimeographed)
2. National Institute of Labor Education Mental Health Project. "A Mental Health Research Program for Labor." Paper read at American Psychological Association Symposium, September, 1960.
3. Avnet, Helen H. *Psychiatric Insurance*. A Research Project Report. Group Health Insurance, Inc., New York, 1962.
4. Bahn, Anita K; Chandler, Caroline A; and Lemkau, Paul V. "Diagnostic Characteristics of Adult Outpatients of Psychiatric Clinics as Related to Type and Outcome of Service." *Milbank Memorial Fund Quarterly*. October, 1962.

2   Advocacy: Strategy or solution?

Slogans are important for inspiration and organization but they do not put bread on the table. Frances Piven has performed a valuable service in reminding us of this old wisdom. She suggests that *radical* social action concepts and strategies, as well as traditional ones, should be judged by their objective consequences in the real political world – not by the subjective intentions of the individuals who espouse and practice them. Whether her estimate of the achievements of advocacy in urban planning will be considered adequate by experts in that field I am in no position to judge. But I hope that the method of analysis she employed in her article will stimulate professionals in all fields to consider the actual impact of the advocacy role in the particular social and political circumstances in which it is employed.

It is timely to begin such a critical assessment. With great rapidity, advocacy has become a central organizing concept among activist professionals in many fields. There are good reasons for its popularity. Advocacy represents a sharp break-away from two longheld tenets of traditional professionalism: the notion that there is some unitary "public" whose interest the professional should serve, and the related notion that the professional serves best by preserving a neutral stance in the social arena. Advocacy grasps the reality of contending class, race and group interests in our society. It recognizes that professional "neutrality" often masks support of dominant interest groups. In today's political context, it represents a call to the professional to put his skills and influence on the side of the poor and unrepresented.

This is the "radical" core of advocacy – its demand for partisan commitment on behalf of the black and minority urban poor. But in our enthusiasm for its

This article originally appeared in *Social Policy* 1 (July–August 1970). Reprinted with the permission of *Social Policy*.

value orientation, we ought not forget that the converse proposition is not necessarily true: commitment to social change and the elimination of poverty does not require the professional to function as a *paid* advocate for some *identifiable client group*. It is one role among many. And when professionals choose to adopt it, the choice should be made deliberately, realistically and with awareness of its limitations as well as its advantages.

Piven's case history highlights one of the most crucial considerations facing the would-be advocate – the choice of the *arena* of advocacy. The common denominator of the advocate role, as it appears to have developed in the various professions, is that it involves representing or championing a client cause in some particular arena where there are contending interests and a decision-making mechanism. The arena may be a magistrate's court, city planning commission, community mental health board or welfare agency. The assumption is that there is some "good" (a right, benefit or position of power) available for the client in this arena. When the particular institution or agency is one which provides specific benefits to individuals, the assumption is a safe one and the advocate's impact beneficial. But where the interests of an entire group or community are at stake and the rights and benefits have broad public policy implications (as in housing, community control of agencies, and the like), the appropriate arena of struggle is not so obvious. In fact, the selection of the arena of conflict may represent the single most important decision confronting the community. From whose perspective is the selection to be made – that of the radical professional, the particular client, or the broader social class or group being served?

Too often the question is settled by the availability of public funds and the special interests of the professional. Assuming the most sincere dedication on the part of the professional, these are hardly the most important considerations on which to base a course of action. The radical lawyer, eager to use the law to create new rights and protections for the poor, may urge that an issue be submitted to court test which might be more successfully prosecuted through political action or direct confrontation. The mental health professional may zealously organize a ghetto community to press for community control of mental health centers at a time when the community could be more effectively mobilized and united against exploiting landlords than the "mental health establishment." The social work activist may be immersed in helping to organize welfare recipients for sit-ins at local agencies while the state legislature with little opposition slashes thousands from the welfare rolls. Ripped out of the existing political context, each cause may be considered "worthwhile" in itself. But the number of causes around which the anger and power of the ghetto community can be effectively marshalled are not unlimited. The crucial questions are: who sets the agenda? what are the priorities? in terms of what superordinate goals are priorities set? If they continue to be set from the limited perspective of the individual profession, poverty leaders and popular movements may easily be led to dissipate their energies in unsuitable arenas, fighting lesser enemies for dubious gains.

The important message in the Piven article is that we cannot naively look upon advocacy as a matter of good professionals fighting a good fight. Advocacy is a selective strategy which requires a choice among alternative issues, arenas and methods of conflict. Advocacy thus *always* has political implications and consequences whether the substantive problem is urban renewal, education or drug addiction. We need only see with what ease major governmental agencies are embracing the advocacy concept to appreciate that advocacy procedures may be used to stabilize a system as well as to change it and to reinforce the status quo as well as effect a redistribution of power. With the same radical rhetoric, advocacy may serve to delay the growth of independent political opposition or to enhance the political consciousness and strength of protest movements. Advocacy is no substitute for sound social and political analysis. Indeed, effective radical advocacy requires some superordinate social and political objectives in the light of which various courses of action can be weighed. Without this, for all its approval, social advocacy may take on the character of other reform movements within the professions: an "ad hoc" response to "new opportunities" which may satisfy professional conscience but achieve only a negligible payoff for the long-range interests of the poor.

3   What is community psychology made of?

"What is community psychology?" appears to have become almost as popular a question among psychologists today as "What is operationism?" some decades ago. This shift in interest certainly testifies to the timeliness of the Swampscott Conference and the launching of Division 27.

The interest is ripe and the question seems right. But the answer proves troublesome. Attempts to specify the common denominator of community psychology vary widely. Some characterize the motivations and value systems of the individuals attracted to the field ("acceptance of responsibility for problems and issues of society," "humanistic goals"); some point to new work settings (community action programs, Peace Corps, Head Start); some emphasize the employment of new skills and techniques ("social interventionist," "social change agent"). Still others speak of a "common point of view" toward the practical uses of psychological knowledge and methodology. But none of these parameters seems to succeed both in setting the community psychologist apart from other professional colleagues or in uniting him with all those who bear the same label. And often as not the way out has been to present community psychology as all things to all men – a tangled skein of crusading spirit, new techniques of psychotherapy, activism, system theory, and God Bless America!

This state of affairs suggests that the question may not be as "right" as it first appears. It is not unusual for other fields in psychology to have a similar difficulty in self-description. What is "social psychology," for example? If we are not content to rely on purely personalistic descriptions but want to characterize the field as it exists in actuality, we usually find ourselves responding to this question by enumerating the kinds of people who are "doing social psychology" and the kinds of problems they are working on.

This same sort of analytic approach might be a fruitful one for Division 27. If

This essay originally appeared in *Introductory Readings in Community Mental Health*, ed. Patrick E. Cook (Merrifield, Va.: Holden-Day, 1970), pp. 13–21. Reprinted with the permission of the publisher.

31

it is the fact – as it appears to be – that community psychology essentially represents the bringing together of various kinds of psychologists who have some concern with the broad question of "man in society" then strictly speaking, *it* isn't anything – neither a homogeneous group, nor a unified body of theory, perhaps not even a single "point of view." We might better ask, Who are these psychologists? What, if anything, do they have in common? If we proceed from an analysis of the component "interest groups" in community psychology, we might be in a better position to evaluate the real (as compared to merely hoped-for) potentialities in the Division for new applications of knowledge, for the development of a "participant-conceptualist generalist" or for the generation of new theories.[1]

Of course, there are many ways to carve up interest groups. I have tried my hand at one classification scheme which I offer more to illustrate how we might go about clarifying the different approaches to community psychology than to furnish an accurate analysis.

In what follows, I will be talking about four different kinds of community psychologists to whom I have given labels of convenience: "social movement" psychologist, "social action" psychologist, "new clinical" psychologist, and "social engineer." These labels are not meant to imply that we are necessarily referring to different people – a social actionist and a clinician may certainly be one and the same. We are using these as aids in delineating points of view, not for the purpose of characterizing individuals.

I. Social movement psychologists

By this phrase I mean to refer to psychologists who identify themselves with the aims and aspirations of political and social movements working for major social change. It is their conviction that fundamental changes in society will only come about through the organized political struggle of sections of the population, and they have committed themselves to support the aggressive political action groups of today – students, the civil rights or black power movements, peace groups, left or independent political groupings of one kind or another. As psychologists, they are involved in working for social change in a *political* way. They may be actively engaged in local actions and community organization, but these activities are viewed within a larger context. Their interest is not only in making progress on some specific social issue but, over and above that, in the gains and growth of the national protest movements which they see as crucial levers for social change.

Even within this sub-grouping there are substantial differences in ideology between those who are concerned with political action as a strategy for making social gains within the existing social system, and the radicals who are interested, not in preserving and reforming, but in profoundly altering the basic economic, political and social structure of our society which they consider a precondition for creating healthy communities.

We are interested here in how these political views and objectives bear on the professional role. Some of these psychologists may be interested in putting their professional skills and talents to work on behalf of national movements. Such a role is not a clear one on the contemporary scene but a historical reference may help to illustrate some of its features. In the thirties, many professionals were attracted to the new CIO industrial unions, either as liberals seeing their potential for social reform or as Marxists who looked toward the working class as the vehicle for remaking society. Economists, social scientists, educators and others worked "on behalf of" these unions. This does not mean that they were necessarily paid employees or consultants; it means only that there was an identification and a devotion to issues that were of concern to labor and application of expert knowledge and skills to the solution of problems most crucial for labor. Some of this work was done under the aegis of autonomous or semi-autonomous bodies; some through professional organizations and some from university bases.

The point of the historical example is not to try to make a forced analogy with the present but only to point up the fact that today, as in the past, there are some professionals concerned with basic social change who are not identifiable by their locus of work (community or laboratory), by their specific function (activist or conceptual), or by a common theoretical frame of reference *within their discipline.* What they share is a certain kind of theorizing about contemporary society and, for some, a form of Marxist analysis of society may constitute the basis for their social involvement.

What are the implications for community psychology? "Social movement psychologists" may work in the same community programs as the social actionists (described below), but the basis for their participation may be quite different. They may work in settings far removed from the community, rendering diversified professional services in a voluntary capacity. They are likely to be concerned with many different kinds of social-political questions related to a number of different fields of psychology, rather than contributing primarily to the creation of a "new field" of community psychology. In terms of potentialities for theory development one thinks particularly of the possibilities of this group enriching the theory and practice of social movements, by subjecting to analysis and/or putting to the test certain "folk psychology" principles of how social and political organizations develop, function, and die.

In sum, in searching for what these psychologists have in common that enables us to "identify" them as a group, I would say that they share essentially a common *extra-psychological* frame of analysis for viewing contemporary social issues and a commitment to organized social movements as the major lever for social change.

II. "Social action" psychologists

There seems to be a substantial group within community psychology that is interested in "social action to promote human betterment" – that is, in participating as professionals in programs directed at some specific social problem. As many have pointed out, there has been a proliferation of government-financed programs for human betterment in the last few years, dominated by the community mental health and poverty programs but encompassing such issues as juvenile delinquency, drug addiction, youth employment, and others. These programs have created certain new employment opportunities for psychologists and have helped to define community psychology as a new field.

In addition to government, other principal employers are philanthropic foundations and non-profit research and service organizations. While these have always been large employers of psychological talent, there has been a shift in the nature of the programs funded[2], creating the demand for different kinds of psychological skills as well as providing the opportunity for social-minded psychologists to engage in new professional responsibilities.

"Social action" psychologists often differ in the emphasis they place upon organizing the community. Some consider that the most significant aspect of contemporary social reform programs is their provision for "participation by the people," and they feel these programs will achieve real human gains only to the extent that they succeed in helping disenfranchised, unorganized persons become actively engaged in common efforts to improve their life conditions. Other psychologists may be disinterested in organizing the recipients of services and feel they can perform a socially useful professional role simply through their own participation in these programs.

Even in programs which encourage people participation, however, the courses of action generally seem to be determined in most instances by the professional staff. *This is basically social action without commitment to political movements as forces for change.* In certain content areas, it may be social action without any clearly specified social goals while in others there may be varying degrees of professional consensus as to what the "desiderata" are.

The many content areas covered by these new programs are a source of great diversity, and so are the theoretical and scientific interests and the values of the participating psychologists. It is hard to see how a common theory or body of knowledge can emerge from a group of practitioners who are not likely to even share a common definition of the psychological problem involved in a particular social problem – say, for example, looting by Negro youths. To some the psychological problem may be that of correcting deviant behavior which interferes with individual progress, to others a matter of reducing inter-group hostility or controlling mass hysteria, or, conversely, a problem of raising the self-esteem of members of minority groups or of changing their child-rearing practices – and so on almost *ad infinitum.* While it undoubtedly would be rare to get any group of psychologists to "define the problem" similarly, it does seem that those who share an extra-psychological frame of reference toward social problems (as in the first group discussed) are more likely to exhibit a narrower conceptual range; their political "frame of reference" may operate, if ever so slightly, as a constraining and/or selective force on the way they identify and formulate issues.

The gain for theory building in the social action group, however, would be that more and more psychologists would be working with populations other than college sophomores and thus would come face to face with the deficiencies of many existing psychological constructs and be pressed to think creatively on their own.

On the level of practice and theory of practice, however, the picture is somewhat different. Working in somewhat similar settings with similar populations, these psychologists will be sharing certain common work interests and will be called upon to utilize certain practical skills not now in the general armamentarium of practitioners – action research, leadership development, adult education, and new forms of consultation, to suggest a few. This would appear to justify the expectation that a new body of knowledge about technique or practice may be developed which will lay the basis for a certain generic approach to the training of a "community psychologist."

One might then consider this grouping of psychologists to be a kind of "conglomerate," made up of subgroups with sub-interests and theories but sharing locations of work that have certain common humanistic goals and orientations and sharing certain common practical techniques.

As to whether a "common cement" of participation in action programs for human betterment will continue to hold together this conglomerate depends not so much on the subjective interests of the psychologists presently or futurely involved, but on social, political and economic events. Will public funding continue for human betterment programs? Will they remain the same in character? Will the corporation replace the foundation as the "intervener" in the ghetto?[3] It is conceivable that changes in social action programs or experiences accumulated in them may promote the movement of some social action psychologists of today toward either the pole of "social movement psychologist" or of "social engineer." This would be the case if the middle ground of applied psychology for human betterment through funded community action programs should disappear leaving psychologists either to affiliate with existing, more traditional public and institutional programs or to ally themselves (in voluntary, if not paid, capacities) with "grass-roots" action groups in the community.

III. "New clinical" psychologists

A group that is both numerically and historically important to community psychology consists of clinical psychologists who are no longer willing to rely on individual, face-to-face psychotherapy as the sole or primary means of remediating individual behavior. Their views have been well discussed in the literature and will not receive extended attention here.

For the future of community psychology, the important development would appear to be that more and more clinicians are departing from the medical model of mental illness, experimenting with new theoretical concepts and new techniques of environmental intervention. Because of these broadened interests and the changes in practice which take the clinician from the office or institution into new locations in the community, there is a growing basis for collaboration between him and the social action psychologist or the social engineer. Nonetheless, the clinical psychologist remains primarily oriented to a target individual and committed to evaluating intervention techniques on this basis.

Since this is the case, some of the questions considered central to the pursuit of community psychology – questions as to "how to achieve institutional change" or "how to involve people in social action" may or may not be relevant to the new clinical psychologists. Conversely, a question meriting consideration is whether and how *their* knowledge and skills may be relevant to the other groupings involved in the community psychology enterprise.

IV. Social engineer

Again, this is a label of convenience intended to distinguish certain participants in community psychology from groups with other focal interests. Some attempt has been made to characterize "social engineers" in terms of the techniques of social change they employ. Generally, the criticism is made that their methods are heavily "manipulative" as compared to those which rely more on involvement of lay people in decision-making and planning.

This distinction by itself seems deficient, however, since social actionists and community organizers may also function in a manipulative way. Perhaps a better way to make a distinction is to suggest that what we mean by "social engineer" is someone directly focused on the system, organization, or institution. In other words, the system is his object and he is only indirectly concerned with the people whose behavior, experience, or ideology is to be modified. The social actionist, on the other hand, is more related to the people who are to be served and/or activated and only indirectly to the system. (Caveats again that any particular Mr. X may wear two hats, or any particular program may embody both approaches). The engineer's stock-in-trade is to diagnose systems and systems effects, to help design and introduce changes in the system which are thought to lead to certain specified changes in people's behavior.

As I see it, the psychologist who participates in drawing up plans for a new kind of public housing is engaged in "social engineering"; so is the psychologist who sits in on meetings of a mayor's cabinet or who reorganizes the basic indoctrination program in the Army. As these examples are meant to suggest, the term "social engineer" is best used neutrally. There seems no reason why negative values should attach to it *per se* as it is sometimes implied in discussions which cast social actionists in the role of "good guys" and "engineers" as the villains. With one as with the other, it would appear that the specific undertaking and its objective consequences should be evaluated, not the *Ding-an-sich*. The trouble arises when claims are made for "social engineering" which are far too sweeping and imply that society will be remade by this approach. Used in this way, the same criticisms can be made against social science technocrats of today as were made against the "Technocracy" of the thirties – criticisms of the social, political and philosophical assumptions and policies of the scientific managers not against their "legitimate" (that is, "technical") concerns. (I would just add that the exaggerated representations of some of the social actionists may equally well be considered unfounded and misleading.)

Applying the term "social engineer" broadly as here clouds over the extremely important consideration that there are many levels of system and system intervention. It has been more popular in the past to reserve the term "social engineer" to those working in the public sector at the higher levels of planning and policy making. The numbers of "top-level" psychologists is likely to increase in the years ahead as professional organizations continue to press for greater participation by social scientists in government "in the national interest." Following the course taken by physical scientists, psychologists, and other social scientists may be expected to take on added responsibilities in government posts, to shift more from the solely consultant role to that of key administrator, to disposal as well as proposal.

Psychologists functioning as social engineers are likely to be involved, too, in an increasing number of content areas as the public planning sphere is enlarged. They will be bringing different kinds of knowledge and expertise to their interventions, and no more than the other groups previously discussed can they be expected to represent a common conceptual base. Moreover, as system intervention or social engineering approaches break into new fields we are likely to see new specializations developing, such as "architectural psychology" or "educational environment specialist." Finally, there is no reason to assume that the values, goals or objectives of psychologists attracted to this professional role are similar or harmonious or "humanistic" in the sense that this phrase is employed by some in community psychology. Recognition of this variance in values and ideology has already given rise to serious efforts to define a responsible role for the social engineer – one that will preserve his freedom to utilize his special knowledge and skills fully but that will ensure that his power to shape public policy is kept subject to the curbs and restraints of the lay citizenry.

What is shared in this group? Broadly speaking, it is a common interest in designing or shaping environments or systems to achieve certain behavioral or experiential consequences. And it is this group that might be expected to enrich psychology with data and theory in the ecological and systems analysis traditions.

Many might not agree with the interest groups that have been sketched out here or what has been said about them. But perhaps there is ground for agreement on some of these propositions:

1. Community psychology at the present time is a convenient umbrella term for psychologists who share a concern for a larger role for psychology on the social problems of the day but who have varying ideologies, values, psychological orientations and knowledge, skills and techniques;

2. Key constructs such as "acceptance of responsibility for problems of society," "social action," and "social change" have different content realms for individual psychologists depending on their interests and frame of reference;

3. It would be helpful in future discussions on the scope of community psychology to move from the level of acceptable but not very meaningful generality ("a new role for the psychologist is that of social change agent") to a more analytic level which specifies the different content realms and explores their implications.

While I have stressed the fact that the differences in background and the nature of present involvement of the various groupings in community psychology create varied potentialities for theory development, it does appear that on the level of practice, all the groupings share a common need – the need for more empirical knowledge about ecological and social system effects on individual behavior and experience. It may well be that the new roles performed by community psychologists will contribute to building a new database which will make it possible for all psychologists – in the community or in the laboratory – to progress toward a more complete theory of human development and functioning.

Notes

1. Reiff, R. Social intervention and the problem of psychological analysis. Presidential address to the Division of Community Psychology (27), American Psychological Association, Washington, D.C., September 1967.
2. Riessman, F. and Rein, M. The third force: an anti-poverty ideology. *The American Child, 47,* November, 1965, 10–14.
3. Cloward R. and Piven, F. Corporate imperialism for the poor. *Nation,* October 16, 1967.

4 *Social class and mental illness:* A critical review

Introduction

Any attempt at a critical review of *Social Class and Mental Illness*[1] must take into account the fact that this work has in a sense earned its own evaluation. In the mental health field it is considered a "classic." Its research findings and their significance have been examined and debated in the professional journals and meetings of clinical and social science disciplines concerned with prevention and treatment of mental illness. Certain conclusions are possible about the impact of this work, and it seems appropriate that these should be the starting point for a "second look" review.

In the first place, *Social Class and Mental Illness* has had a decided ideological impact. It has stimulated critical reappraisal of the psychiatric profession as a social institution incorporating a particular world view and value system. In turn, this re-appraisal has led to greater emphasis on expansion of training programs in social and community psychiatry, on the development of new techniques of treatment for lower economic groups, on movements to enlarge the role of nonpsychiatric personnel, and to introduce indigenous nonprofessional personnel into mental health facilities.

The New Haven study has had considerable influence in the research and action areas as well. Ambitious, large-scale epidemiological studies such as that conducted in Midtown Manhattan[2] have continued the effort to identify sociocultural factors important in the genesis of mental illness. Smaller-scale research, financed in large part by the National Institute of Mental Health, in labor health or public rehabilitation settings has sought to uncover relationships between the work and home worlds of blue-collar workers and their psychological disorders. Whether in basic research aimed at uncovering etiology or

This unpublished review of Hollingshead and Redlich's (1958) book by the same title was written while Scribner was at Rockefeller.

practical research directed at improving treatment programs, the socioeconomic status of the patient has become a more important research datum.

Sweeping changes are taking place, too, on the program planning level as
federal, state and community agencies under recent legislation seek to expand
community health facilities. One of the primary goals of the "community mental
health movement" is to make available outpatient treatment to broader segments of the population – in particular those whose most common treatment
resource has been the state mental hospital. The findings of the New Haven
study that economic and social factors were more of a determinant of treatment
agent than psychiatric factors played no small role in encouraging experimenta-
tions in this direction.

Of course we are not implying that this is the influence of one study, no
matter its excellence and relevance. *Social Class and Mental Illness* was perhaps
as much a product of the changing spirit in the psychiatric and sociological
disciplines as it was a contributor to it. Nevertheless, as judged by objective
consequences, Hollingshead and Redlich made a number of important contributions in bringing out from under the covers the two facts of life "Americans
prefer to avoid" – social class and mental illness. These were both practical and
theoretical and might be summarized as follows.

On a practical level, their research has helped to improve the lot of the
psychologically disturbed especially the poor among them; on a more theoretical
level, the study revealed the value of a social-psychiatric approach to the understanding and treatment of mental illness; it highlighted the enormous importance
of social and institutional factors in the health care field; and on the broadest level,
it went a long way toward establishing or re-establishing the relevance of social
class as an important variable in the analysis of American society.

With these conclusions, the task of present evaluation has just begun. It is
precisely because of the tremendous influence of the book, because it is so often
turned to and quoted as *the* source for all kinds of statements and views on the
relationships between social class and mental illness that it is essential to know
exactly what the study did or did not find. To what extent are the common
interpretations given to it, such as "The lower the class, the greater the mental
illness," justified by the facts? A close examination attempting to disentangle the
proved facts from the inferred should prove useful.

Research plan and methodology

The sociological problem and its translation into research hypotheses

In their introductory chapter, Hollingshead and Redlich state their
broad interest as being one of bridging the gap between the theoretical positions
represented by sociologists and psychiatrists. Mindful of the many unsuccessful

attempts to formulate a unitary theory of behavior which takes into account both the biological and social nature of man, they set themselves the more limited task of investigating possible specific functional linkages between sociocultural and behavioral variables. The particular variable selected for study from the former category was social class status; from the latter, mental illness.

The authors leave no doubt that the aim of their research is explanatory. Moreover they make clear that by "linkage" they mean not merely association or correlation between the two variables, but a causal relationship in which class status functions as the independent or antecedent variable and diagnosis and treatment as the consequent variables.

Two possible linkages were postulated in the research questions: class as a causal factor in the *etiology* of mental illness and class as a causal factor in the *treatment* of mental illness. These initial questions were operationalized in a set of hypotheses which could be tested empirically.[3] The first two are concerned with etiology and attempt to state a testable relationship between *amount* and *kind* of mental illness and class position; the third hypothesis relates psychiatric treatment to the patient's class position.

> *Hypothesis 1.* The prevalence of treated mental illness is related significantly to an individual's position in the class structure.
> *Hypothesis 2.* The types of diagnosed psychiatric disorders are connected significantly to the class structure.
> *Hypothesis 3.* The kind of psychiatric treatment administered by psychiatrists is associated with the patient's position in the class structure.

Every translation of a research question into a working hypothesis involves some transformation in the question itself. The researcher has every right to select how and in what manner the transformation will be made. His decision is, however, critical to an accurate interpretation of the findings. In this study, the important definition was that of mental illness. The hypotheses do not involve mental illness as a disease distributed throughout the general population; they are concerned only with *treated* mental illness – that is, disease distributed throughout a defined patient population. Hollingshead and Redlich explain that they have defined mental illness socially: "Whatever a psychiatrist treats or is expected to treat must be viewed as mental illness."[4] They recognize that the converse of this statement is not true: namely that anything not treated by a psychiatrist is not mental illness. One of the few findings on which most mental health researchers appear to agree is that treated mental illness represents just a small portion of the actual amount of illness present in the population: the "top of the glacier."[5] In the absence of any evidence that treated mental illness is representative of all mental illness, findings based on treated mental illness cannot be simply generalized to all mental illness. This point is stressed because while we do not necessarily require that the title of the book or every reference in the text carry the modifier "treated" in front of "mental illness," we are particularly interested in seeing whether this limitation is in fact lost sight of in the researchers' own interpretation of the find-ings.

The working hypotheses express a second important decision – to test both basic research propositions by using data on treated mental illness. How ade-quate these data will prove to be for evidence of etiological factors is a question we will want to pursue.

Finally, we take note of the choice of a prevalence measure as the indicator of "amount" of mental illness. Without entering into a discussion on the respective merits of prevalence vs. incidence measures in the epidemiological study of illness, we have to take into account the fact that prevalence (the number of cases present in a specified population at any one time or during any one period) reflects not only how many people become ill but also how long they stay ill. If speed of recovery is related to the varying efficacies of different treatment techniques, we have a measure which itself is not independent of treatment practices.

While the interest of the investigators was clearly in showing the influence of a social class on the other variables, the hypotheses state only that it is associated with or related to them. In the case of treatment practices the relationship logically can only be one way. But some have suggested, as in the "drift hypothesis," that mental illness may be the antecedent factor causing a downward shift in the individual's economic and social position. Hollingshead and Redlich deal quite thoroughly with this hypothesis[6] and their analysis of the residential histories of their schizophrenic patients who had lived in the community all their lives failed to support the theory. There seems no reason therefore to question their interpreta-tion of the direction of the significant relationships.

Methodology

The authors present us with a clear, detailed and comprehensive ac-count of the development of their research plan and instruments. These will be reviewed briefly, again from the point of view of their bearing on interpretation of the data.

The psychiatric census

The bold decision was made to try to catch, not a representative selec-tion, but all cases in psychiatric treatment during a stated period (May 31–Dec. 1, 1950).[7] The important question is whether the census operations were so planned and executed as to in fact furnish comprehensive coverage and mini-mize bias from selective inclusion or exclusion of psychiatric patients from the various social classes or from systematic distortions in information transcribed on the patient schedule.

COVERAGE. A psychiatric case was defined as "any person in treatment with a psychiatrist or under the care of a psychiatric clinic or mental hospital between

May 31 and Dec. 1, 1950." This excluded persons being treated in general hospitals unless they were under the care of a psychiatrist and persons being treated by non-medical mental health personnel or by medical, nonmental health personnel – concretely, individuals in treatment with clinical psychologists and social workers and those seeing family doctors for essentially psychiatric illnesses. In 1950 there were probably not too many of the former and these predominantly middle-class. It is common knowledge, however, that the general practitioner is an important treatment resource for working-class individuals with psychological disorders.

The treatment facilities covered in the census were inclusive: private psychiatrists, clinics, private, state, and veterans' hospitals. The thoroughness of the effort to locate every resident in treatment is indicated by the extensions of the "treatment network" to out-of-state practitioners and institutions.

Success of the census depended on cooperation of the practitioners contacted. The authors' analysis of nonrespondents indicates that the level of cooperation was excellent: there was 100% cooperation from all the institutional psychiatrists; 20 out of 66 private practitioners estimated to account for some 40–50 patients refused to cooperate. The pattern of nonrespondents indicates some probable under-estimation of middle and upper social classes which constituted the bulk of the private psychiatrists' patient load. However, this seems more than balanced out by the probable under-coverage of lower-class patients being seen by their family doctors (excluded by definition). This latter exclusion seems somewhat more serious since we have less grounds to infer that the types of mental illness of Class IV and V individuals in treatment with general practitioners were the same as those disorders which brought them to psychiatrists than we have to infer that middle-class patients in treatment with some private psychiatrists were suffering from disorders fairly similar to those exhibited by patients of psychiatrists actually covered in the census.

PATIENT SCHEDULES. Basic demographic and treatment data for the study were secured on the patient schedule. It was filled out in two ways: team psychiatrists conducted direct interviews with the private practitioners and team psychiatrists and sociologists abstracted the pertinent data from the records of patients who were under the care of institutions. The investigators made a careful check of the abstractors' reliability and found it moderately satisfactory. They deplored the fact that the records themselves were often incomplete, confused and contradictory. This known fact – the deficiencies of hospital records for research purposes – does not in my opinion seriously detract from the research findings. There is no reason to expect that errors in the records were "class-biased."

One item on the Patient Schedule requires comment. For the entry "Psychiatric Diagnosis" researchers departed from the customary practice of entering either the raw data as given or first-level judgments (such as "check the *principal* method of treatment"). Hollingshead and Redlich report that they evaluated the diagnosis of each patient given by a treating psychiatrist (or psychiatrists) and where their judgment differed, they rediagnosed the patient's disorder from the record. Seventeen percent of the private practitioners' cases and somewhat under 6% of the hospital and clinic cases were so rediagnosed. Their stated purpose was to improve the validity of the diagnoses – that is, get as close as possible to the "true" mental illness. This may have appeared necessary for testing Hypotheses 1 and 2 but insofar as the study was interested in revealing class-based differences in psychiatric treatment, which begins with diagnosis, the important datum was the diagnosis given to the patient by the treating psychiatrist – "right" or "wrong." Here is an instance where the two research questions – in etiology and in treatment practices – seem to have competing interests.

2. Five percent sample

Test of the hypotheses required that the patient population be compared with the general population, similarly stratified by social class. For this purpose it was crucial to select a sample representative on the criteria used for determining class position. Obviously if the proportion of the general population in a given class were wrongly estimated, it would invalidate any conclusions drawn from a comparison of the proportion of psychiatric patients in that class enumerated by the Census. Occupational and educational data on all New Haven residents were not available but residential data – the third component of the Index of Social Position – was in the form of a City Directory listing all dwellings in the community.

The method of systematic probability sampling was used. Interviewers were trained and the usual safeguards of supervision and spot-checking taken. Of the 3608 household units in the sample, 3559 interviews were completed, an impressive achievement. Refusals were a low 5% and substitutions were made from the same or neighboring dwelling units to preserve the social class distribution.

The sample was tested for representativeness of age, sex and ecological distribution. Discrepancies between the sample count and the Census count for certain age-sex brackets were generally within acceptable sampling variability. On ranking of dwelling units, the sample estimate placed more dwelling units in the middle ranks than ecological ratings based on the Census. Sample estimates were lower than Census on the first, fifth and sixth ranks. Discrepancies were in the 1–2% range. Since residence is only one of three components in the Social Position Index, it is unlikely that the minor under- or over-estimations of ecological rank (scale value) in the sample would result in any significant amount of mis-classification of the individual's class status score.

3. Determination of class status

Psychiatric patients and the 5 percent sample were assigned class positions by use of the Index of Social Position developed by Hollingshead. The manner in which this Index was constructed and validated is clearly set forth in a special Appendix. There is a voluminous literature on the different methods used by sociologists to measure class position and the respective advantages and disadvantages alleged for each. The important facts to be noted about this Index are:

1. A sensible rationale is given for choice of each of the component factors (occupation, education, residence).
2. Acceptable techniques of scale construction were used.
3. The Index was validated before its employment in the study.

Whether or not the Index is acceptable as the best or ultimate measure of social classes in America is not necessary to judge here. There seems little doubt that it served to divide the New Haven population into groups which could be ranked from low to high in socioeconomic position, and that it was a comparatively rigorous and objective method for doing so.

To conclude this summary of research methodology: we have found the research plan and instruments to have been carefully worked out and seemingly free from artifactual biases. We have raised the question as to whether the stretegy of attempting to investigate both etiology and treatment practices through analysis of treated mental illness could do justice to the former, and we will return to this point in our interpretation of findings.

Findings

Social Class and Mental Illness is packed with rich material, comment and analysis on many aspects of the social milieus (both the general community and the psychiatric community) with which the study was concerned. To do justice to the discussions in Parts 2 and 5 would require more extensive treatment than we can give here. We will confine our attention to the quantitative analyses of the data bearing on the test of the three research hypotheses.

Hypothesis 1. Class and prevalence of mental disorders

We will proceed by stating the authors' conclusions and then reviewing the evidence on which they were based.

First conclusion: A definite association exists between class position and being a psychiatric patient.

This was revealed in two types of analysis. The first was a comparison of the proportion of patients in the various classes with the proportion of the general population (5% sample) in these classes. Chi-square tests were applied to determine whether these distributions differed significantly. The second type of analysis involved the computation of prevalence rates based on number of psychiatric cases per 100,000 individuals in each class stratum.

Evidence from the chi-square tests without exception shows highly significant differences related to class. Data were analyzed grossly first, then with selected single factors held constant. Other analytic techniques were used to test associations with two factors at a time held constant and finally with three factors held constant. The three factors selected – age, sex, and marital status – have all been shown in other studies to be related to prevalence of mental illness and thus they were relevant to the proof. The authors state that 90% of the analyses made with two factors held constant and 10 out of the 12 matrices developed for testing with three factors constant displayed a significant association between class and mental illness. Since this is the case, the principal finding can be illustrated by the first table:

Table 8
*Class Status and the Distribution of Patients
and Nonpatients in the Population*

| Class | Population, % | |
	Patients	Nonpatients
I	1.0	3.0
II	7.0	8.4
III	13.7	20.4
IV	40.1	49.8
V	38.2	18.4

Checking through the other presented tables, we find they all show the same general relationships. Not only is there a significant association between class and patient status, but in almost every case, Classes I–IV show fewer patients than their proportion in the population while the proportion of patients in Class V exceeds the population proportion by an extraordinary amount.
The prevalence rates tell a similar story:

Class	Adjusted Rate per 100,000
I–II	553
III	528
IV	665
V	1,668
Total Population	808

While Class IV has a somewhat higher rate than Class I–II, it is the extreme jump from IV to V that commands attention. In Appendix IV, Table 5, where the computational data for the X^2 test of the above table are presented, we find that the difference between observed and expected frequencies in Classes I–IV are all negative; the Class V cell is the only one in which the observed is greater than the expected. As the authors state, the linkage between class status and the distribution of patients in the population follows the "characteristic pattern" of Class V, contributing more patients than its proportion in the population warrants.

Second conclusion: The lower the class, the greater the proportion of patients in the population.

This suggests that the nature of the association between class status and the amount of treated mental illness is a linear one. It seems to be derived from the table of prevalence rates. But simple inspection of this table shows such a statement to be unwarranted: when we move from Class I–II to Class III, we move to a lower class, but the proportion of patients *drops* rather than increases. I have been unable to find any direct evidence for this conclusion.

Third conclusion: The greatest difference is between Classes IV and V in that Class V has a much higher ratio of patients to population than Class IV.

We have already reviewed the evidence leading to this conclusion. It is perhaps the most outstanding of all the findings in this chapter. Indeed, the break is such a sharp one that one might almost speak of a dichotomized population, Population A consisting of Classes I–IV and Population B consisting of Class V. The authors do not view the data this way and while it may be an "optional" view one regrets their failure to draw any implications from the stand-out position of Class V. The concept of class expressed in the Index of Social Position seems to be that of a single dimension, a continuum on which the population can be ordered with classes set off from one another on purely quantitative measures. In the break between Class IV and Class V we seem to have some special factor operating, outside of the class difference measured in the Index. Such an explanatory factor remains to be found.

Hollingshead and Redlich were able to break down their prevalence data into three components: new cases (those arising during the covered period), continued cases (those arising before but continuing into the study period) and re-entry cases (old cases re-activated during the study period). The following table is taken from Appendix IV.

Let us first note the incidence rates.[8] The authors report that differences in incidence rates (as with all the other rates in the table) are significantly associ-

Table 6
Age and Sex Adjusted Rates per 100,000 for
Each Component in Prevalence by Class

Class	Incidence	Reentry	Continuous	Total
I–II	97	88	368	553
III	114	68	346	528
IV	89	59	516	664
V	139	123	1406	1668

Type of Rate

ated with class status. But here the absence of a linear relationship is, if any-thing, more marked than in the total prevalence rates which we had previously examined. Class IV, interestingly enough, has the lowest incidence of any class in the population. The shift in position of Class IV to second highest in total prevalence is accounted for wholly by the fact that there is a disproportionately high number of continuous cases in this class. Moreover, the enormous gap between Class V's prevalence rate and those of the other classes is also seen to be due in the main to the "continuous case" column. Hollingshead and Redlich bring this pileup of cases to the reader's attention with the comment that something seems to be happening to patients in the two lower classes. While they deal most thoroughly and excitingly with this "something" in the chapter on treatment practices, it has an important bearing on the way findings related to class status and prevalence should be interpreted.

In the concluding lines of this chapter, the investigators find that Hypothesis 1 has been proved true and continue: "Stated in different terms, a distinct inverse relationship exists between social class and mental illness." However, as we have repeatedly pointed out, all the evidence presented has related class status only to the probability of being a psychiatric patient; it allows no conclu-sions to be drawn about mental illness in general. We have also raised the question of the validity of suggesting an across-the-board inverse relationship.

In sum, our review of the findings indicates that:

1. The authors have confirmed Hypothesis 1 that an association exists between class position and prevalence of treated mental illness.
2. The linkage between class and prevalence of treated mental illness lies mainly in the fact that the lowest class – Class V – contributes an inordinately high proportion of patients.
3. Class position is linked to prevalence in several ways. It plays a role both in the proportion of the population who become patients and in the proportion of those who remain patients. The greater prevalence of the two lower classes is due (wholly in the case of Class IV and primari-ly in the case of Class V) to the accumulation of cases in treatment.
4. The data have no relevance to the question of how mental illness is distributed among the social classes unless connections are specified between the mentally ill patient group and the mentally ill nonpatient group in each class.

Hypothesis 2. Class position and types of mental illness

In discussing the findings in support of this hypothesis, we encounter a serious difficulty – that is the confusing and inconsistent manner in which the authors state the hypothesis itself.

In the most formal presentation, quoted earlier, the hypothesis read: "The types of *diagnosed psychiatric disorders* are connected significantly to the class structure."[9] The opening statement of this chapter says that Hypothesis 2 "postulated the existence of significant relationships between the *types of disorders patients exhibit* and their positions in the class structure."[10] And, further, ". . . in the second [hypothesis] we examine the *nature of the patient's illnesses* to see if they are associated with class status"[11] (my italicizing throughout).

Clearly a decision was never made as to whether the researchers were looking at illnesses or diagnoses. To look at illnesses required some attempt at an independent evaluation of the patient's history and condition. As already pointed out, the research psychiatrists took a step in this direction by reviewing the records and rediagnosing some of the cases. Nonetheless they persist throughout the text in referring to the "diagnoses the psychiatrists" gave the patients, thus in a sense disowning their own review. The impasse to which this leads us when it comes to giving a coherent interpretation of the data is illustrated in the following statement: "if a significant difference is found . . . we will have empirical evidence of a real relationship between class position and either the *kind* of disorders patients present to psychiatrists or the *way* psychiatrists diagnose the disorders of their patients"[12] (their emphasis).

The greater part of the discussion emphasizes the *way* in which psychiatrists respond to patients of different classes – even when they are exhibiting the same behavior. The authors brilliantly describe how the diagnosis of neurosis, for example, is the "resultant of a social interactional process which involves the patient, the doctor, and the patient's position in the status structure of the community."[13] But in their summary of this section and of the study as a whole they present their research as demonstrating a relationship between class status and the proportion of patients who suffer from different types of psychiatric disorders.

It is hard to be satisfied with this either-or approach because the implications and practical consequences of each are different and because it places no restraints on the way in which inferences are drawn from the data.

In my opinion, there are strong grounds for coming to the conclusion that the data manipulated in these analyses are much closer to the diagnoses given by the treating psychiatrists than to the patient's illnesses. If nothing else, the heavy reliance on transcription from sketchy hospital records for a large number of patients would make it difficult for the researchers to surmount the treatment agent's view of the patients and arrive at a "true" decision as to the nature of the illness. This in itself is not a serious handicap as long as the evidence is taken for what it is.

Again, the researchers give us two tests of the hypothesis, one relying on an examination of the distribution of diagnoses within the patient population (internal test) and one comparing prevalence rates for the various diagnostic categories by class (external test). Both the "within" and "between" comparisons show a decided and consistent relationship between class status and diagnosed mental illness. While these become intricate in the finer analyses they are clear and distinct enough when the patient population is divided into the two categories of "neurosis" and "psychosis." Highlights from the internal test include these findings:

- The diagnosis of neurosis is directly related to class status – the higher the class, the more patients in the neurotic category.
- The diagnosis of psychosis is inversely related to class – the lower the class, the more diagnosed psychotics.
- Patients from different classes are not randomly distributed but are clustered within specific subcategories of neurosis.
- Psychotic patients are also distributed within diagnostic categories in a manner related to class status. The higher the class, the larger the proportion of affective psychotics; the lower the class the higher the proportion of organic disorders.

Prevalence rates for the various diagnostic categories substantiate these differences:

- Amount of diagnosed neurosis differs by class: prevalence rates are higher for higher classes. The rates decline steadily from I–II to IV, with a slight upturn for Class V.
- Amount of diagnosed psychosis varies by class: prevalence rates are higher for lower classes. There are small rises from class to class and a large jump from Class IV to Class V.
- There are significant differences in prevalence rates for each category of neurosis and each category of psychosis.

It is rare indeed that such a mass of evidence when handled this way or that all points in the same direction. The reader as well as the authors conclude the review with considerable conviction that a strong link has been established between social class and the type of diagnosed mental illness.

In the early 1950s this was a startling discovery in itself since the psychiatric profession was engrossed with the subtleties of diagnosis in the calm assumption that the diagnostic process was influenced by psychological factors in the patient only. Hollingshead and Redlich went beyond the unassailable proposition that sociocultural factors played a major role in this process to suggest that their study had yielded "presumptive evidence of the impact of class status upon the various types of mental illness."[14] Such a conclusion, it seems to me, is at least two steps removed from the data we have examined: the facts in the study are concerned with treated mental illness and not with mental illness in the population at large (a point made in our discussion of Hypothesis 1) and, in addition, the facts deal with diagnoses of mental illness as given by existing treatment agencies rather than with "illness" carefully and independently assessed, apart from the ongoing institutional arrangements.

Hypothesis 3. Class status and treatment

In the section dealing with treatment practices, the handling of the data and its interpretation are unequivocal and unambiguous. *Treatment* data are used to draw conclusions about the *treatment* process (rather than about pathologies *per se*) and they unquestionably demonstrate a massive and pervasive effect of class on that process.

As might have been predicted, preliminary analyses showed strong relationships between diagnosis and treatment agency, and diagnosis and principal form of therapy. Therefore it was necessary to test the hypothesized link between class status and psychiatric treatment for groups of patients with the same diagnosis within the same treatment agency.

When this is done, a complex pattern emerges in which the effect of patient class position influences the selection of treatment agency and then, in combination with the psychiatrist's theoretical orientation and class value system, determines to a large extent what is done for him and what chances he has of being restored to a functioning role in the community or of remaining a chronic inmate of a mental institution.

Reviewing the main findings for neurotics:

- No association exists between the overall kinds of diagnoses neurotics receive and kinds of therapy.
- Kind of therapy is significantly associated, however, with where the patients are cared for and their positions in the class system.
- Where they are cared for, in turn, is related to class. Class I individuals are treated exclusively by private practitioners or in private hospitals. At the other end of the spectrum, 81% of Class V patients are treated by public agencies, with 29% hospitalized for treatment.
- Within each treatment agency, there are clear-cut differences in types of therapy provided patients from different economic and social walks of life. Among private practitioners analytic psychotherapy is limited in the main to Classes I and II; the lower the class the higher the percentage receiving an organic therapy for the *same* illnesses. Within the clinics and hospitals, in spite of differing cost and fee arrangements, the same class-related pattern emerges: Class IV and V patients most often get no treatment (custodial care) or shock treatment or lobotomies.

When we turn to patients diagnosed as psychotic we find class influence on treatment even more marked and resulting in appalling social inequities. The outstanding finding here is that patients in the higher classes have a lower rate of institutionalization and when institutionalized are overwhelmingly in private hospitals. The number of patients institutionalized for treatment of diagnosed psychoses increases as we descend the socioeconomic ladder until it is the overwhelmingly predominant form of treatment for Class V. It is not only institutionalization as a form of treatment but kind of institution which varies with class. For Class V patients, the Hollingshead–Redlich data reveal that the first treatment resource and the last treatment resource, the resource for care of alcoholism, schizophrenia or senility is the same – the state hospital.

Even inside the public hospital "equal treatment" eludes the lower class patient. The Class V schizophrenic rarely gets more than custodial care.

Of particular import in light of our earlier discussion on the rise in the over-all prevalence rates with descending class are the data presented on class and duration of treatment. Using a measure of the median number of years in treatment they find that 50% of the psychotics in Classes I and II have been in treatment under three years. This figure climbs steadily until it reaches 10 years for the 50% mark in Class V. Every treatment of the data shows the same story: once a lower class patient is diagnosed as psychotic and committed to a state hospital he tends to stay there. "Treatment" is the end of the road.

Hollingshead and Redlich conclude, as we must, that they have found real differences in where, how, and how long persons in the several classes have been cared for by psychiatrists. Hypothesis 3 is confirmed.

Conclusion

We can now stand off at a distance and look at the book as a whole.

When we do this a principal theme stands out. It is a theme of inequities within society and within one of its major healing professions that result in "two kinds of medicine" – one for the rich and one for the poor. The theme itself is not a novel one, but the way in which it has been explicated by Hollingshead and Redlich transforms it from a moral judgment to an objective statement about existing social practices. Moreover, their study advances our understanding of the way in which class factors operate in modern American society in respect to issues of health care. There are no simple villains of the piece. Rather there are a whole host of complex subjective and objective factors operating toward the same ends. At every step of the way, attitudes and circumstances of class determine who becomes a psychiatric patient and for what, where he goes and what becomes of him. Whether one's psyche is exorcised or part of one's brain removed may depend on your verbal fluency and financial affluency.

Hollingshead and Redlich produced evidence that "shocked" but it has been overwhelmingly corroborated in historical and contemporary studies of psychiatric practice in the United States which have been completed since publication of their study. Every one of the relationships they postulated at the outset of the study in respect to treated mental illness has held up. This is an outstanding research accomplishment.

It is unfortunate that Hollingshead and Redlich encouraged some erroneous interpretations of their work. They were clearly not content to let their analysis rest on the practical level alone. Throughout they express their abiding interest and belief that the conditions of life in the various social strata play an important role in the way mental pathology develops and the kind of symptoms it exhibits. While they repeatedly make the "right" technical statements about the difference between the prevalence of treated illness and illness in general, they often ignore these caveats in their interpretations. The fact is that the stronger the relationship shown to exist between treatment and class, the less useful treatment data become as a means of exploring relationships between class and illness.

It is because Hypothesis 3 was confirmed that the New Haven study could yield no reliable information on the amount of mental illness or the kinds of mental illness endemic among the various classes. Clearly any research directed at the epidemiology of mental illness must in the future depart from reliance on patient data. Killing two birds with one stone is not an available research strategy in the area of mental illness.

One other thing we learn from this book's findings on prevalence of treated mental illness – and that is that the relationships are not well expressed in the simple form of "the lower the class, the greater the number of psychiatric patients." At best it is a short-hand expression concealing some important subclasses of relationships. It is not surprising that the first analysis of these data – startling as they were – should have resulted in a general and somewhat unrefined conclusion. What *Social Class and Mental Illness* shows us on second look is that much remains to be done to unravel the connections between class and mental illness – perhaps to carry to an even more specific level the search for linkages between conditions of life and the risk of illness. Loose interpretations of this pioneering study will only impede this necessary effort.

Notes

1. Hollingshead, August B. and Frederick C. Redlich. *Social Class and Mental Illness: A Community Study.* New York, 1958.
2. Srole, Leo, Thomas Langner et al. *Mental Health in the Metropolis: the Midtown Manhattan Study.* Volume 1. New York, 1962.
3. There were five hypotheses but this volume deals only with the first three.
4. Social Class and Mental Illness, op. cit. p. 11.
5. The 1961 Report of the Joint Commission on Mental Illness and Health cites survey results showing one in ten persons in the population as mentally ill, whereas the number of those coming to professional attention is about one in 100. *Action for Mental Health.* New York. 1961. p. 87.
6. Social Class and Mental Illness, op. cit. pp. 244–248.
7. To my knowledge, a census of outpatient psychiatric treatment facilities was a technical innovation. Most studies of treated mental illness prior to the New Haven study worked exclusively with hospital data.
8. In this discussion, the authors define incidence as a "measure of the way a disease

attacks a population during an interval of time." But this is an obviously mistaken definition in the present context where the data are exclusively concerned with a *patient* population. An incidence rate here tells us only the way individuals in the population become patients. Unfortunately, there are many similar instances of confusion throughout the text.

 9. Social Class and Mental Illness, op. cit., p. 11.
10. Ibid., p. 220.
11. Ibid., p. 220.
12. Ibid., p. 237.
13. Ibid., p. 238.
14. Ibid., p. 231.

5   Research as a social process

The position of the applied researcher in the social sciences is not a very comfortable one today. Like other professionals, we are increasingly challenged to provide some tangible demonstration of our usefulness to society, and while many of us accept the legitimacy of this challenge, we are not sure we know the royal road to relevancy. How and where do we fit on the scene? Granted that there may be roles in which professionals can contribute to the movement for community development, is research one of them?

Those leading the fight for better living conditions and greater political power for ghetto residents are engaged in actions whose outcome seems to be little related to what research has to offer. Impatient with years of fruitless research which has never been reflected in social change in the ghettos, community residents are not inclined to look with favor on the researcher's effort to become relevant by studying them. They want action, not investigation. The concerned researcher thus often confronts a popular verdict that his work is useless.

On the other hand, many professional leaders and key public figures are calling for a vast increase in funds and major reorganization of applied social research to bring its resources directly to bear on problems of urban and community development. They argue that if government could be committed to investing a significant share of the research budget in social science areas, we could make breakthroughs on urban problems similar in magnitude to those made on problems of manned space travel. Here the concerned researcher seems to confront a professional verdict that his work is of critical importance. Properly funded and organized, research has the capability of prescribing to national and community leaders what actions are necessary to solve our most

This paper was originally presented at the American Psychological Association's Symposium on Community Development, Washington, D.C., September 3, 1969.

55

urgent social problems. This is a beautiful illustration of what Krasner (1965) has called the myth of infallibility-fallibility, which is often attached to scientists. Either the researcher is omnipotent – the future course of society may well rest on his ability to come up with the right answers to racism, poverty and violence – or he is impotent, a well-meaning, hopelessly unrelated nuisance who gets in the way of the action.

It is evidently not helpful to look upon the researcher as either God or the Devil. The problem is to search out the specific ways in which he can make a contribution to social reform and community development in his professional capacity as an objective investigator.

In considering this question I think it is useful to start with the recognition that applied research is not only a scientific endeavor but a social process as well. (cf. Warren, 1963) Whatever the topic of investigation, research is always embedded in larger social and political processes which influence its course and outcome. In turn, the research process has an impact upon the larger social processes through the new knowledge it produces and the methodologies it adopts.

The socially concerned researcher will consciously address himself to this reciprocal relationship and seek to structure it in such a way that his research advances the social values and goals he champions. He asks: how can I conduct my research so that its impact within the larger social processes of society will promote political, economic, and social equality?

There is no simple answer to this question. But this paper would like to suggest that one way this can be done is by viewing research as an instrumentality for enhancing the effectiveness of those actors in the social process who are fighting for social reform – that is, by relating research to social action through its service to activist social groups. In specific terms, this calls upon researchers to serve new popular constituencies – community corporations, local school governing boards, student organizations, welfare rights groups, peace groups, consumer and labor groups. Some of these constituencies have organized settings and funds available for the employment of research personnel. Direct employment, however, is not required for researchers to relate to their needs. Investigators in certain traditional settings – universities and public and private agencies – can contribute by entering into collaborative relationships around specific research projects.

In this paper I would like to explore some of the implications of this position. I will do so, first, by contrasting it to a major national research effort which seeks to increase the relevancy of research to the community by focusing on the technological rather than social action potential of research. Then I will examine specifically how new community constituencies might strengthen the research process, and, conversely, how competent research might contribute to action programs within the community.

One of the principal government efforts to bring both social and "hard" research to bear effectively on urban problems is the Research and Development program organized by the Department of Housing and Urban Development under a $10 million 1968 appropriation from Congress. According to Carroll's (1969) analysis of the history and scope of this program, it represents a wholesale, conscious direction of technological activities toward national objectives in the areas of urban development and social affairs. He states:

"In recent years there has been much speculation concerning the potentials of science and technology for urban development. Research and development activities at HUD are designed to determine what the real potentials are." (page 907).

The Department organized its urban R & D effort after the AEC and NASA models which it said demonstrated the successful partnership government and industry could achieve in major research areas and indicated how beneficial a similar partnership might be in nondefense areas. The Department sets priorities for research and then awards contracts for specific projects to commercial and industrial organizations and some academic institutions.

Research projects are intended to have the following characteristics: to join social technology with hard technology – that is to be concerned with managerial and behavioral problems as well as engineering problems; and to take into account the realities of government and public operations on local levels. Carroll also suggests that HUD sees its R & D program as relating to community self-determination movements through an emphasis on "participatory technology."

Stated most broadly, the objectives of HUD's R & D program are: 1) to meld the social and physical sciences into one science of metropolitan development; 2) to relate this science to processes of law and government; and 3) to use it to build "technological bridges" between ghetto communities and the nation at large.

It would be valuable to study HUD's program and proposals for other expanded government-funded and -managed research efforts and analyze the philosophical, scientific and social premises on which they are based. I would merely like to point out two features of the HUD R & D program which bear directly on our topic of a partisan role for applied research.

First, HUD's program appears to be based on the diagnosis that research has failed to contribute extensively to urban and community development mainly because of economic and organizational deficiencies. Social scientists have been isolated one from another in the universities and the social sciences have been isolated from the hard sciences. Both have been isolated from the industrial and public arenas with respect to urban issues. The remedy is to rationalize this research just as NASA rationalized space research. This requires sufficient funding to ensure that the most modern hardware and sophisticated research methodologies are utilized in investigations of urgent social issues.

Money and organization *are* critically important to any enterprise and not less so to urban and community research. But the argument which stresses research technology seems to skip a crucial step. It assumes that the state of knowledge in the behavioral and social sciences is such that there is some scientific consensus about the specific areas most in need of investigation and, most importantly, that there is consensus about the way in which specific research questions within these areas are to be framed. A single example casts doubt upon this assumption. Carroll (1969) reports that the Department of Justice and the Institute for Defense Analyses, a private think tank, are designing a research and development program for public safety. Let us suppose that a contract was awarded to the Legal Services Program within OEO to work in cooperation with Dr. Kenneth Clark's Metropolitan Applied Research Center to develop an R & D program on public safety. What similarities might be expected between the Dept. of Justice and OEO *research* programs? And could one interpret the differences as being related to the differences in research techniques available to or preferred by the different agencies?

Similar contrasts in research programs developed under different sponsorship might be found in other areas. In fact, it is interesting to speculate that the more relevant the area of investigation – that is, the more directly it is related to issues in the public arena – the more variability there is likely to be in the way various scientists formulate the research question.

Given this great variability in the possible formulations of research questions, we have to conclude that the shape of R & D programs on many social issues will be more influenced by the interests of the specific research constituencies and the theoretical predilections, value orientations and social positions of investigators than space or industrial research. The analogy with NASA breaks down. Decisions as to the sponsorship of research, the choice of setting, the selection of investigators will all have a bearing on the range, choice, and formulation of research questions.

These are all problems of social influences on social research and in many ways they are prior to the technological problems. At any rate, if we acknowledge their existence, it does not appear appropriate to create models for the organization of applied social research which do not take them into account or to imply that more money from the government is all that is needed. Nor does it appear warranted to picture the relationship of research to community issues as one of a disinterested research enterprise making an objective diagnosis of community ills and producing tested solutions to specific social problems. It seems more realistic to speak of different research enterprises investigating different aspects of the problem, coming up with different kinds of data leading to different action possibilities.

Some government funding agencies, such as NIMH, have attempted to resolve the dilemma by deliberately adopting a pluralistic policy, sponsoring research in various settings and from various theoretical points of view. This is a position which implies that research can illumine social problems and make possible more informed action but not by itself dictate the course of action.

In areas where many courses of investigation present themselves, some system of research priorities must be established. If the state of scientific knowledge is not such as to unequivocally indicate what line of investigation comes next, research priorities must be worked out on the basis of extra-scientific considerations. Social influences come into play on another level as it were. Now the crucial issues are: Who determines research priorities? Are they exclusively the province of the individual investigator or research organization? Or, as in HUD's program, are they the province of the funding agency? What are the processes by which various groups in the population can declare their interests and be heard?

A second observation that can be made about HUD's R & D program is that it implies that a major reason for government's inability to cope effectively with the urban crisis is the unavailability of the necessary social and engineering technology. The problems are complex and our knowledge of what to do and how to do it inadequate. The entire program seems based on the assumption that government, industry and all significant social forces are committed to urban development and that it is the mission of science and technology to lead the way.

In considering this assumption, it might be useful to make a distinction between broad social objectives and political decisions to carry out these objectives. If we are to take space research as a comparison, we can see clearly that research on space problems was a generally accepted objective for a number of years before President Kennedy responded to Sputnik. But the crash program which produced Apollo came *after* a national political decision was made to beat the Russians to the moon. The target was specified, a time table was set, sufficient resources committed. Estimates of research capability undoubtedly played an important role in determining the feasibility of the target but the decision to pursue the target was made in the larger political arena, not in the research arena.

In what area of domestic social policy has there been a similar national political commitment to invest whatever resources it takes to solve a specific problem within a specified period of time? The Department of Housing and Urban Development has set two of its six top research priorities in the area of low-income housing. Let us suppose that when Congress reconvenes, a decision is made to replace all blighted housing in our twenty largest cities within the next decade. Such a decision would certainly not reduce the importance of HUD research; on the contrary, it would magnify it. Unquestionably it would drastically change the nature of the specific investigations, which would then be clearly committed to finding solutions to *implement* policy rather than producing findings on the basis of which to *recommend* policy.

From whatever aspect we tackle the problem, it seems impossible to disentangle the research process from the larger social and political processes at work in the society or to reduce the relationship between research and social policy to questions of technology. Complex social influences affect the way

social problems are defined for investigation; and equally complex social influences affect whether and how the knowledge produced by research contributes
to the carrying forward of social objectives. These considerations need to be
kept in mind when proposals are made which emphasize the social gains to be
derived from the "utilization of social technology in pursuit of public objectives" (Carroll, 1969, p. 904).

This analysis suggests, then, that the researcher concerned with relevancy
has to take stock of two sets of questions: the scientific ones (those pertaining to
the state of knowledge in the field in which he is working, his own expertise,
and interests) and the social questions (what are the implications and possible
consequences of pursuing certain lines of investigation in certain ways?). In this
light, when we speak of a partisan commitment to new popular constituencies
we are doing no more than proposing that the inherent directionality of much
social research should be explicitly spelled out, and that the researcher should
actively strive to bring the research process into line with the social processes
which will enhance its impact.

This approach does not pose any greater problems to the researcher in
maintaining the objectivity and integrity of his research than he already confronts in working for the traditional constituencies – government, the military,
industry, established institutions. More than a decade ago, Benne and Swanson
(Benne, 1965) made an analysis of the extra-scientific choices which every
behavioral scientist must make in his research role, regardless of his setting.
They identified three areas of choice: What problem will the researcher study?
With whom will he collaborate in the course of his work? And what responsibility will he assume for the utilization of his research results? The researcher
who commits himself to serving the interests of new community constituencies
is simply adopting a consistent principle to guide him in these extra-scientific
choices. The problems will not be new but they are likely to be more out in the
open.

Now I would like to move off this general plane of national research policy
and look at how an individual researcher's commitment to new constituencies is
likely to affect the research process. To make this discussion more concrete, I
will consider the issues from the perspective of a mental health researcher in
the geographical area served by the Hunts Point Multiservice Mental Health
Center, a community-controlled agency in the South Bronx.

The three extra-scientific questions identified by Benne provide a framework
for our discussion.

1. First, a commitment to serve the interests of the residents of this community will help the researcher set his priorities and frame his research questions,
especially since mechanisms now exist through which he can ascertain how the
community perceives its needs.

Lincoln Hospital Mental Health Program until recently conducted a sizable research program in the South Bronx, including the Hunts Point Area. As with most such programs the demands for research and the research interests of the investigators outstripped resources. The Research Director (Struening, 1966) emphasized that a priority task of research was to help formulate program goals appropriate to this particular community's needs. At the same time he noted that neither the research nor administrative personnel had access to the broad segments of the community. Initially the research program concentrated its resources on studies of the population and community, producing area profiles of great usefulness to city-wide and community groups. Without continuing feedback from the community, however, research issues came increasingly to be defined in terms of the frame of reference of the program's professional administrators rather than that of the community residents the program was serving.

This might be illustrated by a decision to invest a major portion of research resources in the development of a five-hour battery of tests, attitude and opinion questionnaires for all mental health aide applicants. The purpose was to develop a screening instrument to enable professionals to predict which applicants would make more effective workers in the Neighborhood Service Centers. The Research Division's Progress Report to NIMH (1966) which described this study also reported that 400 people from the catchment area had applied for this position within a year, of whom 54 could be selected for training. In the same period, the categories "financial problem" and "employment" together accounted for 52% of all problems brought in to the Neighborhood Service Centers. Does it not seem likely that community residents would be dubious of the merit of screening devices to select 50 from 400 and more inclined to welcome research efforts directed at opening up additional employment opportunities within the service agencies for the unemployed? If the researcher asked, "What are the action implications of this screening battery?" community groups might answer "None." On the other hand, program administrators in their capacity as employers might find the action consequences useful.

I want to emphasize that this is not a matter of "bad" or "good" research. What is involved here is a question of the differential social *utilities* that a given piece of research has for different segments of the population: a specific study may be of high utility for mental health program administrators, low for client groups. In the past, to whatever extent considerations of utility have been a factor in the assignment of priorities to research, the utilities that counted were customarily those of the institutional leadership.

This can easily be illustrated in many fields. Until recently a good deal of reading research, for example, was invested in the development of visual discrimination and other tests that would make the best possible instrument for predicting fast and slow readers in the first grade. The utility of this research might have appeared self-evident to school personnel searching for a single way of dividing up pupils for instructional purposes. But how would its utility be perceived by a parents' association in a ghetto school which takes it for granted that the principal function of a school is to teach *all* children, fast and slow, how to read, and who do not see a very good job being done with either group? Commitment to popular-based community organizations may redress this imbalance in research by moving to the fore those questions which have high utility for groups who are served by our institutions. For psychologists, specifically, this might introduce a trend away from preoccupation with diagnostic, screening or predictive instruments which are not directly related to interventions that will benefit those being diagnosed, screened, or predicted.

2. Secondly, if a researcher is committed to serving the interests of local community groups and is accountable to them, he will have greater opportunity to build an implementation component into the research process itself. He can do this by involving the target population and its leaders, not merely in the routine tasks of research, but in the design and conduct of the investigations.

Much applied research is now conducted as though research and implementation have nothing to do with each other. Again drawing an example from Lincoln Hospital's experience: The Mental Health Research program designed a study on the characteristics of mothers and their environments associated with premature births. The study was intended to influence potential mothers to use educational and health services in the area. Suppose a research committee had been organized on which were represented a group of mothers and young marrieds, leaders of the Multiservice Center health programs, and personnel of the hospital medical services. The involvement of these groups in discussions of research objectives would itself have been an important step toward implementation. Program providers and potential users would have become acquainted in a common enterprise. With community representatives collaborating in the production of data and committed to the study's objectives, its findings would be most closely related to the practical needs of the community and stand the best chances of issuing into action.

Warren (1963) has analyzed the close relationship between organization of the research project and its impact on the social systems with which it interacts. Lippitt (1967) and others have also summarized the important organizational considerations in the conduct of research which seeks to produce change in community institutions. A researcher with ties to community groups has unique opportunities for creating research systems which can be transformed into action systems for meaningful social change. This is one of the most significant implications of a popular constituency for applied social research.

3. Finally, concern for the interests of a community constituency and the action implications of research will influence analysis of the data and the forms in which it is communicated. This point is also concerned with utilization of research results but on a broader scale; it deals not only with the researcher's relationship to the specific population involved in his research but with his public educational function. It is an accepted component of the research ethic

that the investigator is obligated to make his findings public. But the public which researchers customarily have in mind is the scientific community. Most researchers consider their reporting obligations discharged when they have completed the required progress report to the sponsoring agency and have prepared journal articles and papers communicating their findings to colleagues. It is characteristic of research reports to conclude with a listing of staff professional publications emanating from the research program. How many publication plans include brochures, leaflets or newpaper articles written for community groups or other popular audiences? How many reports and speeches have been given to communicate research findings to ghetto residents? Again, this process of communication has two-way effects. It not only lets the community in on the research but it forces the researcher to evaluate the meaning and significance of his study to the community.

At the same time, the researcher would destroy his special usefulness if he were so carried away by demands for action implications that he vulgarized or distorted his findings. The obligation of reporting to the community introduces a whole new set of considerations into the interpretation of data. It might, perhaps, be more accurate to say that it forces the researcher to become more explicit about the considerations entering into his interpretation and conclusions. Rather than detracting from his scientific role, this aspect of the researcher's commitment to popular constituencies may be seen as potentially enhancing it, since it imposes on the investigator the necessity for constant scrutiny and refinement of the interpretative process.

Thus far we have been considering the relationship between research and community groups from the point of view of the researcher. This is only half the coin. The researcher cannot contribute to social action programs unless he is valued by the leadership of such programs and unless he values his own special expertise.

Devaluation of research is to be expected in a period when the emphasis of social action is on confrontation, conflict and power struggle.

It need hardly be said that knowledge as well as muscle is power. If research had little to contribute to the practical operations of our society, we could not account for the diffusion of applied research throughout our principal institutions – government, armed forces, corporations, labor organizations, educational institutions, social agencies.

Moreover, a number of reports and analyses in the literature provide tangible evidence of the many ways in which research has contributed specifically to programs for institutional change as well as institutional perpetuation. (Lippitt, 1958; Thelen, 1967). Brooke (1965) and others have shown the substantial contributions of research to community action anti-poverty programs.

If the researcher is willing to lend himself to the purpose of enhancing the effectiveness of community groups, rather than remaining their outside critic, there are two major ways he can contribute: through the *product* of his activities

– the systematic and comprehensive information that his skills make available – and through the self-conscious use of the research *process* to develop leadership and individual growth among participants in the organization's activities.

We have already dealt with the utility of information to action groups in our discussion of selecting and framing the research question. Leaders of community organizations may "know" their communities sufficiently for certain purposes but when it comes to the provision of service programs, more systematic and detailed knowledge is necessary. The researcher can also strengthen the knowledge base for individual action projects. If an Education Committee in Hunts Point Multiservice Center becomes concerned with the large number of suspensions of Puerto Rican and black students from the high schools in its area, it might be helpful for it to know how the rate of suspensions compares to those of schools in other areas of the city, whether they are concentrated in certain schools or among students of a given ethnic group, whether there is a pattern to the circumstances surrounding the suspensions and the like. Such information might help a community group go beyond the immediate objective of reducing the number of suspensions to identifying some of the underlying characteristics of the school environment that contribute to the problem in the first place. The researcher's effort to gather all the relevant information may show up certain factors which the action leader does not see from his position in the "thick of things" (Thelen, 1967, 270).

A prominent role for the house researcher, located within the action organization, is the establishment of record-keeping systems which enable the leadership to know what is actually being done in the various programs, and to modify them, where indicated, to increase their effectiveness. Variously known as social bookkeeping or operational research programs, these serve the dual purpose of improving internal management and meeting the needs for external accounting. If new community control organizations are in fact to be primarily accountable to the residents in the area and the client populations they serve, they need to share information with them as well as with their funding groups and collaborating agencies in some organized, accurate and comprehensible manner.

A record-keeping system which produces a continuous flow of information about the community organization's transactions to its program leadership fills the very important function of strengthening the rational component in decision-making. It enlarges the field of operations which is known to the individual program leaders. It provides the possibility of leadership groups reaching a consensus about next steps on the basis of common, shared information rather than on the basis of fragmentary information and the specialized perspectives and experiences of the individual participants. There is sufficient psychological literature on the influence of needs and personal perspectives on perception for the applied researcher to appreciate that the information he is able to help the organization acquire about its own operations is a potential unifier – another way in which a knowledge base strengthens action.

While the importance of information to action groups is obvious, less attention has been given to the impact of the research process itself. Here again we look upon research as a social process of a particular kind introduced into organizations in which many other kinds of social processes are in operation. The intervention of the research process must have consequences. If the experimental psychologist has been forced in recent years to address himself to the experimenter influence in basic research, it is certainly important for the applied researcher to attempt to bring the consequences of his intervention under control. Since he cannot eliminate these consequences, he will want to maximize the constructive and minimize the negative effects.

What are some of the special characteristics of the research process which distinguish it from other processes in which community leaders and residents may be engaged? In the first place, however the inspiration for research may arrive, the research itself is not a spontaneous activity. Even short-term, single-issue research requires more than a good idea worked out on an *ad hoc* basis if it is to produce reliable and valid information. Research requires a clear specification of objectives and a clear specification of operations leading to them. Research operations generally take the form of planned, integrated and highly structured action sequences in which the ends, the means, and the relationship between them are under maximum control.

This is an idealized picture and most fruitful research operations prove more flexible in practice than researchers are willing to acknowledge in the literature. Nevertheless, as compared to "men of action," they strive for the most precise definition of ends and awareness of the determining influences which different operations have upon the ends. In research, conceptual clarification is the precursor to action. In ghetto communities, residents and indigenous leaders may have had little occasion to participate in this kind of action sequence. Leaders have demonstrated their imaginative, skilled use of practical experience and knowledge in solving problems and meeting objectives. Yet the implementation of community control programs and the carrying through of long-range social objectives gain from the reflective and analytic approaches that research operations require.

The introduction of research into an action setting forces a process of conceptual clarification. This can be illustrated even with the homely example of discussions around the introduction of record-keeping systems. The researcher who eventually has to translate the discussion into research instruments suggests areas of information and pushes the action people to state what it is they want to know and what they will do with it. Should an applicant for job training be asked to describe in detail his contacts with other job training programs? This might help the community determine to what extent its own program is functioning as a substitute resource rather than an additional one, or it might provide a basis for comparison of the new program with old ones. On the other hand, the community may not be interested in comparing its ability to hold trainees in its program vis-à-vis the ability of other programs to hold theirs, they may consider job placement and maintenance a more meaningful criterion of success. In this instance, employment history and job-seeking information may be more relevant kinds of data to collect. A process initiated in the interests of research introduces a process of clarification of program goals. In this process, participants are challenged to go beyond sloganizing, to entertain the different possibilities encompassed in the general objective, to subject these to criticism and finally select a course of action. This is not to suggest that these processes are absent from other kinds of planning operations but rather to point out that they are *essential* to all research operations. Because research discussions usually occur at least one step removed from the heat of action, they provide a climate which encourages the critical and reflective point of view.

Those community leaders and members who are involved in the actual organization of the research including such research operations as interviewing or manipulation of data are enjoying a series of specialized experiences in which they are acquiring and organizing knowledge with which they are not personally implicated – that is, on which they are not personally required to take action. Thus they have the opportunity of participating in the researcher's perspective toward the subject under investigation – one in which some distance is introduced between "what is out there" and "how I see it." There is a growing respect for the value of knowing as fully as possible "what is out there."

For those who participate with the researcher in review of data and preparation of reports, there is the opportunity to participate in the development of a conceptual framework which organizes the facts and makes them useful. There is the important process, never-ending for the professional researcher, of discovering the limitations of his personal knowledge and ambiguity of what appear to be fixed concepts. This is an important aspect of learning because it brings the individual into confrontation with the complexity of problems and helps him achieve sophistication in their analysis and solution.

Finally, those who are involved in the communication of research results to others in the community learn the importance of a shared frame of reference in the communication process and the need for educational efforts to develop common perceptions of the social environment as the basis for sustained effective action.

Summary

In this paper we have examined how the researcher's partisan commitment to popular community constituencies might mutually enhance the research and social action processes. We contrasted this model for increasing the relevancy of applied social research with models emphasizing the technological contribution to urban and community problems which might be achieved through large and rationalized research enterprises. These are clearly not mutually exclusive approaches. We have argued, however, that there is a need and a place for research with a social action orientation; that such an orientation can increase the usefulness of research and contribute to the effectiveness of social reform and community development movements. It would be foolhardy to think there is any simple way of eliminating the natural differences between the man of action and the man of research. We can only direct our effort to bringing research and social action together in such a way that the tension between the two will have the most advantageous yield for both.

6   *Psychology and the problems of society:* A review

This collection of symposium papers and invited addresses on the 1969 APA convention theme, "Psychology and the Problems of Society," presents a satisfyingly varied set of answers to what now appears to be a singularly inappropriate question: What does psychology have to contribute to the solution of current social problems?

The question was formulated by the Convention Committee as an alternative to the theme proposed by the organizing committee of Psychologists for Social Action, then known as the Ad Hoc Committee of Psychologists for Social Responsibility. This group was the first to call upon the profession to take action in opposition to the Vietnam war, racism and poverty, by the introduction of two resolutions to the 1968 APA Convention. One of these, which received the endorsement of the Society for the Psychological Study of Social Issues and other APA Divisions, suggested that the 1969 Convention be organized around the topic, "Psychologists and Social Responsibility," and explore how psychologists might fulfill their ethical and scientific obligation to foster the welfare of man. Some consequences of this shift in topic are discussed below.

The decision to dedicate a convention to psychology's usefulness in the solution of social problems certainly constituted a unique and forward step in the history of organized psychology. It must be counted as a substantial advance, too, that so many psychologists in diverse fields explicitly accepted the moral imperative of relating their work to social needs. With the current debate on "Whither APA?" so commonly presented as a division of the house between "professional activists" and "dedicated scientists" it is important to note that contributors to this volume include numerous university-based experimentalists as well as psychologists engaged in campus and community programs.

This critical review of Korten, Cook, and Lacey's (1970) anthology originally appeared in the PSA newsletter.

Proceeding from a common ethical commitment, the contributors fan out to offer a great array of potential roles for the socially concerned psychologist. George Miller proposes psychologists engage in what Anthony Wallace designated as a cultural revitalization movement, educating people to change their conceptions of themselves and others. Wiesner urges participation in a new discipline of social engineering to monitor social change. New goals and forms of therapy (Spaner) and counseling (Thomas) are suggested. The section on Psychology and Urban Problems describes innovative ways in which psychologists are helping to restructure institutions: advocate to poor communities (Levin): trainer (Bard); evaluator (Guttentag); planner and critic (Clark, Pettigrew); consultant to mass media (Lesser).

As to the social problems to which psychologists are to contribute, Convention Theme Committee Chairman Cook explains the practical considerations which led to the omission of a number of significant topics. Those represented are organized around such issues as problems of minority groups, early education, student unrest, reduction in violence. And herein lies the crucial question: How do social problems become defined? Why emphasize reduction in violence rather than reduction in police surveillance? why student unrest rather than university inadequacies? why population control instead of political repression? Why, as Charles E. Wilson protested, do social scientists continue to ask what they can do for the black community instead of what they can do to build a more humane society?

Kelman, one of the few contributors to get below surface consideration of social scientists' involvement in social issues, suggests that the very definition of what is problematic is itself a social process. Discussing social research, he points out that those who are in a position to sponsor and use social research (the economically and politically powerful) decide what questions are to be asked and provide the framework within which answers will be organized.

This observation might be extended to the definition of what constitutes "society's ills" and what characterizes the curing process. In shifting the Convention theme to a consideration of current social problems, the APA Convention Committee implicitly accepted the prevailing political definitions of these problems. Moreover, it subjected to review only the work directly related to these politically defined social problems. Missing from the Convention was any examination or assessment of the social impact of other areas of psychological work. But it is surely naive to consider that only the work of the "socially concerned" psychologist has social consequences. In a fundamental sense, all psychological work has implications for the problems of society, whether that work is conducted in a laboratory, a classroom, a mental hospital, or an army recruiting center. The very choice of which psychological functions are to be performed and the integration of these functions into the operation of specific institutions and in society at large have real consequences, whether these are intended or unintended, recognized or undetected. It is to be hoped that this volume will promote greater consciousness among psychologists as to the many different ways in which they contribute either to the perpetuation of the status quo or to its transformation.

This volume is also a stunning revelation of the limitations of efforts to relate psychology to specific social problems without an analysis of the basic social forces operating in our present-day capitalist society. In spite of the best of intentions, such efforts may be not only inadequate but self-defeating. As Russell Nixon made abundantly clear in his presentation to this year's convention of APA on the limits of human advancement under capitalism, several decades of reform efforts including wars on poverty, welfare dependency, juvenile delinquency and crime, have left us with a society in which inequities have become more extreme and social crises more frequent. It is encouraging and important that psychologists are awakening to their social responsibilities. To act responsibly on such aroused social consciousness, however, requires not only a scientific knowledge of psychology but a scientific understanding of society and the dynamic forces operating within it. Relating psychology to the basic mechanisms of social change in a class society is an enterprise that truly calls on all psychologists for their most serious and scholarly effort as well as their more extended participation in the day-by-day struggles of social movements.

7   Psychologists, process, and performance

The topic assigned me – to provide some assessment of the state of knowledge on the comparative study of cognition and its policy implications – seems like an eminently reasonable one.

For the past twenty years or so, considerations of educational goals and policies have centered around the ugly and inescapable fact that our schools, like many of our institutions, are failing children of the poor and working classes, Black children and those of other ethnic minorities. However sharp the controversy as to what programmatic course to take, there has been common consensus that changes are required that will enable schools to "take into account" cultural differences in the background of the children. There has been common consensus as well that psychological research can provide the basic facts about cultural differences to guide school reform.

In the light of this reasonableness and consensus, I hope it won't appear capricious of me to reject the assignment of making broad generalizations about comparative research. The assignment carries with it certain implications. It implies that there *is* some integrated domain of psychological inquiry that can be subsumed under the general rubric of "comparative study of cognition." It implies that the evidence of investigators in this domain can be marshalled and weighed, that the golden kernels can be gleaned and the chaff thrown away, and that with the proper commitment and sensible course of action the golden kernels can be brought to bear in the formation of more equitable social and educational policies.

This paper was originally presented at the Technology and Culture Seminar, MIT, Cambridge, Mass., 1975, and appeared in *Merit and Equality in a Just Society: Report of the Technology and Culture Seminar.* Reprinted with the permission of MIT.

71

Two approaches to culture and cognition

I would like to follow another course – one that sheds the neutral banner of "the comparative study of cognition" and deals with the several distinct research enterprises or practices carried on under this banner. At least two approaches can be distinguished. Although they share certain common concepts and methods, they pose different questions, yield different evidence, and have vastly different implications for public policy and, in particular, for the future of our schools. In my discussion, I will accentuate their contrasting features because I believe this will help illuminate the process by which "findings" from comparative research come to constitute "evidence" that is considered relevant for policy-making decisions. And, conversely, it may serve as a reminder to those concerned with the ethical and social implications of research that we need to specify what kind of research practice we are talking about when we look to science for policy guidelines.

Let me give my brief and oversimplified characterization. One psychological approach to culture and cognition is easily identifiable. This approach simply takes culture as given, as a way of "marking off" populations who can be differentiated according to some characteristic – ethnic group membership, language, or socioeconomic status. Its concern is to employ the tools of psychology to compare these "marked off" populations and determine whether they differ in one or another basic cognitive capacity – attention, or memory, or logical reasoning, for example. The science of psychology was involved from its infant years in this endeavor when W.H.R. Rivers joined an anthropological expedition to the Torres Straits at the turn of the century to see how the inhabitants of these exotic places would do on laboratory-developed tests of perceptual acuity. Over the years, the specific areas of interest have shifted: in one decade Rorschach tests circled the globe, in another Piagetian conservation tests, but the tradition has carried on unbroken to the present day.

The careful and theoretically well-motivated examples of this research, have yielded many important and useful findings for our understanding of the variety of ways in which people manifest perceptual and cognitive skills. In its simplistic form – and this, unfortunately, has characterized the bulk of this research – psychologists have contributed to dividing the people of the world into "haves" and "have nots" in terms of their psychological resources, much as economic and political analysts have divided the world into "have" and "have-not" nations in terms of their material resources.

The basic assumption underlying this research is that psychological tests and experimental tasks can be used as measuring instruments for assessing the cognitive capacities of people. Although it does not require any assumption about the universality or culture-specificity of basic processes, in actual practice, it has often led to a characterization of different cultural groups as being deficient in the higher order skills presumably essential for participation in a technologically complex society and in formal school settings. It is this comparative psychological enterprise which is most often turned to as having something relevant to say about the determination of national educational policies and goals. It interprets the problems of education in this country or in third world countries in terms of competencies or incompetencies of peoples, not inadequacies or adequacies of societal institutions.

Another approach to culture and cognition has a shorter lineage. It is one that our laboratory, along with many other investigators, has been trying to develop. This approach considers *culture* to be as important a part of the inquiry as *cognition*. It accepts as a sound starting point anthropological findings of the universality of basic psychological processes – remembering, generalizing, reasoning. It maintains that a wide diversity of informal learning situations all nurture these basic processes but there are culturally-fostered differences in the way these skills are integrated and brought into play in various problem-solving situations. It considers the psychological problem to be one of specifying the particular mechanisms which promote such different organizations of skills. Experimental tasks are seen as specially-contrived situations for investigating the interaction between task demands and skills. It interprets the problems of education as finding ways to maximize the match among the many cultural institutions, both formal and informal, in which children and adults learn, and learn to solve problems. Its findings are piecemeal, complicated, not easily visible and its utility is not readily apparent to educators and policy makers who seek early solutions to critical problems.

Resulting diverse estimates of social and moral responsibilities

A. Arthur Jensen's research: Assumptions, procedures, and inferences

I think the contrasting ethical and policy considerations that emerge from these two approaches can best be explored through an examination of a particular piece of experimental research on subcultural variations in the U.S. The research I have selected to examine is a series of experiments by Arthur Jensen and his students using the free recall paradigm for investigating memory processes. Some of the reasons for my choice are obvious. For one thing, Jensen's two-level theory of mental abilities and the tracking system it proposes for our schools is already a major position in the public arena. It poses the most immediate questions of the ethical and social responsibilities of comparative psychological research.

Secondly, this particular set of studies on free recall is cited by Jensen as a major support for the two-level theory. The paradigm he employed is one of the most intensively used paradigms in human learning. A formidable literature has developed around it, based on the findings of dozens of studies with college students and elementary school children, and theoretical controversies have raged for years over their proper interpretation. Thus, we can bring considerable background knowledge and sophisticated analysis to bear on an evaluation of how Jensen uses this task in comparative research and what conclusions he draws from it.

The only way to assess Jensen's use of the "hard science" capability of psychology is to examine in detail the assumptions he brings to the experiment, the materials and procedures he uses, and the nature of the inferences he draws from the data. Such a critique inevitably involves us in some of the technical aspects of this very specialized area of research. I think this exercise will help give us a better grasp of how evidence purporting to speak to the question of population differences in cognition is generated in many psychological laboratories today. Jensen's experiment is not a "horror example" of poor research; rather (and this is what makes it significant) it is typical of a common genre of psychological research dealing with cognitive processes.

The experiment I will be analyzing is reported in the *Journal of Educational Psychology* (1973) under the title "Free recall of categorized and uncategorized lists: A test of the Jensen Hypothesis." (Jensen & Frederiksen, 1973). What I am going to do is concentrate on the core difficulties investigators face when they attempt to use experimental tasks as yardsticks to measure what various cultural groups "have" and "have not" in the way of psychological capacities.

First, let me briefly remind you of Jensen's theory of mental abilities so we can see why he looks upon this experiment as a test of his hypothesis. As Jensen describes it, his theory posits "two broad classes of mental abilities called Level I and Level II. Level I involves rote learning and memory; Level II involves intelligence – that is analytical understanding, reasoning, abstraction and conceptual thinking" (Jensen & Frederiksen, 1973). Jensen maintains that intellectual differences among populations arise as a consequence of the differential distribution of Level II abilities: while rote learning may be equally distributed across populations, Level II abilities are more highly developed among whites and middle- and upper-class Americans than among black and poor Americans.

Jensen says the method of free recall can be used to investigate some of these aspects of the Level I–Level II hypothesis. This method consists of presenting a list of words to subjects and asking them to recall as many as they can in any order they choose. The phenomenon that has excited psychological interest is that the adult populations regularly give back the words in a different order from the one in which they were presented. Over repeated trials the order tends to become stable. Even though the order of presentation of the words is changed from trial to trial, groups of words tend to appear together consistently in the subject's recall, a phenomenon that is known as *recall clustering.* Now,

Jensen makes the following claim: "Associative clustering in verbal free recall is one of the clearest forms of evidence of conceptual hierarchical processes. For clustering to occur, the subject must actively organize the stimulus input according to certain self-provided superordinate categories" (Jensen and Fredericksen, 1973). He goes on to say that lists can be made to differ in the degree to which they elicit clustering. A list can be made up of items belonging to several distinct semantic categories – for example, food, clothes, animals. A list can also be made up of items that do not have these categorical relationships with one another – a list that is called an uncategorized list. Recall of an uncategorized list is more likely to involve rote learning and possibly simple pairwise association while learning on the categorized list involves the use of hierarchically organized categories.

The experiment follows rather straightforwardly from these guiding assumptions. Experimental subjects were age-matched black and white second and fourth grade children drawn from two public schools in California – a ghetto school provided the black population and a school in a middle-class neighborhood the white population. Children were tested individually for recall of a list of 20 toy objects. In one list the items were drawn from four semantic categories – clothing, tableware, furniture, animals. A second uncategorized list was composed of unrelated items. The categorized list was presented in a blocked and random order, but since Jensen had no specific hypotheses about the blocked presentation, we will not include it in our analysis. Ten white and ten black children at each grade level received one of the lists.

To predict recall performance on the different lists, Jensen added a developmental hypothesis – namely that Level I and Level II abilities have different growth curves, with Level II coming into prominence later in development. Assuming that black and white children differ only in Level II abilities, Jensen predicted that these ethnic groups should show little or no difference in recall of the Level I uncategorized list in either grade but on the Level II categorized list, the white group should manifest higher recall and more clustering than the black group at the upper grade level.

Jensen reports that the results bear out his predictions – on the uncategorized list there were no differences in amount recalled between black and white children at either grade level. On the categorized list, there were similarly no differences between black and white children in amount recalled or semantic clustering at the second grade level, but there was a difference in both scores on the fourth grade level. As Jensen acknowledges, this finding of significant difference rested on the "peculiar fact" (this is his terminology) that there was no age-related difference in the performance of the black children: fourth graders performed at or slightly below second graders. This fact is peculiar because in over hundreds of developmental studies with children of every ethnic and social class background, no other investigator has failed to find an age-related improvement in performance. Nevertheless Jensen goes on to draw his conclusions and for the present purposes, it is not necessary to question the way this peculiar fact was treated nor the statistical techniques employed to establish the performance difference, although they departed from those customarily applied to date of these studies.

As a guide to an evaluation of this experiment, it may be helpful to list the assumptions involved in Jensen's use of this task as a *test* of differential mental abilities. These include (though are not limited to) the following:

1. The populations have been selected in such a way that we can specify the relevant variations between them by their characterization in terms of ethnic group membership.
2. The task and materials are comparable for the populations being compared so that performance differences represent variations in population characteristics.
3. Level I and Level II processes may be distinguished by performance on different word lists.
4. Performance on a task in a single experimental situation provides a sufficient database from which to make inferences about underlying cognitive competencies.

With respect to the first assumption about the characteristics of the populations being compared, we know that in this, as in all his studies, Jensen confounds ethnic group membership and social class so that we are hard put to know just what populations the findings from his experimental samples are to be generalized to. But let's go along with his generalization in terms of ethnicity.

Regarding the comparability of materials for the groups being compared: we know from years of diligent and dull laboratory investigations that many seemingly prosaic characteristics of the words or items making up such lists do affect the performance of college students in this task. Word familiarity, the closeness of the association of a particular word to the category label, how many items go to make up the categories, are among some of the properties of word lists. We know from common sense and from extensive anthropological and linguistic research that individuals with differing cultural backgrounds have differences in vocabulary (it's not likely that "chittlin's" would be a common food item in white supermarkets in Berkeley) and in the way their vocabularies are mapped into categories. To make sure the lists were functionally equivalent, Jensen would have had to collect data on vocabulary and category norms for younger and older children, for black and white children. We know, however, that he presented the same list to all groups without testing for its equivalency.

This brings us to what is the heart of the matter – the last two assumptions – that performance on a particular list can be used to distinguish between Level I and Level II processes and that performance in a single experimental task is sufficient to allow inferences about the *absence* of certain processes. What I have to say about these assumptions might be said with respect to both Jensen's so-called Level I task (the uncategorized list) and his Level II task (the categorized list), but I will confine my remarks to the categorized list only.

First let us consider what recall clustering on this list means in terms of psychological processes. Jensen's position is that such clustering is clear-cut evidence for use of superordinate categories in recall, a Level II process. In simple terms what does this mean? It means that the child on seeing the list items presented (for example: *chair, mouse, shoe*) discovers the categories in the list: "Aha, chair is furniture; mouse is animal." As each item is presented, he orders it to its appropriate category. When asked for recall, he summons up the category and then proceeds to pull out the items on the list belonging to that category. The efficiency with which he does this is an index of the magnitude of his Level II abilities.

Now this model of what underlies clustering in free recall has indeed guided considerable research on random categorized lists. But this is only one model attempting to account for clustering. The outstanding fact is that ever since the random categorized list was introduced into learning laboratories over twenty years ago, no investigator has succeeded either in demonstrating that this model represents the actual operations of any subject population or that the processes it describes are both necessary and sufficient to produce clustering in recall output.

Associative theorists have long contended that the same outcome might be the result of simple associative processes rather than hierarchical ones, or, to stick to Jensen's terminology, Level I processes rather than Level II. Certain pairs of items may cluster together because they are high associates of each other – for example, on Jensen's list, *hat* and *coat*, and *table* and *chair*. Besides that, taken as a group, items belonging to one category are likely to be more closely related to one another than to items in other categories, at least for such contrasting categories as those used in the Jensen list: *shirt* is more likely to bring out *shoe* as the next word in recall than it is to bring out *mouse*. According to these accounts, when a run of category items appear together in recall, we do not have to evoke superordinate categories at all to explain the results.

While this debate may take on the appearance of a scholastic argument about angels and pins, its import is clear: the present understanding is that it is possible for cluster scores to represent a wide range of processes, from a purely hierarchical retrieval plan to a purely chain associative plan or a mixture of both.

Attempts to distinguish among these components from performance data have gone on uninterrupted for years, with the claims and counterclaims for special techniques of analysis filling up a good part of the mountain of literature earlier alluded to. No one has announced a victory. One upshot of this non-conclusive controversy is that some leading investigators have taken the position that, contrary to previous opinion, there is no substantive conflict between stimulus-response association and organizational accounts of free recall. One veteran of the field, Leo Postman, a staunch defender for many years of the associationist point of view has recently stated that "the differences between the two positions appear to reduce largely to matters of language" (Postman, 1972).

Not all will agree with this no-difference view or accept the conclusion that it is impossible in principle to construct a task with enough analytic power to distinguish between associative pairing and use of superordinate categories. But that is not the point. What is the point is that the theoretical debate over what clustering scores mean and the impasse in the field as to how to get behind cluster scores to the processes responsible for them – a well publicized debate – is nowhere reflected in Jensen's work.

We can see why. Jensen's use of a cluster score as a diagnostic of Level II abilities must rest on the assumption that there is a Level II ability there to be measured. To acknowledge the complexity of the processes involved and the tremendous obstacles in identifying them would be to acknowledge that the categorized list is not in itself a workable device for distinguishing between qualitatively different cognitive processes.

So much for the interpretation of what clustering signifies. What does its absence signify? According to Jensen, it signifies absence of conceptual organizing activities.

There are a number of difficulties with this interpretation. For one thing, while Jensen uses a generic term such as "conceptual" in describing Level II abilities, in practice he restricts the term to activities involved in grouping by membership in a common *taxonomic* category. But taxonomic relations do not exhaust the possible forms of conceptual, meaningful organization. Examination of recall organization according to these categories alone introduces a special bias in comparative research, because it leads to a systematic underestimation of recall organizing activities of populations whose preferred mode of organization is non-taxonomic. Psychologists specializing in studies of children's memory processes have for some time recognized and tried to overcome this particular bias. My own work among the Kpelle, a traditional, rice farming tribal group in West Africa, illustrates the misleading conclusions that can follow from failure to take into account subject-preferred modes of organization.

I worked with schooled and nonschooled children and adults and began my investigation with a simple sorting task – 25 items belonging to five indigenous taxonomic categories. Subjects were asked to put items into groups of things that belonged together. They were given repeated trials until they grouped all items in identical fashion on two consecutive trials. After some stable organization had been achieved, they were asked to recall the items in any order they chose. Recall output was analyzed to determine the extent to which order of recall reflected the subject's own personal organizational structure as well as how it reflected the taxonomic organization of the list. Age, years of schooling, and participation in the cash economy significantly affected the taxonomic cluster scores, but there was no significant difference whatsoever among any population in cluster scores computed for subjects' *own* groupings. This lack of difference in use of structure for recall purposes was somewhat surprising since subjects represented such a wide age range – six years up to sixty – and educational levels from zero to high school. To adopt Jensen's terminology, by one criterion (taxonomic clustering) different groups might be said to differ in conceptual organizing abilities. But all groups showed equal skills in using an organizational class structure to order their recall. Jensen's assumption that all subjects share the same categorical structure for these materials hinders discovery of processes his own theory says are important for performance.

But let's say, for the moment, there is something special about taxonomic organizing. Suppose an investigator fails to find evidence of this process in one experimental situation – what inferences can be drawn from this fact? Jensen draws two inferences about underlying competencies from his cluster score on recall of a categorized list. Jensen says that if subjects fail to reorganize items by taxonomic category, this failure can be taken as diagnostic of their *inability* to do so, and, further, as an indication that they lack the kind of mental structure that would support such organizing processes. Jensen has explicitly stated in a theoretical paper reviewing his Levels position that categorical organizing activities in the free recall task indicate the presence or absence of a "hierarchically arranged verbal associative network" (Jensen, 1971).

Perhaps someone should break this news to Professor George Miller or to Johnson-Laird and other scientists who have been working for years to develop a theory of how lexical knowledge, and especially semantic information, is organized and represented in adults and how this organization and representation changes and develops as children acquire greater mastery of their language. But the incredibility of leaping from organizing activities in a single experimental task to the inference of how mental structures are or are not organized does not have to be dramatized by theoretical arguments. There is strong empirical evidence from two converging lines of research that demonstrates the implausibility of such an inference.

B. "Induced" recall clustering (Cole, Flavell, Scribner)

One line of research is our own comparative work among the Kpelle and Vai people of Liberia. Early studies by Cole and other colleagues using procedures almost identical to those employed by Jensen showed that non-schooled traditional adults in general did not remember many items and did not cluster their recall. Instead of concluding that Kpelle lack "hierarchically arranged verbal networks," the investigators introduced modifications into the task to see whether and under what conditions Kpelle might be induced to organize their recall by taxonomic categories. After failing with some experi-

mental manipulations they hit on three tasks that dramatically shifted performance. In one, the objects to be remembered were associated with external
cues, such as chairs; in another, to-be-remembered words were embedded in
narrative stories of a traditional style; in the third, subjects were asked at recall
to give back the items of one category at a time – the experimenter instructed
the subject to recall all the *foods*, then all the *clothes*, and so on. In all these
situations there was not only an increase in the amount recalled, but analysis of
recall order showed subjects were engaging in grouping operations in accordance with the taxonomic categories. The constrained recall condition (in
which subjects were instructed to recall one category at a time) is an especially
direct piece of evidence that Kpelle villagers who performed so poorly in the
standard task did indeed know the taxonomic categories and could indeed use
them. If they did not have the requisite cognitive structure, such variability in
performance would be inexplicable.

Research conducted by Flavell and his associates on memory development
among American school children has produced similar findings. In one study,
young children who, like Jensen's second graders, showed little spontaneous
taxonomic clustering in free recall, were able to sort the items correctly into
their respective classes when asked to do so. Furthermore, once they were
induced to sort the items, they made use of this organizational structure in a
subsequent recall task. This phenomenon of "induced" recall clustering has
been replicated in a number of studies using a variety of techniques for drawing
children's attention to the categories in the list, and investigators have used
similar techniques to boost clustering performance of children of lower socioeconomic levels.

These studies have drawn attention to the importance of distinguishing between basic processes such as categorical or conceptual organizing, and the
application of these processes in specific tasks or across certain domains. There
are a variety of ways of making this distinction. Some investigators differentiate
between cognitive operations and the executive routines that bring them into
action when they make for efficient performance on a task. Others speak of the
presence or absence of generalization of skills from task to task. Frequently the
distinction is made between underlying competence and how it is reflected or
not reflected in the performance requirements of different tasks.

One does not have to subscribe to any of these views, but it seems mandatory
that comparative research take into account the evidence that members of the
same age group or ethnic group or social class will exhibit their knowledge of
taxonomic relationships (or any other competency) in some tasks and not in
others. In the face of such variability in performance, an explanation that
equates the occurrence or absence of a process or activity in a single experimental situation with some fixed underlying capacity appears to be both logically indefensible and empirically false.

The inadequacy of a "yardstick" approach to comparative research

It seems patently clear that the evidence offered by Jensen from this set of experiments to establish the inherent stupidity of millions of children must be considered totally inadequate by any scientific standards. But the logic of the argument requires us to recognize that the evidence of other similarly-conducted studies is equally unreliable, whether or not their rankings of different ethnic and social groups agrees or disagrees with Jensen's. The "yardstick" approach to comparative research, in spite of its appeal, does not represent the best psychology has to offer, and it is doubtful that it can lead to sound policy.

It is not necessary to thoroughly analyze the underlying assumptions and methodology of the contrasting approach to the comparative study of cognition that I briefly outlined in my introductory remarks (See Cole and Scribner, 1974 and Scribner and Cole, 1972). But the direction this approach leads to is clear. It leads away from an obsession with measuring "cognitive abilities in general" to an analysis of how particular abilities are brought into play in particular tasks, how particular cultural activities help shape the development and application of skills. This is an enormous undertaking. It encompasses all the problems *experimental* psychologists face in trying to uncover the psychological processes responsible for performance. It embraces all the problems *developmental* psychologists face in trying to relate specific experiences to the growth of specific skills. And it exceeds these, because, linking culture and cognition requires the knowledge and expertise of anthropologists and sociologists as well as psychologists. It is unreasonable to expect that any single field of knowledge, any single research technique, or any single discipline will be able to come up with sturdy conclusions about cultural universals or differences in cognitive processes.

As a collaborative effort, the comparative study of cognition offers exciting possibilities for the growth of social science theory and for social policy. As a one-discipline enterprise, focused on the assessment of what different people "have " or "have not," this area of research represents such an oversimplification of the issues that it is unlikely to contribute to basic knowledge or to informed and sound social practice.

References

Cole, M. & Scribner, S. *Culture and Thought.* New York: John Wiley & Sons, 1974.
Jensen, A. R. The role of verbal mediation in mental development. *The J. of Genetic Psychology*, 1971, *118*, 39–70.

Jensen, A. R. & Frederiksen, J. Free recall of categorized and uncategorized lists: A test of the Jensen hypothesis. *J. of Educational Psychology*, 1973, *65*, 304–312.

Postman, L. A pragmatic view of organization theory. In Endel Tulving and Wayne Donaldson (Eds.) *Organization of memory*. New York: Academic Press, 1972.

Scribner, S. & Cole, M. Effects of constrained recall training on children's performance in a verbal memory task. *Child Development*, 1972, *43*, 845–857.

What will we do tomorrow?
Tomorrow
We'll walk to berry hill
Where bush smells sweet
And birds' light feet
Trace grace
Notes on the ground.

The earth is round.

Tomorrow
We'll walk to ocean shore
Where waves of brine
Heap sand with shine
And seagulls soar.

The earth's no more.

Tomorrow
We'll walk down city street
Beneath our feet
No sidewalks meet
Cracks spread across
A flat gray sheet.

The earth's concrete.
                              Sylvia Scribner

PART 2

Thinking and cultural systems

Introduction

When she first undertook the work included in this section, Scribner had joined Rockefeller University as part of Michael Cole's laboratory of comparative cognition. While a doctoral student at the New School for Social Research, she had formulated a programmatic societal and cultural analysis of literacy that informed her work on that topic in subsequent years. The writings in this section appeared more or less concurrently with those on literacy included in Part 3, and the two lines of investigation are interwoven theoretically.

Much of Scribner's work on thinking and culture during that period was conducted in collaboration with Michael Cole and their associates in the multiple forms that collaboration takes, from joint working out of an empirical project to theoretical dialogue, and this is reflected in the list of selected coauthored works at the end of this introduction. Scribner's broad view on experimental methodology, stressing the need to hold a cultural interpretation of the experiment and to recognize that people assimilate the problem to current cultural forms, is one she shared with Cole and other members of his research group. All also shared a theoretical perspective grounded in activity theory and substantive questions on thinking and culture.

As in any collaboration, throughout the dialectical give and take individual voices are distinct. Scribner's single-authored works on thinking, culture, and society in this section reveal the continuity of her concerns about the societal context of thought and action. These writings, as well as the paper on intelligence tests at the end of this section, written during the same period, reflect the organic relationship among question, purpose, and method that was a stamp of Scribner's research. They interweave analytical, broadly political, methodological, and substantive concerns seamlessly.

As described in the introduction and in Aggie Scribner Kapelman's narrative, the research took Scribner to Liberia for several extended periods, where she lived among Kpelle people in the village, working closely with Kpelle collaborators and living the life of a respectful researcher-participant in alternation with that of a scientist in the urban corridors of Rockefeller University.

In Scribner's concerns about societal dimensions of science, the organization of knowledge in different disciplines was central. In particular, it was evident to her that psychology and anthropology had strong theoretical and substantive relations. Yet the history of the disciplines produced differences in conceptualization and formulation of research. Throughout the articles in this section, she stresses the need to integrate the psychological and anthropological analysis of cognitive processes.

The two reviews at the beginning of this section address those issues and stress the need for psychological theories that incorporate sociocultural factors *within* psychological systems, so as to provide a unified framework for analyzing processes both within and across cultures, a key aspect of Scribner's formulation of the anthropology–psychology interplay. Her review of *Societal Structures of the Mind*, in its critical form, stresses the societal level of analysis at which anthropological and psychological investigations must rely and calls into question the reductionism of the interpersonal formulation of social phenomena traditional in those disciplines. In her review of *Culture and Cognition: Readings in Cross-Cultural Psychology*, she focuses on the political agenda embodied in much of cross-cultural research in its early days, and, along with those editors, raises fundamental questions regarding the ethics and politics of cross-cultural investigations.

Scribner's methodological discussion, "Situating the Experiment in Cross-Cultural Research," lays the foundation for her empirical papers. Her approach, always, was to tailor the instrument to fit the question and the question to fit the broader societal purpose of the research. In this article, Scribner formulates a "quasi-experimental" research strategy that spans experimental and naturally occurring manifestations of cognitive phenomena, and that integrates psychological and anthropological descriptions. She would continue to work out this problem and to refine the articulation of psychological and systemic elements of theorizing throughout her work, up to her rich and elegant method in the research on thinking at work in Part 5.

The article "Recall of Classical Syllogisms: A Cross-Cultural Investigation of Error on Logical Problems" is a major advance in discussions at the time, providing a theoretical reinterpretation of those responses to syllogisms that rely on empirical knowledge rather than logical form. In contrast to previous interpretations of these responses as reflecting logical failures ("empiric bias"), Scribner's analysis grounds them in broad cultural context.

The suggestions she outlines here are subsequently developed explicitly in her classic article "Modes of Thinking and Ways of Speaking," where she introduces to this field of research the important construct of "genres." She integrates the analytical framework outlined in "Situating the Experiment" and the previous empirical article into an incisive theoretical description of empiric and theoretical modes of reasoning. Kpelle people, she observes, reason hypothetically about the actual while denying the possibility of reasoning hypothetically about the postulated, and indeed describe the latter as futile. She makes the important point that "empirical biases . . . operate as an 'organizer,' characterizing the individual's entire mode of engagement with the material."

Thus, empiric reasoning, far from reflecting a shortcoming in hypothetical thinking, reflects a grounded epistemology and a functionally guided use of hypothetical thinking. Scribner's systemic interpretation of those phenomena moves their analysis beyond the dichotomies between abstract and concrete thinking prevalent at the time, and provides an integrated description of thinking in culture and society.

Her insistence that the definition of problems and the methods of study are always rooted in society and politics is also reflected in the article "Intelligence

Tests: A Comparative Perspective." This article, written during the same period, was prompted by the controversy about intelligence then raging in response to Jensen's genetic determinism. Scribner stresses that the purpose for which testing is conducted shapes its practical consequences. Whereas in medical settings testing is aimed at improving treatment outcome, in educational/institutional settings testing is used to deny learning opportunities to some individuals, often those discriminated against on the basis of class and ethnicity. The article reviews the history of the Binet test and shows how the agendas of those who do the testing distort its original function.

Scribner's analysis of the characteristics of cultures and their relation to individual thought incorporates historical-cultural development as theorized by Vygotsky, whose work she was coediting at the time. Her analysis demonstrates the dialectical relationship between the general and the specific that must be synthesized for a genuine understanding to obtain. Her view that sociocultural factors must be incorporated within psychological systems informs all her work, as is evident in Parts 3, 4, and 5. In her writings on literacy in Part 3 she would introduce the concept of practice as providing the material basis through which links between the sociocultural and psychological levels are established.

Selected coauthored works

Scribner, S.; Cole, M. (1973): Cognitive consequences of formal and informal education. *Science* 182, 553–59.

Cole, M.; Scribner, S. (1974): *Culture and thought: a psychological introduction.* John Wiley & Sons, New York.

Cassallas, M.; Cole, M.; Hall, W.; Meissner, J.; Scribner, S.; Traupmann, K. (1976): Memory span for nouns, verbs and function words in low SES children: a replication and critique of Schutz and Keislar. *Journal of Verbal Learning and Verbal Behavior* 15, 431–35.

Cole, M.; Scribner, S. (1977): Cross-cultural studies of memory and cognition. In: *Perspectives on the development of memory and cognition* (Eds.: Kail, R. V.; Hagen, J. W.). Lawrence Erlbaum Associates, Hillsdale, N.J., 239–71.

8   *Societal structures of the mind:*
A review

Although its title promises consideration of social events on a *societal* level, this volume actually deals with phenomena on the *interpersonal* level, a reductionist transformation not uncommon among social psychologists. The authors conceive of social events as acts of resource exchange in which two individuals in some role relationship (parent-child, wife-husband) give to, or take something away from, the other. How are these transactions "given meaning" (p. 3) so that the individual member of society comes to understand and control his social world? The answer, according to the authors, lies in the fact that the child, growing to adulthood, develops a set of basic categories for understanding the structure of such social encounters. This book presents a theory of how these categories come into being and how they are organized into stable cognitive structures that regulate the interactions between individuals in various social settings. The theory, and data supporting it, represent several decades of work by the Foas and their colleagues, and the book clearly reflects this sustained, consistent involvement. Their structural models of social concepts are elaborated in great detail as an "integrative framework" for the social sciences. A number of chapters examine the usefulness of these models in tying together presently unrelated areas of social psychological research. A final section explores the practical implications of the theory for social institutions and the improvement of "society as a whole."

In a final chapter, the authors propose that the structural models of roles and resource exchanges will be invariant across cultures, providing the basis for a

This review of the book edited by V. G. Foa and E. B. Foa (Springfield, Ill.: C. C. Thomas, 1974), originally appeared in *American Anthropology* 78 (1976): 655. Reprinted with the permission of the American Anthropological Association.

"comparison of cultures." Studies cited in support of this proposition are limited both as to culture and population. Except for an undescribed Senegalese group, no other of their non-American samples is drawn from a traditional, tribal culture. (Israel, Greece, India, and Japan are the most frequently investigated cultures, and students the most researched group.) Perhaps this limitation accounts for the survival of *money* as a universal resource category and for father-mother-daughter-son as central family role categories. No details are given as to how the instruments were generated or validated for non-American samples, and no evidence from observations of actual behavior in natural or contrived settings is furnished to supplement or check out the questionnaire data for non-American samples.

The theory presented may have value, as the authors suggest, in providing a coherent framework for interpreting currently unrelated areas in social psychological research. As for its broader significance as a theory of society, one cannot help wondering about the survival value of a society in which all social experiences are interpersonal encounters for the exchange of resources (p. 174) and none are encounters for resource production.

9   *Culture and cognition:* A review

Berry and Dasen, co-editors of this new book of readings on the relationship between culture and cognition, modestly describe their primary goal as providing a handy volume of studies which have not been readily accessible to investigators, teachers or students. In this new and rapidly developing area of research – not yet situated scientifically, but lying "somewhere" between the traditional disciplines of anthropology and psychology – their goal is addressed to an actual and felt need. For several years, Price Williams' (1969) collection of papers was the only one-cover source of information on the state of the art in cross-cultural psychology. That volume had the broad-gauged mission of representing all leading areas of research, including the classic issues of socialization training and personality as well as emerging lines of work on perceptual and cognitive development. The Al-Issa and Dennis volume (1970), published shortly thereafter, brought together additional material on the various sub-areas of cross-cultural psychology, but as in any attempt at general coverage, the representation of work in a particular field was necessarily limited. With the upsurge of activity in the experimental study of cognitive processes in the last decade, the need has grown for greater visibility of major cross-cultural research contributions.

The Berry and Dasen volume serves this purpose admirably. Its contributors exemplify almost all major and currently active lines of exploration of the intricate links between aspects of culture and aspects of mental functioning. Their single focus on "comparative cognitive psychology" enabled the editors to go beyond the mere assembling of papers in handy form to review and reflect upon the mission and methods of the field. Berry and Dasen have not missed this opportunity. In their introductory material to the various sections of the book, they have provided the necessary historical background and critical view-

This review of the book edited by J. W. Berry and P. R. Dasen (London: Methuen, 1974) originally appeared in the *Journal of Cross-Cultural Psychology* 6 (1975): 122–26. Reprinted with the permission of SAGE Publications.

points to enable the reader not only to catch up on current work but to begin an assessment of its strengths and weaknesses. They do not hesitate to question the presuppositions that many prefer remain silent: Is the cross-cultural enterprise legitimate? What does it have to contribute to our basic knowledge of thought processes?

The organization of the book reflects these concerns with fundamental issues. In a general introduction, the editors trace the intellectual history of speculation about possible cultural variations in mental processes and place contemporaneous psychological investigation in the context of the Great Debate between social scientists stressing uniformities in human cognition and those stressing qualitative differences or "discontinuities". This chapter is distinguished by an original contribution in which Berry attempts a synthesis of the two sides to this controversy: he suggests that the study of cultural variables that make a difference *within* cultural systems may lead to the discovery of higher-level uniformities in cognitive functioning *across* cultural systems.

Selections in Part I are concerned primarily with the variations in cognitive processes inferred from performance on experimental tasks. The most interesting contributions in this section are reports of research which have put aside the old and trivial objective of demonstrating that differences "exist" between two human groups for the important and challenging task of testing hypotheses about specific cultural differences that might account for observed performance differences. Thus, Berry, in a sophisticated series of studies of perceptual skills, attempts to explicate the influences of a number of interrelated variables: characteristics of particular environments, the subsistence activities they foster and the socialization practices adapted to these activities. Doob's classic paper on eidetic imagery raises the question of a possible link between modality of memory representation and literacy. Ross and Millson test for the effect of an oral versus written tradition on mnemonic skills. Cole, Gay and Glick, in studies of quantitative behavior among the Kpelle, and Maclay, in sorting experiments with the Navaho, explore the effects of linguistic structure on concept learning and classification. This concern with the mechanisms linking culture and cognitive behavior is a relatively new development among cross-cultural psychologists and reflects a growing appreciation of the relevance of anthropological constructs and methods to experimental work.

Part II deals with a more traditional psychological preoccupation – the measurement and comparison of intellectual "capacities" among different human groups. How much of the total product of cross-cultural research in the twentieth century is represented by studies attempting to determine whether members of another culture do well or poorly on our intelligence tests is hard to estimate. But the expenditure of time and money has been considerable. The main thrust of the papers in this section is the suggestion that the achievements of this enterprise are less than equal to the effort. Indeed, the radical suggestion is made by several investigators that "comparative intelligence testing" is not only of doubtful heuristic value but may well be impossible *in principle*. The argument of noncomparability of intelligence testing is strengthened by issuing from investigators who have personally pioneered in the adaptation of tests and testing methods to nonWestern cultural contexts. S. Biesheuvel, for example, who has carried out extensive studies of abilities of Bantu and Western communities in South Africa concludes that such a "multitude of circumstances" divide the two groups – material conditions, habits of child rearing, customary pursuits and value systems – that no inferences can be drawn from differences in test performance about differences in underlying cognitive capacities. Measures of intelligence, he contends, "are strictly comparable only within homogeneous cultures. There is no possibility of comparing the ultimate intellectual capacity of different ethnic or cultural groups, except perhaps by means of elaborate experimental designs, involving the training of members of one group within the culture of the other and even there uncontrolled or sampling factors are likely to invalidate the findings" (p. 223).

Cole and Bruner, reviewing research that indicates members of different cultures may differ in the situations to which they apply particular cognitive skills, conclude that inferences from performance to competence require testing in a wide range of ecologically valid situations. This is close to the classic position of Florence Goodenough (1936, cited in Berry's paper in this section) that test items are valid only if they are representative samples of the intellectual activities of a given culture-group. Wober carries the position one step further. He reports an investigation of an indigenous African society's conception of "intelligence" and proposes that investigators seek to discover and analyze the specific intellectual skills developed and valued in traditional cultures so that members of these cultures can be assessed on the basis of how well they perform their own skills, rather than ours. Taken together, the papers in this section draw on the experience of cross-cultural research to make new contributions to the critique of the testing movement.

The third and final part of this volume, under the primary editorship of Dasen, deals with questions of cognitive development as they are reflected in Piagetian studies. Readers will welcome the appearance here in English of Piaget's article on cultural factors influencing intellectual development, originally published in the International Journal of Psychology (1966). The final review paper by Dasen, in addition to presenting a coherent and useful summary of the evidence for universality of Piaget's stages, brings the theory into confrontation with some "surprising" data from studies of conservation performance in New Guinea, Australia, Ivory Coast, Sicily and Sardinia. In these investigations, a substantial number of nonliterate adults failed to demonstrate conservation behavior on one or more of the Piagetian tests; Dasen concludes that, while these results do not threaten the generality of Piaget's system, they underscore the fact that cultural variables might play a more important role in cognitive development than has been previously hypothesized.

Since the editors invite us to take a critical attitude, we may well ask what the volume, on balance, has to say about the worthwhileness of the cross-cultural approach. Although the editors have made an estimable attempt to present the studies in a coherent framework, it must be acknowledged that the search for cultural influences on cognitive processes remains clouded by theoretical ambiguities – how is performance related to underlying competencies? skills and styles to process? quantitative differences to qualitative? Again, while psychologists have made an effort to break away from cultural ethnocentricism, the new paradigms and experimental techniques required to evaluate thinking in traditional cultures are slow in appearing and the old kit of tools is still carried from one society to another.

In the face of these weaknesses in theory and method, cross-cultural work on cognition, as this volume and other recent works indicate (Cole & Scribner, 1974; Lloyd, B., 1972), is beginning to make a substantial contribution to the science of psychology – in illuminating the role of experience in development, and in dramatizing inadequacies of existing comparative methodologies. In a recent symposium on new approaches to intelligence, Jacqueline Goodnow (Resnick, 1975) credited cross-cultural research with forcing upon psychologists everywhere the task of re-defining intelligent behavior and devising new ways of measuring it. Cross-cultural psychology may be coming of age.

References

Al-Issa, I. and Dennis, W. *Cross-cultural studies of behavior.* New York: Holt, Rinehart and Winston, 1970.

Cole, M. and Scribner, S. *Cultural and thought: a psychological introduction.* New York: John Wiley and Sons, 1974.

Goodnow, J. The nature of intelligent behavior: questions raised by cross-cultural studies. To appear in Resnick, L. (Ed.) *New approaches to intelligence.* New York: Erlbaum, 1975.

Lloyd, B. *Perception and cognition.* Middlesex, England: Penguin Books, 1972.

Piaget, J. Necessité et signification des recherches comparatives en psychologie genetique. *International Journal of Psychology, 1,* 1966.

Price-Williams, D. R. *Cross-cultural studies.* Middlesex, England: Penguin Books, 1969.

10 Situating the experiment in cross-cultural research

Of the many methodological problems in cross-cultural research I have selected the experiment as the point of emphasis because it seems to me that the role of the experiment needs to be clarified if we hope to resolve a central dilemma in the field of culture and cognition.

In a sense, the experiment has created the dilemma. In the last several decades, there has been a substantial increase in the number of cross-cultural psychological studies of cognition in which the principal research tool has been the experiment or a task derived from an experiment. In the same period, there has been an upsurge of interest in cognitive phenomena among anthropologists and the initiation of new lines of research based principally on the methods of field observation and interview.

Ordinarily, this shared interest and intensive research effort by two disciplines should promote a more rapid growth of knowledge and understanding. This seems to have been the case in the field of culture and personality, which also arose as a specialized domain of inquiry sitting astride the two disciplines of psychology and anthropology. But in culture and cognition, the multiplication of psychological and anthropological studies has not yet resulted in an integrated body of data or in a set of unifying constructs. On the contrary, it has brought sharply into focus the discontinuities in the evidence each of these sciences presents of cultural variations in cognition.

This essay originally appeared in *The Developing Individual in a Changing World*, vol. 1, *Historical and Cultural Issues*, ed. K. F. Riegel and J. A. Meacham (Berlin: Walter de Gruyter, 1976), pp. 310–21. Reprinted with the permission of Walter de Gruyter.

Discontinuities between anthropology and psychology

I will illustrate the problem with a few sketchy and admittedly over-simplified examples. Many carefully conducted experiments using Piagetian tasks have found a considerable number of *adults* in nontechnical societies failing to show behavior associated with the possession of logical structures of intelligence assumed to be characteristic of 8 to 12-year-old children in techno-logical societies (Dasen 1972 reviews many of these studies). Yet anthropologists by means of new analytic techniques are identifying complex logical structures underlying conceptual systems within these cultures (Wallace 1962, for example). Moreover, ethnographic studies reveal that individuals within these cultures engage in elegant processes of inferential reasoning as they go about the everyday business of settling disputes (Gibbs 1962), or the more exotic business of bargaining on the terms of their participation in some Western-inspired research project (Kulah 1973).

Evans-Pritchard (1963), Albert (1964), Bellman (1968), and other anthropologists have documented the complex communication skills involved in patterns of verbal exchange among the Zande, Burundi, and Kpelle peoples of Africa. Cole and his associates, on the other hand (1969), found that Kpelle adults performed poorly in an experimental situation that was specifically designed to tap communication skills.

As a final example, anthropological reports of feats of memory on the part of nonliterate people in traditional societies date back to as early as the seventeenth century (Evreux 1864). But ever since the 1920s, psychologists using methods and procedures developed in the laboratory to test memory performance have failed to confirm these generalizations about extraordinary mnemonic powers.

These examples indicate that the divergences in data and generalizations between anthropology and psychology on various topics of cognition generally run in the same direction; contemporary anthropological evidence highlights the commonality in the cognitive skills of populations in technological and nontechnological societies; psychological evidence, for the most part, emphasizes either the absence of certain skills or the lower levels of skill of non-technological peoples. The problem and dilemma is how to reconcile these two sets of data and interpretations.

One response to this problem has been the denial that there is any need for reconciliation because the two research approaches and two sets of evidence really speak to different questions. Thus, some psychologists feel that ethnographic descriptions of performance in naturally occurring situations are useful for many purposes but have little to contribute to an understanding of the basic psychological processes underlying performance in different cultures.

They feel that such knowledge can only be generated by the laboratory experiment which permits the isolation and systematic manipulation of various components of the performance.

Critiques of experimental method

Some anthropologists, on the other hand, question whether the laboratory situation yields findings that have any trans-situational generality at all. One objection is that experimental materials, tasks, and procedures developed in industrial societies are ethnocentric and culturally biased. Others go beyond this in asserting that the experiment itself, as a context for the elicitation of behavior, has no ecological validity in the cultures to which it has been transported. Whatever limitations are imposed by the artificiality of the experiment in the societies in which it originated, they argue, are magnified many times over in traditional societies whose people lack experience with test-like situations. Granted that experimental methods make it possible to analyze processes underlying performance. But if the performance itself is nonrepresentative and distorted, what can be learned from such an analysis that has any relevance for the understanding of cultural determinants of behavior?

This position, which is essentially an attempt to draw a line between what anthropology and psychology can tell us about cognition, does not seem to be a very fruitful way of handling the problem. Psychologists would hardly be willing to accept the conclusion that experiments can do little to illuminate the problem of cultural influences on cognition. And anthropologists, I am sure, would be equally resistant to the notion that evidence of cultural skills is not relevant to an understanding of individual cognitive processes. But even if, as psychologists, we were ready to ply our narrow trade, we would still have to take into account the questions that have been raised about the use of the experiment as a tool in cross-cultural research. It certainly seems precarious to pursue ambitious investigations that seek to compare cognitive processes among populations of *different* cultures, if we cannot reconcile the comparative evidence of psychological and anthropological studies of cognitive processes within the *same* culture.

To meet some of these criticisms, cross-cultural psychologists have devoted considerable attention in recent years to reducing sources of cultural bias in the experiment. The idea that an experiment consists of a fixed set of materials and operations that can be taken abroad like a piece of luggage has been replaced by an emphasis on the need to adapt features of the experiment to the culture in which the research is being carried out. The contemporary view, as Glick (1975) puts it, is that 'The logic of comparative study involves the testing of people in a *comparable* (note, not *identical*) manner'. Lloyd (1972) agrees that the investigator's concern is not to duplicate the original experiment but to 'ensure that it will produce data in the new setting which can be compared with that collected in the original Euro-American situation' (p. 21). Frijda and Jahoda (1966), Berry (1969), and others have made important contributions toward solution of problems of comparability in materials, procedures, experimenter-subject communication, motivations, etc.

While these are important, they leave untouched the perhaps more fundamental criticism that the experiment, by its very nature, rather than by this or that feature of it, cannot be considered an equivalent or comparable performance situation in all societies. To handle this criticism, we have to go beyond the consideration of specific features of the experiment and explore what the experiment represents as a context for the manifestation of cognitive skills within the traditional cultures to which we carry it. What are the naturally occurring contexts in the culture in which these same skills are elicited? How does the experimental paradigm compare to these naturally occurring situations? Are there situations similar to the experimental situation (such as test-taking in school, for example) that individuals encounter in some cultures and not in others? (See Scribner and Cole, 1973.) These are some of the questions we would want to ask simply to meet the criterion of establishing comparability between experimental investigations in one culture and another.

The experiment as an unnatural situation

But this is essentially the same set of questions that arises when we confront the problem of comparing and integrating data from psychological experiments with data for field research within *one* culture. To relate the two sets of data to each other we are led to ask questions about the contexts in which the behavior we are investigating was elicited. When we observe a Kpelle child trying to memorize word lists in a free recall experiment and when we observe him trying to memorize the names of nine leaves in a singing game on the road behind his house, we are in each case studying the act of memorizing as it occurs in a given situation with a given set of features. Looking upon the experiment this way it makes sense to ask about the similarities and differences between these situations and, most particularly, about the similarities and differences in the *cognitive demands* they make upon the child. Can these differences be characterized in any generalized or formal way? If we can identify dimensions along which the experimental situation can be compared to the naturally occurring situation we will have a better possibility of achieving some integrated interpretation of performance in the two situations.

This approach suggests that it might be valuable to make the experiment itself an object of cross-cultural inquiry. Our aim would then be to identify certain distinctive features of the experimental situation as a context for cognitive behavior and to fit it into the range of situations in the culture in which this behavior is manifested.

This is a very general statement and an ambitious manifesto. I have no blueprint to propose and no developed line of investigation to use as a model. But some contemporary lines of research suggest certain techniques that might be useful in helping us understand what is going on in the experiment when we are investigating cognitive phenomena in other cultures. I will pick up on these and draw them out to show that this line of inquiry is a feasible one.

Investigating subject's understanding of the experiment

A number of years ago Webb, Campbell, and their colleagues (Webb, Campbell, Schwartz and Sechrest 1966) analyzed the special problems involved in drawing inferences from experimental data which stem from the fact that the experiment is a reactive situation. By this term, they emphasized that the performance outcome in an experiment is determined not merely by the conditions the investigator establishes but by the subject's awareness that he is an object of study.

Orne (1970) has systematically investigated the contribution this awareness makes to a variety of behavioral responses in experimental situations, ranging from hypnotic phenomena to galvanic skin responses. He identified as significant variables such factors as the subject's construction of the hypothesis under investigation – what he thinks the experimental question really is, what he identifies as the relevant variables, and what he thinks constitutes appropriate behavior in the experimental situation. Orne calls these the 'demand characteristics' of the experiment – the information the experimental situation conveys to the subject over and beyond what the experimenter tells him. One of the most interesting features of Orne's work is that, in spite of the investment of a great deal of effort and ingenuity, he found it impossible to design an experiment *without* demand characteristics — that is, an experiment that was totally meaningless to his subjects!

If, as Orne has demonstrated, it is important for the experimenter to take the subject's definition of the experiment into account, even when he is working with a familiar and relatively homogenous subject population, how much more crucial this is when an experimenter is working in an unfamiliar culture with subjects for whom the experiment is an alien situation. Yet, to my knowledge, there has been no systematic attempt to study demand characteristics in a cross-cultural setting. There is some anecdotal material, however, that suggests how this might be done.

Glick (1969), for example, was investigating what attributes of objects traditional Kpelle rice farmers use in classification tasks. His experimental procedure was the standard one in which the subject is presented with an array of familiar objects and told to put together those that belong together. He found that the great majority of subjects made groupings that were based on functional or perceptual relations between items rather than on their common membership in a taxonomic category. Other investigators have interpreted similar findings as an indication that individuals displaying this behavior are deficient in conceptual thinking. Glick, however, asked his subjects why they grouped the items in the way they did. Many answered that this was the clever way to do it, the way that made 'Kpelle sense'. This reply suggested to him that subjects were construing his request to group the items as a test of their cleverness and were responding according to the culturally accepted view of what cleverness is. Glick followed up his hunch, asking a subject to group the items again, this time as a stupid person might do it. Interestingly, under these instructions, he secured perfect taxonomic grouping!

This can be construed as a role-playing approach and many modifications come to mind: Villagers might be asked to group the objects as students attending school might do it, as Westerners might do it, or as elders might do it. Another manipulation might be to vary the role of the experimenter instead of the subject: Are different task expectations conveyed by an experimenter identified with traditional ways and one identified with foreign ways?

In doing pilot work among Kpelle villagers in West Africa on solution of verbal syllogisms, I tried another technique for eliciting information on subject's perception of the task. I was asking individuals to answer classical syllogisms of the following type: All stores in Kpelleland are in a town. Mr. Ukatu has a store in Kpelleland. It is in a town? Earlier research by Cole and his colleagues (Cole *et al.* 1971) showed that traditional Kpelle villagers handled these problems on no better than a chance basis while young Kpelle adults attending high school performed in a manner comparable to that of American students. I was interested in finding out what features might account for the poor performance of the villagers.

One hypothesis was that they were failing to grasp the nature of the task as one that involved reasoning to reach a conclusion. It seemed from other evidence that they might be conceiving of the problem as a test of their knowledge of facts. So, working with expert translators, we prepared a set of instructions carefully explaining the hypothetical nature of the problems. We also gave a series of practice problems in which we helped the subject arrive at the right answer and demonstrated the peculiarities of the syllogism – how the answer can be derived simply from the information contained in the premises of the problem without any knowledge of the factual situation to which the premises refer.

After the series of test problems, we asked the subject some questions about the experiment and then requested him to give us a problem just like the ones we had given him. This was our test of how the subject construed the experimental task. Here is a typical problem offered by a village tailor: 'Suppose you see your son climbing up in a palm tree and start cutting nuts. You go and begin cooking for him. You hear a sound. How can you find out whether the palm nut fell down or your son?'

This problem and others like it are very instructive. First it tells us that the tailor had correctly grasped the purpose of the psychological game we were playing – his problem, indeed, is one that involves a reasoning process. But it also tells us that he did not grasp the *distinctive* features of the verbal syllogism. An important characteristic of the tailor's problem is that it has a number of correct answers. Among several possibilities, you can find out what has happened to your son by going to the palm tree and looking for him or by staying home near the cooking fire and listening for another sound. The information given in the problem does not in any way dictate the choice of a particular alternative. We know from previous ethnographic research that this problem is similar to a whole class of Kpelle riddle problems that furnish the material for verbal battles of wit in the villages. These problems do not have a single right answer, nor is there necessarily a social consensus as to which answer is the best one; honors go to the participant who delivers the most persuasive and unshakeable argument for the answer he chooses to give. In this respect, traditional Kpelle reasoning problems stand in sharp contrast to the verbal syllogisms we were using in our experiment. The defining attribute of a syllogism is that the answer or conclusion is a necessary one, whether or not it is reasonable, sensible, or clever.

We also learn from the problems given us about the limitations of verbal instructions and brief practice procedures. Our instructions seemed to meet all formal requirements in the sense that they covered the essential features of the task, and they seemed to meet all linguistic requirements as well – they simply failed to communicate what we thought we were communicating, and that was the special nature of the problem material.

The repertoire of problems we secured from our subjects also helps us in interpreting their performance on our test problems. We have the suggestion that one of the factors leading to poor performance might be the assimilation of the syllogism to the traditional riddle problem. If this were the case, subjects may have considered the choice of a Yes or No answer relatively unimportant in comparison to the clever reason they could construct to support it.

Certain testable hypotheses open up from this line of reasoning. One is that villagers might do better when the content of verbal syllogisms is made as unfamiliar as possible since this might counter their tendency to assimilate syllogisms to the traditional problem form. This would be an interesting hypothesis to test because it implies that achieving equal familiarity of problem content in two cultures or in two population groups within a culture does not ensure comparable task difficulty; the dimension of familiarity may be an irrelevant dimension for one group, a facilitating dimension for a second, and a disruptive dimension for a third.

In addition to suggesting modifications in the experiment, this hypothesis suggests a new line of ethnographic research which might help us link the investigation of reasoning processes in the laboratory with those occurring in everyday life. Is there an analog of the Western logic problem in the language games of the Kpelle – that is, a language game in which the response is determined by the formal or structural features of the material and not by its content? If so, we might have more suitable material for experimental purposes. If not, we might want to identify individuals renowned for their skill at traditional riddle-problems to see how they do on our syllogistic problems. Do we observe negative transfer from one class of problems to another or do we observe a generalized verbal problem-solving skill? Through an interweaving of experimental and ethnographic research, we should make progress toward identifying the characteristics of problems and problem-solving situations that influence how reasoning processes are manifested.

Experimenting with the experiment

A second strategy for studying the cognitive demands of a particular experimental paradigm, proposed by Cole (Cole *et al.* 1971), is to subject it to systematic variation until the investigator achieves equal levels of performance among populations that may have initially differed in performance. This research strategy shifts the principal class of independent variables under investigation from those related to characteristics of populations to those related to characteristics of experiments. Instead of carrying one fixed paradigm to many different cultures, the researcher works with many different variations of a single paradigm within one culture. This approach is exemplified by a series of free recall studies conducted by Cole, Gay, Glick and Sharp (1971). These began with the standard free recall paradigm in which the experimenter read a list of disconnected words naming objects belonging to four Kpelle language semantic categories (food, tools, clothes, utensils). In the United States, when lists of this kind are presented in random order, school children from the upper elementary grades on, and middle-class adults, typically reorder the list and recall words clustered together by category rather than in their original order. The amount of clustering in recall has been found to be positively associated with number of words recalled. In the first studies, Kpelle villagers showed little learning of the list and little evidence of clustering.

Cole and his colleagues, however, did not terminate the experimentation at this point. They raised the question: What does it take in the way of experimental procedure to secure clustering and recall performance among the Kpelle villagers comparable to that of educated populations? After failing with some experimental manipulations, they hit on three tasks that dramatically shifted performance. In one, the objects to be remembered were associated with external cues, such as chairs; in another, to-be-remembered words were embedded in narrative stories of a traditional style; in the third successful manipulation, subjects were asked at recall to give back the items of one category at a time – that is, the experimenter instructed the subject to recall all the *foods*, then all the *clothes*, and so on. In all these situations, there was not only an increase in the amount recalled but an analysis of the order in which the items were recalled showed that villagers were engaging in grouping or categorizing operations.

Under these special conditions, the retrieval processes of nonliterate Kpelle farmers seemed very much like those of American or Kpelle students: both intracultural and intercultural differences were greatly reduced. Cole (1972) offers the following interpretation of these findings:

'This series of experiments taken as a unit certainly seems to bear out the dictum that people will be able to perform well at tasks they find normal and which they often encounter. As such, it confirms anthropological doctrine. But . . . it specifies somewhat more closely than usual what "normal" conditions are. And it turns out that "normal" cannot be simply equated with "encounter often". Some of the experimental situations eliciting fine recall were *abnormal* in the sense of infrequently encountered . . . What the successful conditions seem to share with "frequently encountered" situations is a lot of structure. Where life or the experimental procedures do not structure the memory task, the traditional person has great difficulty. "Normal" in this case refers to the presence of certain structural features.'

This work is interesting from our present point of view because it identifies a specific cognitive demand present in the experimental situation that is presumed absent from naturally occurring situations. The argument is that the free recall paradigm, unlike situations in everyday life, fails to provide external cues or structure for recall and requires the subject to produce internal cues or structure to support the mnemonic performance. How well he does this, or whether he adopts this strategy at all, may depend on how often his culture confronts him with a similar cognitive demand. This leads to a specific hypothesis about how cultural circumstances may contribute to differences in memory performance – that is, the hypothesis that a member of a traditional society will rarely encounter situations in everyday life that require him to make his own retrieval plan.

To confirm that this is the case among the Kpelle requires an extensive program of field research to identify the contexts in which Kpelle need to learn, store, and retrieve masses of information. The leader of a cooperative work group must remember the work days, hours, and places put in by every one of the twenty or more individuals who constitute the group. Does he have any specific devices for doing this? What are the memory demands required by other activities, such as ritual ceremonies or instruction of the young in bush schools? Can we identify any devices built into these contexts that may serve as retrieval cues?

I am not suggesting that this kind of research will yield analytic knowledge of component processes of recall. But that is not its purpose. Its purpose is to tell us something about how situations vary in their cognitive demands and how the particular experimental paradigm we are using fits into this spectrum.

Studying naturally occurring and quasi-experimental situations

We have seen in all these examples how questions arising in experimental research lead to questions that can best be explored in field research, and the other way around. In closing, I should like to take this approach one step further and suggest the value of a research strategy that seeks from the outset to investigate some particular cognitive phenomenon in a range of situations, from the naturally occurring to the experimental. This strategy requires that we go beyond the use of ethnographic data to set a performance baseline for experimental findings and beyond their use as a source of hypotheses to be tested in experimental research. It means employing a full range of research techniques – both those of anthropology and those of psychology – to study a *single question* concerning cognitive performance.

Without trying to push the parallel, this strategy has been fruitfully employed in the comparative study of animal behavior, principally by Schneirla and his associates (Aronson, Tobach, Rosenblatt & Lehrman, 1970). Schneirla's own studies of ant behavior show the complementary nature of observation in the field and experimentation in the laboratory. Field work gives the investigator access to the complete natural phenomenon; selected aspects of this phenomenon can then be isolated and studied quantitatively in the laboratory. One of Schneirla's contributions that has a special relevance for our topic is his emphasis on the possibility of intervention in the field – that is, introducing some experimental manipulation in the naturally occurring situation to test a specific hypothesis about conditions controlling the behavior in question (Aronson, Tobach, Rosenblatt & Lehrman, 1971). I have borrowed the term *quasi-experiment* (Campbell and Stanley 1963) to designate this manipulation of conditions in the field.

Again, to keep the discussion concrete, let me work out a specific example. Dr. Akki Kulah, a Kpelle colleague, has described a game called *kolon* (1973), widely played by young and old, whose function seems to be that of teaching young children proverbs. *Kolon* is a competitive game played by two opposing teams whose members vary in age from six to adulthood. The game begins when the leader of one team calls out a phrase to the youngest member of the opposing team who must respond with the 'answer' which is a particular proverb. If the child fails to respond correctly the turn passes to the next older team member.

Kulah has recorded a number of *kolon* games and is now analyzing this material to stipulate the rules of the game and to develop some hypotheses about the relations between the stimulus material and the proverb responses. This analysis will not in itself tell us much about component learning and memory processes of the individual players. Since we do not know the history of the participants, we cannot tell when a child fails to respond correctly whether he has lost the association between the stimulus and the proverb, whether he has forgotten the proverb, or whether he never knew it. When we fully understand the structure of the game, however, we can intervene in it, turning it into a quasi-experimental situation. We might introduce new material to be learned in a format similar to the customary one so that rounds of the game are equivalent to learning trials. We might then begin to manipulate features of the game to see how learning and memory are affected – what happens when we change the structure of the material, that is, vary the relations between the stimulus and response members? What is the influence of the social structure of the game – are there memory cues in the interrelationships of game participants? What happens when it is converted into an individual learning situation? At this point we might return to the laboratory and set up a formal paired associate learning experiment and then gradually reintroduce features of the *kolon* game.

This strategy will clearly not be equally useful for the study of all cognitive phenomena, and for some it may be inapplicable. But it seems feasible and appropriate for pursuing many controversial issues in memory, problem-solving, classification, learning, communication, and related areas. At the least, the systematic study of a given phenomenon in a range of situations, including the quasi-experimental, should help us use the experiment to greater advantage in cross-cultural research. At the best it will move us along toward identifying the formal features of situations that affect cognitive performance. As we develop a framework which relates cognitive processes to their contexts, we may overcome the old dichotomies that have stood in the way of our fuller understanding of the interrelations between culture and cognition.

Note

The views here expressed have developed in the course of collaborative work with Michael Cole and owe much to his formulations on cross-cultural experimentation. Preparation of this paper was supported by a grant from the Carnegie foundation to Michael Cole and U.S.P.H.S. Grant GM 16735 from the Institute of General Medical Sciences to C. Pfaffman.

References

Albert, E. M. (1964). 'Rhetoric', 'logic', and 'poetics' in Burundi culture patterning of speech behavior. *American Anthropologist, 66,* 35–54.

Aronson, L. R., Tobach, E., Rosenblatt, J. S., & Lehrman, D. S. (Eds.) (1970). *Development and evolution of behavior: Essays in memory of T. C. Schneirla.* San Francisco: W. H. Freeman Press.

Aronson, L. R., Tobach, E., Lehrman, D. S., & Rosenblatt, J. S. (Eds.) (1971). *Selected writings of T. C. Schneirla.* San Francisco: W. H. Freeman Press.

Bellman, B. L. (1968). Unpublished field notes.

Berry, J. (1969). On cross-cultural comparability. *International Journal of Psychology, 4,* 119–128.

Campbell, D. T., & Stanley, J. C. (1963). *Experimental and quasi-experimental designs for research.* Chicago: Rand McNally.

Cole, M. (1972, April). *Toward an experimental anthropology of thinking.* Paper presented at the joint meeting of the American Ethnological Society Council on Anthropology and Education, Montreal.

Cole, M., Gay, J., & Glick, J. (1969, March). *Communication skills among the Kpelle of Liberia.* Paper presented at the Society for Research in Child Development Meeting, Santa Monica, CA.

Cole, M., Gay, J., Glick, J., & Sharp, D. W. (1971). *The cultural context of learning and thinking.* New York: Basic Books.

Dasen, P. (1972). Cross-cultural Piagetian research: A summary. *Journal of Cross-Cultural Psychology, 3,* 23–39.

Evans-Pritchard, E. E. (1963). Sanza, a characteristic feature of Zande language and thought. In Evans-Pritchard (Ed.), *Essays in social anthropology.* New York: Free Press.

Evreux, Y. (1864). Voyage dans le nord du Bresil fait durant les annees 1613 et 1614. Paris and Leipzig, Frank, 1864. (New Haven Human Relations Area Files.)

Frijda, N., & Jahoda, G. (1966). On the scope and methods of cross-cultural research, *International Journal of Psychology, 1,* 110–127.

Gibbs, J. (1962). Poro values and courtroom procedures in Kpelle chiefdom. *Southwestern Journal of Anthropology, 18,* 341–350.

Glick, J. (1969, November). *Culture and cognition: Some theoretical and methodological concerns.* Paper presented at the American Anthropological Association meetings, New Orleans.

Glick, J. (1975). Cognitive development in cross-cultural perspective. In J. Horowitz (Ed.), *Review of child development research, vol. 4,* pp. 595–654.

Kulah, A. A. (1973). *The organization and learning of proverbs among the Kpelle of Liberia.* Unpublished doctoral dissertation, Harvard University.

Lloyd, B. B. (1972). *Perception and cognition: A cross-cultural perspective.* Middlesex, England: Penguin Books.

Orne, M. T. (1970). Hypnosis, motivation, and the ecological validity of the psychological experiment. In W. J. Arnold, & M. M. Page (Eds.), *Nebraska symposium on motivation* (pp. 187–265). Lincoln: University of Nebraska Press.

Scribner, S., & Cole, M. (1973). The cognitive consequences of formal and informal education. *Science, 182,* 553–559.

Wallace, A. F. C. (1962). Culture and cognition. *Science, 135,* 351–357.

Webb, E. J., Campbell, D. T., Schwartz, R. D., & Sechrest, L. (1966). *Unobtrusive measures: Non-reactive research in the social sciences.* Chicago: Rand McNally.

11   Recall of classical syllogisms: A cross-cultural investigation of error on logical problems

These exploratory studies of logical reasoning among members of a West African tribal society face in two directions. As part of a long-term research program investigating the role of cultural factors in cognitive development,[1] they attempt to bring modern evidence to bear on the old controversy as to whether traditional people "think differently from us." (Is "logic" related to "culture"?) At the same time, their investigative techniques and findings are closely related to new lines of research and theorizing about logical thinking and the course of its development – work that seeks to identify the component processes involved in inferential reasoning within one culture (what is "logic"?).

To preserve both these interests – the historical, cross-cultural and the contemporary, theoretical – we will adopt the following course. We will first describe the background of the research and immediate questions motivating it, and present the principal findings and their implications. We will then discuss recent studies in the United States, using similar experimental techniques, to reexamine the cross-cultural data in relation to theoretical issues of the psychology of thinking posed by these studies.

Background

In the early nineteenth century, Western scholars inspired by reports of the strange beliefs and customs of colonial people began debating whether the *manner* of thinking of these people, as well as its *content*, was qualitatively different from their own.[2] In the twentieth century, after publication of the works of the French sociologist, Levy-Bruhl, this debate took the more specific form of querying whether the "logic" of primitive peoples conformed to West-

This essay originally appeared in *Reasoning: Representation and Process,* ed. R. J. Falmagne (Hillsdale, N.J.: Lawrence Erlbaum Associates, 1975), pp. 153–73. Reprinted with the permission of Lawrence Erlbaum Associates.

ern logic. From his analysis of the literature, Levy-Bruhl concluded that it did not. He characterized primitive mentality as "prelogical," by which he meant that "it does not bind itself down as our thought does, to avoiding contradictions" (Levy-Bruhl, 1966, p. 63).

Similar views have been expressed within psychology. For example, the developmental psychologist Heinz Werner (1961) maintained that logical processes in members of primitive cultures differ from those of normal adults in Western societies: "It is one of the most important tasks of developmental psychology to show that the advanced form of thinking characteristic of Western civilization is only one form among many, and that more primitive forms are not so much lacking in logic as based on logic of a different kind [p. 15]."

In a more contemporary framework, the question of possible differences in logic arises with respect to the universality of Piaget's stages of logical operations. Piaget himself (1972) recently suggested that under some cultural conditions the "final stage" of formal propositional thinking may not appear.

Anthropologists have turned powerful critical arguments, buttressed by a mass of historical and observational evidence, against this view of two logics, but experimental research methods of psychology have rarely been brought to bear on this problem. The earliest investigation was conducted by the Soviet psychologist Luria and his colleagues (Luria, 1971) among peasant families in Central Asia. Their experimental material consisted of various types of classical syllogisms, a task long employed by psychologists to investigate the rules of reasoning (Woodworth & Sells, 1935). Similarly, Cole (Cole, Gay, Glick, & Sharp, 1971) employed a variety of verbal logic problems in both naturalistic and experimental settings to study inferential processes among the Kpelle in West Africa. In both investigations, adults with some minimal education solved the majority of problems correctly, whereas those lacking formal schooling (Cole *et al.*, 1971) or literacy (Luria, 1971) had no better than a chance solution rate. Explanations traditional Kpelle farmers gave Cole for their answers were strikingly similar to those given Luria by the geographically and culturally distant Siberians. Both frequently justified their answers by appealing to fact or common knowledge:. "Because that's the way things are – I know it myself" (Luria, 1971, p. 270).

The following excerpt from an interview with a nonliterate Kpelle farmer illustrates the force of this empiric approach.

The problem has just been read by the experimenter. It is:

All Kpelle men are rice farmers. Mr. Smith (this is a Western name) is not a rice farmer. Is he a Kpelle man?

The subject replies:

S: I don't know the man in person. I have not laid eyes on the man himself.
E: Just think about the statement.

S: If I know him in person, I can answer that question, but since I do not know him in person I cannot answer that question.
E: Try and answer from your Kpelle sense.
S: If you know a person, if a question comes up about him you are able to answer. But if you do not know the person, if a question comes up about him, it's hard for you to answer it. (Scribner, this study).

This Kpelle man clearly fails to grasp the nature of the task as one involving logical implication in the sense in which Cohen and Nagle (1962) define it – inference determined solely by the structural relations between the stated propositions, independent of their factual status.

Both Luria and Cole identified this empirical bias as an important determinant of the poor problem performance of nonliterate traditional people, but they left unexplained the mechanisms by which such bias might operate to affect performance. A study by Henle (1962) suggested possible mechanisms. She gave American graduate students short written narratives that contained arguments in syllogistic form drawing conclusions about problems of everyday life. Students were required to evaluate the logical adequacy of the conclusions and to write out their judgments and the grounds for them. In her analysis of the written protocols, she identified a number of processes leading to erroneous judgments. These included omission of entire premises, modification of premises, and importation of new evidence. Henle (1962) concluded that "Where error occurs, it need not involve faulty reasoning but may be a function of the individual's understanding of the task or materials presented to him [p. 273]."

Whether or not one agrees with Henle's conclusion, the implication of her analysis is that it cannot be taken for granted that a logic task embedded in a verbal syllogism will elicit a process of inferential reasoning confined to the terms of the problem presented by the experimenter. Before drawing conclusions about the subject's reasoning processes, then, the investigator must determine what problem the subject is actually attempting to solve. This approach is rendered more specific by Evans (1972), who urges that experimental investigations of syllogistic reasoning should distinguish between two different task components: the first, the subject's encoding and interpretation of the sentences constituting the logical premises of the problem, and the second consisting of the operations the subject performs on the encoded information to reach a conclusion. Falmagne (this volume) similarly analyzes the operations involved in logical reasoning tasks in terms of stages – one or more stages in which linguistic information is encoded into a mental representation and a stage in which inferences are drawn from this representation.

This analysis of task components suggests one possible source of "error" for traditional people. Encoding and interpretive requirements of syllogisms may present special difficulty to them and, accordingly, differences in solution rates between traditional and schooled populations may reflect differences in the way

these populations represent the problem rather than differences in their inferential operational processes.

To investigate this hypothesis among nonliterate people, the studies reported here used a recall procedure as an initial attempt to secure data on problem representation that could be analyzed independently of problem solution data. The notion of using problem recall as an indicator of subject's encoding and interpretation of the problem was suggested by an observation of Luria's that farmers who had difficulty in solving his problems also had difficulty in repeating them.

Study I

Research was conducted in central Liberia among the Kpelle with whom Cole *et al.* had conducted earlier investigations. The Kpelle are a subsistence rice-farming people who preserve many old tribal ways of life while adapting to the new (for ethnographic descriptions, see Gibbs, 1965; Cole *et al.*, 1971). The subjects were 36 nonliterate men and women farmers living in an isolated village off the road and an equal number of young adults attending a junior high school in the vicinity. To relate findings to other studies on logical reasoning, comparable problems were presented to young New York City adults whose education level ranged from completion of high school to completion of college. An effort was made to screen out students who had taken courses in formal logic but this did not insure that they were without prior instruction in rules of inference.

Experimental material was modeled after that used by Hill (1961) and consisted of three eight-problem lists, one of classical syllogisms and the other two of sentential logic problems. Twelve subjects in each population were randomly assigned to each list. The present analysis deals only with data on classical syllogisms.

The problems represented four figures of the syllogism (*AA, AE, IA, OA*) each one appearing in two content versions (Table 11.1). In one content version, the two premises express factually true propositions leading to a conclusion not only logically correct but also factually true. For example, the logically required conclusion on Problem 1, "Yes, the store is in town," is in accord with the social fact that stores in Kpelleland are located in towns. In the other content version, at lest one premise asserts a factually false proposition (in Problem 4, for example, the premise that "All women who live in this town are married"), leading to a logically valid conclusion that is either factually false or ambiguous. Factual truth and falsity are only approximate judgments. Extensive pilot testing made it clear that for individual subjects there was considerable variation in evocation of "exceptions to the rule" (knowledge of a particular store on the road just outside of town, for example).

Instructions and experimental procedures were designed to make the task as

Table 11.1. *Classical syllogisms, study I (Kpelle)*

1. All stores in Kpelleland are in a town.
   Mr. Ukatu has a store in Kpelleland.
   Is it in a town?
2. All houses in Kpelleland are made of iron.
   My friend's house is in Kpelleland.
   Is it made of iron?
3. All Kpelle men are rice farmers.
   Mr. Smith is not a rice farmer.
   Is he a Kpelle man?
4. All women who live in this town are married.
   Lorpu is not married.
   Does she live in this town?
5. Some people we know are not in school.
   All the people we know are in Liberia.
   Are all people in Liberia in school?
6. Some animals we know do not have Kpelle names.
   All animals we know are in Kpelleland.
   Do all animals in Kpelleland have Kpelle names?
7. Some kwi (Western) people are wealthy.
   All wealthy people are powerful.
   Are some kwi people powerful?
8. Some Kpelle chiefs are children.
   All children are single.
   Are some Kpelle chiefs single?

meaningful as possible to Kpelle. Problems were described as word games and the individual was told he could answer them by simply listening to the words and, as a colloquial Kpelle expression puts it, "taking them to be true." Instructions emphasized, "You don't need to know anything to answer these word games. All you have to do to find the answer is to listen carefully to the words and think about them." Each session began with a practice problem that the experimenter read aloud and answered. He then explained that he found the answer by putting the words together.

The experimental procedure is outlined in Table 11.2. For each experimental problem, the procedure consisted of the following steps: the experimenter read the problem and the subject gave a "Yes" or "No" answer followed by the reason for his answer. He was then instructed to repeat the problem exactly as it had been read to him. Following this, the experimenter read the problem again and secured another subject repetition. The experimenters were two Kpelle men, one a high school graduate and the other a doctoral student in anthropology. Both were local residents of the area with extensive experience in experimental

Table 11.2. *Steps in experimental procedure*

1. *E* reads problem.
2. *S* answers "yes" or "no."
3. *S* states reason for his answer.
4. *S* repeats problem: Repetition # 1.
5. *E* rereads problem slowly.
6. *S* repeats problem: Repetition # 2.

investigations of this kind. All sessions were conducted in Kpelle and were tape recorded. They were later transcribed into English by one of the experimenters and, as a check for accuracy, a sample was also transcribed by a Kpelle college student with training in translation.

The necessity of translation from one language to another presents serious difficulties in an analysis depending wholly on linguistic responses as data. They caution against making a more fine-grained analysis of recall errors than the data warrant. As will be seen, however, recall protocols of the Kpelle subjects share a number of features with those of American subjects and a great deal of commonality with protocols secured in a subsequent study with the Vai tribe, another language group in Liberia. As far as basic phenomena are concerned, therefore, we can be confident that we are not dealing merely with artifacts of translation or unique properties of the Kpelle language.

Results on problem solution and explanation

Before the recall data are analyzed, and as a means of placing this study in relation to previous research, the summary outcome on problem solution, will be reported.

Kpelle villagers answered 53% of the problems correctly (a chance solution rate), Kpelle students 80%, and American students 90%. Results among the Kpelle are in line with the Cole and Luria studies and indicate that present findings are not specific to the materials and procedures used in this study. Performance of American high school and college students, as expected, is above the 86% solution rate of the third grade pupils whom Hill (1961) tested on similar problems.

Reasons given to support answers to the problems were classified into three categories. The first, theoretic, includes those statements explicitly relating the conclusion to the information contained in the premises of the problem as given by the experimenter; the second, empiric, includes statements justifying the conclusion on the basis of what the subject knows or believes to be true; the third, irrelevant, covers idiosyncratic and arbitrary answers as well as "don't

Table 11.3. *Reasons justifying answers to problems, study I (Kpelle)*

	Percent justifications		
	Theoretic	Empiric	Arbitrary
Kpelle villagers	22.3	68.1	9.6
Kpelle students	75.0	21.9	3.1
American students	82.3	3.1	14.6

know" responses. The respective percentages are shown in Table 11.3 for the three groups of subjects.

Villagers almost always justified their answers on the basis of belief or fact, whether or not their answers were correct or incorrect. There is a dramatic shift from empiric to theoretic explanations among Kpelle students and empiric reasons all but disappear from protocols of American students, although some give idiosyncratic replies.

Recall accuracy

For evidence on how problem information was handled by the various subject groups, transcripts of problem repetitions were analyzed with respect to two questions: how much of the original problem content was retained in recall reproductions (a quantitative analysis of retention of meaning, or recall accuracy) and the nature of changes introduced into the material (a qualitative analysis of recall error).

As a measure of recall accuracy, protocols were scored for the extent to which recall repetitions preserved the meaning of each of the several parts of the syllogism – the two premises and the question. Changes in the material, such as word substitutions, transpositions, and paraphrases, that did not affect propositional meaning were ignored. "Recall accuracy," therefore, refers to semantic, not verbatim, reproduction. Comparative results are reported in Table 11.4.[3]

Columns 1 and 5 in Table 11.4 report the proportion of problems correctly repeated in their entirety for each of the experimental groups. In each group, some problem repetitions fall into this category, indicating that the recall demands of the task have been understood by individuals in all the populations being compared. As expected, every group improved on the second recall, since it occurred immediately after the experimenter reread the problem and it was the second time the subject heard it. Even on this recall, however, a great deal of information was lost. Villagers' reproductions were highly fragmentary. Thirty-seven percent failed to preserve the meaning of either premise; 42% preserved the meaning of one premise; only 25% reproduced the sense of all the information contained in the original problem. This appears as striking confirmation of

Table 11.4. *Proportion of problems totally or partially recalled, study I (Kpelle)*

	First recall				Second recall			
	(1)	(2) Both[a] premises	(3) One Premise	(4) No premise	(5)	(6) Both[a] premises	(7) One Premise	(8) No Premise
	Total				Total			
Kpelle villagers (N = 87)	11.5	16.1	28.7	55.2	18.4	24.1	39.1	36.8
Kpelle students (N = 93)	28.9	34.4	31.2	34.4	35.5	48.4	31.2	20.4
American students (N = 90)	47.9	55.3	28.7	16.0	63.2	69.5	26.3	4.2

[a]This is a total count of problems in which both premises were correctly reproduced and therefore overlaps with Column 1.

Luria's observation. However, an unexpected finding is that villagers were not unique in faulty recall. Fully one-half of Kpelle students and nearly one-third of American students failed to reproduce all the information in the two premises that would have been essential to problem solution.

Recall accuracy was analyzed with respect to two characteristics of the problem material – their logical structure and the factual truth or falsity of their content. The response measure used in this analysis was the proportion of problems correctly repeated in their entirety on the second recall – that is, repetitions given immediately after rehearing the problem that preserved the meaning of both premises and the question of the syllogism.

To investigate the effect of problem structure, the problem list was divided into two sets, one set containing problems with only universal propositions (the "universal set") and the second containing problems with both universal and particular propositions (the "particular set").

As shown in Table 11.5, every group recalled the universal set more fully and accurately. Kpelle villagers reproduced 45% of the universal problems in their entirety as compared to only 2% of the particular; Kpelle students reproduced 64% of the universal and 8% of the particular; American students reproduced 79% of the universal and 46% of the particular.

Although the pattern of error is consistent across groups, impairment of recall performance on the "particular set" is extreme for both schooled and traditional Kpelle. The explanation is not obvious. The Kpelle language has specific lexical terms for *all* (every one of) and *some* (a few of) and no problems

Table 11.5. *Effect of quantifiers on recall accuracy, study I (Kpelle)*

		Percent problems completely recalled, 2nd recall			
		Kpelle villagers		Kpelle students	American students
Universal set					
Problem 1		36.3		81.8	100.0
2		0.0		50.0	100.0
3		50.0		64.0	72.7
4		50.0		64.0	41.6
Total	45.4		64.4		78.7
Particular set					
Problem 5		0.0		8.3	16.6
6		0.0		8.3	41.6
7		0.0		8.3	58.3
8		9.1		8.3	66.6
Total	2.3		8.3		45.8

are encountered into translation of these terms from English into Kpelle or retranslation into English. This does not rule out the possibility that these terms introduce linguistic difficulties for the Kpelle of a different nature than those involved in English and this requires further investigation. However, the qualitative analysis of errors involving the quantifiers *some* and *all* (see Discussion, below) and findings in the second study reported in this chapter suggest that extralinguistic factors are also in operation.

In contrast, division of the problem lists into sets of factual truth or falsity showed no difference in recall accuracy for any group related to this aspect of problem content. Villagers had complete reproductions of six of the factually true and six of the factually false problems; Kpelle students reproduced 15 of the true and 18 of the false; Rockefeller University students reproduced 30 of the true and 29 of the false. This result, however, cannot be taken as a determinative demonstration of lack of content influence. In this study, factuality was not varied independently of problem structure and its effects might well have been masked by the overwhelming quantifier effect.

The relationship of recall accuracy to correct solution rate is of special relevance to the problem of identifying components of the syllogistic task that may contribute to differential performance of tribal villagers and school-educated individuals. A comparison of group averages shows that recall accuracy parallels solution accuracy: groups more successful in giving correct answers to the problems as they were presented are also more accurate in recalling them. Because both American students and Kpelle students had such a high proportion of correct answers, no meaningful within-group comparative analyses could be made for these subjects. For the villagers, recall accuracy was assessed independently for problems with "right" and "wrong" answers, using as a response measure the number of problems in which the meaning of both premises was retained in the second recall. Of the 48 problems answered correctly, 11 recalls reproduced both premises; of the 40 problems answered incorrectly, 11 recalls reproduced both premises.

It would be desirable to use the recall data to throw light on the logicality of the reasoning processes involved in the task and not merely on the attainment of some experimentally defined performance criterion. This would require that subjects' answers be related to their own representations of the problem. Unfortunately, this could not be done in the present study. The nature of the transformations made in the material, as presented below, was such that in the great majority of cases is was not possible to derive a logically valid inference. This was especially true with respect to the fragmentary villagers' reproductions.

Analysis of errors in recall

Measures of recall accuracy confirm the fact that the experimental problems undergo transformations in the course of subjects' operations with them. What is the nature of these changes and are they the same or different for the various experimental groups?

To introduce the discussion of problem transformation during recall, a complete transcript of one Kpelle villager's efforts at problem repetition is presented here:

Problem: Some kwi (Western) people are wealthy.
       All wealthy people are powerful.
       Are some kwi people powerful?

Subject's answer and reason: Yes . . . it is because some kwi are wealthy and have power.
Subject's first repeat: Some kwi in this town are wealthy. They have power.
Experimenter: What question did I ask you?
Subject: Do some kwi have power?
(Experimenter reads the problem again.)
Subject's second repeat: Some kwi are wealthy. They have power. Do many wealthy men have power?

This example illustrates some common and interrelated errors. Considering the second repetition only, observe that the question, "Are some kwi people powerful?" has been transformed into a piece of evidence – "They have power." What was given as evidence – "All wealthy people are powerful" – has been turned into a question – "Do many wealthy people have power?" The term *many* has been substituted for the universal quantifier *all*. Although such examples are rare among Kpelle and American students, there are individual cases of similarly radical problem transformation within these groups.

We will now turn to a more systematic consideration of errors drawing on illustrative material from subjects' second recalls, supported where appropriate by qualitative data. A definitive or exhaustive classification of errors has not been attempted in this preliminary experiment. The major purpose has been to determine what kinds of evidence recall protocols may contribute to an understanding of information-processing difficulties in verbal syllogisms.

Omission of a premise

A principal form of error among the Kpelle was the complete omission, not merely distortion, of a premise. The premise overwhelmingly dropped was the second or minor premise; it disappeared from 40% of villagers' reproductions and 20% of Kpelle students'. American adults, in contrast, were rarely caught dropping a premise in its entirety. Here are the typical illustrations of otherwise accurate villagers' reproductions in which the minor premise is not present in any form.

All the stores in Kpelleland are in a town.
Then is Mr. Ukatu's store in town?

Omitted: the proposition that Mr. Ukatu's store is in Kpelleland.

Some of the people we know are not in school.
Then are all the people in Liberia in school?

Omitted: the proposition that all the people we know are in Liberia.

Dropping of or nonstatement of premises has been observed to be characteristic of reasoning on problems in everyday life. Cohen and Nagle (1962) point out that practical reasoning often proceeds on the basis of incompletely stated premises; implicit knowledge is combined with explicit statement to provide the basis for a conclusion. Henle (1962) has found that students sometimes drop entire premises when they are reconstructing their chain of reasoning, even though they are working from written texts. The data presented here indicate that this phenomenon may also occur when the individual's assigned task is not that of carrying forward an argument or reaching a solution but merely repeating a syllogism that he has heard.

Displacement of terms

Numerous reproduction errors involve displacement of subjects or predicates from one premise to another, destroying the implicative relations between them. These occur, with differing frequencies, among all populations and can be illustrated by transformations in problems presented to American students. The problem is this:

All children who were born in this country are citizens.
Achebe is not a citizen.
Was he born in this country?

Several American students reproduced this problem as follows:

All children who were born in this country are citizens.
Achebe was not born in this country.
Is he a citizen?

A second illustration is the problem:

Some oil men are wealthy.
All wealthy men are powerful.
Are some oil men powerful?

This was reproduced by several students as:

Some oil men are wealthy.
All oil men are powerful.
Are some oil men wealthy?

Changes in quantifiers

The largest class of errors involved the quantifier and appeared in the protocols of all populations, including American students, most frequently in villagers' reproductions.

A problem-by-problem analysis of villagers' errors with quantifiers showed that all errors occurred on problems containing both terms. In those problems in which *all* appeared in the first premise and no quantifier was used in the second, *all* was correctly reproduced in every repetition that included the first premise. In the four problems in which the term *all* appeared in the second premise and *some* in the first, there were errors involving *all* in 38% of the second premise repetitions and errors involving *some* in 41% of first premise repetitions.

There were many examples in which *all* or *some* substituted for each other or switched locations in the syllogism. Here is one version in which *all* has been replaced by *some* in the second premise, destroying the possibility of a valid conclusion: "Some Kpelle chiefs are children. *Some* children are single. Then are some Kpelle chiefs single?" Another reproduction of the same problem transposes the *all* of the second premise and the *some* of the question: "Some Kpelle chiefs are children. Some children are single. Then are all Kpelle chiefs single?"

Confusability of quantifiers is shown directly in recall protocols that present both terms in the same proposition. Kpelle villagers often give propositions in this form: "*all* the children, *some* are single." A New York adult recalled a problem in this fashion: "Some cardinals are religious. All religious people are married. Are all relig – are all cardinals married? Are some cardinals married?"

Recall errors involving the quantifier *some* are especially interesting because this quantifier has been consistently identified as a prime source of difficulty in other performance tasks using syllogistic material. Wilkins (1928), in her classical study of syllogistic reasoning among college men, attributed the greatest number of invalid conclusions to the ambiguity of the word *some*. In logic, it means at least some, whereas in ordinary usage, it often carries the implication *not all*. Wason and Johnson-Laird (1972), using a matching task to study subject's interpretations of single propositions, also found there was a tendency to interpret statements of the type "Some X are *not* Y" as implying "Some X *are* Y." Our recall protocols show frequent examples of denials and affirmations of this kind appearing in sequence. Here are two recalls of the problem containing the proposition "Some people we know are not in school":

> Some people we know are going to school.
> Some people we know are not going to school.
> Then are they all in school?

> All the people here in Liberia, some are going to school.
> There are some who are not going to school.
> Are those people going to school?

Conversion to the factual

Villagers' recall protocols showed a variety of ways in which the hypothetical or theoretical status of the problem statements was transformed into a factual basis. Educated subjects, both African and American, did not show this bias. Problem questions were sometimes converted into statements of fact and incorporated into the problem. When retained as questions, they were frequently recalled as queries of fact or belief. Here are some examples from the protocols: "Do you *think* he can be a bachelor?" "All the people in Liberia, do you *believe* they are in school?" "Do you *know* some Westerners have power?" "Why is it Mr. Smith *cannot* make rice farm?" "Is Mr. Ukatu's store in the town or in the bush?" "Does Lorpu have a husband or doesn't she have a husband?"

Although other examples can be cited, this analysis clearly demonstrates that subjects engaged in the task of repeating syllogisms make errors similar in kind to those made by subjects engaged in the task of evaluating single propositions or drawing conclusions from syllogisms.

Certain features of the experimental procedure, however, limit the extent to which such recall errors can be attributed to the encoding components of the task. Although the second recall was elicited immediately after a new presentation of the problem, it occurred at a point in the procedure when the subject had already produced an answer, a reason, and an initial repeat. In this context, the recall task may have reflected distortions introduced into the material by prior cognitive operations. A followup study attempted to get some measure of this effect by varying the point in the procedure at which the subject was asked to recall the problem.

Study II

This study was conducted among members of the Vai tribe living in small villages in Grand Cape Mount County, Liberia. Like the Kpelle, most Vai earn their living by subsistence farming. Their social and cultural life also shares certain common characteristics with the Kpelle and neighboring tribes and their language belongs to the same Mende language family. (A description of the Vai people is available in *Area Handbook for Liberia*, 1972).

All subjects were nonliterate adult men and women engaged in traditional occupations and speaking no English. With the aid of Vai informants, four syllogistic problems were prepared and presented in random order to all subjects under varying instructions. The four experimental groups, each with 12 subjects, were given different combinations of recall and solution tasks. In Group 1, subjects followed the procedure of the first study – answering each problem after it was read, stating the reason for their answer, and then, on the experimenter's request, repeating the problem. In Group 2, subjects first repeated the problem and then answered it and explained their answers. Group 3 subjects repeated the problem after hearing it but were not asked to provide an answer. Group 4 subjects were given an opportunity to hear and repeat each part of the problem, one sentence at a time. They were included in the study as a control to insure that features of individual sentences were not a major source of recall error.

Considering the control condition first, it was found that subjects repeating one sentence at a time almost perfectly preserved the meaning of the premises (91% correct repetitions) and the question (75%). In contrast, under all conditions requiring repetition of the complete syllogisms, recall was faulty and fragmentary (Table 11.6). On all measures except the 100% accuracy rate (Column 1), recall in Group 1 was inferior to that in Groups 2 and 3. This outcome might be expected on two grounds – first, recall in Group 1 was delayed rather than immediate and, second, the process of problem solution intervened between presentation and recall.

It is impossible to measure the effect of problem solution unconfounded by the recall delay factor but a comparison of Groups 2 and 3 gives some measure of the effect of instructions to answer on recall accuracy. Subjects engaged in the task as one only requiring recall (Group 3) have substantially more com-

Table 11.6. *Proportion of problems totally or partially recalled,*
as a function of time of recall, study II (Vai)

	Percent problems			
			Partial	
Time of recall	Total, both premises and question	Both[a] premises	One premise	No premise
Group 1: Recall after answering	22.9	27.1	35.4	37.5
Group 2: Recall before answering	20.8	37.5	47.9	14.5
Group 3: Recall only	34.1	43.2	27.3	29.5

[a] This is a total count of problems in which both premises were correctly reproduced and therefore overlaps with the first column.

pletely accurate recalls than those oriented to problem solution (Group 2), but this is offset by the fact that they also have more recalls that are completely incorrect. Results are therefore, inconclusive with respect to whether or not a solution set is an independent contributor to recall error. However, a solution set is clearly not a necessary condition for recall error to occur. Subjects whose only task is to listen to the syllogism under instruction to remember it retain its full meaning in no more than one-third of their recalls. Analysis of the recall protocols shows distortions in material similar to those found in other conditions and in the Kpelle study. It is accordingly clear that Study 1 findings on recall error do not depend on the condition that recall followed problem solution.

Discussion

The introduction of a recall procedure in the syllogistic reasoning task was initially motivated by an interest in locating sources of error in performance of traditional people on such tasks and in bringing new evidence to bear on the question of "two logics." It had been anticipated that this procedure would permit a comparison of subjects' answers with their own constructions of the problems as represented in their problem repetitions. The fragmentary nature of problem repetitions and the destruction of the implicative relationship between propositions in the great majority of these repetitions makes it impossible to draw any inferences about the logicality of villagers' reasoning processes from data obtained in these studies.

This very fact, however, substantiates the hypothesis that the syllogistic task imposes encoding and representational difficulties for unschooled tribal people not ordinarily encompassed in the category of deductive processes. It emphasizes that investigators have no warrant for drawing conclusions about logical processes from solution data alone.

A significant finding from the point of view of cross-cultural comparisons was that encoding difficulties were not confined to Kpelle villagers. Not only did the Kpelle and American student groups show considerable "forgetting" but they introduced changes in the material paralleling in most respects the transformations made by the villagers. There were many commonalities in error patterns: effect of problem structure on recall accuracy, confusion of quantifiers, displacement of terms, and omission of entire or partial premises. Such commonality in classes of error suggests commonality in some underlying operational processes.

The difference in the magnitude of error between villagers and student groups remains striking, however, and requires further investigation. One clue to the discrepancy may be found in the single class of error unique to unschooled villagers – the importation of such truth statements as *think, believe,* and *know* into the syllogisms. Their reformulation of the problem from a hypothetical to a factual one, even when they are endeavoring to repeat it exactly, taken together with the empiric nature of their justifications for their answers, suggests that the formal reasoning problems of the type used in these experiments are "heard" and apprehended quite differently by traditional people and those exposed to formal schooling. The "empiric bias" appears to enter as soon as the subject becomes engaged with the material. Why this may be so and whether formal problems can be devised that are meaningful in a nonempiric sense to tribal people are challenging questions for future research.

Considered from the point of view of their theoretical implications for the psychology of thinking, the findings are most interesting in the correspondence they demonstrate between the nature of errors made in recall and errors other investigators have identified in tasks requiring inferential reasoning. Most compelling is the fact that retention of meaning is markedly affected by introduction of the quantifier *some*, which is known to be a prime source of difficulty in other performance tasks using syllogistic material. An explanation for the quantifier effect on recall is not immediately obvious. Problems 7 and 8, which not a single villager recalled correctly (i.e., gave a paraphrase preserving the meaning of the problem), were among the shortest on the list. They posed no greater overall memory burden than Problems 1–4, for example, yet the latter were recalled more accurately.

Neimark and Chapman (this volume) present direct evidence of the difficulties subjects encounter in representing the relationships stated in "particular" propositions. They required subjects ranging in age from 12 to 20 years to match logical propositions of the type "*All* A *are* B, *Some* A *are* B," and the like, to Venn diagrams exhibiting all possible set inclusion relationships. They found a dramatic difference between response accuracy to the universal propositions and to the particular propositions, with only a minority even of college students interpreting *some* and *some are not* correctly. Errors on compound propositions ("*All* A *are* B and *All* B *are* A," for example) paralleled those on single propositions and were not significantly greater in amount, leading the investigators to conclude that the major source of error on compounds arose from restrictive interpretations of the quantifiers in the simple propositions. They point out that the compound propositions they used did not provide an analog of the processes underlying syllogistic reasoning because they contained no middle term; however, they suggested that their data supported analyses of errors in syllogistic reasoning that attributed them to inaccurate interpretations of individual premises (Ceraso & Provitera, 1971).

The findings presented here, however, suggest that error in recall was largely a result of the combination of quantifiers in two premises rather than the effect of the single term *some* in individual propositions. In Study II, subjects required to repeat a syllogism containing a universal and a particular proposition one sentence at a time gave almost perfect reproductions, only three errors occurring in repetitions of the premises.[4] This result dismisses the possibility that the difficulties in recalling "particular" problems might be due to specific linguistic factors related to the term *some*.

Neimark and Chapman have directly tapped difficulties involved in representation of set inclusion relationships expressed in logical propositions. Similarities in errors revealed by their matching task and the recall task in the present study furnish some basis for considering these as converging operations from which inferences can be drawn about the mental organization or representation of logical propositions. They suggest, as a specific hypothesis for future testing, that integration and representation of information in syllogistic problems may be crucial to both recall and solution performance.

Barclay's (1973) assimilation theory of sentence memory provides a useful framework within which this hypothesis may be tested. He holds that, with the exception of the special case in which individuals are required to memorize the literal wording of sentences, memory for connected sentences is an active, constructive process that cannot be understood in terms of linguistic analysis of individual sentences. The constructive process of comprehension consists in relating the information given in the single sentences, and assimilating it to existing knowledge (both lexical and nonlexical) and to task demands. The outcome of this constructive process is a semantic representation (comprehension), which in turn serves as a memory representation. The process of retrieval, then, consists of reconstructing the information from this representation. Barclay's outstanding experimental finding is that American college students, given a set of sentences describing some ordered array, "recall" certain sentences describing relationships among the items that have not been included in the set of sentences given by the experimenter but constitute correct inferences from that set. Similarly, subjects recognize as "old" new sentences describing true relationships in the array.

Paris and Carter (1973) found the same false recognition for new sentences semantically consistent with old sentences among second and fifth grade children. They presented three-sentence stories comprised of two premise sentences and a filler sentence (for example, "The bird is inside the cage, the cage is under the table, the bird is yellow"). On a later recognition test, both younger and older children consistently responded that they had previously heard the true inference statement, "The bird is under the table," when, in fact, they had not. In a related study, Kevin (1971, referred to in Barclay, 1973) read subjects partial syllogisms lacking conclusions. False recognitions were more frequent for valid than invalid conclusions, suggesting that subjects' memory representations "contained" the conclusion. Paris and Carter concluded from these findings that subjects' semantic representations for connected sentences embodied more information than was available from the linguistic inputs alone.

One implication from this work is that the converse proposition may also hold true: if subjects fail to achieve an integrated representation, either because they do not synthesize information in the individual sentences or do not assimilate it to existing knowledge, their memory representations may embody less information than is predicted by an analysis of the linguistic inputs alone. This implication is a matter for empirical confirmation.

A second implication goes to the adequacy of the conceptual framework within which the present studies have been conducted. The research proceeded from the assumption, suggested by temporal stage models of logical reasoning, that inference operations occur *after* information has been encoded and formalized in some representation – the deduction, as it were, being "read off" from the relationships expressed in the representation. Such a model makes a separation between the processes involved in understanding premises and those involved in reaching conclusions. The import of the work reported on memory for sentences is that understanding related sentences involves logical operations of inference and integration. Without identifying such inferential processes with those involved in reaching conclusions or answering questions, it nevertheless seems useful to approach future investigations of the syllogistic reasoning task on the assumption that thinking may be involved in memory representation as much as memory representation is involved in thinking.

Notes

1. This research was supported by Office of Education Grant 0-71-1695 and Carnegie Corporation Grant 5-2917-230, both to Michael Cole and National Institute of Medical Sciences Grant GM 16735. We want to thank Dr. Akki Kulah and Messrs. Paul Ricks, Kiemu Kollie and Edward Yakpazuo for their assistance in research among the Kpelle; and Dr. Ethan Gologor and Messrs. Budu Sherman and Abraham Paasawe for help in work among the Vai. An earlier version of this paper was presented at Eastern Psychological Association, May 1973.

2. The terminology used in the works cited does not reflect modern usage, but for simplicity's sake the authors' original terms have been retained in the exposition of their views. The reader should supply quotation marks for the term "primitive."

3. Table 4 is given in percentages because experimenters occasionally failed to secure first or second repetitions on some problems. Out of a possible total of 192 repetitions, the corpus available for analysis consisted of 179 among Kpelle villagers, 183 among Kpelle students, and 180 among American students.
4. These errors did involve substitutions or omission of the quantifier, however, and it might be that the single-sentence immediate recall task used was unsuited to an investigation of this question because it produced too little total error to permit differential analysis of error.

References

Area Handbook for Liberia. Washington, D.C.: The American University, 1972.

Barclay, J. R. The role of comprehension in remembering sentences. *Cognitive Psychology*, 1973, **4**, 229–254.

Ceraso, J., & Provitera, A. Sources of error in syllogistic reasoning. *Cognitive Psychology*, 1971, **2**, 400–410.

Cohen, M. R., & Nagel, E. *An introduction to logic.* New York: Harcourt, Brace & World, 1962.

Cole, M., Gay, J., Glick, J. A. & Sharp, D. W. *The cultural context of learning and thinking.* New York: Basic Books, 1971.

Evans, J. St. B. T. On the problems of interpreting reasoning data. *Cognition*, 1972, **1**, 373–384.

Gibbs, J. L., Jr. *Peoples of Africa.* New York: Holt, Rinehart & Winston, Inc., 1965.

Henle, M. On the relation between logic and thinking. *Psychological Review*, 1962, **69**, 366–378.

Hill, S. A study of the logical abilities of children. Unpublished doctoral dissertation. Stanford University, 1961.

Kevin, R. C. The generative nature of memory for inferences. Unpublished master's thesis, University of Texas at Austin, 1971. (Cited in Barclay, J. R., 1973).

Levy-Bruhl, L. *How natives think* (1910). New York: Washington Square Press, 1966.

Luria, A. R. Towards the problem of the historical nature of psychological processes. *International Journal of Psychology*, 1971, **6**, 259–272.

Paris, S. G., & Carter, A. Y. Semantic and constructive aspects of sentence memory in children. *Developmental Psychology*, 1973, **9**, 109–113.

Piaget, J. Intellectual evolution from adolescence to adulthood. *Human Development*, 1972, **15**, 1–12.

Wallace, A. F. C. *Culture and personality.* (2nd. ed.) New York: Random House, 1970.

Wason, P. C., & Johnson-Laird, P. N. *Psychology of reasoning: Structure and content.* Cambridge, Massachusetts: Harvard University Press, 1972.

Werner, H. *Comparative psychology of mental development.* New York: Science Editions. 1961. (first published 1948.)

Wilkins, M. C. The effect of changed material on ability to do formal syllogistic reasoning. *Archives of Psychology* No. 102, 1928, 1–79.

Woodworth, R. S., & Sells, S. B. An atmosphere effect in formal syllogistic reasoning. *Journal of Experimental Psychology*, 1935, **18**, 451–460.

12 Modes of thinking and ways of speaking: Culture and logic reconsidered[1]

> Our attitude towards what we listen to is determined by our habits. We expect things to be said in the way in which we are accustomed to talk ourselves: things that are said some other way do not seem the same at all but seem rather incomprehensible. . . Thus, one needs already to have been educated in the way to approach each subject.
>
> (Aristotle *Metaphysics* book II)

Of the many issues relating to culture and thought that have been a matter of scholarly concern in the last century, the question of whether industrialized and traditional people share the same logical processes has provoked the most bitter controversy. Initially centered within sociology and anthropology, the debate has largely shifted to the psychological arena. Here it has taken its most prominent form in the clash over the proper interpretation of cross-cultural Piagetian experiments on logical competencies: Do they, or do they not, demonstrate the universality of logical structures of intelligence? (For a historical review of theoretical positions on cultural differences and logical thinking, see Cole and Scribner, 1974. Dasen, 1972a, provides a summary and analysis of cross-cultural Piagetian research.)

In the last few years, quite a different line of psychological evidence has become available. Following a time-honoured tradition in psychological laboratories (see Woodworth, 1938), a number of cross-cultural investigators have made use of syllogisms and other formal logical problems as tools for studying processes of inference in verbal thinking. While still in its early stages, this work

This essay originally appeared in *Discourse Production and Comprehension*, vol. 2, ed. R. O. Freedle (Hillsdale, N.J.: Lawrence Erlbaum Associates, 1977). Reprinted with the permission of Lawrence Erlbaum Associates.

125

has produced a coherent body of findings which suggest the fruitfulness of a new strategy in the pursuit of cultural influences on logical processes – a strategy uniting the psychological study of thinking processes with the ethnographic study of ways of speaking.

This paper reviews the principal findings of this research and offers a first, speculative framework for their interpretation. We begin with a brief description of the studies that furnish the data for discussion, while Aristotle, the inventor of the syllogism and the analyst of discourse, waits in the wings.

Cross-cultural studies on verbal reasoning

Verbal logic problems were first used to investigate cultural influences on reasoning by the Soviet psychologist Luria (1971) and his colleagues in studies conducted in 1931–2 in remote regions of Uzbekistan, Central Asia. Inspired by Vygotsky's theory of mental development which holds that the specific characteristics of complex intellectual processes are determined by conditions of social life and practical activity, these psychologists sought to determine whether the social and economic reforms introduced in Uzbekistan after the revolution had effected changes in the perceptual and cognitive skills of the local people.

To investigate reasoning, Luria prepared simple syllogisms and used them in a semi-experimental, semi-interview format with four basic populations, differing in the extent to which they participated in modern social institutions: nonliterate Muslim women in remote villages who were not engaged in productive activity; nonliterate men in the same villages who carried on traditional modes of farming; young activists involved in collective farming, some of whom had minimal literacy training; women enrolled in courses at teacher training schools. Marked differences in performance between the 'traditional' and 'modern' groups (described below) were taken as confirmation of Vygotsky's theory.

Some decades later, Cole, Gay, Glick, and Sharp (1971) incorporated verbal logic problems in their extensive series of studies on learning and thinking among the Kpelle, a rice-farming tribal people in Liberia, West Africa. To determine the specific situational and experiential features affecting performance, they used a wide variety of problem materials (sentential and syllogistic problems), tasks (drawing conclusions or judging validity) and settings (individual interviews and group discussions). Comparative populations were nonliterate men and women in traditional occupations and young people with varying amounts of education in the English curricula of government and mission schools. Their finding of what appeared to be massive 'error' on the part of traditional populations prompted Scribner (1975) to undertake a series of recall studies among the Kpelle and Vai (a neighbouring people), seeking to test the

Table 12.1. *Representative problems in cross-cultural studies on verbal reasoning*

Central Asia

Cotton grows where it is hot and humid.
In the village it is hot and humid.
Does cotton grow there or not?

In the far north all bears are white.
Novaya Zemyla is in the far north.
What colours are the bears there?

West Africa

All people who own houses pay house tax.
Boima does not pay a house tax.
Does he own a house?

Some of the people we know are not in school.
All of the people we know are in Liberia.
Are all of the people in Liberia in schools?

Mexico

A dog and a horse are always together.
The horse is here now.
Where do you think the dog might be now?

So that Jose can carry corn from his farm to the town, he needs a cart and a horse.
He has the horse but doesn't have the cart.
Can Jose carry his corn from his farm?

hypothesis that failure to integrate and retain the information on the problems was the source of apparent 'nonlogical' performance.

In an attempt to further specify the effects of particular cultural factors on performance, Sharp and Cole (1975) replicated the Kpelle studies among Mayan-speaking and Spanish-speaking villagers in the Yucatan, Mexico. Comparison groups were rural and semi-urban, schooled and non-schooled adult and child populations. Finally, Cole and Scribner administered a set of syllogisms to a sample of 750 Vai adults as part of a project to investigate the cognitive consequences of literacy (the Vai Literacy Project is briefly described in Scribner and Cole, 1974).

The type of problem material used in these studies is illustrated in table 12.1. Considering the diversity of people, settings, tasks, and materials covered in these studies and of the special problems of 'nonreplicability' in cross-cultural research, the consistency of basic findings is impressive. Not only are quantitative results strikingly uniform from study to study, but certain qualitative aspects of performance are so similar that it is often difficult to distinguish the trans-

Table 12.2. *Summary of cross-cultural studies: Percentages of correct answers
to verbal logic problems*

	Nonschooled	Schooled
Cole, Gay, Glick, and Sharp (Kpelle)		
Study 3	35	91 (high school)
Study 4	61	100 (high school)
Study 5	65	
	64* (10–14 yrs)	82* (10–14 yrs, 2nd–3rd gr.)
		89* (10–14 yrs, 4th–6th gr.)
Scribner (Kpelle)		
Study 1	63	83 (jr high school)
Study 2	62	
Scribner (Vai)	52	
Cole and Scribner (Vai)	69	87 (all grades)
Sharp and Cole (Yucatecans)	45* (Mayan, trad. town)	73* (3rd gr. educ.)
	62* (Mayan, trans. town)	76* (4th gr. educ.)
		55 (1st–2nd gr.)
		78 (4th–6th gr.)
		97 (secondary school)
Scribner, Orasanu, Lazarov, Woodring (United States)		
Study 1		74 (2nd gr.)
		77 (5th gr.)
Study 2		72 (2nd gr.)
		74 (5th gr.)

*Indicates age-controlled studies.

lated interview protocol of a Uzbekistanian from that of a Vai – cultural and
geographical distance notwithstanding.

Performance consistency with respect to problem solution is displayed in
table 12.2, which summarizes findings in simplified form. (Luria's studies are
omitted, since his method, adapted to each individual respondent, does not
yield a 'tally' of scores). Basic comparisons are made with respect to the contrast
feature of schooling/no schooling, the only characteristic of populations that
was systematically investigated across studies. Two studies of U.S. school-
children are included to extend the range of comparisons. In several studies,
social conditions made it possible to vary age and schooling independently and
these studies are indicated by an asterisk.

Taken as a group, these studies appear to support a number of generalizations.

1. *In all cultures*, populations designated as 'traditional' or 'nonliterate' have just somewhat better than a chance solution rate across all types of problem material. (In the majority of studies cited, subjects were confronted with a two-choice judgment decision so that the 50 percent level may be taken as a crude indicator of 'chance'). Absolute levels vary with tasks and materials.

2. *Within each culture* there is a large discrepancy in performance between schooled and nonschooled. The major jump seems to occur at levels of education as low as two to three years of school (Luria also reports 'educational effects' with minimal literacy training), and there is continued improvement at the secondary school and college level.

3. With schooling, there is little *between-culture* variation in performance for the cultures studied. Grade, rather than society, is most determinative of performance. The two studies of U.S. elementary school children included in the table show the consistency of the grade-level/performance relationship.

A significant finding, not represented in the summary statistics of table 12.2, is that there was considerable diversity of performance among nonliterate adults. Accuracy of solution varied from problem to problem (see Cole, *et al.* 1971; Scribner, 1975; and Sharp and Cole, 1975, for detailed problem analyses) and from population to population. These diversities constitute an important line of evidence for the argument developed in this paper. Nonetheless, the overall level of performance of nonschooled traditional people and the within-culture differences in performance between schooled and nonschooled groups suggest that logical problems pose special difficulties for traditional nonliterate people. Uniformities in patterns *across* cultures indicate that the source of these difficulties is not likely to reside in aspects of culture that are unique to any one of the given cultures.

Logical thinking versus logical error

Is the source of difficulty in these problems the fact that traditional people do not reason logically? Even minimal familiarity with daily life in these communities makes such a conclusion untenable with respect to everyday thinking. Levy-Bruhl (1966), who first formulated the notion of a 'different logic' characterizing primitive thought, specifically exempted the sphere of practical activity from this generalization.

Is it then the case that traditional people do not apply their logical skills to *verbal* material? Internal evidence from the experimental situation itself argues against such a notion. Many of the nonliterate people demonstrated in the course of the interviews that they were perfectly capable of valid inferential reasoning with information presented in the verbal mode. This is well illustrated in the following protocol from a Kpelle farmer:

> *Experimenter:* If Sumo or Saki drinks palm wine, the Town Chief gets vexed. Sumo is not drinking palm wine. Saki is drinking palm wine. Is the Town Chief vexed?
>
> *Subject:* People do not get vexed with two persons.
>
> *E:* (Repeats the problem.)
>
> *S:* The Town Chief was not vexed on that day.
>
> *E.* The Town Chief was not vexed? What is the reason?
>
> *S:* The reason is that he doesn't love Sumo.
>
> *E:* He doesn't love Sumo? Go on with the reason.
>
> *S:* The reason is that Sumo's drinking is a hard time. That is why when he drinks palm wine, the Town Chief gets vexed. But sometimes when Saki drinks palm juice he will not give a hard time to people. He goes to lie down to sleep. At that rate people do not get vexed with him. But people who drink and go about fighting – the Town Chief cannot love them in the town.

While this man's answer is 'wrong' as far as the experimental problem is concerned, it is the outcome of an elegant piece of logical reasoning from new evidence. We can easily see this by recasting his statements into more traditional syllogistic form:

Sumo's drinking gives people a hard time. (Explicit premise)
Saki's drinking does not give people a hard time. (Explicit premise)
People do not get vexed when they are not given a hard time. (Explicit premise)
The Town Chief is a person. (Implicit premise)
Therefore, the Town Chief is not vexed at Saki. (Conclusion)

This is not an isolated example. Scribner (unpublished notes) analysed interviews with eight adults in one of the Cole *et al.* studies, each of whom had received at least three problems to solve. Wherever there was sufficient information to reconstruct the chain of reasoning leading to the answer it was found to follow logically from the evidence used by the subject.

The critical factor is that the 'evidence used by the subject', in many cases (as in the illustration given above), bore little resemblance to the evidence supplied in the experimental problem. Cole *et al.* (1971, p. 188) concluded: 'The subjects were (or seem to have been) responding to conventional situations in which their past experience dictated the answer. . . In short, it appears that the particular verbal context and content dictate the response rather than the arbitrarily imposed relations among the elements in the problem.'

Luria had earlier reported the same tendency for Uzbekistanians to respond in terms of direct personal experience. By manipulating the content of the problems, however, he demonstrated that where the subject matter was related to practical *knowledge* but did not deal with already known *facts*, responses were not merely verbalizations of conventional answers but were new conclusions reached through step-by-step reasoning from the problem premises. 'Reasoning and deduction . . . follow well-known rules . . . subjects make excellent judgments about facts without displaying any deviation from the 'rules' and revealing a great deal of worldly intelligence' (Luria, 1977).

These observations make it clear that inferences about a generalized incapacity of traditional people to reason logically are unwarranted. Moreover, they suggest that any inference about reasoning abilities of members of a traditional culture requires some specification of what they are reasoning *about*. Are subjects making their judgments on the basis of assertions made in the problem statements or are they drawing upon real world knowledge to generate conclusions? Is the *functional* evidence (the information actually used by the subject) the same or different from the *formal* evidence (the information supplied in the premises)? Fortunately, there are data which help us identify the functional evidence used in problem solutions; an examination of the nature of this evidence deepens our understanding of the factors affecting performance on logic problems.

'Empirical' vs. 'theoretical' explanations

In some studies, subjects were asked not only to draw conclusions but to justify or explain their answers as well. Scribner took these explanations as indicators of whether subjects were responding to the information contained in the problem or to information external to it. All statements that *explicitly* related the conclusion to the problem premises were coded as 'theoretical'; all statements justifying the conclusion on the basis of what the subject knew or believed to be true, and nonresponsive replies, were classified as 'empirical'. Examples of each will clarify the distinction.

The problem is:

> All people who own houses pay a house tax.
> Boima does not pay a house tax.
> Does Boima own a house?

A theoretical justification: 'If you say Boima does not pay a house tax, he cannot own a house.' An empirical justification: 'Boima does not have money to pay a house tax.'

Table 12.3 presents the proportion of theoretical explanations given by the principal comparative groups in four studies.

Population differences here are even more marked than those relating to solution rates and again the dimension of schooling/nonschooling serves as a significant discriminator. Nonschooled villagers overwhelmingly support their answers by appeals to fact, belief or opinion. With comparable consistency, schooled groups adopt a theoretical approach to the task; even 7-year-old second-graders in school systems known for emphasizing rote learning rather than the development of critical thinking tend to refer to what the problems *say* when asked to account for their answers. These data not only corroborate

Table 12.3. *Percentages of theoretical reasons for problem answers*

	Nonschooled	Schooled	
Scribner (Kpelle)	22·3	75·0	(students, jr high school)
Scribner (Vai)	8·3	—	
Cole and Scribner (Vai)	29·5*	72·2*	(adults, all grades)
Sharp and Cole (Yucatecans)			
Mayan, trad. town	43·0	75·9	(Mestizo adults, grs. 1–6)
Mayan, trans. town	58·5	46·5	(2n gr.)
		80·8	(4th–6th gr.)
		97·4	(secondary school)
Scribner, Orasanu, Lazarov, Woodring (United States)			
Study 1		77·6	(2nd gr.)
		93·2	(5th gr.)
Study 2		76·0	(2nd gr.)
		95·1	(5th gr.)

*Sample from survey

anecdotal reports of the several investigators, but document the pervasiveness of villagers' resort to the concrete example or particular circumstance. This appeal to real world knowledge and experience, which for the time being we will call 'empirical bias', is the single most prominent characteristic of villagers' performance and merits detailed analysis.

What is empirical bias? Some examples

As ordinarily used in studies on reasoning, empirical bias refers to the subtle effects of problem content which 'seduce' the reasoner from the formal task; it operates as a 'distractor'. In the cross-cultural research reported here such distracting effects are also found, but, among some traditional groups, empirical bias takes a new form: it operates as an 'organizer', characterizing the individual's entire mode of engagement with the material.

At an extreme, such bias is shown in a refusal of some individuals to engage in the reasoning task at all, on the grounds that the problems presented are, *in principle*, unanswerable. This is illustrated in the following protocol of a non-literate Kpelle farmer who has been presented with a description of this word game and shown how to solve a practice problem by 'listening to the words and taking them to the true' (a colloquial Kpelle expression). The problem:

All Kpelle men are rice farmers.
Mr Smith is not a rice farmer.
Is he a Kpelle man?

The subject replies:

S: I don't know the man in person. I have not laid eyes on the man himself.
E: Just think about the statement.
S: If I know him in person, I can answer that question, but since I do not know him in person I cannot answer that question.
E: Try and answer from your Kpelle sense.
S: If you know a person, if a question comes up about him you are able to answer. But if you do not know the person, if a question comes up about him, it's hard for you to answer it.

This man firmly rejects the possibility of coming to a conclusion on the basis of propositions which make assertions about matters on which he has no personal information. He is not distinguishing between the process of drawing conclusions from statements asserting relationships and the process of evaluating information. At the same time, the protocol illustrates that his failure to grasp the nature of this reasoning task should not be confused with failure to adopt a hypothetical attitude. In fact, on several occasions this Kpelle man reasoned hypothetically (i.e. from a conditional statement) in his exposition of why he *couldn't* answer the question ('If you know a person . . . you are able to answer. . .'), but his hypothetical reasoning was within the empirical mode. One might say he was reasoning hypothetically about the *actual* while denying the possibility of reasoning hypothetically about the *postulated*.

Luria's (1977) transcripts have many such examples drawn from interviews with nonliterate Uzbekistanian women, who seem to have been the most isolated of the groups worked with thus far. To the problem: 'In the far north all bears are white; Novaya Zemyla is in the far north. What color are the bears there?' the women often suggested, 'You should ask the people who have been there and seen them'; 'We always speak of only what we see; we don't talk about what we haven't seen.' These represent the extreme examples and were only occasionally encountered in contemporary studies, but no similar cases, to our knowledge, have been reported outside of the cross-cultural literature.

For the majority of traditional adults, empirical bias entered the problem solution process primarily as selector and editor of the 'evidence'. Personal knowledge and experience were used as (1) the criterion for acceptance or rejection of particular information conveyed in the premises, (2) the source of new information from which to derive a conclusion, (3) 'proof' or verification of a conclusion reached through use of problem information. These functions are illustrated in the following protocols from Vai respondents, all adult men and women without schooling.

Problem	*Answer and explanation*
Rejection of problem information	
(1) All women who live in Monrovia are married. Kemu is not married. Does she live in Monrovia?	Yes. Monrovia is not for any one kind of people, so Kemu came to live there. (denial of first premise)
(2) Some government officials are wealthy. All wealthy men are powerful. Are some government officials powerful?	No. Because all government officials are wealthy, but not all wealthy people have power. (denial of second premise)
Importing new evidence	
(3) All people who own houses pay house tax. Boima does not pay a house tax. Doe he own a house?	Yes. Boima has a house but he is exempted from paying house tax. The government appointed Boima to collect house tax so they exempted him from paying house tax. (discussion indicated that this was exception proving the rule that all people pay house tax)
Verifying a conclusion	
Problem (3) above.	No. If he has a house, he would pay the government tax *as required by the Liberian government.* (factual corroboration)
(4) Some of the people we know are not in school. All of the people we know are in Liberia. Are all of the people in Liberia in school?	No. Because you said you know some people who do not go to school and *myself know a lot of them too.* (corroboration of the formal evidence by personal experience)
(5) All schools in Vai land are in a town. I know a school in Vai land. Is it in a town?	Yes. All schools are in a town. A school *should* be for the *fact human beings are attending it so it can't be built in the bush.* (corroboration by common sense)

As these examples show, evidence from the problem and evidence from personal knowledge can be interwoven in any designs to sustain a reasoning process and yield an inference.

For populations at the extreme end of formal education and/or modernity, theoretical approaches may be an all-or-none matter; at the extreme of rural isolation (as among Luria's Muslim women) empirical approaches may be all-or-none. In the present analysis, formal evidence in a problem controls performance of the schooled groups. The nonschooled groups show no such homogeneity: some respondents appear at either end of the spectrum, handling all problems empirically or, in fewer numbers, handling them all theoretically. The great majority have a mixed strategy, relying now on the formal information in the problem, now on evidence external to it. Adoption of a particular mode is influenced in varying degrees by specific features of the material, especially the factual status of the information supplied in the premises. Several problems in the Vai research evoked empirical responses from more than 75 per cent of respondents while others drew such responses from only 30 per cent of the sample. The fact that most nonliterate individuals respond theoretically to at least one problem demonstrates that while their approach to the task is dominated by empirical bias, it is not wholly controlled by it.

Empirical vs. theoretical explanations and wrong answers

The presence of within-subject as well as between-group variability in empirically and theoretically based answers raises an interesting possibility. If we separate out the problems in which individuals used evidence contained in the premises, as indicated by their theoretical justifications, we should expect to find a high proportion of correct answers. Indeed, theoretical responses should *invariably* be associated with correct responses, provided the subject is able to meet the logical demands of the problem. If people are making judgments on the basis of their own experience, however, as evidenced by empirical justifications, their conclusions could be either correct or incorrect, depending on the factual status of the information given in the problem.

To test this line of reasoning, we made a detailed problem-by-problem analysis of the relationship between explanations and answers for the first 100 respondents in a village picked at random from the current Vai survey study. This was a heterogeneous sample in which the majority of respondents were nonliterate, but it included some men literate in the indigenous Vai script and several individuals who had attended English school. Of the 600 cases (100 subjects × six syllogistic problems) there are 171 wrong answers, *but not a single case in which a theoretical reason is given for a wrong answer* (see table 12.4).

To determine the generality of this relationship for logical problems of a different type and for members of another culture, a similar analysis was made for the Sharp–Cole studies. Although, as we have seen, the distribution of empirical and theoretical explanations differs markedly from one group to another, the relationship between theoretical justifications and correct answers is robust. Summing across populations as well as problems, of 233 wrong answers to problems, only 17 are associated with theoretical reasons.

Not only is this relationship constant across groups, but it holds for *any given individual* within every population group: men and women from a traditional culture who give theoretical reasons on particular problems produce the logically correct answers on these problems, even though all their other answers may be wrong.

. . . While theoretical reasons almost always predict accuracy, empirical reasons, as we conjectured, were used to justify right as well as wrong answers. In

Table 12.4. *Type of reason and error in problem solution*

	Proportion of theoretical reasons with wrong answers	Proportion of empirical reasons with wrong answers
Sharp and Cole, 1975 (Mexico)		
Mayan, trad.	0·02	0·21
Mayan, trans.	0·01	0·15
Mestizo adults		
(elementary school)	(<0·01)	0·08
2nd gr. children	0·01	0·18
4th–6th gr. children	0·02	0·09
Secondary school students	(<0·01)	0·00
Scribner and Cole, 1975 (Africa)		
Vai adults	0·01	0·42

some problems, the validly correct conclusions coincide with facts that would be known through direct personal experience, e.g. conclusions such as 'Not everyone in Liberia goes to school', derived from the premises 'Some of the people we know are not in school' and 'All of the people we know are in Liberia.' Correct answers on these problems could either represent reasoning about familiar situations or merely the person's assent to a true fact of life. In the absence of extended discussion with the subject, we cannot tell which process was involved. In contrast, other problems contained one or more premises that denied a commonly accepted truth, thus setting the valid problem conclusion into opposition with experienced reality. One problem in the Vai research asserted the 'absurd' proposition that 'All women who live in Monrovia (the capital city of Liberia) are married'; the second proposition stated that 'Kemu is not married'; and the question asked, 'Does Kemu live in Monrovia?' Respondents working from real-life knowledge-acquaintance with a particular Kemu, for example, or from the known fact that there *are* unmarried women in Monrovia – could arrive at an incorrect answer through logical reasoning.

. . . The significant comparative conclusion is that, in those instances where they deal with the problem as a formal 'theoretical' one, nonschooled nonliterate men and women display exactly the same logicality as adults and children exposed to Western-type schooling. In the sample at hand, when they are 'theoretical,' they are virtually never wrong.

This evidence, of course, does not rule out the possibility of error attributable to reasoning processes or other sources. It is well known (Wason and Johnson-Laird, 1972; Henle, 1962) that even test-sophisticated U.S. and British university students err on logic problems, depending on their structural complexity, content, and linguistic features. The present conclusion holds only for the problems used in the two studies analyzed, and the degree of complexity they represent; it may be that the problem sample was weighted toward the structurally simple, 'easy' end of the spectrum. . . .

The constancy of the relationship between theoretical approaches and accurate solutions represents the strongest evidence to date that traditional people can and do engage in valid deductive reasoning on verbal logic problems, provided they put brackets about what they know to be true and confine their reasoning to the terms of the problems. More often than not, traditional villagers fail to do just that, under conditions in which educated subjects almost always do just that. It appears characteristic for villagers to approach informally 'as a matter of course' a task that students approach formally 'as a matter of course.' Those living in the most rural and isolated towns bring to the arbitrary problems of the experiment a reasoning system, at play in everyday life, in which inference is intricately interwoven with evaluation and interpretation of semantic information; others, adopting a formal mode for some problems tend to lapse into the semantic-evaluative approach to other problems. Performance on the formal task is rarely free from intrusions of real-world knowledge.

The question originally motivating the research – what is the relation between cultural influences and verbal reasoning – involves us in the exploration of another: What is the relation between cultural experiences and empirical bias? How do we pin down the specific activities within a given cultural milieu that contribute to a 'break' between empirical approaches to everyday problems and theoretical approaches to problems whose subject matter does not 'count'?

Empirical bias: Task dependent?

Before turning to some hypotheses suggested in the ethnographic literature, we would like to examine another set of cross-cultural experimental data involving somewhat different operations with syllogisms. Scribner (1975) conducted several studies among the Kpelle and Vai in which she asked subjects to *repeat* the syllogisms after they were read, or to *recall* them after they had been solved. Results from these studies help us to determine whether the phenomenon of empirical bias in the reasoning experiments was a function of the specific task demands set in those experiments. We know that, at least in some of the cultures studied, riddles and disputations are common forms of verbal exchange. It may be that the experimental situation conveyed to the subjects the implied expectation that cleverness – 'good argumentation' – was called for, and thus encouraged the production of culturally valued types of proof. No such expectation is implied, however, when subjects are asked to repeat as accurately as possible exactly what they have heard. In Scribner's initial studies conducted among the Kpelle, subjects were asked to repeat each syllogism on two occasions: once after having answered and explained it, and a second time, immediately after hearing the problem restated. In follow-up

Table 12.5. *Percentages of problems with accurately recalled premises (Kpelle)**

	Both premises	One premise	No premise
Kpelle villagers (N = 87)	24·1	39·1	36·8
Kpelle students (N = 93)	48·4	31·2	20·4
U.S. students (N = 90)	69·5	26·3	4·2

*Data presented are from subjects' second recall involving repetition of problems immediately after they were read.

studies among the Vai, additional groups were added in which the only task was to repeat the syllogism in its entirety or sentence-by-sentence. In the one-sentence-at-a-time procedure, repetition was almost perfect, indicating that the surface structure of individual propositions did not pose any special encoding problems. In the other experimental condition recall errors were similar to those among the Kpelle (results are presented in table 12.5) and the discussion will be based on the Kpelle data.

Recall was scored for preservation of meaning rather than verbatim accuracy; lexical substitutions, omissions, and changes in word order that did not change the meaning were scored as accurate. Even on this basis, recall of the problem as a whole was highly fragmentary; in only a small number of cases did villagers reproduce the sense of the problem as such. Information was omitted or transformed in such a way that implicative relationships were destroyed and questions posed that did not follow from what had gone before.

A Kpelle farmer attempts to recall:

Problem:
> All the stores in Kpelleland are in a town.
> Mr Ukatu's store is in Kpelleland.
> Is Mr Ukatu's store in a town?

First repeat:
> You told me Mr Ukatu came from his home and built his store in the Kpelleland. Then you asked me, is it in a town?

Second repeat (immediately after hearing problem reread):
> All stores are in the land. Mr Ukatu's store is the one in Kpelleland. Is it in the town?

In the first repetition the subject has assimilated the problem to a narrative form. He imported new information pertaining to a personally known Mr Ukatu ('came from his home and built his store'), but omitted the major premise entirely. In the second repetition, the surface form more closely approximates the syllogism, but the major proposition – that all stores in Kpelleland are built in towns – is still omitted. In each case, the question, 'Is Mr Ukatu's store in a town?' does not follow from the information reproduced and appears only as a question of fact, unrelated to the preceding material.

The most common classes of error included changes or omissions in quantifiers that converted generalizing statements into particular statements of fact, omission of entire premises and displacement of terms. These changes in many instances had the effect of 'destroying the syllogism as a unified system' (Luria, 1977) and replacing it with a series of discrete statements that shared the same topic but were not logically related to each other.

In a number of recall reproductions the hypothetical or theoretical status of the problem was converted to a factual status. 'Remembering' new information from personal experience was one form this conversion took; another was the rephrasing of the problem question such that it referred, not to the antecedent information, but to matters of belief or fact: 'Do you *think* he can be a bachelor?' 'Why is it Mr Zerby *cannot* make rice farm?' 'Then, Mr Ukatu's store, do you *know* it is in town?' '*For what reason do you think* any of them can be a bachelor?' 'All the people in Liberia, do you *believe* they are in schools?'

Replication recall studies with Kpelle and US students showed, as did the problem solving studies, both commonalities and differences with the villagers. Again, magnitude of error was considerably greater for unschooled villagers than for either student group. Educated subjects, both African and American, resembled villagers in that their most common form of error was confusion of quantifiers, and, like the villagers, they sometimes omitted entire premises and switched terms from one premise to another. The one class of errors students did not make was conversion to the factual. Even when their problem repetitions were inaccurate with respect to the originals, students almost invariably preserved their hypothetical status.

It appears that among population groups for whom logical relations do not control problem solving in the experimental situation, such relations often fail to control memory as well. The dominance of an empirical approach to problem solving is thus not necessarily a reflection of the fact that individuals are required to draw or justify conclusions. The recall data, taken together with evidence from earlier studies, suggests that more general processes of 'understanding' the material may underline both recall *and* solution.

In what follows, we will sketch one approach to the special characteristics of formal problems and what may be involved in understanding them. This approach is not in any way dictated by the evidence at hand, but it is offered as one framework within which to search for the relationship between culture and the formal approach to problem solving.

Schemas and genres

The theory of comprehension and sentence memory proposed by Bransford, Barclay, and Franks (1972) and Barclay (1973) provides a starting point for the integration of recall and problem-solving findings. They maintain that, with the exception of the special case in which individuals are required to memorize the literal wording of sentences, memory for connected discourse is an active constructive process of comprehension. Comprehension involves relating or integrating the information presented in the individual sentences and assimilating it to existing lexical and nonlexical knowledge schemas. They have demonstrated experimentally that memory for a text may be 'richer' than the information explicitly contained in its constituent sentences – incorporating additional conceptual information from the schemas into which the material was assimilated.

Data from recall studies with syllogisms illustrate the converse case: memory for these connected sentences not only failed to incorporate new logical inferences but often failed to preserve the logical and conceptual information in the original. In Bransford and Barclay's terms, this may be interpreted as an indication that the material was not integrated and assimilated to preexisting schemas.

This interpretation raises a general question: *What are* (how can we conceive the nature of) *the pre-existing schemas into which verbal logic problems can be assimilated?* If the information the problems contain is completely congruent with practical knowledge, their assimilation could follow the course of comprehension of other forms of connected discourse. (Recall Luria's excellent results with material involving practical knowledge but not directly related to people's own personal experiences.) If the relations the problems express are arbitrary, not consonant with or in opposition to accumulated knowledge, their assimilation into pre-existing schemas may militate *against*, rather than facilitate, comprehension, recall, and problem solving. Such assimilation would manifest itself in 'empirical bias', as pre-existing schemas become the field of operation for remembering and reasoning activities. For a formal or theoretical approach to be maintained, with operations restricted to the arbitrary terms of the problems, the schema to which the material is assimilated must be based on relationships rather than subject matter.

In addition to the concept of schemas, the general interpretive framework we would like to develop makes use of another analytic category, that of *genre*. Hymes (1974) has proposed that *genres* and *performances* be considered basic categories for the study of ways of speaking in different speech communities. As he uses the term, *genre* refers to stylistic structures or organized verbal forms with a beginning and an end, 'and a pattern to what comes between' (1974, p. 442). Greetings, farewells, riddles, proverbs, prayers, are among well-known elementary genres, and tales and myths representative of complex genres. *Per-*

formances refers to the use of genres in particular contexts. Both genres and performances may vary from one speech community to another, and the relationship between them may vary as well: certain genres in certain communities may be context-bound while in others they range over diverse events and situations.

Let us entertain the proposition that verbal logic problems (along with other 'formal problems' which we shall not attempt to specify at this point) constitute a specialized language genre that stands apart from other genres in ways that may be difficult to define but are readily recognizable (just as poetry may be distinguished from prose by readers who may never exactly agree on what poetry 'is').

It is, of course, true that people do not 'speak in syllogisms' in any community we know of, but we have good authority for considering logic problems a specialized form of discourse. In one of his definitions of a syllogism, Aristotle referred to it as 'discourse in which certain things being stated, something other than what is stated follows of necessity from their being so' ('Prior analytics,' quoted in Jager, 1963, p. 14). Or, again, he defined the component parts of the syllogism as premises, each of which is a 'form of speech which affirms or denies something' and is itself composed of terms which predicate something of something else (Bochenski, 1970, p. 45). Aristotle is here developing new terminology ('premises,' 'terms') to talk about a language function that has hitherto not been isolated from the other functions in which it is ordinarily embedded. As Bochenski points out, new technical terminology was required to convey the distinction between two customarily related, but conceptually independent, aspects of sentences – the truth value they express (dependent on subject matter) and the relations authorizing necessary inferences that they express and that are independent of subject matter.

In ordinary discourse, these aspects interpenetrate. Discourse that uses language primarily to convey necessary relations between propositions constitutes what we have been calling the 'logical genre.' In its focus on topic-neutral relations rather than topic-bound content, the logical genre stands in contrast to other genres, both formal and informal (see Bricker, 1975, for an analysis of formal and informal Mayan speech genres).

With these constructs – *schema, genre, performance* – we can suggest an interpretation for the findings of both the memory and reasoning studies. Through experience with the genre (a socially evolved language structure) individuals develop a cognitive schema through which they assimilate increasingly varied and more complex examples of the genre. They will remember the form of a problem (the general relationship between premises) even when they forget the particular subjects and predicates used. In a reasoning task, they will grasp an example (e.g. approach a problem formally) even though they may not be able on a particular occasion to handle successfully its specific content.

An example from memory research makes this point more concretely. In societies in which narrative is a developed genre, recall of 'stories' will be facilitated by their assimilation to the narrative structure. This structure confers 'sense' on the presented material and serves as a guide to the retention and retrieval of the specific informational content in the given example. The narrative, like the formal problem, may be considered a socially evolved genre that individuals in varying degrees, depending on their own personal life experiences, acquire or, in Vygotsky's terms, internalize. Like narrative, when the formal problem's structure is internalized, it helps to make sense of the material presented and serves as a device that guides and constrains remembering and reasoning.

In the studies we have reviewed, there were some individuals who seem not to have developed the requisite schema for handling the type of discourse represented in the logic problem. They denied the sense of the question or failed to retain the logical system in their recall reproductions. The overwhelming bulk of respondents in all cultural groups, however, showed some grasp of the genre. For most nonschooled adults this was a transient phenomenon. Several possibilities exist here. Schemas may not be generalized across all content and may be more vulnerable to certain subject matters than others. Alternatively, or concurrently, the experimental or interview context may not have provided the appropriate cues to elicit the desired performance – the use of the logical genre (cf. Hymes, 1974).

We know very little about the social conditions which give rise to the logical genre, how cultures define the occasions for its use, through what experiences individuals acquire its schema. Within Western academic institutions, examples of the genre are not uncommon. Verbal and arithmetical problems would seem to fall into the class of problems whose content is arbitrary and whose meaning resides in the relationships expressed. If the teacher presents a problem: 'Johnny has one red apple and Mary has one red apple, how many apples do Johnny and Mary have altogether?' it will not do for a child to look around the room to see who else may have an apple or to question whether apples are really red. An empirical approach to the problem will not earn a passing grade. Specialized studies – algebra, geometry, chemistry – and other fields that use technical notational systems may be considered to present 'arbitrary problems' in the sense that the problems derive from a system outside the learner's own personal experience and must be taken in their own terms. It would be interesting to examine school curricula to find to what extent students must learn to work with other verbal problems that represent the genre of logical discourse.

More challenging is the question of what activities outside of school, and especially what activities in traditional cultures, might give rise to this form of discourse. Ryle (1963) has made the provocative suggestion that the 'logical idiom' arises when societies face pressures for 'special kinds of talk,' especially involving commercial transactions, contracts and treaties, legal and administrative services. To our knowledge, no researches in the ethnography of speaking have yet identified and analyzed examples of this genre, but it appears to be an important direction in which to carry studies of specialized language functions.

For the psychologist, the leading developmental question becomes that of specifying under what circumstances and as a result of what experiences individuals possessing this genre internalize it as a schema available for cognitive activities. The leading functional question becomes that of specifying the experimental conditions, as well as everyday conditions, under which a given example of this form of discourse is assimilated in the logical schema.

Note

1. An edited version of a chapter to appear in R. O. Freedle (ed.) *Discourse Production and Comprehension* (Hillsdale, N.J.: Lawrence Erlbaum Associates, in press). Reprinted with the permission of the author and publishers.

References

Barclay, J. R. The role of comprehension in remembering sentences. *Cognitive Psychology*, 1973, *4*, 229–254.

Bochenski, I. M. *A history of formal logic*. 2nd edition. Notre Dame, Indiana: University of Notre Dame Press, 1970.

Bransford, J. D., Barclay, J. R., & Franks, J. J. Sentence memory: a constructive versus interpretive approach. *Cognitive Psychology*, 1972, *3*, 193–209.

Bricker, V. R. The ethnographic context of some traditional Mayan speech genres. In R. Bauman, & J. Scherzer (Eds.), *Explorations in the ethnography of speaking*. London: Cambridge University Press, 1974.

Cole, M., Gay, J., Glick, J., & Sharp, D. *Cultural context of learning and thinking*. New York: Basic Books, 1971.

Cole, M., & Scribner, S. *Culture and thought*. New York: Wiley, 1974.

Dasen, P. R. Cross-cultural Piagetian research: a summary. In J. W. Berry & P. R. Dasen (Eds.), *Culture and cognition: readings in crosss-cultural psychology*. London: Methuen, 1974.

Henle, M. On the relation between logic and thinking. *Psychological Review*, 1962, *69*, 366–378.

Hymes, D. Ways of speaking. In R. Bauman & J. Sherzer (Eds.), *Explorations in the ethnography of speaking*. London: Cambridge University Press, 1974.

Jager, R. *Essays in logic*. Englewood Cliffs, N.J.: Prentice-Hall, 1963.

Levy-Bruhl, L. *How natives think* (1910). New York: Washington Square Press, 1966.

Luria, A. R. Towards the problem of the historical nature of psychological processes. *International Journal of Psychology*, 1971, *6*, 259–272.

Luria, A. R. *Cognitive development. Its cultural and social foundations*. Cambridge: Harvard University Press, 1976.

Ryle, G. Formal and informal logic. In R. Jager, *Essays in logic*. Englewood Cliffs, N.J.: Prentice Hall, 1963.

Scribner, S. Developmental aspects of categorized recall in a West African society. *Cognitive Psychology*, 1974, *6*, 475–494.

Scribner, S., & Cole, M. Research program on Vai literacy and its cognitive consequences. *Cross-cultural psychology newsletter*, 1974, *8*, 2–4.

Scribner, S. Recall of classical syllogisms: a cross-cultural investigation of error on logical problems. In R. J. Falmagne (Ed.), *Reasoning: representation and process.* Hillsdale, N.J.: Lawrence Erlbaum Associates, 1975.

Sharp, D. W., & Cole, M. The influence of educational experience on the development of cognitive skills as measured in formal tests and experiments. Final Report to Office of Education. New York: Rockefeller University, 1975. (mimeo, 87 pp.)

Vygotsky, L. *Mind in society.* (Cole, M., John-Steiner, V., Scribner, S., Souberman, E., Eds.). Cambridge: Harvard University Press, 1978.

Wason, P. C., & Johnson-Laird, P. N. *Psychology of reasoning: structure and content.* Cambridge: Harvard University Press, 1972.

Woodworth, R. S. *Experimental psychology.* New York: Holt, 1938.

13 Intelligence tests: A comparative perspective

At night
in sweat
i woke from dream
error with two tails
dilemma with horns
distributions with best fit
a graphic hell
with no confidence.
Sylvia Scribner

In the hope of providing a fresh perspective from which to consider the social determinants of intelligence testing, I have developed a comparison of testing in two human service domains, medicine and education.

The comparison is not an uncommon one. In part, it is a natural outgrowth of the fact that psychological testing is often carried out in medical settings, providing a bridge between the two fields. Psychological test literature frequently uses the existence and widespread acceptance of medical tests to enhance the perceived value of educational tests. Thus, the report of a special committee on tests of the American Psychological Association (Cleary, et al., 1975), in justifying its pre-technical assumptions about the value of testing, states that: "Diagnosis, prognosis, prescription and measurement of outcome are as important in education as in medicine." (p. 18)

Such comparisons are typically no more than surface analogies, but, if carried deeper, they reveal certain fundamental differences in the motivation for testing, the manner of testing, and the consequences of testing in these two domains. This discussion focuses on these differences and sharpens them, to

This paper was originally presented at the Conference on Alternatives to Standardized Testing, Pittsburg, May 14–15, 1976.

bring into prominence the interrelationships between the institutional and social contexts of testing, its technical apparatus, and its consequences.

The comparison is directed to the following questions: What is the nature of
testing in the two domains? How do test outcomes affect the individual's life?
What impact do they have within the institutions? What are their broader social
consequences?

Testing in the medical domain

An initial observation about medical tests is that they are primarily
special-purpose: they are administered on particular occasions for particular
diagnostic purposes. There is no general physical ability test analogous to the
general mental ability test. In recent years, with increasing emphasis on health
maintenance needs, new instruments have been developed to assess an individual's overall state of health. Interestingly, these "health inventory" assessments
are designed to secure as detailed a picture as possible of the functioning of
different physical systems that can be used both as the basis for individual care
and for projecting the health-care needs of the population as a whole. The
health inventory does not yield a single summary figure purporting to measure
an individual's health capacity – a health quotient, as it were. That there are no
H.Q.'s comparable to I.Q.'s is less likely to reflect technical incapabilities than
the fact that the concept has no perceived utility.

Of the three standard functions of tests – prediction (prognosis), diagnosis,
and selection – the leading function in medical testing is diagnosis; prognosis
and selection are byproducts of diagnostic procedures. When a patient reports
to a clinic complaining of blurred vision and dizzy spells, he is likely to be given
a battery of tests, from an eye chart to an EEG. The purpose of the tests is to
enable the clinical team to penetrate beneath the reported and observed symptoms to determine what processes are responsible for the condition. Does the
patient suffer from near-sightedness or from a brain tumor? More than one test
may be necessary to rule out alternative hypotheses. Individual tests will be
more or less useful, depending on the degree to which test data permit unambiguous inferences about underlying processes. The information-value of test
responses determines the efficacy of the tests. Note that the concept of "right"
or "wrong," "good" or "poor" responses does not arise in the diagnostic context.

The central role of diagnosis in medical testing is related to the fact that
medical institutions are mandated to provide treatment and that differential
forms of treatment are available. Diagnosis and treatment form an interactive
system, with sometimes one and sometimes the other making new advances. As
scientific knowledge increases and diagnostic procedures become more sophisticated, illnesses may be labeled and identified even in the absence of known
effective treatment interventions. And treatment methods may be hit upon

through practical experiments that are effective in controlling the disease process or relieving symptoms, even though there is only partial knowledge of the nature of that process. The scientific-technical enterprise, however, moves toward an ever-closer relationship between the two, such that available treatments provide guidelines for diagnosis and diagnosis informs treatment.

In addition, prediction is not practiced for prediction's sake, outside of a research context. There is no mass testing of individuals for prognostic purposes only. Suppose a test were developed that permitted almost perfect prediction of glaucoma from eye color. What would the response be to a proposal for mass testing, the only outcome of which would be the labeling of individuals as high or low glaucoma risks? Such mass testing, independent of a program for either treatment or prevention, would not win easy acceptance among the public at large or in the health professions.

In the individual case, a diagnostic work-up providing information about the patient's condition will also yield information about chances of benefiting from available methods of treatment. In most cases, however, the patient's prognosis does not determine her admission to health care; the patient with a poor prognosis is not turned away. We said "in most cases," for the restrictions on this rule are important indicators of the social conditions under which prediction does or does not assume a leading role in testing. "Poor prognosis" *may* have no-treatment consequences if treatment facilities are limited and must be allocated rationally. Too few hospital beds, insufficient supplies of medicine, a doctor shortage – these are the conditions in which some social decision-making process comes into play to determine the beneficiaries of the limited goods. A priority plan that selects beneficiaries of treatment on a risk basis (treat those who have the best chance of profiting from available methods) may be considered optimal under such conditions. Whether such a selection system is more or less desirable than other possible priority plans is not important for the present discussion. What is illuminating is that prediction and its associated function of selection assume importance under conditions of scarcity – insufficient resources to meet the need. At that point, some assessment instrument may be pressed into service to differentiate among those who will and those who won't receive treatment. Functions served by testing are clearly responsive to supply and demand factors in the human services.

What are the consequences of medical testing for the individual? Although tests may not lead to interventions that enhance the individual's life chances, they do not, on the whole, reduce them significantly. An important aspect of test improvement is reduction of the risk accompanying test administration. The development of nonintrusive diagnostic tests is now a major effort in clinical practice.

The impact on the individual tested is potentially broader, however, for testing often entails labeling and classification, and labels, as such, may have undesirable consequences. It is customary in medical practice to label the disease rather than the person – classification procedures are nosological, not "personological." Significant exceptions, we might note, occur in psychological pathology, when labels such as "mentally retarded" or "mentally ill" are commonly affixed to the patient and may result in the adverse side-consequences of stigmatization and loss of opportunities for personal achievement.

We can recall that, in the not too distant past, stigmatization was also attached to certain physical illnesses. There were "dirty" diseases that "dirty" people contracted: gout was a high-status symbol, tuberculosis the unmentionable affliction of the working girl. We like to believe it a sign of progress that evaluative practices of this kind are diminishing, but even if they persist in certain areas with respect to certain conditions, such practices do not rest on alleged scientific support. Because medical testing is special-purpose and oriented to individual diagnosis, the evaluative group-comparison aspect is minimized.

Finally, we would like to make an observation about the relationship among medical tests, treatment, and outcome. Regardless of how the individual has been tested, the medical institution and its practitioners stand accountable for outcome of treatment. Treatments that are ineffective reflect on insufficiencies in our knowledge or inadequacies of our practice. There is no institutionalized policy of blaming the patient for failure to recover. For several years we have been in the midst of a national debate as to the best means of improving the delivery of national health care to many sections of the population whose needs are now inadequately served – rural communities, urban poor, elderly, and minority groups. Whatever the outcome of this political process, it has opened up for review both the practices within medical and health care institutions and the relations of these to the political and economic institutions that regulate their function. There is recognition that the problem is societal in scope and that the responsibility for basic change rests on the social, not the personal, level.

We make no claim that this brief description captures the reality of medical practice today. But we think that it does accurately highlight the way in which social goals, policies, and priorities, as well as institutional practices, determine the functions of testing.

Testing in the educational domain

Educational tests resist easy characterization because they have developed in various formats and for various purposes. It is customary to group them into two broad categories: general mental-ability tests, including both IQ and aptitude tests; and achievement tests. The conventional wisdom is that the first category gives some measure of the potential that the child or youth brings into the educational system and the second measures the outcome of the educational process. Historians of psychology (see Boring, 1950, for example) consider the first category to be the unique contribution of the American testing movement. Indeed this type of test dominates testing practice and, today, as in the past, is the center of controversy over testing. The American Psychological Association educational tests report (Cleary, et al., 1975) notes that the tests of most concern in the schools are the so-called general intelligence tests and tests of the narrower aptitudes that make up "intelligence." On the basis that ability tests have the most widespread use and have been subject to the most "widespread misuse and misinterpretation" (p. 17), the report restricts its discussion to such tests. We will follow a similar course.

Mental ability tests are "general purpose" instruments that lack the specificity of medical tests. Such nonspecificity is consonant with their main functions, which historically have been those of prediction and selection rather than of diagnosis. Cronbach's (1960) comparison between the objectives Binet outlined for testing and those of Terman and other early testers indicates that, from the outset, American instruments were intended to serve the function of mass evaluation rather than individual diagnosis geared to treatment. Binet was concerned with the description and explanation of individual differences, and he saw this task as involving two types of diagnostic study:

1.   The study of how psychic processes vary from individual to individual, what the variable properties of these processes are, and to what extent they vary.
2.   "The study of relations among the different psychic processes in a single individual. . . ." (1895, quoted in Herrnstein and Boring, 1965, p. 429).

Binet believed that these studies could be carried out by mental tests, but he explicitly rejected the notion that a single mental test could be devised that would shed light on individual psychology or permit comparisons across groups of individuals differing in knowledge and background:

We must first select the cases where the persons to be examined are of like background and practice the same professions, the persons whom we would compare with each other in order to determine their most important and characteristic differences. These cases must be treated separately from the cases in which we plan to compare individuals in different professions. We must, for example, use different tests in comparing two students in the same field from those in comparing a juggler with one of these students. That, believe us, is evident. Next the tests must be appropriate to the background and everyday occupations of the individuals. We cannot use the same tests in comparing two bricklayers as in comparing two students or two school children. (Herrnstein and Boring, 1965, p. 431)

As it has evolved in common practice, the IQ test is in every respect the antithesis of Binet's scheme. Rather than illuminating various psychic processes within the individual and the relations among them, it seeks to measure a generalized faculty. Instead of tailoring the test to the background of the individuals being tested, test developers emphasize standardization of instruments and procedure, ignoring individual and cultural differences. Whereas in the medical context tests may simultaneously serve both diagnostic and predictive-selective functions, in educational testing these functions have become bifurcated. The heavy emphasis placed on prediction has diverted attention from the diagnostic potential of psychological tests. This is not to say that tests have not been used for diagnostic purposes. But for those purposes, testers most frequently depart from a standardized format of administration, and de-emphasize the total summary score in favor of interpreting scores on the test subscales (Rapaport, Gill and Schafer, 1968). Moreover, it stands to reason that tests *designed* to be diagnostic could more usefully serve this purpose. Diagnosis is a peripheral practice, however, within the school system, where standardized group testing holds sway.

The very success of IQ tests in predicting children's careers through school has served to freeze the tests in essentially their original form. Cronbach (1960) and others point out that although the psychometric properties of IQ tests have improved and models of prediction have become increasingly sophisticated, test instruments of today are not very different from those of the 1920s and their original prototype, the World War I Army Alpha test. A half-century of continuous psychological investigation of learning processes, memory, and reasoning skills have not eventuated in the development of tests yielding information of the kind Binet sought. The scientific technical enterprise of testing has become increasingly divorced from the diagnostic and treatment enterprise.

Many factors are undoubtedly implicated in the failure to develop diagnostic tests with prescriptive value in education. For one thing, the task of diagnosis has turned out to be infinitely more complicated than Binet envisioned. But the difficulty of the task strikes us as a lesser factor than the strong social functions which the tests fulfill in their present form.

Indeed, it was the *social* utility of IQ tests, rather than their educational worth, that was advanced initially as the key argument for their widespread adoption in the public school system. This utility was located in the "sorting out" function of the public school system and the facilitative role of mental tests in this process.

During the early decades of this century, when mass immigration changed the composition of urban populations, school superintendents and other educators became alarmed at survey data which showed that a large percentage of children were behind their age-expected grade levels. This age-grade discrepancy, interpreted as a problem of "massive retardation," suggested that the uniform standard curriculum was not equally effective for all groups of children, and led to interest in developing differentiated curricula. Impressed by the success of the Army Alpha test in sorting recruits into military occupations, educators turned to the new "science of IQ" to provide efficient and objective means of sorting children for purposes of instruction. Some educators believed that varied modes of instruction would be provided to different IQ categories to meet their special needs. However, the curricula that developed were not differentiated by modes of instruction to meet the same end, but by the adoption of different educational end points for particular groups of children. The academic curriculum for the allegedly slow groups was impoverished or eliminated altogether in favor of vocational training. The requirement that schools should teach all children what society felt it valuable to transmit was converted into the practice of preparing children for their "station in life." IQ tests predicted what level the children could reach, and the end-point was built into the differentiated school curriculum (see Tyack, 1974, for a detailed historical account of this development).

Terman, for example, argued that occupations could be ranked by the level of intelligence they required and that children could be matched to occupations by IQ tests:

Intelligence tests can tell us whether a child's native brightness corresponds more nearly to the median of (1) the professional classes, (2) those in the semi-professional pursuits, (3) ordinary skilled workers, (4) semi-skilled workers, or (5) unskilled laborers. This information will be of great value in planning the education of a particular child and also in planning the differentiated curriculum here recommended (Terman, 1920, p. 23).

Terman advocated a three-track system, supplemented by a special track for the gifted and a special track for the intellectually disadvantaged, all of which corresponded to the five classes of occupations into which he saw the child population channeled. For some, that long-range selection function of the public school system was of greater utility than its traditional function of education. This position was made explicit by Professor Pillsbury (1920), who argued against the accepted wisdom that "education is essentially a process of creating intelligence" (p. 62). Schools, he thought, mainly winnow out the unintelligent and select the capable. Pillsbury foresaw the possibility that improved mental measurements would speed up the whole process: Why should unintelligent children be accepted into the regular curriculum in the first place?

It might be questioned whether it is worthwhile to spend so much time selecting through the slow process of the school system if selection is so large a function of that system. One might urge that we develop a set of tests similar to the army tests and apply them to the youth when they present themselves at the kindergarten and then assign them to the form of instruction that would prepare them for the function in life that is suited to their abilities (1920, p. 73).

We have digressed to present this historical background, because the discussions revolving around the introduction of IQ testing and ability grouping in the schools reveal the intimate relationships between the functions of tests, the functions of educational institutions, and the hierarchical social relations in society. While differentiated curricula are no longer explicitly advocated as a means of fitting children to their place in the occupational and social class structure, a number of analysts of contemporary education have concluded that the social selection function of the school system continues to be a major one (see, for example, Bowles and Gintis, 1973; Leacock, 1969; Tyack, 1974). If medical institutions served an analogous function ("matching station in life" to "health capacity") it is reasonable to suppose that medical test construction would move toward increasing the predictive, rather than the diagnostic, power of testing instruments and procedures.

What is lacking in the educational domain, of course, is any demonstration of significant relations among diagnosis, treatment, and outcome. Indeed, *individualized treatment*, the function that both legitimizes and makes necessary the development and use of medical tests, remains an external consideration in the educational testing movement. In historical perspective, the interaction between testing and treatment in the educational domain has taken a form quite different from that in medicine. To a considerable extent, test results have been used as the basis for modifying treatment *goals* (varying the content and end point of education for different groups of children), rather than modifying treatment *practice* (e.g., adapting teaching methods of a single curriculum to specific skills or disabilities of individual children). As McClelland (1973) has persuasively argued, such present-day practices as the system of tracking within elementary schools and selective access to higher levels of schooling on the basis of IQ and aptitude tests have had the result that such tests both predict treatment outcome and help to produce it. The prevailing paradigm of IQ tests as "independent predictors" of an educational outcome criterion can be maintained only if one ignores the instrumental role of test scores in determining educational *input*.

Moreover, the effects of test scores on educational input may be more than a matter of track or group placement. Test scores can also affect educational input by helping define teachers' expectations of individual children, and thus subtly influencing the quality of interaction between teacher and student, which itself constitutes an important aspect of the learning experience.

In thus reducing academic opportunities for low-scorers, IQ tests have had adverse reactive consequences for millions of children. But the adverse consequences of mental testing extend beyond the dilution of treatment programs to the attribution of responsibility for treatment outcome. Poor prognosis or unsatisfactory response to treatment is commonly attributed to inadequacies in the individuals being served by the educational system, rather than in deficiencies in the system's knowledge base or institutional and pedagogical practices. Lowered expectations, impaired self-image, and other psychological consequences that accompany labeling and attribution may materially alter life chances well beyond the school years.

Such adverse effects are not uniformly distributed among children of all socioeconomic and cultural backgrounds within the population; historically and in the present, they have been systematically related to social class and ethnic-group membership. Classification and grouping on the basis of IQ tests has reproduced in the schools the social and occupational stratification of the larger society and its patterns of ethnic and racial segregation. As we have seen, Terman's linking of occupational level to intelligence level provided the conceptual framework for different educational programs for working-class and middle-class children. In early debates on testing, labor groups, such as the Chicago Federation of Labor, vigorously attacked Terman's position and characterized the testing movement as one attempting to justify existing societal inequities by giving them the force of natural law: "The alleged 'mental levels' representing natural ability, it will be seen, correspond in a most startling way to the social levels of the groups named. It is as though the relative social positions of each group are determined by an irresistible natural law" (Chicago Federation of Labor, in Counts, 1928, p. 107). It was clear to the Federation that IQ tests merely reflected different life conditions determined by the unequal distribution of wealth and social status in industrial America, and it vociferously protested the use of the schools to perpetuate this order.

The argument that occupational social stratification is the consequence of innate differences in intelligence has been vigorously revived in the last decade (Herrnstein, 1971). According to some analysts (see, for example, Bowles and Gintis, 1973), the role of the IQ test in supporting this ideological position provides the principal social justification for its continued use. To the extent that mental testing serves as rationale and support for unequal opportunities based on color, class and ethnicity, in a profound sense, it has serious implications for society as a whole.

References

Boring, E. G. 1950. *A History of Experimental Psychology.* New York: Appleton-Century-Crofts.

Bowles, S., and Gintis, H. 1973. I.Q. in the U.S. class structure. *Social Policy*, January-February, pp. 65–96.

Cleary, T. A., Humphreys, L. G., Kendrick, S. A., and Wesman, A. 1975. Educational uses of tests with disadvantaged students. *American Psychologist, 30:* 15–41.

Counts, G. S. 1928. *School and Society in Chicago.* New York: Harcourt, Brace.

Cronbach, L. 1960. *Essentials of Psychological Testing.* New York: Harper and Row.

Herrnstein, R. J. 1971. I.Q. *Atlantic Monthly.* September, pp. 43–64.

Herrnstein, R. J., and Boring, E. G. 1965. *A Source Book in the History of Psychology.* Cambridge, Massachusetts: Harvard University Press.

Karier, C. J., Violas, P., and Spring, J. 1973. *Roots of Crisis: American Education in the 20th Century.* Chicago: Rand McNally.

Leacock, E. B. 1969. *Teaching and Learning in City Schools.* New York: Basic Books.

McClelland, D. 1973. Testing for competence rather than for "intelligence". *American Psychologist, 28:* 1–14.

Pillsbury, W. B. 1920. Selection – an unnoticed function of education. *The Scientific Monthly, 12:* 62.

Rapaport, D., Gill, M., and Schafer, R. 1968. *Diagnostic Psychological Testing.* New York: International Universities Press.

Terman, L. M. 1920. The use of intelligence tests in the grading of school children. *Journal of Educational Research, 1:* 20–32.

Tyack, David. 1974. *The One Best System: A History of American Urban Education.* Cambridge, Massachusetts: Harvard University Press.

My sentences (and most of me)
Run to incoherency
Broken phrases, there are lots.
In writing
They come down to dots.
Capitals can't clear the way
Of indeterminates I can't say.
Nor punctuation stop
The flow.
More is said
Than I can know . . .
                                Sylvia Scribner

PART III
Literacy: Mind and society

Introduction

The writings in this section span more than sixteen years and several periods of Sylvia Scribner's life. They include "The Cognitive Consequences of Literacy," written in 1968 while she was a doctoral student at the New School for Social Research; "Literacy in Three Metaphors" (1984), a paper originating from a planning document on research on literacy she wrote as Associate Director of NIE; and "Studying Literacy at Work," a paper delivered while she was at the Center for Applied Linguistics. Her social and intellectual commitment to considering thinking in its societal context shapes the theoretical formulation in the initial paper and the methods and questions she subsequently developed, and infused her policy undertaking while she was at NIE. She saw that research and policy were inherently related and, at NIE, was able to strengthen educational practice through stimulating significant research, and to strengthen research efforts of the academy and other institutions.

In "The Cognitive Consequences of Literacy" she poses the question of how writing, as a social invention and a "tool system used by man to alter and control his environment," (p. 161) may transform not only human culture but human mind as well. She states: "Like technological inventions, [these conceptual inventions] become part of the real world outside of man, the world with which he interacts, which he reflects and symbolizes. Thus, conceptual inventions which are social in origin and part of the human legacy have the potential through cultural transmission of being internalized by the individual and becoming part of his inner world." (p. 161) She identifies several hypotheses, based on her elegant review and analysis of the material and the cognitive properties of written language. Her discussion lays out the parameters for a rich empirical research program on those questions and previews lines of research she would later pursue at Rockefeller in collaboration with Michael Cole.

While the problems outlined in this early programmatic paper shaped her research questions for many years, Scribner's specific explanatory framework for cognitive effects changed substantially in the course of studying literacy with the Vai people, work reported in Scribner and Cole's *The Psychology of Literacy* and other writings. She would critique as insufficiently grounded conceptualizations that posited cognitive effects produced by the properties of the symbol system per se. She struggled with the complexities of data interpretation with her fundamental theoretical preferences as a guide until she developed a functional formulation of literacy and its effects as social practice, integrating the societal with the cognitive.

In an oral presentation, "The Concept of Practice in Research on Culture and Thought" (not included here), given in 1980 while Scribner was at the Center for Applied Linguistics, she discussed the Vai work reported in the Scribner and Cole volume, and described literacy in terms of social practice, a construct she saw as critical. She states: "In the course of the Vai research, I

157

developed a framework for interpreting the findings and their significance, and to guide further development of theory and method in the study of how socially organized activities come to have consequences for human thought. I called this framework a 'practice account of literacy' to emphasize that it is not a formal model nor grand theory. I present it briefly here because it appears to have a number of points of convergence with the theory of activity developed by Soviet psychologists." This formulation, to be further developed in her paper "Mind in Action" (Part 5) as a practice framework for cognition, links the theoretical and substantive concerns of the research in this section and of the program she developed at NIE. Here and in later work, Scribner uses practice as a key construct that provides a material foundation to cross-cultural cognitive analysis and to research on thinking at work.

The shift in interpretive framework is reflected in "The Practice of Literacy: Where Mind and Society Meet," a discussion of the Vai research in which social practice is the explanatory construct through which she interprets cognitive changes. The shift is especially clear in "Literacy in Three Metaphors," in which she emphasizes that literacy is a social, not an individual achievement. The meaning of literacy in a particular society is bound to societal values, and her splendid discussion considers three metaphorical meanings literacy may have: literacy as adaptation, as power, or as a state of grace. Her stress on social values in this paper is particularly noteworthy because it is based on a planning document for the White House Conference on Library and Information Services in 1979.

The next paper, "Observations on Literacy Education in China," is a report from Scribner's participation in a scientific delegation to the People's Republic of China as Associate Director of NIE. In it, she considers issues of literacy on a societal scale, discussing the textbook as an instrument of educational practice and evaluating China's success in becoming a predominantly literate society.

"Studying Literacy at Work" extends questions of literacy to practical work situations. We include the existing draft of this presentation given at the NIE conference on basic skills. This paper discusses the research on work Scribner was conducting while at the Center for Applied Linguistics, with a focus on "cognitive and linguistic operations involved in on-the-job literacy." The description of the three-tier method she was developing, from ethnography of the plant to description of literacy-related tasks under normal working conditions to task analysis and experimentation, reflects once again Scribner's commitment to tailor the method to the question and to study thinking as embedded within the real work situation with its attendant social constraints.

Scribner's consideration of societal and individual processes as linked and mutually transformative had philosophical as well as political dimensions. In her introduction to *The Future of Literacy in a Changing World,* she explores theoretical formulations of the relation between the psychological and the social afforded by the concept of levels of integration and by activity theory. Her discussion is both substantive and analytical, addressing the theoretical problem of how to relate psychological, ethnographic, and historical dimensions of literacy as well as evaluating alternative approaches to this issue. Scribner articulates the dialectical-materialist foundation of both the levels of organization concept and activity theory. The research program on thinking at work that she was primarily engaged in at that time would continue to concretize those ideas.

Selected coauthored works

Scribner, S; Goody, J.; Cole, M. (1977): Writing and formal operations: a case study among the Vai. *Africa* 47, 289–304.

Scribner, S.; Cole, M. (1978): Literacy without schooling: testing for intellectual effects. *Harvard Educational Review* 48, 4, 448–61.

Scribner, S.; Cole, M. (1981): *The psychology of literacy*. Harvard University Press, Cambridge, Mass.

14   The cognitive consequences of literacy

Introduction

The supreme challenge confronting social scientists, C. Wright Mills (1963, 425) observed, is that of developing a "concept of mind which incorporates social processes as intrinsic to mental operations."

If this problem is central to the analysis of human society and its history, it appears no less central to the study of the growth of the individual mind. It is a challenge to the psychologist as well as the sociologist, and in this paper, I should like to consider – in a free-ranging and speculative manner – one possible psychological response to this challenge.

We may begin with the observation that a number of social scientists in recent years have sought a link between mind and society by assigning to psychological processes the function of "mediating mechanisms" in cultural development and social change. Some, in fact, have found the role of these mediating mechanisms to be so crucial as to consider mind, rather than society, their rightful object of study.

We are not proposing that psychologists respond by "taking over" society as their scientific domain. But we do suggest that the converse proposition – namely, that social processes function as mediating mechanisms in psychological change and development – may be of major theoretical and practical importance for psychology.

My own interest has been in exploring one aspect of this general hypothesis – the possible interconnections between social inventions and cognitive development. To suggest that inventions modify thought processes may appear at first sight either odd or trivial: odd because the term "invention" usually brings

This paper was written in 1968 while Scribner was a doctoral student at the New School for Social Research.

160

visions of hardware to mind – the ax, the wheel, the printing press or computer; trivial because there does not seem much new to be said about man, the tool-making animal, whose interaction with the environment proceeds by technological rather than biological change. Yet among the most significant social inventions whose implications are still to be fully explored are the magnificent conceptual systems that lie at the base of all human culture. Many of these truly involve "stupefying leaps of the imagination": systems for reckoning time using units which have no counterpart in nature (hours and minutes); number systems based on the discovery of zero, the nothing quantity; or writing systems which construct an arbitrary equivalency between two sensory modalities (sight and hearing).

These, too, are "tool systems" used by man to control and alter his environment. If we accept the validity of the brilliant insight – that the tools man uses to shape nature to his purpose in turn help shape his own nature – we should be prepared to find that these conceptual inventions lead to significant transformations, not only in human culture, but in the mind of man. Like technological inventions, they become part of the real world outside of man, the world with which he interacts, which he reflects and symbolizes. Thus conceptual inventions which are social in origin and part of the human legacy, have the potential through processes of cultural transmission of being internalized by the individual and becoming part of his inner world.

In this paper we will be indulging in speculation about the possible psychological consequences of one such conceptual system, a system widespread but not yet universally shared – writing. We wish to explore the thesis that writing, which objectifies the spoken language and creates new symbolic languages for man to manipulate, makes possible the attainment of a new higher level of conceptual thought. Seen from the viewpoint of society, the consequences of literacy will be manifested in new kinds of intellectual systems and cultural products; from the viewpoint of the individual, in new modes of concept formation and in awareness of the act of thought itself.

Our exploration of this thesis will lean heavily on extrapolations from social science and psychological literature. There are no experimental data now available to support our hypotheses directly but there are sufficiently provocative suggestions from field and laboratory studies, we believe, to argue for its cogency. In the final section of this paper, we will present some of the relevant empirical data but we have first to consider the question: What is the basis for singling out "writing" as a possible significant mechanism in cognitive growth?

It must be acknowledged that few psychologists to date have considered writing worthy of special interest and attention.[1] While there has been a remarkable growth of research in language development and the role of language in various cognitive processes in recent years, most investigators have conceptualized language as internalized speech only and have not addressed themselves to the possible special characteristics of its written form. Anthropologists and historians, on the other hand, have long been intrigued by the circumstances surrounding the invention and evolution of writing. Far from being merely a recording device for speech, writing[2] is known to be an item of culture quite distinct from language with a different origin and history (Hoijer, 1960, 216).

There is first the fact of writing's very late invention. While we do not know "man" without "language," it is conservatively estimated that at least one million years intervened between man's first appearance and the beginnings of written record (Movius, 1960, 49). Many great arts of civilization (pottery, weaving, agriculture, domestication of animals) were mastered in early stages of the Neolithic period but systematic writing systems did not appear until approximately 3,000 B.C. Like the "great arts," however, writing, too, was invented independently by different peoples in different corners of the globe at different times in world history.

Interesting, too, is the fact that the first writing systems had nothing to do with speech. They were completely independent systems of communication. The "conventional visible signs" utilized in different scripts may have had their origin in direct pictorial representation of the events to be communicated, or they may have been symbolic from the outset (as in various mnemonic devices), but in either event they communicated directly without mediation of the spoken word. Phonetic writing systems which establish an equivalency between word and visible sign did not come into existence until 1,000–700 B.C. (Gelb, 1952).

Even in these most highly developed systems which make it possible for man to write anything that he can say, writing has continued to make use of "purely visible signs" to express distinctions and meanings not found in speech.[3]

At the same time that phonetic writing systems have drawn speech and writing closer together, writing has been used to create original languages having no counterpart whatsoever in oral communication. We refer to the many and varied notational systems used by the sciences and to mathematical and logical languages, which all exemplify the "trans-speech" nature of writing.

But the aspect of writing that has most captured imagination is the regularity with which its appearance has always been accompanied by far-reaching changes in all important spheres of life, by rapid and remarkable developments in government, art, commerce, industry and agriculture. This "co-appearance" of writing and technological and intellectual development has led most scholars to date the beginning of "civilization" from the advent of writing, and to use written language as the "bench-mark" separating the primitive from the complex society. Whether the particular view of the historical impact of writing is negative (Writing, says Levi-Strauss, introduced exploitation of man by man into human society) or positive (". . . an immense stride forward in the history of mankind, more profound in its own way than the discovery of fire or the wheel," says Diringer, 1962, 19) it appears incontestable that its invention played a profound role in the transformation of human culture.

An interesting and unusual attempt to explicate the relationship between the development of writing and the appearance of new cultural products is found in a study by Goody and Watt (1963), which examines the consequences of the diffusion of the alphabetic writing system on Greek philosophy. They suggest that the mastery of a phonetic writing system by relatively broad strata of the population in early Greece was instrumental for the emergence of two new forms of human intellectual endeavor – the origin of history as distinct from myth, and the founding of formal logic. Alphabetic writing played this role, they maintain, not merely because it preserved the content of man's knowledge in easily accessible form, but because it was a mode of communication whose characteristics facilitated the development of skeptical and analytic modes of thought.

This interpretation clearly suggests that psychological processes formed the link binding together three distinct social phenomena – the spread of literacy, the origin of history, and the appearance of formal logic. History and logic, like all other intellectual systems, are products of human thought. It is in the writings of a Xenophanes (and his unrecorded counterparts) that we find rejection of myth; in those of an Aristotle the rules of logic. While one could think of their intellectual creations as arising from old ways of thought furnished with an expanded store of information and different tools of communication, it is not unreasonable to look upon them as arising from changed ways of thinking made possible by the mastery of the written language. In this light, history and logic can be taken to represent the externalization and formalization of new thought-ways attained by the philosopher-scientists of early Greece through the spread of literacy.

This leads us quite directly to the more general hypothesis with which this paper is concerned – that literacy, a skill by which the individual appropriates a social product (writing) for private use, is a pivotal mechanism in cognitive growth.

Literacy is a fact of history not only in respect to whole cultures but in respect to the individual as well. The process of cultural development is collapsed and condensed, as it were, in the life-span of the individual. Each man, whatever the culture into which he is born, must acquire and assimilate some portion of the knowledge and techniques developed over past centuries by his predecessors. Whether he does in fact appropriate these cultural products and when he does so are, to a large extent, socially determined matters. Thus, reading and writing skills became instrumental during adolescence in ancient Greece and are introduced to the child of six in the United States today. For the vast majority of mankind – child or adult – they have yet to become operational skills. This very fact of the independence of literacy from age and biological processes of maturation makes it an attractive point of entry for scientific inquiry into the relationship between "society" and "mind."

Even considered apart from this grand design and simply from the point of view of specific issues in developmental psychology, literacy commends itself as an object of study. Developmental psychologists have made considerable progress in delineating the changes in cognitive processes that take place as the infant grows to adolescence. But, as Flavell (1963) and others remind us, we have not made corresponding progress in identifying the specific mechanisms which bring about the transition from one mode of operation to another. Rather than engage in debate over the global concepts of "culture" and "constitution," an analytic investigation of the effects of specific skills such as those involved in literacy cannot fail to deepen our understanding of the intricate and varied ways in which individual and cultural factors relate to each other in the course of intellectual growth.

Our plan is to begin with an examination of the spoken and written language systems to identify their differentiating characteristics. We will then proceed to an analysis of the mental operations involved in learning how to use the written language and those which the existence of the written language, in turn, makes possible. On the basis of this theoretical analysis, we will formulate "guiding hypotheses" about the specific changes in thought processes which may be either dependent upon (or nurtured by) the attainment and exercise of reading and writing skills. We will then consider these hypotheses in the light of research findings from two fields of work – studies of nonliterate thought in primitive cultures and studies of nonliterate thought of children.

Our hope is that this excursion into the literature will lend sufficient support to our thesis to encourage a direct research attack on literacy as a mechanism of cognitive growth.

Reading and writing, the traditional concerns of educator and psychologist alike, may yet provide us with new clues about the nature of mental life if we broaden our concerns from what their mastery requires to what such mastery contributes to the process of cognitive development.

The spoken and the written language

It has been common for linguists to dismiss language as a derivative form, hardly worthy of study in its own right. Bloomfield (1933, 282) says: "A speech utterance is the same whether it receives a written record or not . . . For the linguist, writing is, except for certain matters of detail, merely an external device like the use of the phonograph which happens to preserve for our observation some features of the speech of past times." Lotz (1961, 2), a linguist who stresses the symbolic rather than the behavioral aspects of language, fleetingly refers to "script" as one of the secondary symbolic systems "which lends permanency to the expression."

In recent years, greater interest has been shown by linguists in written language, and their relative neglect of this area until now is somewhat understandable in view of the fact that comparative linguistics must deal with many language systems that exist only in oral form. It appears doubtful, however, that psychologists who are interested in language from the standpoint of human behavior can afford to ignore the many ways in which written language[4] differs from spoken language. In actual usage, the lexicon, grammar and style of both forms of language are radically different. Basil Bernstein (1964, 253), well-known for his comparative studies of spoken English, has identified two different kinds of language systems, which he designates as "formal" and "public" languages.[5]

The chief characteristics of formal language are:

1. Accurate grammatical order and syntax regulate what is said.
2. Logical modifications are mediated through a grammatically complex sentence structure, especially through the use of conjunctions and subordinate clauses.
3. There is frequent use of prepositions to indicate logical relationships as well as temporal and spatial contiguity.
4. There is frequent use of impersonal pronouns.
5. There is a discriminative selection from a range of adjectives and adverbs.

In contrast, the chief characteristics of public language are:

1. Short, grammatically simple, often unfinished sentences with a poor syntactical form.
2. Simple and repetitive use of conjunctions.
3. Little use of subordinate clauses to break down the initial categories of the dominant subject.
4. Infrequent use of impersonal pronouns as subjects of conditional clauses or sentences.
5. Rigid and limited use of adjectives and adverbs.
6. A large number of statements which signal a requirement for the previous . . . sequence to be reinforced: "Wouldn't it? You see? You know?"
7. Idiomatic selection from a group of idiomatic phrases will frequently occur.
8. *It is a language of implicit meaning.* (italics in the original)

The "formal" and "public" languages described in this manner are terms used by Bernstein to designate the speech systems of the English middle-class and working class respectively. But we see how aptly they can be used to highlight some of the common distinctions between written and oral forms of discourse! Without invalidating Bernstein's argument that speech systems are generated from, and in turn, reflect the differing social relationships within the several classes, it does not seem out of line to suggest that some of the differences between working-class and middle-class speech may simply be those of fully literate versus basically nonliterate[6] speech. This is to say that written language, once acquired and internalized, turns back upon and interacts with oral language so that subsequent language development issues from the mutual influence of the one upon the other. We can think of these two language systems as two intersecting circles which partially overlap but have independent areas as well. They move closer together as the individual becomes "more literate." From this point of view, although the genesis of the systems is inextricably linked with their form, any one language specimen of an individual who has attained competency in both system may more closely approximate either the oral or the written system irrespective of the particular form in which it is expressed. Thus we can have oral written language (as in formal argument, speechmaking, dictation) and written oral language (as dialogue in plays and novels). We have only to think of the difficulties and special arts involved in such transpositions to appreciate that written and oral languages are in behavioral respects different "systems."

We would now like to take our comparison a little deeper by considering some of the characteristics of reading and writing which we feel may be of significance to the psychology of cognition.

1. Writing produces a material product.

Every act of writing in any writing system with the use of any implements gives language a corporeal form, objectifies it.

This process of objectification changes the relationship of the individual to language in a number of ways. Through writing, language is converted from a temporal to a spatial dimension. Once spatialized, it is freed from a given temporal sequence and is available for what Piaget would call reversible operations. "Timeless" language can be stopped, run backwards as well as forwards, broken up into all kinds of units and sequences, organized and re-organized in countless ways – in short, it comes under the language user's control. As this implies, although written language is static and contrasts in this respect with spoken language which is always "language in action," it enables the language user to play a more active role; he can manipulate its symbols in ways more varied and complex than speech alone makes possible.

Another way of looking at this is to observe that writing separates the producer from the product. Oral language exists only at the very moment that the individual is in the act of creating it, whereas writing separates our language from us and sets it in the outer world, making it available for inspection and contemplation by its creator as well as by others. In this way language itself becomes an object upon which we work, not merely an instrumentality through which we work to gain other (non-language) ends.[7]

2. Writing externalizes thought.

Insofar as thought is expressed in language and language is objectified in writing, writing in some part represents objectified thought. In this sense the writer, looking upon what he has written, reviews his own thought. While the analysis of external reality can be carried out by conceptual thought embodied in oral language,[8] conceptual thought embodied in *written* language may well be the necessary condition for the analysis of thought itself.

Vygotsky (1962) looked upon inner speech as the end state of a process of internalization and abbreviation of social speech. The use of inner speech for reasoning (thinking) about one's own thought processes might similarly represent the internalization of a process of criticism which initially takes place in interpersonal dialogue and goes "inside" via an intermediate stage which makes use of the written statement as the "other." The Socratic dialogue became famous as a method of arriving at "clear thinking," as a technique of education in the art of reasoning. It proceeded by making ideas the object of investigation through oral interrogation conducted by two people; one expressed the idea and the other examined and criticized it. With ideas given permanent form in writing, however, the two roles are more readily combined in the same person: the author of the idea can "stand back" (in Socrates' shoes, as it were!) and subject it to a critical "second" look. This particular usefulness of the written statement is quite explicitly recognized by many who turn to pen and paper for help in clarifying their thoughts. Once the role of critic of one's own thinking becomes stabilized through the technique of writing and editing, it may become internalized and the "editing" come to precede (and not necessarily always eventuate) in the writing.

3. Written language is more abstract[9] than spoken language.

Written language has sometimes been called an abstract activity because it is a second order symbolization – one in which the symbol is twice removed from its referent; the visual symbol represents, not the referent, but a symbol in another sensory modality.

This analysis seems appropriate for the period of written language acquisition. Visual marks initially have no direct semantic significance; their meaning is mediated through corresponding sequences of phonemes. As the reader or writer acquires skill, however, spoken words and phrases may drop out of this mediating position so that in time the written marks are themselves directly comprehended.[10] From the external point of view, writing would remain a second order symbolization, but from the individual cognitive point of view, we would have to identify the actual stage of the process to determine whether or not it could be characterized as "second-order" symbolic activity.[11]

There is another sense in which we can speak of reading and writing as more "abstract" than speaking. Every utterance is made in the context of a concrete situation. According to Werner (1963) and others, it is this situation as a whole, including the child's activity in it, which for the child just beginning to talk constitutes the diffuse meaning of verbal expressions. Only slowly are specific word meanings differentiated out of this total context. Even for adults, situational factors continue to play an important role in spoken language signification.

In written language, the "situation" is not concretely given but itself has to be constructed through the text. Thus the words carry a double burden: they not only have to convey a specific communication but the same words have to convey the "context as a whole." In this light it is interesting to speculate on the ease with which comic strips are grasped by otherwise poor readers. Perhaps one of the facilitating factors is that the comic strip anchors words and expressions in a concretely given situation; it exactly specifies, in pictorial fashion that can be "directly apprehended" (i.e., nonverbally), who is talking, to whom, and under what circumstances.

"Being taken out of context" also means that written language is stripped of all the expressive features of direct communication – inflection and tempo of speech, facial expression, gesture, and the like, which enrich language meaning. Comprehension of a written text is divorced from such aids and to a much greater extent than obtains in oral speech has to become a more purely cognitive activity.

We should take note of the fact, too, that spoken language ordinarily receives direct semantic ratification through the responses of others. Meaning in written language is ratified (or supplied) only through other symbols. Here indeed we may speak of second- and third- and fourth-order symbolization.

Finally, we may consider the manner in which the relationship between the physical and semantic properties of words change as they undergo transformation from the auditory to the visual modality. To some extent, however slight, there is an integrative bond between the two sets of properties in oral language. As we have indicated, there are occasions when pitch, stress, and other physical features play an important role in conveying the meaning. Word appearance in the written text does not ordinarily serve this end. For usual purposes,[12] so long as certain minimum standards of legibility are met, variations in word size or letter formation are of no account. When reading, we handle words as semantic units and have no commerce with their physical properties. We are considered to have achieved excellence in reading when we do, in fact, read for meaning and *not* for words. And the dominance of word meaning over word form in the written text is tacitly acknowledged in the advice that "Poetry to be appreciated should be read aloud"; it is in the oral condition that attention is paid to word form.

4. Literacy skills require an analytic approach.

It seems to make psychological sense to think of the unit of spoken speech as being the whole utterance. From a developmental point of view at least, it appears to be the case that word meanings are only gradually differentiated from the child's early holophrastic expression. In contrast, written language cannot be mastered by a progression from the "whole expression" to the component unit. Whether the particular reading method employed selects the word, part of the word, or the letter as the initial unit, the student is required to analyze the familiar utterance into unfamiliar parts and then to re-synthesize them.[13]

This analytical translation of sound into visual form or visual form into sound through syllabification or discovery of "grapheme-phoneme correspondences" is a formal activity, not directly meaningful in itself. It is merely a means to an end (reading comprehension or writing facility). Thus, in the acquisition of written language, technical skills must to some extent be considered independently of the content. In spoken communication it is only in cases of defect (speech or hearing impairment) that the technical skills required in language production have to be specifically trained apart from the functional use of the language.

It follow that there is a greater separability or differentiation of the various processes involved in the utilization of written language. It is sometimes true in oral language that utterances are run off as automatic sensori-motor habits, but it is more generally the case that the physical utterance and its signification are integrally related. In written language, on the other hand, it is not uncommon to have meaning, sound and sight functioning independently. Once we acquire skill in reading, we "recognize" words which we cannot pronounce and may not understand; we may grasp the meaning of a word without being able to pronounce it; or pronounce it without knowing its meaning. Similarly in writing, we may find that we know a word but we are not at all sure of its correct visible sign.

Thus from the outset, the individual undertaking to learn how to read or write confronts the "machinery of the language"; he has to become aware of its components and of the various operations required to produce or comprehend it.

5. Literacy skills must be acquired consciously and intentionally.

Psychologists studying the cognitive development of the child can hardly find two more contrasting "learning situations" than those involved in the acquisition of speech and written language. In the former case we are hard put to it to discover how the language is "learned"; in the latter, we encounter difficulties in explaining why the language is *not* learned.

When it is said that speech is acquired spontaneously and written language deliberately, one refers first of all to the fact that literacy is systematically taught over a long period of time and that direct teaching plays a relatively minor role in the child's mastery of speech. But more than this is involved in the distinction. The crucial role in learning written language is not played by the teacher but by the child himself, who must direct the process, participate in it actively and intentionally and keep it under conscious control.

Why this must be so has already been indicated in the previous sections where we reviewed the abstract aspect of writing, which requires the child to create the situation and the context, and its analytic characteristics, which require him to become aware of its component processes so that he can manipulate them.

Vygotsky (1962, 99) has very beautifully expressed still another characteristic of written language which makes imperative its conscious direction:

Written language demands conscious work because its relationship to inner speech is different from that of oral speech. The latter precedes inner speech in the course of development while written speech follows inner speech and presupposes its existence (the act of writing implying a translation from inner speech). But the grammar of thought is not the same in the two cases. . . . Inner speech is condensed, abbreviated speech. Written speech is deployed to its fullest extent, more complete than oral speech. . . The change from maximally compact inner speech to maximally detailed written speech requires what may be called deliberate semantics – deliberate structuring of the web of meaning.

Vygotsky concluded that the difficulties in the development of written speech and the lag between it and oral speech can be attributed to these intrinsic features. "The discrepancy is caused," he said, "by the child's proficiency in spontaneous, unconscious activity and his lack of skill in abstract, deliberate activity" (1962, 100).

It remains only to be added that not only during childhood but throughout life the act of writing remains a deliberate act. Unlike other highly developed skills which become automatized, writing must always be consciously attended to. When our attention wanders or control falters, errors creep into our productions – errors of a kind rarely encountered in spoken language, such as the omission or transposition of key words necessary to carry the meaning of the sentence.

It cannot be maintained that reading and writing skills are necessarily the very first skills which children acquire intentionally and consciously. But in our society, they are among the first *cognitive* skills to be brought under conscious self-direction, and so can be expected to exert the greatest influence on the developing intellectual functions.

6. Written language is essentially private.

Reading and writing are private acts and they therefore provide an individual relationship to words and thought. In oral language there are always at least two people involved at the same time with the same set of words. Under these circumstances, language is embedded in a shared situation, and it fulfills its communicative function, at least in part, because there is some commonality of perception and understanding among the speakers. Spoken language, in fact, is often modulated so as to enhance this commonality among the participants of the conversation or the members of a particular language community.

The user of written language is performing in a solitary rather than a social manner. The intellectual operations involved are detached from the "common perceptual world"; they cannot spontaneously reflect commonalities but rather must construct them anew whenever the reader works upon a new communication, and this construction must be carried out without the benefit of "feed-back".

While reading is a private act it does not mean that it is more "personal" than speech. We have already seen that writing objectifies language and thought. This means that at the same time they are withdrawn from the social world, they are also "depersonalized" and can be more effectively utilized because the self is in some measure detached from them.

This analysis has been concerned with the distinguishing features of written language and with the nature of the intellectual operations required for its mastery. We have suggested that writing is a new form of communication, a new "modality" as it were, through which the individual acquires information about, and interacts with, others and his environment. We have also suggested that the mental skills involved in reading and writing are qualitatively different from those developed spontaneously in the acquisition and use of oral language.

What consequences for thinking processes would this analysis lead us to postulate? On an *a priori* basis only, we might hypothesize two principal effects of literacy,[14] one deriving from the product of writing, the other from the psychological operations that it involves.

> *Hypothesis 1. Literacy moves thinking to a new conceptual level.* Writing changes the relationship between word and thought. By giving language a corporeal form, writing provides thought with word-objects to manipulate. We may expect that thought based on manipulation of word-objects will attain a conceptual level further removed from the physical world of things than is possible for oral thought.
> *Hypothesis 2. Literacy moves thinking from the spontaneous to the conscious level.* Reading and writing are consciously controlled activities which require awareness of one's own thought processes, as in translating "inner speech" to outer form. High levels of proficiency in reading and writing should facilitate the development of reflective thought – thought which thinks about itself and can give an account of itself. Another way of saying this is that the individual acquires the ability to make the act of thought itself an object of thought.

If literacy is a mechanism through which a new level of conceptual thought is attained, then the speculations we have made should prove congruent with observations of differences between "literate thought" and "non literate thought" in two major fields of inquiry – anthropology and developmental psychology. By maintaining that the empirical data derived from investigations in both of these fields are relevant to our hypotheses, we are not allying ourselves with the position that child thought and primitive thought are "alike" nor with the now discredited position that people in primitive societies are of "inferior" mentalities. We do maintain that, if conceptual systems help shape the mental life of man, man's mental products should be *predictably* different in cultures which possess or fail to possess the particularly important tool system of the written language.[15] If a comparative study should reveal this to be the case, we would have no grounds for inferring that the mental capacities or laws of thought are different in adults of more or less technologically advanced societies. We would have grounds, rather, for inferring that the existence of a written language system (probably along with other technological systems)[16] is related to changes in the way man *utilizes* his mental capacity. To substantiate this inference of a relationship between literacy and certain modes of thought, we would need to turn to psychological studies of the development of thought processes in the individual to see what differences there are, if any, between literate and non-literate children or adults *within one culture*. Developmental psychology offers some relevant data. For confirmation of the "strong hypothesis" that literacy operates as a causal mechanism giving rise to the emergence of certain kinds of thinking, we require a series of experiments in which the factor of literacy is independently manipulated to determine whether predicted changes in intellective function occur as individuals acquire a level of proficiency in the uses of reading and writing.

With these clarifying comments let us turn first to some interesting comparisons that have been made between thought systems in oral and literate cultures. These analyses have been selected, not for their representativeness, but for their particular relevance to the point of view we have been advancing here.

Thought systems in oral and literate cultures: Some selected observations

Levi-Strauss' description of the "Savage Mind" makes an especially interesting starting point – first, because he is widely recognized for his original contributions to the analysis of primitive thought systems, and second, because he is the leading contemporary opponent to a developmental point of view in respect to the intellectual attainments of simple and complex societies. Primitive thought and modern science, he maintains (1966, 15), are not to be considered a function of different stages of the human mind but rather as two different strategic levels at which nature is accessible to scientific inquiry. They are two parallel modes of acquiring knowledge.

In opposition to the view that primitive thought is in any way less scientific or logical than modern thought, he cites generic terms in primitive vocabularies (such as "animate," "rational" and the like) which he believes to evidence "abstract" thought. He stresses other commonalities: both mythic and modern scientific thought demonstrate a thirst for objective knowledge of the universe; both proceed by ordering, classifying, and systematizing information; both are based on the principle of determinism; both use techniques of active and methodical observation, of experimentation based on hypotheses; both combine interest in the practical and the theoretical; both create logic systems based on selected fundamental antimonies. These commonalities lead Levi-Strauss to conclude that the two thought systems require the "same sort of mental operations."

Given this central theme, it is all the more interesting to follow Levi-Strauss's *differentiation* of mythic and modern thought. Characterizing mythic thought as a "science of the concrete," he describes it as concerning itself with the organization and exploitation of the "sensible" world in "sensible" terms – as working with phenomena adapted to the functions of perception and imagination. Mythic thought seeks the interconnections of objects through their "secondary" qualities – those that are part of living experience – whereas modern science travels a road more "remote from sensible intuition" and searches for necessary relations in the structural qualities of things. The distinctive attribute of mythic thought is that it stands "midway between percepts and concepts." It makes use of signs which "like images are concrete entities but have some limited capacity for reference." Terms that enter into logical systems as signs always carry with them the manifold properties of their referents, and while their meaning can be sufficiently generalized to serve the purpose of the system into which they enter, they are not capable, as concepts are, of entering into *unlimited* relations with other entities of the same kind. The possible combinations of signs are restricted by the tangible properties they possess which limit their deployment.

Classification systems composed of signs in which tangible properties inhere have a "polyvalent logic" which appeals to "several, formally distinct types of connection at the same time" (1966, 61). Connections, or meaning equivalences, may be based on contiguity (the Anthill Clan is linked with the Snake Clan because snakes hide on anthills and with the Grass Clan because grass grows on anthills); on resemblance (red ants and cobras are linked by color); on common function (bees and carpenters belong together because they both build) or historical association (elephants and clay are associated because in the old days women used elephant footprints to cook in before clay pots were invented).[17] But what is especially important to an understanding of primitive theory is that several different kinds of relationships between terms may characterize any given classification system.

We have selected the following example to illustrate this "polyvalent logic". The Osage system of classification divides all animate and inanimate things into the three categories of sky, land, and water as follows:

Sky	*Water*	*Dry Land*
Sun	Turtle	Bear
Star	Mist	Porcupine
Crane	Rush plant	Deer
Night	Fish	Eagle
Heavenly bodies		

The position of "eagle" in the "dry land" category would be incomprehensible, Levi-Strauss points out, if it were not known that in Osage thought eagles are associated with lightning, lightning with fire, fire with coal, coal with earth. Eagles qualify as land animals because they are "masters of coal." Here we see existing connections between things making up a chain of associations that eventually results in the categorization of eagle as a land animal. But note that when eagle is so classified, it is on the basis of a symbolic connection – master of coal – derived from the association chain, whereas the other terms enter the system on the basis of direct factual connections (bear and deer *live* on land) or actual physical properties (mist *is* a form of water).

Levi-Strauss is convincing in his demonstration that primitive thought is conceptual in the sense that it is capable of generalization. At the same time, and outstandingly, it is conceptual thought rooted in concrete experience, tied to the actual properties of things or events, "entangled in imagery." As Levi-Strauss puts it, mythic thought lacks the kind of concept which is open for relations with terms with which it has no *existent* connections, direct or derived. This kind of concept is present in modern scientific thought where it plays a decisive role in creating new meanings and in projecting the merely possible as opposed to the actual.

Since Levi-Strauss's methodology relegates historical questions to the realm of the contingent, when he rejects the notion of "stages or phases in the evolution of knowledge" (1966, 22) he supplies no alternative explanation for the difference between mythic and scientific thought nor of their historical order of appearance.

In the analyses of Stanley Diamond (1964), an anthropologist with extensive field experience among the people of West Africa, we meet again with the distinction between primitive thought and the "pure concept" but combined with some speculation as to "historical causation." Primitive thought is a mix, both concrete and abstract. It is abstract because, "in the basic sense every linguistic system is a system of abstractions; each sorting out of experience and conclusion from it is an abstract endeavor; every tool is a symbol of abstract thinking; indeed, all cultural convention, all custom is testimony to the generic human capacity for abstracting." At the same time, the abstractions of primitives ". . . are indissolubly wedded to the concrete; they are nourished by the concrete . . . ultimately induced, not deduced" (1964, 186). If this sounds like a contradiction to us, it is only because we in the Western world have come to reserve the term "abstract" for a particular form of abstraction, the Platonic abstraction. Plato's definition of the abstract as pure idea stripped of all concrete properties coincided with the rise of the political state, which destroyed primitive community and severed the thinker from the man of action, leaving one to pursue the "abstract" in philosophy, the other to labor with the "concrete" in life. This specifically Platonic abstraction has become so entrenched in Western thought that we erroneously conclude that primitives are deficient in the abstract capacity because they do not think like Platonists.

In the works of the classicist Eric Havelock (1963), Plato again emerges as the pivotal historical figure proclaiming the movement from one mode of thought to a qualitatively different one. But these contrasting modes of thought are now designated "poetic" and "philosophical" – the one imagistic, temporally organized, subjective; the other conceptual, analytic, and objective; the one Homeric, the other Platonic. Each mode requires a language appropriate to its material and intellectual style. And Havelock's original contribution is to suggest that the language appropriate to the Platonic mode of thought could arise only when the technology of preserved communication changed from oral recitation to written record.

In the days before Homer and for many generations after him, the Greek cultural book – all the accumulated public and private law, traditions, customs, and mores – was perpetuated by being stored in personal, living memory. The epic poem, narrated, recited and memorized, was the vehicle of its transmission. The several hundred years intervening between Homer and Plato saw the gradual extension of writing from occasional use by a privileged few in fragmentary memoranda to general use in plays, speeches and other texts of connected discourse read by many. Paralleling this extension of literacy was the development by pre-Socratic philosophers of a new language with a syntax and lexicon suitable for the expression of conceptual thought.

Plato both reflected the impact of these new language habits and heralded their hegemony in fields of the intellect. He was the outstanding, perhaps never surpassed, advocate of the new (written) language of philosophical knowledge, foe of the poetized (oral) statement. How do these "knowledges" differ? Knowledge that must be preserved in the oral state is compelled to be obedient to the psychological requirements of memorization: it must be stated in language that is regularly patterned, that is visually rich and imagic, that personifies impersonal phenomena, a language of action depicting events and doings – a language, in short, that is designed to excite emotion and promote subjective identification with the material so that it will more easily become "part of oneself." The epic poem or other form of oral narrative thus presents knowledge in the form of concrete events, organized in a time sequence; it cannot present knowledge in the form of timeless data, organized in a hierarchical system of relations or categories.

But Havelock is not engaged in a literary critique. His contention is that this style of oral composition represents a particular cast of thought, an "oral state of mind." In this state, thought and language are tied to the concrete; concepts such as wrath, piety, justice exist only in specific instances of behavior. Affective and cognitive attitudes are intertwined, making for a knowledge which is both subjective and objective at the same time. Most importantly, when all phenomena are described as present events or doings you do not have generalizations couched in the language of universals.

These characteristics of oral thought were unnecessary, even impedimental, in the new literate society. When knowledge no longer had to be shaped to the needs of memorization, retention, and recall, the writer became free to abandon the narrative form for a reflective reorganization of the material. The reader could refrain from emotional identification with the content and adopt an analytic, critical attitude toward it. With the written sign present to refresh memory, the concept need no longer be embedded in character or event – it could exist in its "simple purity," uncontaminated by specific instances. Plato, says Havelock, conformed to the literal meaning of the Latin term "abstraction." He tore the "object" out of context and recreated it by an act of intellectual isolation and integration (256).

It is not the justice of Havelock's interpretation of Plato nor his judgments of the poetic statement that concern us here. Rather we are interested in the fact that the three authorities we have cited (and others might have been chosen), in spite of their different starting points[18] and variations in their analyses of the characteristics of primitive thought, all appear to have similar views on what primitive thinking *lacks*. Absent from such thought is the "pure concept," the universally generalizable or deployable term which has been emptied of tangible properties. In certain forms of post-literate thought – call it "modern scientific" (Levi-Strauss), "Platonic abstraction" (Diamond) or the "language of philosophy" (Havelock) – new meaning systems are created with just such concepts. Here we believe lies the "heart of the difference" between modes of thought which operate with the oral language only and those that arise in societies in which the written language has been disseminated.

This difference is clearly quite closely related to our first hypothesis in which we suggested that mastery of the written word should make possible the attainment of a new conceptual level. We should like to refine this hypothesis further in the light of our discussion of primitive thought, but before we can do so it is important for us to clarify our vocabulary. We intentionally defined the "universally deployable concept" as one "emptied of physical properties" in order to avoid the ambiguities inherent in the usual modifiers "concrete" and "abstract." The meaning of these terms in the passages quoted is unstable and unclear. But in their imprecise usage of these psychological concepts, social scientists only mirror and magnify the confused usage in the psychological literature.

The two principal senses in which "abstract" has been used in these discussions of primitive thought have been to indicate 1) presence and extent of generalization (a generalization-differentiation dimension) and 2) distance of the meaning term (sign or concept) from the actual properties of things (a sensory-nonsensory dimension). Thus Levi-Strauss argues that primitive thought is abstract because it engages in extensive classification that involves generalization and differentiation. Here he relies on the first meaning. Primitive thought, on the other hand, is concrete because it is entangled with imagery and tied to the sensible world. This is the second meaning. "Concrete" and "abstract" are here not antonymic but obviously ordered on different dimensions of meaning.

As a first step toward trying to clarify the relationship between these terms, let us apply the term "generalization" to one or more processes of thinking[19] that result in the establishment of meaning equivalences among things. Psychological investigations demonstrate that a number of different kinds of processes may be involved in generalization, often, but not necessarily, including the process of abstraction. The Pavlovian generalization phenomenon takes place on the basis of perceptual similarity. Generalization of the grasping reflex in the infant, according to Piaget, occurs on the basis of functional equivalence (the "nutritional" value to the reflex activity that various objects possess). These are examples of non-abstractive generalization in the behavioral realm. In the cognitive realm, psychologists investigating language development and concept formation have shown that young children generalize on the basis of maximal similarity among things or on other points of contact among "whole" items (items whose properties have not been analyzed). These, too, are examples of non-abstractive generalization.

On the verbal level, however, the great majority of generalizations among adults occurs on the basis of abstraction, defined here as the thought process by which one isolates a single aspect of an object from the whole.

An abstracted attribute may be more or less close to material reality. It may be a sensory feature (hue, sound), or a real function ("things to smoke"). But it may also be a nonmaterial attribute which for want of a better name we will refer to here as a "semantic" property – a meaning that an item has by virtue of its subsumption in a certain class within a classification system. Certain attributes are "isolatable" on either a perceptual or a semantic basis (color is a case in point[20]) and there is no hard and fast line between them but every investigator has had to take into account the dimension from sensory-to-semantic and struggle for proper terms with which to describe it.

Thus we find several sets of distinctions to be considered. There are non-abstractive and abstractive generalizations and, within the latter category, we can further distinguish between generalizations based on an isolated sensory and those based on an isolated semantic attribute. Clearly, generalizations that are based on the abstraction of non-material attributes will have the greatest flexibility and broadest reach.

"Generalization" and "abstraction" then, because they vary in kind, are inadequate terms unless further qualified for discriminating between primitive and modern scientific thought.

We confront a similar difficulty with "concept-conceptual." Some psychologists apply the term "concept" as a label for any generalization or meaning equivalence. They insist that all verbal thought is conceptual. According to them, the word, by which we name discrete objects that differ in many respects as the same thing, functions as a concept. While this has some face validity, it is such an all-embracing definition that it becomes difficult to distinguish between levels of word meaning. Others think it necessary to reserve the term "concept" to only those meaning equivalences that are based on abstractions of a nonsensory attribute consistently applied (as by "rule"). The difficulty here is that this "strict" definition frequently leads to the foolish dilemma of our having to characterize the primitive scientist-philosopher as "nonconceptual" because his meaning systems lacked this kind of concept, while we describe tens of thousands of school children in technically developed societies as "conceptual" because they have attained this kind of concept.

What is clearly needed, it appears, is some differentiation of levels of conceptual thought that will permit us to remain loyal to observed differences between modes of thinking without denying to any normal human thought the generic capacities for generalization and abstraction. As we elaborate more refined tools of experimentation and a more analytic theoretical approach, we may in time develop a scheme that will do full justice to both the universals in mental functioning and to its diversity and complexity. At the present time, let us try to integrate what has been said about distinctions between nonliterate and literate thought in a theoretical framework that makes use of a two-way distinction only – a distinction that roughly parallels the observations of the differences between mythic thought bound to the world of things and scientific-philosophic thought created with the "pure concept."[21] Our hypotheses about the influence of literacy on cognitive processes are found to fit well in this scheme.

The primary distinction we make between the two levels of conceptual thought is that in one the referent content of the concept is an object or some aspect of an object or material reality, while in the other the referent concept is another concept. The existence of the first level is necessary for the emergence of the second, since the concepts of the first level are the "objects" of the second. First-level concepts are formed through commerce with physical and social reality mediated by oral language. In the formation of this kind of concept, the word directs attention to properties objects have in common and it functions as a name or label for this "commonness." On the second level, the word directs attention to the semantic properties of other words (verbal concepts) or, to put it a little differently, to some attribute or aspect of a concept. These concepts are more likely to be formed through the process of verbal definition than through direct encounter with some aspect of material reality.

On both levels, concepts are organized in hierarchical systems representing different kinds and degrees of generalization. However, on the level of object-concept, generalization may be nonabstractive whereas all generalization of the "word-object" concept is abstractive generalization. On both levels the meaning of the concept is to some extent dependent upon its position within the system of which it is a member, but the word-object concept's meaning may be wholly defined by its position in that system. An illustration of a concept on the first level is a particular number – "five" for example. The number is a concept which stands for a set of objects. "X" in algebra, however, is a concept which stands for a set of numbers. The meaning of "five" can be expressed by pointing; the meaning of "X," only through verbal definition by means of which the term is related to the whole system of which it is a part.

At the earlier stage certain aspects of objects had been abstracted and generalized into ideas of numbers. Algebraic concepts represent abstractions and generalizations of certain aspects of numbers, not objects and thus signify a new departure – a new higher level of thought (Vygotsky, 1962, 114–115).

The following table presents the comparison schematically and simplistically.

THEORETICAL COMPARISON OF CONCEPTUAL LEVELS

Level 1 *Object Concept*	*Level 2* *"Word Object" Concept*
1. Direct relationship to some object or attribute of an object. Object of thought is an object.	1. Indirect relationship to object; object is mediated by some other concept. Object of thought is a verbal concept (word).
2. Generalization on the basis of objects or attributes of objects; generalization of things.	2. Generalization of earlier generalizations (concepts) – therefore, generalization of thought.
3. We are aware of the object of thought, not of our mental activity.	3. We are aware of the act of thought.
4. Language internalized as inner speech regulates our behavior. Through language we become conscious of our behavior; we describe it and reflect upon it.	4. Written language that is internalized regulates our thinking. Through this new system of language, we become conscious of our thought; we can describe it and reflect upon it.
Function: "Analysis of reality with aid of concepts" (Vygotsky).	Function: "Analysis of thought with aid of concepts" (Vygotsky).

Within this schema, primitive thought – that is oral thought – is conceptual thought on the first level; modern thought is conceptual thought on both levels, the second made possible by the invention and diffusion of writing.

This schema, however, is essentially a statement about the nature of cognitive growth. The questions that flood to mind are many. What is the evidence for the development of "two levels" of thought in children? Does it appear to be a universal stage of cognitive growth or is it dependent on cultural factors? Is there any evidence that literacy is implicated in its development?

Just as in the case of the anthropological literature, we will find the psychological literature merely suggestive. Developmental psychologists have only slowly moved away from major concern with changes which are a "function of age" to interest in the possible influence of cultural factors on cognitive growth. Nevertheless, there have already been some exciting findings which bear on our hypotheses. Let us turn to some of these studies.

Schooling and thought: Suggestions from developmental psychology

Vygotsky (1962), a pioneer in research on concept formation, was led by the outcome of his experiments to differentiate between two kinds of concepts – the "everyday concept," that develops spontaneously in the course of living and the "scientific concept," which is acquired through verbal definition and is usually transmitted through formal (school) instruction. "Brother" is an example of the first type; "slavery," of the second. The course of development of the two differs: the everyday concept becomes crystallized as a result of contact with numerous examples; its referents are known and the concept develops "upward" from these, slowly becoming related to other concepts and becoming incorporated in a conceptual system. The scientific concept, on the other hand, starts from the "top down"; its relationship to other concepts and its place in the system are given theoretically but its specific referents or exemplars must be acquired by its application to given instances.

In a comparative study with school children aged 8–10, Vygotsky found that the development of scientific concepts runs ahead of everyday concepts. Children were asked to complete sentences expressing causal relations using simple familiar material from everyday life and material taken from social science courses: "He fell off his bicycle because. . ." and "Planned economy is impossible in the U.S.S.R. because. . ." Nearly 80% of the 8-year-olds could correctly complete the sentence fragments using scientific material whereas only 59% were able to do so with the everyday material. The intriguing fact is that the 8-year-olds who completed the "bicycle" sentence by adding the phrase "Because he broke his leg" were never guilty of such non sequiturs in their spontaneous conversation. They were able to use "because" correctly in daily speech but unable to do so deliberately, Vygotsky says, because conscious usage requires that one be aware of "because" as a concept – i.e., know its meaning and use and the specific relationship it expresses between terms.

Since scientific concepts are formed in the process of instruction and the child is questioned, corrected, and forced to explain them, he becomes conscious of their meanings and interrelationships from the very outset. This helps him achieve a grasp of terms like "because" which express these relationships. Consciousness and control of the scientific concept lead the child to become conscious of his everyday concepts and these, too, become systematized and their relationships understood. By the age of 10 in Vygotsky's investigation, there was no longer a disparity in expression of causal relationships: "The formal discipline of scientific concepts gradually transforms the structure of the child's spontaneous concepts and helps organize them into a system; this furthers the child's ascent to higher developmental levels" (Vygotsky, 1962, 116).

As can be seen, Vygotsky stressed the role of school as a crucial lever for intellectual development. In a series of experiments concluded with his students,[22] he attempted to elucidate the relationship between formal instruction in other school subjects such as reading and writing, grammar, and arithmetic and such intellectual functions as the child's awareness of his own operations in problem solving, his concept of number and understanding of figurative meanings and relationships. These investigations compared the "level of maturity of psychic functions" at the beginning of schooling and after a prolonged period of instruction. Vygotsky concluded 1) that the psychological functions studied unfold in a continuous interaction with the contributions of instruction; and 2) instruction usually precedes development. But what is most interesting is that Vygotsky does not hold the customary view that instruction is instrumental because of the *information* it transmits. He wryly notes that the superiority of the child's control of scientific concepts can hardly be due to "knowledge" since fact and familiarity are all on the side of everyday concepts. The significant influences of school instruction seem to be two: imparting to the child already organized systems of verbal concepts which interact with and move on the development of his spontaneously acquired concepts (as discussed above) and giving the child practice in certain *mental operations*. This latter point can be clarified by citing Vygotsky's own analogy between the formative influence on scientific concepts and that of foreign language learning.[23]

The influence of scientific concepts on the mental development of the child is analagous to the effect of learning a foreign language, a process which is conscious and deliberate at the start. In one's native language, the primitive aspects of speech are acquired before the more complex ones. The latter presupposes some awareness of phonetic, grammatical and syntactic forms. With a foreign language, the higher forms develop before spontaneous, fluent speech. . . In his own language, the child conjugates and declines correctly, but without realizing it. He cannot tell the gender, the case, or the tense of the word he is using. In a foreign language, he distinguishes between masculine and feminine gender and is conscious of grammatical forms from the beginning (1962, 109–110).

This comparison is closely akin to our analysis of the differences between the spontaneous use of speech and the use of written language. And, as we know, Vygotsky himself applied the same analysis to writing; he repeatedly stressed its analytic and abstract nature, and its dependence on conscious control of one's own mental operations. Scientific concepts, foreign language, grammar, and "written speech" all represented new functional systems to him – systems which required and helped to establish in the child an abstract, self-conscious and controlled level of thinking. These systems which "drive on" the process of cognitive development are products of "schooling," not life.

Piaget, as is well known, differs from Vygotsky on the role of instruction in cognitive growth, denying it any role in effect, but he has presented us with a coherent theory and systematically obtained data on certain qualitative changes in thinking which occur from birth to adolescence. Piaget considers that intelligence progresses through a fixed order of stages, each of which is characterized by thought structures which enable the child to master and perform certain specific kinds of intellectual operations. We are mainly interested in his characterization of the last two stages – that of concrete operations, marking the period from 7 to 10 or 11, and formal operations, which are fully achieved in late adolescence and constitute "adult thought."[24]

During the period of concrete operations, the child masters the logic of classes and relationships, but only in relation to the manipulation of actual things. He groups and classifies according to actual connections among objects or events, and he can handle relations of order among things (serialize them) when he is dealing with their perceptible properties. He has difficulty, however, in stating the general rule for a classification or handling relationships that are expressed verbally. An illustration given by Piaget is the following:

Ten year old children are asked to order objects in one or more series – let us say, pieces of paper of different sizes and varying shades of gray. Most of them will handle this problem successfully and arrange the paper in series that range from lighter to darker and smaller to larger. But confronted with a classical reasoning test such as Burt's (Edith is fairer than Susan; Edith is darker than Lily; Who is the darkest of the three?) they are unable to handle the relationships correctly. In sum, the child can *put things* together in a way that shows a logical grasp of their relations but cannot deal logically with verbal expressions of these relations.

By 11–12 the child enters the period of formal operations and becomes capable of handling classifications and relationships in terms of verbal propositions. As Piaget puts it, the child becomes capable of intellectual operations about reality rather than being confined to working on reality itself.

On the level of propositional thought, when the child is operating with verbal statements about things, many relations among things become possible that have never been encountered in actuality. Propositional thinking, therefore, takes account not only of the real but of the possible and hypothetical. It can develop classification schemes by formulating theoretical possibilities without proceeding from the observation of actual properties. It is not consistent with Piaget's theoretical framework to discuss these differences in terms of concept formation but we cannot fail to be struck by the correspondence between his characterization of "propositional thinking" and Levi-Strauss' definition of modern "scientific thought" which differs from mythic thought in possessing a concept that has been freed from its connection with actual things and is capable of projecting the "merely possible." The changes Piaget describes as involved in the transition from concrete to formal operations are certainly concordant with our hypothesis about the development of "second-order concepts" which are based on other concepts and their semantic properties rather than on objects and their material properties.

Piaget's investigations have also revealed certain other characteristics of propositional thinking which are in line with our speculations and the observations of Vygotsky. At this stage, the child is capable of reflective thinking. He can give a logical account of his own operations – what he did and why it worked – and can think logically about thought. Protocols of young teen-age subjects attempting to solve certain scientific problems (Inhelder and Piaget, 1958) indicate that attainment of a "solution" involves not only getting "b" to follow "a" but being able to grasp and to state the *necessity* for this sequence.

As Piaget describes the operations which he considers characteristic of formal operational thought – the highest stage of thought – the conviction mounts that many if not all of these would be inconceivable if it were not for the existence of written languages and the child's acquired skill in manipulating the symbols of these language. This, of course, is far removed from Piaget's own view, but it seems to be a reasonable extension of his principal dictum, "penser, c'est operer." To *think* in abstract propositional terms must be a consequence of having acted upon or manipulated abstract propositions externally. Such actions would seem to be dependent upon the possession of reading and writing skills. It is difficult to imagine that oral speech alone could provide the mechanism for such continuing and extensive symbol manipulation. And, of course, by the age of 11 or 12, the child in Geneva and other industrialized societies has had four or five years of experience in reading, writing, and arithmetic.

Unfortunately there have thus far been few attempts to replicate Piaget's studies and observations on the stage of formal thinking among adolescent populations of other cultures. One follow-up study conducted in England with boys in junior high grades up through training college concluded that ability to solve the experimental problems was not dependent on knowledge of specific subject matter but that the "cultural milieu, climate of opinion or the general experience to which the person is subject is of the greatest importance in developing thinking skills" (Lovell, 1961, 152).

In a comparative study of school children in the U.S.A. and Hong Kong (Goodnow and Benton, 1966), it was found that lack of schooling among the

Hong Kong children upset their ability to solve a combinatorial reasoning task which Piaget uses to illustrate certain cardinal characteristics of propositional thinking.

The effect of schooling, as distinct from other differences in culture, has been most extensively explored in a recent series of comparative studies by Bruner and his associates (Bruner et al, 1967). These psychologists tested several hundreds of children in such varied social settings as the suburbs of Massachusetts, Mexico, Alaska, and Africa. In these studies an attempt was made to vary independently three major cultural factors which are usually treated as one conglomerate: national culture, living environment (urban vs. rural setting), and schooling. While there are a number of interesting observations emerging from these comparisons, the most pronounced and most general conclusion reached by the investigators was that, of all the three dimensions explored, *schooling is by far the most influential in affecting cognitive skills.*

The effect of schooling was most dramatically demonstrated in studies conduced among the Wolof people in Senegal, West Africa. A number of families in the bush now send their children to school whereas others of similar status have not enrolled their children in the educational system. This aspect of a culture in transition enabled the investigators to construct matched groups of schooled and unschooled children within one village and to compare these to a group of Wolof children living in the metropolitan center of Dakar and attending school there. Here then for the first time in cross-cultural studies in cognition there was an opportunity to evaluate intellectual performance along independent dimensions of village vs. city life, school vs. no school, and village school vs. village, no school.

Cognitive processes were assessed on two concept tasks: Piaget's conservation task involving judgments of equality of liquid poured into different size beakers and a concept formation task developed by Bruner. On the Piagetian problem, school children from the bush performed in a manner that was highly similar to the performance of their school compatriots in Dakar. But what is even more interesting, their performance was almost indistinguishable from that of American and Swiss children of the urban middle classes! Analyzing performance at the various stages from non-conservation to conservation, the investigators found that the bush children were on the average one year older than their American and European counterparts when they achieved the various levels, but in terms of *school grade level*, their progress was identical. Unschooled Wolof children, on the other hand, showed an entirely different pattern of performance and, in this study, fully one-half failed to achieve conservation even at the highest age tested (11–13). A follow-up study conducted by the same research team among unschooled Wolof adults showed the same proportion failing to achieve conservation, leading the authors to suggest (Bruner *et al*, 1967, 234) that "without school, intellectual development defined as any qualitative change, ceases shortly after age 9."

While these findings of "no-conservation" are in conflict with those of another study of African children (Price-Williams, 1961) and need further confirmation before acceptance, the existence and nature of the intellectual differences between Wolof schooled and unschooled children is a finding of great importance.

The authors have this to say about this crucial difference (1967, 234–235): "The parallel findings [between bush schooled, Dakar schooled, American and Swiss children] cast strong doubts on any simple maturational notion of development. Rural Wolof children exposed to a certain set of cultural influences, namely the school, differ more from other rural Wolof children raised without school than they do from European children."

The qualitative nature of the difference between schooled and unschooled as described by the investigators is of special interest because it accords quite closely with our hypothesized difference between literate and nonliterate thought. Take this one illustration: The unschooled children did not understand the standard experimental question, "Why do you *think* this glass had (more) or (equal) water?" The investigators were forced to change the question to, "Why *does* this glass have (more) or (equal) water?"

It would seem that the unschooled Wolof children . . . do not distinguish between their own thought or a statement about something and the thing itself. *Thought and the object of thought seems to be one.* Consequently, the idea of explaining a statement is meaningless; it is the external event that is to be explained (1967, 232), (*Emphasis supplied*).

The fact that playmates who went to school had no difficulty with this question lends weight to the point of view that it is not membership in a technologically complex society *per se* but specific educational experiences which make possible the development of reflective thought.

Tests involving Bruner's concept formation task (conceived along the more traditional line of requiring statements of likenesses and differences among items) yield further support for the suggested link between school and the development of reflective thought. Wolof children showed the same developmental pattern as all other national groups studied in respect to what Bruner calls the "structure" of concepts: as age increased, items were more frequently grouped together by the use of some superordinate rule which governed whether they were considered "alike" or "different." This age-related change cut across the rural-urban and school-no school divisions. But, only the school children showed a growth in the ability to *state* the rule that was governing their groupings. To state the rule you are using requires that you be aware, not only of the task, but of your own approach to the task – a kind or level of thinking apparently absent among the unschooled children in this study and present among their student friends.

Finally, Bruner reports a similar developmental pattern among American, Eskimo, Mexican, and Senegalese school children in the attributes of objects selected as the basis for an equivalence grouping. Between the ages of 8-13, children in all of these countries shift from reliance on perceptual attributes to wider use of functional and nominal[25] attributes as grouping criteria – a shift which has been traditionally considered a shift from "concreteness" to "abstraction." Rural Wolof school children also make this shift although they do not attain the same proportion of functional and nominal responses as their "city cousins." *Unschooled* rural Wolof children, however, depart from the observed pattern: they continue to rely almost wholly on perceptual attributes such as color or other distinctive properties making for observable physical similarity among things.

With these data in hand, it is not surprising to find Bruner (1967, 315) concluding that "schooling appears to be the single most powerful factor we have found in the stimulation of abstraction."

Like Vygotsky, Bruner attempts to push further into "the school experience" to identify the specific factors at work and like him, but in accord with his own theory of the importance of systems of cognitive representation, Bruner speculates about the crucial role of language:

Where there is difference [between schooled and unschooled] is in how language is used and what opportunities are provided for different uses. Here again school is important. For it is the school children who have the greater opportunity to practice language in contexts that do not carry the meaning for them automatically, who are forced thereby to use sentences to the full. They are the ones who, moreover, are led by the nature of school lessons to translate their experiences and actions into words and sentences that will satisfy a teacher and thereby learn to reorganize experience and action to conform to the requirements of language (Bruner, et al., 1967, 316–317).

And, finally, Bruner points explicitly to the use in school of the written form of language, which heightens linguistic competence and thus symbolic functions in general.

The contemporary developmental studies we have reviewed, then, are beginning to lay an empirical base for studies of the interactional effects of specific cultural institutions and specific cognitive processes. In this "unravelling" of the cultural web, the school appears to be emerging as a crucial factor in cognitive growth. While the written language is an indispensable and inseparable feature of the school experience, the converse does not hold. The opportunity still remains to investigate the impact of written language acquisition divorced from the school context – a step which the pioneer studies of Vygotsky, Piaget and Bruner suggest may further unravel the complex ties between culture and mind.

Notes

1. Vygotsky is a notable exception and the views presented here are greatly indebted to his work.

2. For the purpose of this discussion, we will accept Gelb's (1952, 12) definition of writing as "Human intercommunication by means of conventional visible signs".
3. There are special signs such as . . . for an omission, modifications in spelling to distinguish between two words not differentiated in speech, such as "sea . . . see," and identifying labels or symbols used extensively in commercial and cartoon literature.
4. "Written language" here and throughout most of this paper will refer mainly to the alphabetic system, although with modifications many of the same observations could apply to other systems.
5. In this presentation I have eliminated a number of characteristics given by Bernstein and simplified his wording to some extent.
6. Non-literate is not to be taken as illiterate. The distinction is between levels of mastery and utilization of reading and writing skills. As I am using the terms here, "illiteracy" denotes the complete absence of skill; the existence of some skills with only minimal utilization is here termed "nonliteracy." "Full literacy" defines a stage where the written language has been internalized. In between there are many levels of varying proficiency. When we hypothesize that literacy will have certain cognitive consequences, we are of course referring not to the minimal but the higher levels of literacy and to actual use of literacy skills.
7. Magic offers the most dramatic examples of language used instrumentally to impose subjective wishes on reality.
8. See discussion below of Levi-Strauss' views on the science of pre-literate peoples.
9. The term "abstract" has a multiplicity of meanings which reduces its usefulness in discussions of cognitive processes. We discuss these varied usages below but here we are letting the word stand as a convenient label for a number of written language features having to do with the "greater distance" of the written than the oral word from the social and physical context.
10. McLuhan (1962), a severe critic of the phonetic alphabet, speaks of it as a system which "abstracts meaning from sound" and then "translates sound into a visual code" – an interesting analysis which leaves us with both visual and auditory signs bereft of meaning. It would seem that both our oral and written languages are incomprehensible!
11. deGroot's (1966) analysis of the superiority of chess masters in solving chess problems has led him to the interesting conclusion that their skills have transformed what was initially an inferential analysis of the open moves on the chessboard into direct perception of the possibilities. In other words, he conceives of a progression at a certain high level of skill from "conceptual" to "perceptual" information processing. This observation seems pertinent to the reading situation as well.
12. We will let the special cases of advertising and other exhortatory material stand as major exceptions, and the use of bold-faced and italicized type in various kinds of texts stand as a minor exception.
13. Gibson, Pick et al. (1962, 554) define the learning-to-read task as that of discovering the higher-order invariants that are the appropriate units of analysis. They call these spelling-to-sound correlations "grapheme-phoneme correspondences."
14. These hypotheses may be stated either in "weak" or "strong" form. The weak form would be that literacy is a facilitative mechanism; the strong form that it is a causal

mechanism in the effects postulated. Although the distinction is clearly crucial for research purposes, we do not feel that it is necessary to develop it for the purpose of this speculative analysis.

15. As we have noted, writing is a prerequisite for the development of many of the conceptual systems which furnish the building blocks of modern science.

16. Any approach which starts off to "demonstrate a link" between literacy and cognition is likely to oversimplify and overexaggerate the "uniqueness" and "significance" of the skills involved in literacy. In the modern as well as ancient world, the spread of literacy is always accompanied by other significant social changes, and it is difficult to single it out from the entire complex of conditions as being *the* factor responsible for change. With this caution in mind, however, it would still seem necessary to balance the risk of oversimplifying the effects of a single social phenomenon taken in isolation with the risk of continued avoidance by psychology of the significant dimensions of social life.

17. These illustrations given by Levi-Strauss show remarkably similar principles of grouping to those described by Vygotsky (1962) as characteristic of "complex thinking." In complex thinking, as distinct from concept thinking, items are grouped together on the basis of contiguity, resemblance, or being found together in nature.

18. One was seeking the invariant characteristics of human mind, another the factors responsible for the demise of the primitive community, and the third a meaningful explanation for Plato's attack on poetry.

19. "Generalization" is also commonly applied to the *outcome* of acts of thought, but that is not our usage.

20. Several "blue" items may be classed together because they look alike, but even if they have such different values of hue as not to appear similar they may still be grouped together as representatives of a theoretical color category "blue." The actual basis for grouping would have to be tested by observation of the grouping performance. As is clear by now, the same word – "blue" – may represent different kinds of generalizations.

21. It will be seen that our characterization of these two conceptual levels draws heavily on Vygotsky's analysis of the differences in stages of generalization. We have drawn freely from his presentations and those of his colleagues and successors (see especially Davydov, 1967) but we have modified, reformulated and added to them in line with our own views of the role of literacy in the attainment of a new conceptual level. Our starting point is the changed relationship between word and thought as a result of mastery of writing, a point of view never expressed as far as we know by Vygotsky.

22. Unfortunately, Vygotsky does not describe these studies in detail, and his bibliographic reference is to unpublished student theses.

23. Vygotsky was obviously referring to the traditional form of language instruction which stressed mastery of grammar and the written language rather than conversational use.

24. Piaget uses ages as approximate only, acknowledging that they will differ from culture to culture within an invariant sequence of stages.

25. Bruner uses this term to refer to the use of a superordinate class term to group items, such as "fruit", "clothing" and the like.

References

Bernstein, B., Social class, speech systems and psycho-therapy. In Riessman, F. et. al. (Eds.) *Mental health of the poor.* New York: The Free Press of Glencoe, 1964.

Bloomfield, L. *Language.* New York: Henry Holt and Company, 1933.

Bruner, J. S., Olver, Rose and Greenfield, Patricia, et. al. *Studies in cognitive growth.* New York: John Wiley & Sons, Inc., 1967.

Davydov, V. V. The problem of generalization in the works of L. S. Vygotsky. *Soviet Psychology,* V, Spring, 1967, 42–52.

deGroot, A. D. Perception and memory versus thought. In Kleinmuntz, B. (Ed.) *Problem solving.* New York: John Wiley & Sons, Inc., 1966.

Diamond, S. Plato and the definition of the primitive. In Diamond, S. (Ed.) *Primitive views of the world.* New York: Columbia University Press, 1964.

Diringer, D. *Writing.* London, 1962.

Flavell, J. H. *The developmental psychology of Jean Piaget.* Princeton: D. Van Nostrand Company, Inc., 1963.

Gelb, I. J. *A study of writing.* Chicago: University of Chicago Press, 1952.

Gibson, Eleanor J., Pick, Anne, Osser, H., and Hammond, Marcia. The role of grapheme-phoneme correspondence in the perception of words. *Am. J. of Psychol.,* 1962, *75,* 554–570.

Goodnow, Jacqueline J. and Benton, Gloria. Piaget's tasks: the effects of schooling and intelligence. *Child Development,* 1966, *37,* 574–582.

Goody, J. and Watt, I. The consequences of literacy. *Comparative Studies in Society and History,* V, 1963.

Havelock, E. *Preface to Plato.* Cambridge: Harvard University Press, 1963.

Hoijer, H. Language and writing. In Shapiro, H. (Ed.) *Man, culture and society.* New York: Oxford University Press, 1960.

Inhelder, B. and Piaget, J. *The growth of logical thinking.* New York: Basic Books, Inc., 1958.

Levi-Strauss, C. *The savage mind.* Chicago: The University of Chicago Press, 1966.

Lotz, J. Linguistics: symbols make man. In Saporta, S. (Ed.) *Psycholinguistics.* New York: Holt, Rinehart & Winston, 1961.

Lovell, K. A follow-up study of Inhelder and Piaget's "The growth of logical thinking." *Brit. J. Psychol.,* 1961, *52,* 143–153.

McLuhan, M. *The Gutenberg galaxy.* Canada: Univ. of Toronto Press, 1962.

Mills, C. W. Language, logic and culture. In Horowitz, I. L. (Ed.) *Power, politics and people.* New York: Oxford Univ. Press, 1963.

Movius, H. L., Jr. The old stone age. In Shapiro, H. (Ed.) *Man, culture and society.* New York: Oxford University Press, 1960.

Price-Williams, D. R. A study concerning concepts of conservation of quantities among primitive children. *Acta Psychol.,* 1961, *18,* 297–305.

Vygotsky, L. S. *Thought and language.* Cambridge: The M.I.T. Press, 1962.

Werner, H. and Kaplan, B. *Symbol formation.* New York: John Wiley & Sons, Inc., 1963.

15 The practice of literacy: Where mind and society meet

It is seventy-five years since Edmund Burke Huey[1] published his pioneering work on the psychology and pedagogy of reading. His research instruments were rudimentary and his knowledge base limited, but few, even now, rival his deep understanding of the phenomenon of reading and the challenge it poses to the human sciences. Huey said:

... to completely analyze what we do when we read would be almost the acme of a psychologist's achievements, for it would be to describe very many of the most intricate workings of the human mind, as well as to unravel the tangled story of the most remarkable specific performance that civilization has learned in all its history. (p. 6)

Embedded in this short statement are three important concepts about reading which serve as an introduction to the topic of this paper – how cultural practices affect the reading process. I will review current research which demonstrates a link between social uses of literacy and the psychological operations required for certain reading tasks, and Huey's concepts provide a useful starting point.

First, Huey describes reading as something we *do*, "what we *do* when we read." In terms of contemporary cognitive science, Huey is claiming that reading is performance as well as competence. Whether or not one subscribes to a competence-performance distinction, it is certain that the concept of reading as performance requires us to take into account aspects of behavior that are not typically catalogued as "basic reading competencies." If reading is performance, we need to understand *why* a person undertakes to do it – the purposes and goals of reading – and we need to inquire into the conditions under which reading is carried out – the features of the social and physical settings that

This article originally appeared in the *Annals of the New York Academy of Sciences* 433 (1984): 5–19. Reprinted with the permission of the New York Academy of Sciences.

contextualize and constrain particular acts of reading. A performance framework of analysis requires attention not only to a *reader* and a *text* but to the *task* the reader is trying to fulfill through engagement with a text. (For current work on the influence of purpose and task on reading, see Collins *et al.*,[2] Gibson and Levin,[3] and Sticht.[4])

Huey's second concept is that reading should be viewed as the outcome of "very many workings of mind," not as some unitary process. Increasingly today, reading researchers[5] are turning away from attempts to work out a single-process analysis of reading, and are emphasizing that every act of reading involves processes on many levels – linguistic, perceptual, and cognitive. Huey, however, went beyond this observation to emphasize that full understanding of reading requires a knowledge of how component processes are assembled, how they are synthesized on particular occasions of performance to accomplish "reading." He likened the synthesis in reading to the synthesis that occurs in skilled motor performances such as tennis or piano playing. By making this comparison, he drew attention to the fact that an outstanding characteristic of all complex skills is their flexibility: a skilled performer adapts strategies and techniques to the task at hand.

Finally, Huey emphasizes the social dependency of reading skills. Individuals do not become expert readers as a consequence of maturation or, in Piagetian[6] terms, by passing through successive intellectual stages. Society – civilization is the term Huey used – is involved in the acquisition process. Whether or not physiologically normal individuals attain literacy skills is entirely dependent on whether written symbol systems are available in their culture and what meanings and uses are assigned to them. According to one UNESCO projection,[7] one billion people throughout the world are nonliterate today. No amount of study of reading as an individual phenomenon can account for that fact.

If Huey's concepts are brought together and paraphrased somewhat loosely, they yield a functional approach to reading which can be defined as follows: *reading* is a term that refers to a variety of performances with written language; it involves many and varied skills depending on the task and purpose of the performance; these skills and tasks are somehow bound up with the social milieu in which individuals learn to read.

The rest of this article will proceed from this functional definition of reading and will be devoted to a discussion of recent research that seeks to explicate that "somehow" – the specific ways in which the social milieu affects the reading process. Research evidence for cultural influences on reading skills will be drawn from a multidisciplinary investigation conducted among a traditional rice-farming people of West Africa, the Vai people of Liberia and Sierra Leone.[8] Because Vai society is both culturally and geographically distant, it offers us a fresh perspective from which to view literacy activities in our own society, activities whose very familiarity blurs our vision of the social factors affecting them.

Background of Vai research

My colleagues and I[9] undertook the Vai research to test age-old speculations that learning how to read and write fosters the development of higher intellectual skills. Such claims have been with us ever since Plato mediated about the effect of writing on men's minds.[10] In recent years, communication specialists such as McLuhan,[11] Ong,[12] and others have popularized the notion that the processing of alphabetic writing involves a particular form of linear, logical thought. Greenfield[13] and Greenfield and Bruner[14] have argued that comprehension of written language, because it presents decontextualized information, requires a form of abstract thinking which is not necessary for the interpretation of spoken language. Another leading cognitive psychologist, David Olson,[15] has maintained that in learning how to read essayist text, individuals acquire a particular kind of logical competence – the ability to make inferences from language alone.

These claims have far-reaching implications for both theory and practice. If certain thinking skills are intimately bound up with reading and writing, it follows that there may be deep qualitative differences between the thought of literate and nonliterate individuals. If nonliterates are incapable of abstract or logical thought, it also follows that programs for economic and social advancement may be seriously handicapped by these human limitations. For these reasons, it is important to go beyond rhetoric and traditional wisdom to bring empirical evidence to the discussion. Researching the psychological impact of literacy, however, proves a difficult enterprise. One reason is that we rarely find literacy in the raw. In our own and other industrialized societies, literacy and schooling go hand in hand. As children progress through the grades learning how to read and write, they are also acquiring knowledge, becoming familiar with science, and engaging in classroom dialogue and inquiry. With these experiences all intertwined, it is difficult to determine whether literacy *in itself* is a driving force for intellectual advancement. The logical requirements for research on literacy are that we find a place where there are literate people who have never gone to school and compare their thinking with people of similar background who are neither literate nor schooled. If group differences are found on cognitive tasks, we may have identified intellectual skills uniquely associated with literacy.

While the logical requirements are simple, the logistical conditions for meeting them are not. Countries with universal schooling do not allow us to separate literacy from education. In many third-world countries, nonliterate groups are sufficiently dissimilar from literate groups in language, custom and socio-economic status to disqualify comparisons. Vai society, however, has a configuration of literacy practices which are ideal for research purposes. The Vai are one of the few peoples in the world with an original writing system, invented 160 years ago. This system is a syllabary with approximately 200 characters representing the syllabic structure of the Vai language. The arts of reading and writing in this script are passed on from one villager to another through individual tutoring; no schooling or education in the larger sense is involved. Thus literacy in the Vai script offers an unusual opportunity to examine the cognitive implications of literacy acquired without schooling. Moreover, since literates and nonliterates alike pursue the same farming and craft occupations, group comparisons are reasonable.

Vai society is unusual, too, in hosting literacy in two international scripts in addition to the local writing system. The official language in Liberia is English and government-sponsored English schools modelled after United States schools are scattered throughout country villages, so that English literacy is becoming increasingly widespread. In addition, the Vai are a Muslim people and have a century-old tradition of Qur'anic study. Thus three literacies, each with its own script and its own mode of transmission, flourish among a people whose primary economic activity is slash-and-burn rice farming and whose way of life remains largely traditional. These exceptional historical circumstances created in Vai society an "experiment in nature," ideally suited to testing questions about social influences on literacy and the skills uniquely associated with reading and writing activities.

Social uses of literacy among the Vai

While our principal interest was in analyzing intellectual operations involved in literacy activities, it was apparent that we could not undertake such psychological analysis until we knew exactly what these activities were and how they were distributed throughout the population. The initial phase of the research, therefore, concentrated on securing a detailed description of the social functions of reading and writing. Methods were both quantitative and qualitative. We conducted a sample interview survey involving 700 adults in all parts of Vai country, and in-depth ethnographic studies of literacy practices in two typical towns.

First, some findings on the extent of literacy. Approximately one-third of Vai men are literate in one of the three scripts (few women are literate). The majority know and use the indigenous Vai script, the next largest group is literate in Arabic and the smallest in English. A substantial number of literate men are knowledgeable in both Vai script and the Arabic alphabet and a few have mastered all three scripts. Since each literacy involves a different orthography and a different course of study, multiple literacy is no mean accomplishment.

As in other multiliterate societies,[16] social functions of literacy are distributed in regularly patterned ways across the scripts. English is the official writing system of government and commerce and of institutions operating on a national scale. In the capital city of Monrovia, English writing is part of the natural landscape as it is among us – it is displayed on street signs and billboards, and English-language newspapers and books are available in stores. Upcountry, however, English has a limited role. Some chiefs retain clerks to record court matters in English and maintain official correspondence with government agencies. Some villagers who formerly attended schools use their literacy for personal affairs but even these individuals get their news by radio or word of mouth.

English is learned exclusively in government-run schools, but not all villages have schools, and commonly these continue only up to the 5th grade. Students are thus forced to leave home to pursue their education; if they contrive to complete high school, they rarely return to the farm but remain in the city seeking to win a place for themselves in the modern sector.

Arabic writing, on the other hand, is an organic part of village life. Almost every town of any size has a Qur'anic school conducted by a learned Muslim. These are usually schools without walls – groups of boys ranging in age from approximately 4 to 24 years who meet around the fire twice a day for hours of recitation and memorization of Qur'anic verses. In Islamic tradition, committing the Qur'an to memory is a holy act, and the student's progress through the text is marked at fixed intervals by religious observances and feasting. Initially, since Arabic is a foreign language to the Vai, learning is by rote repetition: students can neither decode the written passage nor understand the sounds they produce. But boys who persevere learn at some point to match symbol with sound; they become able to sing out passages from the text without having heard them before and to write new verses from dictation. For those who go on to learn Arabic as a foreign language, Qur'anic reading passes through other stages until text memorization is fully supported by comprehension.[17] Memorization of the entire Qur'an requires from five to seven years of concentrated effort. Among the Vai, a few who complete the Qur'an arrange for tutorial instruction in religious, legal and other texts. Some outstanding individuals acquire libraries and lead scholarly lives in the countryside teaching, studying and participating in textual commentary and disputation. Thus Arabic literacy relates individuals to text on both the lowest level (repetition without comprehension) and highest level (analysis of textual meaning). Vai script uses, in contrast, are overwhelmingly secular, pragmatic, and personal. Script learning may begin any time in adolescence or throughout adulthood. No special occasions are set aside for it. The would-be literate arranges to get the help of a friend, relative or coworker who teaches him the characters and gives him practice in reading. Typically, this instruction begins with individual words such as names of things and progresses to text. The teacher uses whatever Vai script material he has on hand, and when he thinks the student has made sufficient progress he sends him a letter in the script with instructions to write a reply. On the average, most students are able to pass this test after two to four weeks.

While learning is individual, the practice of Vai script literacy is often a social enterprise. For reasons discussed later, the orthography is ambiguous and often hard to decipher. Accordingly, it is not uncommon to see several village men reading a letter out loud together, sometimes consulting each other about a particular character, at other times arguing about whether the author's spelling is correct or his writing style "good Vai." Reading and writing are cooperative as well as individual phenomena.

Uses of the Vai script involve both textual and nontextual materials. Nontextual uses range from very simple activities such as labelling a piece of property to systematic record-keeping. Records fulfill both social cohesion and economic functions: lists of dowry items and of funeral contributions, for example, help to regulate the reciprocal rights and obligations of the kinship system. Records also enlarge the scope and planning aspects of commercial transactions such as cash-crop farming or carpentry, tailoring, and other traditional crafts. In every village, some expert scribes keep public records for the town, maintaining lists of house tax payments, work contributions to public projects such as road or bridge-building, population counts and the like.

Letter-writing is the principal textual use of the script. Every literate interviewed reported that he corresponded with one or more people. Letters may pass from hand to hand within a town, or may be carried by taxi to distant parts of Liberia. Many Vai people who are not personally literate participate in this form of exchange through the service of scribes. For all its popularity, however, letter-writing is circumscribed in ways which simplify its cognitive demands; four out of five literates in the survey reported that they correspond only with persons already known to them and never with a stranger. Written communication among the Vai draws heavily upon shared background knowledge against which the figural news is exchanged.

As for other textual material, it is interesting to note that it is all held in private. Texts are rarely circulated to others to be read, though on occasion they might be made available for copying. This ownership arrangement has several important consequences. One is that reading typically involves familiar material (works written by oneself) rather than assimilation of new knowledge. When we showed literates an unfamiliar story written in Vai script, they often expressed surprise that we would expect them to "read" something they did not "know." Another consequence of the private holding of written materials is that existing texts reflect what individuals choose to write about and what they think writing is "for." Much of the writing is journal style; literates maintain diaries or notebooks in which they enter various items: autobiographical facts, for example, snippets of town history, or family birth dates. We also discovered books of maxims for the young, clan histories, and on one occasion, a collection of traditional Vai folk tales. Texts of this kind were rare, however, and certain genres entirely missing. For example, we found no poetics or expository prose or textbooks in the Vai script.

This is a brief review but it supports certain general observations. In spite of its three-script literacy, Vai society's uses of written language are considerably more restricted than those of an industrial society such as ours. Many traditional educational, cultural and economic activities are carried on without the intervention of the written word. Yet within the spheres of cultural activities in which literacy is a factor, reading and writing are used for a variety of purposes – practical, intellectual and ideological – and many routes lead to learning.

Modal reading tasks

Comparative studies of Vai script, Arabic and English literacy suggest that each type presents the learner and the practitioner with a particular modal reading task. Oversimplifying in order to highlight differences, we can summarize the principal goals of reading in each script as follows: In English schools, Vai students, like United States students, pass through the first grades *learning to read,* but then their major requirement is *reading to learn.* Their reading material consists overwhelmingly of expository prose material that is meant to convey new information. Once outside of school, English literates will occasionally read newspapers, government announcements, and other material communicating "news." In Vai script literacy, *reading* is importantly *related to action.* Letters typically carry news and requests of one kind or another; records are used to better carry out practical activities. Even recorded histories and stories are given instrumental significance: they are often read aloud at ceremonial occasions to instruct young people and strangers in Vai ways. As for Qur'anic literacy, much of it clearly consists of *reading to remember.* The goal of study is to ingest the holy word, literally to take it inside oneself through memorization.

Harking back to Huey's language, we can say that in these literacies people are doing different things with reading – learning, acting, remembering. They are also interacting with different writing systems – a syllabary whose characters represent syllables in the native language, and two alphabetic systems, Arabic and Roman, which represent phonemes in foreign tongues.

Cognitive analysis of literacy skills

Thus far we have been considering the social organization of literacy among the Vai and how social practices pose different kinds of reading and writing tasks to individuals. Our aim, however, was to determine what processing skills underlay these differences and whether they had any general intellectual implications. Were certain psycholinguistic and cognitive skills common to all literacies? Or were some specific to particular scripts and/or reading tasks?

To pursue these questions we turned to psychological studies. Taking advantage of the multiliteracy situation among the Vai, we set up a comparative research design to ferret out commonalities and differences among groups with different literacy experiences. One group consisted of youth and adults who either were in English school at the time or who had once attended school. Groups of Vai script literates and Arabic literates represented nonschooled literacy. In most studies we contrasted individuals who knew only one of these scripts with those who were biliterate, that is, knowledgeable in both Vai and Arabic. Comparable groups of nonliterates were included and, in keeping with the social reality of literacy among the Vai, we conducted most of our studies among men only.

In the first set of studies, we administered a set of experimental cognitive tasks tapping abstraction, memory and other cognitive processes that have been speculatively linked to literacy. Results on this battery were clear-cut. In keeping with previous research, we found that schooling improved performance on many of these tasks, especially those involving verbal explanations. But there was no indication that the mere ability to use language in written form had any general impact. Vai script and Arabic literates were no different in average performance from nonliterates. Moreover, some nonliterates performed on every task as well as literates or those with schooling. If for the time being we accept these tasks as indicators of higher-order intellectual processes, the conclusion is unmistakable that literacy per se does not play a formative role. The failure of Qur'anic schooling to make a difference in general cognitive performance was interesting because of the argument, cited earlier, that alphabetic writing systems are especially likely to foster abstract forms of thinking. These conclusions are, of course, relative to the circumstances of Qur'anic and other literacies obtaining among the Vai.

The second set of studies represented a shift in research strategy from testing general hypotheses about literacy to a more functional, context-sensitive approach. Instead of relying on psychological theories to suggest literacy-related skills, we developed specific hypotheses on the basis of our ethnographic observations. We selected certain literacy activities for which we had detailed descriptions – memorizing the Qur'an, for example, and writing a letter in Vai script. We made functional analyses of the skills these activities seemed to involve, and designed experimental tasks with different content but hypothetically similar skills to determine whether practice in the original activity enhanced performance. The logic of the enterprise was to demonstrate the link between a particular literacy practice and specific cognitive skills through evidence that literates displayed those skills on a related but new task while nonliterates did not. This is a reversal of the mainstream of research on reading which asks what skills are *necessary* for literacy; through our transfer paradigm, we proposed to determine what skills are *promoted* by literacy.

Several lines of experimentation modeled processes involved in reading letters composed in Vai script. The first series focused on perceptual-linguistic processes and was prompted by our observations of how script readers went about decoding the message in personal letters that came to them by taxi or by hand. Making out the sense of a letter seemed a difficult task for many. Some difficulties appeared to be related to features of the writing system which introduce ambiguity into the written message. As previously pointed out, the Vai language is represented by its script at the level of a syllable; a single character stands for one spoken syllable. Although characters map the syllabic structure of the language in a comprehensive and systematic manner, there is not always a direct one-to-one correspondence between a single character and the unit of sound it represents. Vowel tone, a phonological feature that is semantically crucial, is not marked in the script, and, as a consequence, the same character may have more than one sound referent. Representation of vowel length, another semantically distinctive feature of the language, varies from one writer to another. Finally, writing conventions, like those of ancient Greece, do not segment lines of text into words or other semantic or syntactic units. Each syllable stands alone with space surrounding it (Figure 15.1). Since Vai words may consist of more than one syllable, readers must find a way of integrating the individual syllables on the page into meaningful chunks of language. A common solution to these problems is reading aloud – grouping and regrouping strings of syllables until they are organized into such meaningful chunks. In this recycling process, readers must keep separate syllables in mind until they can be integrated into words or phrases: We supposed that this experience might foster skills in integration of syllabic units of languages and that these skills might apply to language processing in contexts that did not involve the script. To test this idea, we developed an oral language comprehension task. We asked nonliterates and members of the various literate groups to listen to tape recordings of a native Vai speaker. The speaker presented meaningful Vai sentences, one at a time, without tonal variations, pausing between linguistic units in a mimicry of early stages of reading. One set of sentences was segmented into syllable units, as is the script, while another set was segmented into an equal number of word units. The sentence composed of word units was used as a baseline control for possible individual or group differences in memory. To illustrate this material with English examples, a sentence separated into words might be:

Momo/travelled/upcountry/yesterday.

The same sentence segmented into syllable units was:

Mo/mo/tra/velled/up/coun/try/yes/ter/day.

The listener was asked to repeat the sentence immediately after hearing it, and answer a comprehension question.

Results (Table 15.1) reveal a striking interaction between literacy group and task. First consider sentences containing word units. Literacy in every script enhanced performance on this task with all groups of literates, schooled and

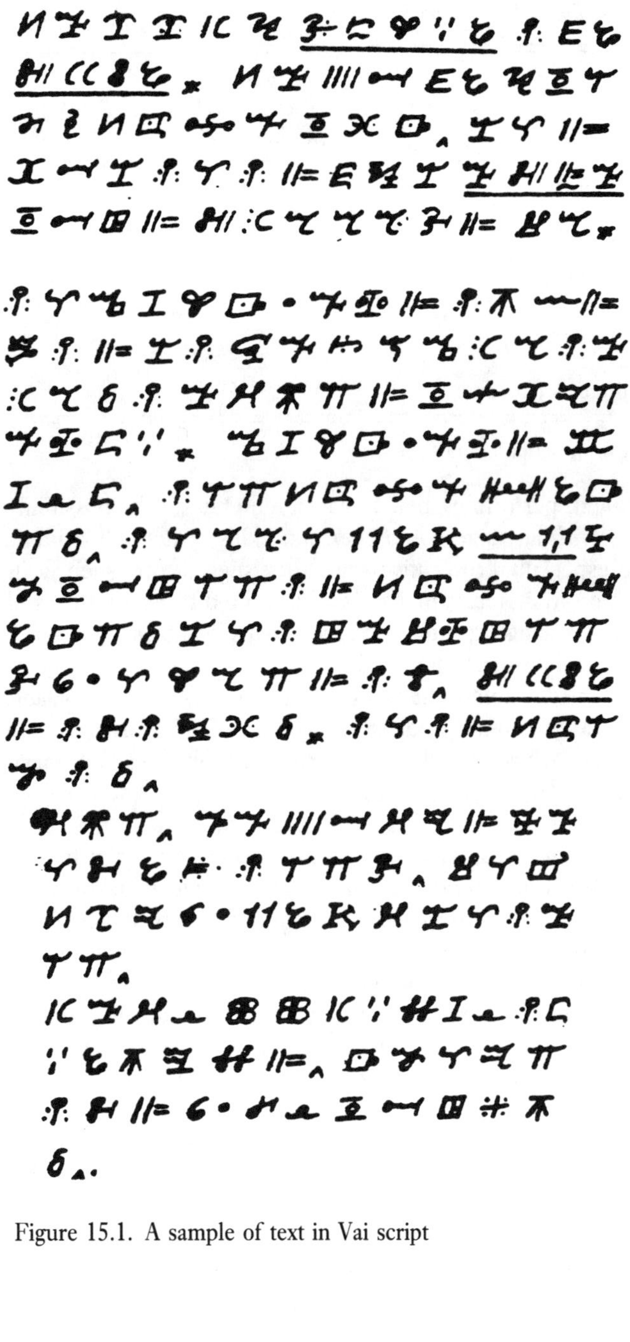

Figure 15.1. A sample of text in Vai script

Table 15.1. *Relationship between literacy and oral language comprehension: mean scores on auditory integration task[a]*

Literacy group	Word sentences perfectly recalled (maximum 5)	Syllable sentences perfectly recalled (maximum 5)
Nonliterate men	1.45	.90
Arabic literates		
Qur'anic only	2.50	1.00
Arabic language	2.60	1.10
Vai script literates		
Beginning	2.80	1.10
Advanced	2.85	2.40
English literates (students)	3.45	2.00

[a]Adapted from Scribner and Cole.

nonschooled, performing better than nonliterates. The possibility that literacy facilitates *oral* language comprehension skills is not self-evident, and results here are especially provocative since they suggest that such facilitative effects are common to literacies in scripts with quite different patterns of relationship to the spoken language (the Vai script maps syllables, for example, while the English alphabet maps phonemes).

Next, consider comprehension of sentences containing syllable units. With this material, the only group showing superior performance was that of Vai script readers whose tested reading proficiency was at an advanced level. Other literate groups dropped to the level of nonliterates. The performance of individuals with English schooling is especially interesting: they turned in the best comprehension performance for word sentences, but they, too, dropped below advanced Vai script literates on the syllable sentence task.

Group levels of performance thus upheld the hypothesis that the specific processing requirements of the Vai script, as distinguished from those in other writing systems, fostered comprehension of syllabic speech. Through techniques of multiple regression, we subjected this outcome to a more stringent test, controlling for personal background factors. We also entered each person's score for word sentences as a control factor for memory and other task variables. In equations predicting comprehension of syllable sentences, we found that, among some twenty background factors, only one affected performance – advanced reading score in Vai script.

These results are the first derived from experimental studies to establish a formative role for literacy skills on comprehension and memory for spoken language. All Vai people in these studies were, of course, native speakers; no group had more or less experience listening to naturally spoken Vai than any other. Vai script readers, however, also hear their language in syllabic form during the reading process, and perhaps on that account, were better equipped to hear and understand Vai when it was presented in syllabic form during a purely auditory task. The skills involved were clearly script-specific.

Now let us turn to a study involving higher-order cognitive skills such as those required in composing and writing personal letters. Effective written communication requires a greater elaboration of meaning than does face to face oral communication. We thought it reasonable to expect that Vai script literates with extensive letter-writing experience might have acquired special skills for composing well-organized and unambiguous messages. We tested this proposition with an instructional task that required the transmission of information in a well-structured form. We taught people to play a simple board game in which markers were moved to a finish line by a procedure similar to the throw of a die. After learning the game, each individual was asked to describe it to someone unfamiliar with it. In addition, we asked informants to dictate a letter explaining the game to someone far away who have never seen it before. Board games are popular among the Vai who play a game called "ludo" which has a similar racing format and is somewhat like Parcheesi. We transcribed the instructions and coded them for the amount of game-related information they contained and for the presence of statements describing the materials of the game. On both these measures – information and description – men literate in the Vai script were far superior to nonliterates and were also superior to Qur'anic literates who lacked experience in letter-writing. When we analyzed outcomes using multiple regression techniques so that we could control for possible background differences among the groups, we secured strong effects for Vai script literacy. What is more, Vai script effects were strongest for literates who reported the most extensive letter-writing experiences.

We also analyzed instruction protocols to see whether they reflected characteristics of Vai literates' style of communication in their day-to-day letter-writing practices. Over the years Vai letters have evolved certain stylized formats. Here is an example:

This letter belongs to Pa Lamii in Vonzuan. My greeting to you, and my greeting to Mother.

This is your information. I am asking you to do me a favor. The people I called to saw my timber charged me $160.00. I paid them $120.00 and $40.00 still needed, but business is hard this time. I am therefore sending your child to you to please credit me amount of $40.00 to pay these people. Please do not let me down.

I stopped so far.

I am Moley Doma
Vaitown

The statements "This is your information. I am asking you to do me a favor" serve to contextualize or frame the communication. They tell the recipient what the communication is about and what information to expect. This aspect of an effective communication was well understood by Vai literates and clearly explained in the interviews. In one discussion on the characteristics of a good letter, a middle-aged farmer said: "You must first make the person to understand that you are informing him through words. Then he will give his attention there. It is the correct way of writing the Vai script."

Transcribed protocols of game instructions were analyzed for the presence or absence of this stylistic feature. Over a range of experimental conditions, we found that Vai script literates more commonly contextualized their instructions by beginning with a general characterization of the game in a manner analogous to the introduction of the topic in a personal letter. Here is an example of such an opening: "This is a game I am coming to tell you about where two people take a race and one of them wins." This stylistic consistency strengthens the case for considering the better performance of Vai script literates on this task to be the result of a generalization of skills they had acquired in their letter-writing practices.

In other studies, we uncovered specific effects associated with Qur'anic literacy and with literacy acquired through participation in English schooling.

The entire program of research and its pattern of findings can be summed up in the following statement: over and above a common core of decoding and encoding skills associated with all three literacies, we found specific processing skills related to the characteristics of particular writing systems and to the cognitive demands of particular reading and writing tasks. Literacy tasks characteristic of the classroom environment in English schools differed in certain respects from those in the daily environment of the Vai script literate and these in turn from those of the Qur'anic schoolboy or the Arabic scholar. Insofar as we could identify them, processing skills, whether primarily perceptual, linguistic, or cognitive, tended to reflect the functional requirements of well-practiced literacy tasks in each of these literacy domains.

Implications of the Vai research

The skills associated with literacy in Vai country are not necessarily associated with everyday literacy practices in our society; there is a world of difference between the two settings. The general significance of this research, therefore, lies not so much in its specific findings as in the broader framework it suggests for understanding the interrelationship between social and psychological processes involved in literacy. We describe this framework as a practice approach to literacy.[18] "Practice" is used here to denote a recurrent set of goal-directed activities with some common object, carried out with a particular technology and involving the application of particular knowledge. A practice is a usual mode or method of doing something and cultural practices exist in all domains. Growing rice, for example, is an agricultural practice, sewing trousers is a craft practice, and writing letters is a literacy practice.

Literacy practices involve a common "object" – a written language. They employ a particular technology – an orthography and the conventions of written representation, as well as the mode of production and distribution of writing. They draw on particular domains of knowledge – information and concepts needed to read and write with understanding and to accomplish particular purposes. Recent historical and anthropological studies[19] support the observations of the Vai research that the literacy practices that arise in a given society are dependent on that society's history and structure. Societies differ in the functions they generate for literacy and in their perceptions of its instrumental and ideological values. Detailed comparative case studies also show that, as among the Vai, in most societies literacy has a plurality of functions even when only one writing system is in use. The more complex the society and the more developed the technologies for producing writing, the greater the variety of social functions which are mediated by written language – in our terms, the more diverse are the literacy practices within that society. Among the Vai it was possible to trace the connections between particular spheres of activity and kinds of literacy practices with great clarity because of the division of literacy work across three scripts which were differentially employed in various domains. Links between social functions of literacy and personal practices of literacy in our society are extraordinarily complex, but wherever there is a reader, there is an individual involved in the use of a social technology and socially created knowledge for purposes which have a social origin.

For sound scientific and educational reasons, a considerable amount of reading research concentrates on the individual reader as a unit of analysis. But ignoring the socially embedded nature of reading and reading skills limits the scope of this research, and undermines its applicability to educational programs.

One limitation is an underestimation of the context-dependent nature of reading skills. Reading research is almost wholly devoted to the study of a small set of reading tasks that typically occur in the classroom. Important as these are, and no one suggests that they are not, it is still the case that school-like literacy tasks are not necessarily representative of the many productive literacy practices encountered in daily life. A lack of ability to perform school tasks may not preclude ability to perform others; school and nonschool literacies, Vai research suggests, do not exhaust each other. One implication is that reading research should be extended to a wider range of tasks in an effort to specify distinctive as well as common underlying processes in what people do when they read.

Failure to take into account the social nature of literacy practices also leads to an underestimation of the many learning opportunities for acquiring skills that arise outside of the classroom. The relationship between ability and performance, between can and do, is interactive, not a one-way street. As the Vai research suggests, participation in well-motivated reading and writing activities may promote the acquisition of certain skills, not merely reflect already formed skills. Although evidence for the formative role of particular literacy tasks on linguistic and cognitive skills is still only suggestive, what we know argues for more deliberate attention to the kind of reading and writing we ask students to do. If specific reading tasks invoke specific processing operations, pedagogy needs to take that fact into account. Treating reading as a single phenomenon rather than as a rich variety of activities with written language is not consonant with the research described here. On the other hand, a functional approach to reading, which values both its social meaning and personal significance, may contribute to our educational horizons as well as deepen our understanding of what Huey called the "most remarkable performance" in human history.

Notes

1. Huey, E. B. 1908. *The Psychology and Pedagogy of Reading.* Macmillan. New York.
2. Collins, A. M., A. L. Brown, J. L. Morgan & W. F. Brewer. 1977. The analysis of reading tasks and texts. Technical Reports No. 43. Center for the Study of Reading. Champaign, Ill.
3. Gibson, E. J. & H. Levin. 1975. *The Psychology of Reading.* The MIT Press. Cambridge, Mass.
4. Sticht, T., Ed. 1975. *Reading for Working: A Functional Literacy Anthology.* Human Resources Research Organization. Alexandria, VA.
5. Just, M. A. & P. A. Carpenter. 1980. A theory of reading: From eye fixation to comprehension. *Psychol. Rev.* 87: 329–353; Farnham-Diggory, S. 1984. Why reading? *Devel. Rev.* 4: 62–71; Rumelhart, D. 1977. Toward an interactive model of reading. In *Attention and Performance,* Vi. S. Dornie, Ed. Erlbaum. Hillsdale, N.J.
6. Piaget, P. & B. Inhelder. 1969. *The Psychology of the Child.* Basic Books. New York
7. Piaget, P. & B. Inhelder. 1979. *The World of Literacy: Policy, Research and Action.* International Development Research Centre. Ottawa, Canada.
8. Scribner, S. & M. Cole. 1981. *The Psychology of Literacy.* Harvard University Press. Cambridge, Mass.
9. This research, funded by the Ford Foundation, is fully described in S. Scribner & M. Cole, *The Psychology of Literacy* (Cambridge, Mass.: Harvard University Press, 1981). Other research participants and their publications are: S. Reder, "The Functional Impact of Writing on Vai Speech," Ph.D. dissertation (New York: The Rockefeller University, 1977); and M. R. Smith, "An Ethnography of the Vai People," Ph.D. dissertation (Cambridge, England: Cambridge University, 1982).
10. Plato. *The Republic.* Translated, with an introduction and notes by F. M. Cornford. 1945. Oxford University Press. London.
11. McLuhan, M. 1962. *The Gutenberg Galaxy.* University of Toronto Press. Toronto, Canada; McLuhan, M. 1965. *Understanding Media: The Extensions of Man.* McGraw-Hill Book Company. New York.
12. Ong, W. J. 1970. *The Presence of the Word.* Simon and Shuster. New York; Ong, W. J.

1971. *Rhetoric, Romance and Technology: Studies on the Interaction of Expression and Culture.* Cornell University Press. Ithaca, N.Y.

13. Greenfield, P. 1972. Oral or written language: The consequences for cognitive development in Africa, the United States and England. *Language & Speech* **15**: 169–178.
14. Greenfield, P. & J. Bruner. 1969. Culture and cognitive growth. In *Handbook of Socialization Theory and Research.* D. A. Goslin, Ed. Rand McNally. New York.
15. Olson, D. R. 1977. From utterance to text: The bias of language in speech and writing. *Harvard Ed. Rev.* **47**: 257–281.
16. Reder, S. & K. R. Green. 1979. Literacy as a functional component of social structure in an Alaska fishing village. Paper presented at the 78th Annual Meeting of the American Anthropological Association, Ohio.
17. Wagner, D. A. & A. Lotfi. 1983. Learning to read by "rote." In *Literacy and Ethnicity.* Special issue of the *International Journal of the Sociology of Language* **42**(4).
18. Scribner, S. Literacy as a cultural practice. Paper delivered at American Anthropological Association Annual Meeting, Houston, Texas, 1977.
19. Oxenham, J. 1980. *Literacy, Reading, Writing and Social Organization.* Routledge & Kegan Paul. London; Cipolla, C. 1969. *Literacy and Development in the West.* Penguin. Baltimore, Md.; Laquer, T. W. 1976. The cultural origins of popular literacy in England. *Oxford Rev. Ed.* **2**: 255–275; Cressy, D. 1980. *Literacy and the Social Order.* Cambridge University Press. Cambridge; Graff, H. J. 1979. *The Literacy Myth: Literacy and Social Structure in the 19th Century City.* Academic Press. New York; Stone, L. 1969. Literacy and education in England, 1640–1800. *Past & Present* **42**: 61–139; Goody, J., Ed. 1968. *Literacy in Traditional Societies.* Cambridge University Press. Cambridge; Heath, S. B. 1980. The functions and uses of literacy. *J. Commun.* **30**: 123–133; Smith, M. R. S. 1982. An Ethnography of the Vai People. Ph.D. dissertation, Cambridge University.

16   Literacy in three metaphors

I will discuss literacy in three metaphors and around one theme.

The metaphors organize different, and often opposing, views about the nature and functions of literacy in our society. The theme is that each metaphor, taken by itself, gives us only a partial grasp of the social and psychological forces sustaining literacy; it leads to the conclusion that effective literacy education requires acceptance of diversity of aim and interest.

To illustrate my theme, I will draw on the literacy experiences of a people distant from us both geographically and culturally – the Vai people of Liberia and Sierre Leone, West Africa. These are a subsistence rice-farming people with iron-tool technology. But they are a people who invented their own script and who use three different writing systems. Their uses of literacy may help illuminate controversies over the role of literacy of our own society.

Bringing a perspective from the Third World to an understanding of our literacy problems is especially appropriate because it is a radical departure from the framework in which literacy goals have been discussed and debated for the last half century. International and national forums have addressed questions of literacy in nations with massive and visible amounts of *il*literacy. Problems of defining literacy, setting national goals, measuring literacy, determining the effectiveness of different educational programs – discussions of these problems have had conditions in Third World nations as their reference point. Basically, *we* have been discussing *them*. Here lies one of our difficulties. Today, disclosures about the extent of functional illiteracy in the United States are forcing us to a reexamination of what literacy is and means to us. Surprisingly, we find few guidelines for this reappraisal. Little systematic attention has been given to

An article based on this talk given at the Planning Conference for a White House Conference on Library and Information Services, Washington, April 1979, appeared in the *American Journal of Education* 93 (1984): 6–22.

examining the role and future of literacy in technologically advanced countries of the world: countries with universal schooling, developed economies, and continual rapid advances in information-handling technologies. Our present educational programs rest on implicit assumptions that we know what basic literacy skills these social conditions require, and we are agreed as to what their utility will be in the years ahead for both society and the individual. We educate, after all, with a purpose in mind. But as soon as we question the effectiveness of existing programs, as soon as we attempt to design new programs to better meet the needs of populations now ill served, our disagreements surface: What counts as literacy today? What competencies are reasonable as minimal national standards? How should we determine long-range goals for the future? Should our educational programs acknowledge that literacy is a fading art of the past, or insist that it is a social and political necessity of the future?

Many points of view are urged on us, but I will organize my examination of prevailing concepts around three metaphoric labels: literacy as adaptation, literacy as power, and literacy as a state of grace. Each of these literacies has implicit in it different educational policies and goals; each makes certain assumptions about the social motivations for literacy and about the way literacy is practiced in our society. I will consider these metaphors schematically, attempting to show the limitations of each as a sole guide for educational and public policy programs.

Literacy as adaptation

This metaphor is designed to capture concepts of literacy that emphasize its survival or pragmatic value. When the term "functional literacy" was originally introduced during World War I, it specified the literacy skills required to meet the tasks of modern soldiering. Today, functional literacy is conceived broadly as the level of proficiency necessary for effective performance in a range of settings and customary activities.

This concept has a broad common-sense appeal. The necessity for literacy skills in daily life is obvious – on the job, riding around town, shopping for groceries – we all encounter situations requiring us to read or produce written symbols. No justification is needed to insist that schools are obligated to equip children with the literacy skills that will enable them to fulfill these mundane situational demands. And basic educational programs have a similar obligation to equip adults with the skills they must have to secure jobs or advance to better ones, receive the training and benefits to which they are entitled, and assume their civic and political responsibilities. Within the United States, as in the international arena, literacy programs with these practical aims are considered efforts at human resource development, and as such, contributors to economic growth and stability.

The conception of literacy as adaptive functional skills applied in the world –

not merely in schools – has given a powerful impetus to the improvement of educational programs. Yet functional literacy approaches are neither as straightforward nor as unproblematic as they first appear. Attempts to define "minimal functional competencies" to support specific instructional curricula have foundered on lack of information and divided goals. Is it realistic to try to specify some fixed set of skills as "functional literacy"? To what extent are the tasks included in functional literacy assessment surveys or tests representative of tasks individuals encounter in their daily lives? Are they equally representative of all economic and cultural groups? If not, how do they differ? If we were to consider the level of reading and writing activities carried out in small and isolated rural communities as the standard for functional literacy, educational objectives would be unduly restricted. At the other extreme, we might not want to use the literacy activities of college teachers as the standard determining the functional competencies required for high school graduation. We know little about the range of literacy activities practiced in different cultural communities within the United States nor how, and by whom, the required literacy work gets done. Lacking such knowledge, public discussions fluctuate between narrow definitions of functional skills pegged to immediate vocational and personal needs and sweeping definitions that virtually reinstate the ability to cope with college subject matter as the hallmark of literacy.

Adapting literacy standards to today's needs, personal or social, would be shortsighted. What about tomorrow's requirements? Controversy is sharper here. Forecasts based on the same projected trends come to different conclusions. Some argue that as economic and other activities become increasingly subject to computerized techniques of production and information-handling, even higher levels of literacy will be required of all. An equally plausible, contrary view is that the new technologies – talking typewriters, videodiscs – may reduce literacy requirements for all. Others argue that these technologies are in effect new systems of literacy: the ability to use minicomputers as information storage and retrieval devices requires mastery of symbol systems which would build on word literacy; they are second-order literacies, as it were. One possible scenario is that in coming decades, literacy requirements may be increased for some and reduced for others, accenting the present uneven, primarily class-based, distribution of literacy functions.

From the perspective of social needs, the seemingly well-defined concept of functional competency becomes fuzzy at the edges. Equally as many questions arise about functionality from the individual's point of view. Functional needs have not yet been assessed from the perspective of those who purportedly experience them. To what extent do adults whom tests assess as functionally illiterate perceive themselves as lacking the necessary skills to be adequate parents, neighbors, workers? Inner-city youngsters may have no desire to write letters to each other; raising one's reading level by a few grades may not be seen as a magic ticket to a job; not everyone has a bank account which requires the mastery of unusual forms. Appeals to individuals to enhance their functional skills might founder on the different subjective utilities communities and groups attach to reading and writing activities.

The functional approach has been hailed as a major advance over more traditional concepts of reading and writing because it takes into account the goals and settings of people's activities with written language. Yet even tender probing reveals the many questions of fact, value, and purpose that complicate its application to educational curricula.

We now turn to the second metaphor.

Literacy as power

While functional literacy stresses the importance of literacy to the adaptation of the individual, the literacy-as-power metaphor emphasizes a relationship between literacy and group or community advancement.

Historically, literacy has been a potent tool in maintaining the hegemony of elites and dominant classes in certain societies, while laying the basis for increased social and political participation in others. In a contemporary framework, expansion of literacy skills is often viewed as a means for poor and politically powerless groups to claim their place in the world. The International Symposium for Literacy, meeting in Persepolis, appealed to national governments to consider literacy as an instrument for human liberation and social change. Paulo Freire bases his influential theory of literacy education on the need to make literacy a resource for fundamental social transformation. Effective literacy education, in his view, creates a critical consciousness through which a community can analyze its conditions of social existence and engage in effective action for a more just society. Not to be literate is a state of victimization.

Yet the capacity of literacy to confer power or to be the primary impetus for significant and lasting economic or social change has proved problematic in developing countries. Studies of UNESCO's experimental world literacy program have raised doubts about earlier notions that increased literacy rates would automatically enhance national development and improve the social and material conditions of the very poor. The relationship between social change and literacy education, it is now suggested, may be stronger in the other direction. When masses of people have been mobilized for fundamental changes in social conditions – as in USSR, China, Cuba, Tanzania – rapid extensions of literacy have been accomplished. Movements to transform social reality appear to have been effective in some parts of the world in bringing whole populations into participation in modern literacy activities. The validity of the converse proposition – that literacy *per se* mobilizes people for action to change their social reality – remains to be established.

What does this mean for us? The one undisputed fact about illiteracy in

America is its concentration among poor, black, elderly, and minority language groups – groups without effective participation in our country's economic and educational institutions. Problems of poverty and political powerlessness are, as among some populations in developing nations, inseparably intertwined with problems of access to knowledge and levels of literacy skills. Some (e.g., Kozol) maintain that a Freire approach to literacy education is demanded in these conditions. Others (e.g., Hunter and Harman) advocate a more limited approach to community mobilization, seeing community social action as a first step in creating the conditions for effective literacy instruction and for educational equity.

The possibilities and limits of the literacy-as-power metaphor within our present-day social and political structure are not at all clear. To what extent can instructional experiences and programs be lifted out of their social contexts in other countries and applied here? Do assumptions about community integrity and the functionality of literacy in poor communities in the United States warrant further consideration? How are communities best mobilized for literacy: around local needs and through small-scale activism? or as part of some broader political or social goal? If literacy has not emerged as a grass-roots demand, should governmental and private agencies undertake to mobilize communities around this goal?

Literacy as a state of grace

Now we come to the third metaphor. I have variously called it literacy as salvation or literacy as a state of grace. Both labels are unsatisfactory because they give a specific religious interpretation to the broader phenomenon I want to depict – that is the tendency in many societies to endow the literate person with special virtues. A concern with preserving and understanding scripture is at the core of many religious traditions, Western and non-Western alike. As studies by the Resnicks have shown, the literacy-as-a-salvation metaphor had an almost literal interpretation in the practice of post-Luther Protestant groups to require of the faithful the ability to read and remember the Bible and other religious material. Older religious traditions – Hebraic and Islamic – have also traditionally invested the written word with great power and respect. "This is a perfect book. There is no doubt in it," reads a passage from the Qur'an. Memorizing the Qur'an – literally taking its words into you and making them part of yourself – is simultaneously a process of becoming both literate and holy.

The attribution of special powers to those who are literate has its ancient secular roots as well. Plato and Aristotle strove to distinguish the man of letters from the poet of oral tradition. In the perspective of Western humanism, literateness has come to be considered synonymous with being "cultured" – using the term in the old-fashioned sense to refer to a person who is knowledgeable about the content and techniques of the sciences, arts, and humanities as they have evolved historically. The term sounds elitist and archaic but the notion that participation in a literate – that is, bookish – tradition enlarges and develops a person's essential self is pervasive and still undergirds the concept of a liberal education. No one shows more eloquently than George Steiner the continuity of the culture of the book in Western traditions, the extent to which "cultured-ness" consists of knowing the book that begins before Plato and may now, in his view, be entering its last edition. In the literacy-as-a-state-of-grace concept, the power and functionality of literacy is not bounded by political or economic parameters, but in a sense transcends them; the literate individual's life derives its meaning and significance from intellectual, aesthetic, and spiritual participation in the accumulated creations and knowledge of humankind made available through the written word.

The self-enhancing aspects of literacy are often given a cognitive interpretation. For centuries, and increasingly in our own generation, appeals have been made for increased attention to literacy as a way of developing minds. An individual who is illiterate, says a recent UN publication, is bound to concrete thinking and cannot learn new material. Teachers of college English in the United States urge greater prominence for writing in the curriculum as a way of promoting logical reasoning and critical thinking. Literate and nonliterate individuals presumably are not only in different states of grace but in different stages of intellectual development as well.

But, again, we run into boundary problems of this metaphor. For one thing, we need to know how widely dispersed in our society is this admiration of book knowledge? To what extent are beliefs about the value of literateness shared across social classes? ethnic groups? religious groups? How does book culture – more accurately, how do book cultures articulate with the multiple and diverse oral cultures flourishing in the United States? Which people value literacy as a preserver of their history? or endow their folk heroes with book learning? Are there broad cultural supports for book learning among wide sectors of the population? Or, as some maintain, is written literacy culture created by the ethno-centric interests of a small elite? McLuhan and others have insisted that written literacy is a vestige of a disappearing "culture." Is this point of view defensible? And if so, what implications does it pose for our educational objectives?

I have described some current positions toward literacy education in terms of three metaphors. I have tried to indicate that each metaphor arises from other, more fundamental concepts of conditions fostering individual literacy, concepts and assumptions that until recently were not subject to study. Today, many scholars and educators are beginning to examine actual literacy practices and attitudes to arrive at a more fully rounded approach to literacy education than any single metaphor encompasses.

My own consideration of the question "what is literacy" was prompted by my research experiences in a traditional West African society. Together with my colleagues, I spent five years studying the social and intellectual consequences of literacy among the Vai people of West Africa. If you picture a National Geographic photograph of a bush village in equatorial Africa, you will have a sense of the material conditions of Vai life – wattle and mud or concrete houses in a clearing; no electricity, water, or telephone; few clinics, few schools, dirt roads often impassable in the rainy season. To the casual observer Vai society is the very prototype of traditional nonliterate subsistence farming societies. Yet the Vai have invented an original phonetic writing system. This script – a syllabary of over 200 characters – has been in use in village life for over 150 years. It has been passed on in tutorial fashion without benefit of an institution like a school or the formation of a professional teacher group. In addition to this indigenous script, literacy in the Arabic and Roman alphabets also flourishes in the countryside. The Vai are a Muslim people and the Arabic script is the literacy for religious practice and theological learning. Missionaries and, more recently, the Liberian government have been disseminating English literacy, the official government literacy, through the establishment of Western-style schools. About one-third of the Vai male population is literate in one of these scripts, the majority in the Vai script. Many read and write both Vai and Arabic and some outstanding scholars are literate in all three scripts. Since each writing system has a different orthography, represents a different language, and is learned in a different setting, becoming literate in two or more scripts is an impressive intellectual accomplishment. Why do people take the trouble to do it? And, in particular, what has maintained the Vai script in the face of competition from two universal and institutionally powerful scripts?

Certain obvious answers are ruled out. Literacy is clearly not a necessity for personal survival. As far as we would determine, nonliteracy status does not exclude a person from full participation in economic activities or in town or society life. As we look around Vai country and see the major activities and institutions continuing to function in the traditional oral mode, we are at a loss to define the literacy competencies that might be useful in everyday life. But Vai literates have not been at such a loss and have found no end of useful functions. On the average, for example, they write two to forty letters a month in personal correspondence. Letters commonly pass from hand to hand in one small town. The arrival of a taxi often brings letters in Vai script from relatives or friends in distant parts of Liberia – bearing family news or appeals for credit, or begging for release from debts. Since Vai society, like other traditional societies, maintains an effective oral grapevine system, reasons for the popularity of letter-writing are not self-evident – especially since all letters must be personally sent and hand delivered. Yet literates find the advantage of secrecy and guarantee of delivery more than compensation for the time and trouble spent in writing. Scholars speculate that the usefulness of the Vai script in protecting secrets and allowing clandestine resistance to the central governing machinery of Libera, whose official literacy was English, were important factors in the establishment and longevity of the script.

On closer study, we find that Vai script literacy also serves many personal and public record-keeping functions. Household heads keep albums for family births, deaths, and marriages; some maintain lists of dowry items and death feast contributions that help to regulate kinship exchanges. Records also enlarge the scope and planful aspects of commercial transactions: artisans maintain lists of customers; farmers record the yield and income from cash-crop farming. The script also serves a variety of administrative purposes such as recording house tax payments and political contributions. Some fraternal and religious organizations maintain records in Vai script. All of these activities fit nicely into the metaphor of literacy as functional adaptation, and the only surprising aspect is that so many varieties of pragmatic uses occur under circumstances which would seem to generate little environmental press for literacy.

But not all literacy uses are so narrowly adaptive. Vai script has not been used to produce public books or manuscripts; there is no recorded cultural archive, nor has the script been developed as an educational medium to impart new knowledge and information. In this sense, Vai script literacy is restricted. Yet in the privacy of their homes, Vai literates engage in creative acts of composition with the script. Almost everyone keeps a diary; some write down maxims and traditional tales in copybooks; others maintain rudimentary town histories; some write down their dreams and tales of advice to their children; a few who might qualify as scholars produce extended family and clan histories. Townspeople, when questioned about the value of the script, will often cite its utilitarian functions, but will equally as often speak about its importance for self-education and knowledge. Vai script literates are known in the community, are accorded respect, and are sought out for their information and help as personal scribes or as town clerks. A Vai parable about the relative merits of money, power, and book learning for success in this world concludes with the judgment that the "man who knoweth book passeth all."

Why this excursion into a case of African literacy after our metaphoric discussion of the goals of literacy education in a technological society? Perhaps because Vai society – much simpler than ours in the range of literacy functions it calls for – nonetheless serves to highlight some of our unnecessary simplicities in attempting to define the one best set of goals in literacy education. Suppose we were called on as experts to devise literacy education programs for the Vai people – which metaphor would dominate our recommendations? Would we emphasize the spread of functional competencies, urging all farmers to keep crop records and all carpenters to list customers? This surely would be an effective approach for some but, just as surely, it would neglect the interests and aspirations of others. Should we appeal to the cultural pride of the populace, suggesting Vai script literacy be extended as an instrument for group cohesion and social change? We might count on support for this appeal, but resistance as well: Qur'anic schools and the network of Muslim teachers and scholars are a powerful counterforce to the Vai script and a countervailing center for cultural cohesion. Moreover, families participating in the Vai script tradition do not necessarily repudiate participation in English literacy as well; it is prudent to have one or more children in English school as well as Qur'anic school. As for literacy as a state of grace, aspirations for self-improvement and social status clearly sustain many aspects of Vai literacy both in the Arabic religious and Vai secular traditions. A diversity of pragmatic, ideological, and intellectual factors sustains popular literacy among the Vai.

Is there any reason for us to expect literacy aspirations of our diverse population to be more uniform and impoverished or to fit more neatly into the favorite metaphors we employ for establishing literacy education goals?

None of the three aspects of literacy we examined in our metaphors is exclusive of the others, and none captures the full reality of the complex social aspects of literacy in our own society. Our analysis suggests that there is no one best answer to the question, what is literacy? Even the more focused question of what is the role of or the future of literacy in America needs to take into account the different aspects of literacy. One might imagine, for example, that in the years ahead literacy will become vocationally less important but maintain its current level of political importance; or that literateness will outstrip functional competence as a literacy ideal for certain sections of the population – or one can write other combinations of the future. If we want to make best use of the resources we have for advancing literacy in all its aspects, it appears we need to begin by broadening our vocabulary of metaphors.

17   Observations on literacy education
in China

Functional literacy has emerged in our own and other industrialized countries as a distinctive, and publicly prominent, educational concern. At one time, many believed that "literacy" and "schooling" are co-terminous; today we recognize that the relationship between schooling and functional literacy skills is a complicated matter. As issues involving literacy have become more complex, United States educational researchers have broadened their learning and teaching questions beyond those traditionally covered in classical reading research. Experiences of other nations are of particular interest now, because of the innovative educational approaches these countries have devised to meet inherited problems of widespread child and adult literacy.

Even if literacy had not been a priority research topic of several of us on the 1980 NIE delegation, a study of educational research in China would not have been complete without a look at its literacy programs, which are considered an outstanding world achievement (*World of Literacy*, 1979[1]). Also, I can offer a personal interest: much of my professional life in the past ten years has been devoted to studying social and psychological factors involved in popular literacy. I hoped to learn more about what lay behind China's success story – and to satisfy as well a haunting skepticism: Given the complexities of China's writing system and shortages of teaching personnel, could mass popular literacy actually be achieved through short-term literacy campaigns?

As it turned out, we had time only to nibble away at these questions. We obtained almost all of our information on literacy in one meeting in Chengdu[2] with the head of the adult education unit of the municipal education bureau

This essay originally appeared in *The Linguistic Reporter* 25, 3 (1–4). Reprinted with the permission of the Center for Applied Linguistics.

and his counterpart from the Sichuan provincial bureau. Other discussions provided some corroborative information and useful background knowledge, but our report remains factually meagre, with detailed statistics only for Sichuan Province. It may still be useful as an up-date of earlier information and for the broader research questions it suggests.

I will begin with a factual description of the status of literacy education and research as reported to us and then make some interpretive comments on issues that are of general concern.

Extent of literacy

Since 1955, the People's Republic of China has been engaged in a massive national effort to achieve universal literacy. Before liberation in 1949, the illiteracy rate was an estimated 80%–90% (*World of Literacy*). Today, according to officials of the Chinese Central Educational Research Institute, some 140 million individuals are illiterate, representing approximately 14% of the total population (estimated here as one billion). We are told that this figure is the outcome of a nationwide count in which literacy was assessed by the administration of locally developed tests. (We have no detailed information on the date or nature of this census nor its verification. It was not clear, for example, whether the count of illiterates includes children or is confined to youth and adults. We have some suggestion that the reference population is the working population. Recent estimates by outside demographers give this population as 622 million people (15–64 year age range). Measured against this base, the illiteracy rate would amount to 22.5%.)

As in other nations, nonliteracy is unevenly distributed throughout the populace; it is concentrated among the peasantry and inhabitants of more isolated mountain regions. Statistics provided for Sichuan Province give some sense of the distribution pattern. In this county, the age range of 12–45 years is the main target for literacy efforts. Among peasants in this bracket, 27% are reported as still nonliterate; in contrast, fewer than 1% of office and factory workers in the same age range in Chengdu municipality are nonliterate; and the literacy rate for farmers on the outskirts of that city is reported as higher than for the Province as a whole.

The city-country differential is familiar to literacy workers world-wide, but the discrepancies reported to us in Sichuan Province reflect, at least in part, priorities established by educational authorities there. With a limited number of teachers, the ministry decided to work first in the big cities and communities in the plains regions; proceed to hill regions; then to remote mountain areas, and finally to minority nationalities. "We started our work in easier places and then went step by step to more difficult places" (Mr. Gong Chenhen).

Chengdu municipality also observed a set of priorities when "big literacy movements" unfolded after liberation: first office workers, then in descending order, factory workers, peasants in the outskirts, and citizens of the city. By 1955, "most office and factory workers had reached the level of graduates of junior middle school" (Mr. Lung Kuiyan). During the ten years of the cultural revolution, adult education programs were scuttled, we were told. We have no current figures on overall educational levels of the urban work force to compare with those offered for 1955. The personnel of the #1 Cotton Mill on the outskirts of Chengdu, however, a factory that has somewhat more than 10,000 employees (60% female), confirmed that workers' educational needs now are primarily at middle school and technical levels, and that basic literacy among them is a near-universal. Today, Chengdu municipal literacy activities are concentrated on "peasants in the outskirts," with gains reported for post-cultural-revolution years as follows: 70,000 peasants reached literacy levels in 1979 and 30,000 in 1980. Chengdu expected to realize the Central Ministry of Education's target of 80% literacy among the peasants in its municipality by 1981. By self-report, Chengdu has one of the best records in the country in literacy education.

Measures of literacy

Standards of basic literacy are set by the Central Ministry of Education; current guidelines were issued in 1978. In light of the many definitional controversies surrounding literacy and its measurement, China's solution to the problem of determining minimal literacy levels is an interesting amalgam of traditional and contemporary approaches. Basic literacy is measured by the number of script characters an individual has learned; this measure reflects the emphasis on a set amount of knowledge and skill that is characteristic of traditional literacy assessments. This criterion, however, is in turn determined by functional considerations – what a person must know to function in his/her milieu – the dominant conception of literacy in present-day international literacy programs. China has chosen to define functionality as reading newspapers and writing letters, and has determined the number of characters required for these activities. In practice, however, more seems to be involved in functional competence than newspaper reading and letter-writing; different standards have been set for industrial and agricultural populations. A criterion of 1,500 characters is considered sufficient for literacy tasks peasants are likely to encounter whereas workers are thought to need 2,000 characters to fulfill literacy requirements in production.

To put these numbers in some perspective we can compare them to the 2,500 characters children are required to learn in the first two or three years of school (learning time varies with instructional method); with the 3,000 "most often used characters" and with the 6,196 standardized script characters used in printed material. Using a simple arithmetic comparison, minimal functional literacy for peasants at work is approximately 60% of the level of children in their fourth year of primary school; it may well be that neither number represents an acceptable functional level but is rather considered a "generative threshold" for further learning, each adapted to its special setting. School children, for example, are expected to go on to master 3,000–3,500 characters by the end of the sixth grade and the set of 1,500 characters constituting the minimal adult standard includes 500 independent characters, which, the Chengdu representative told us, might rapidly lead to learning additional combined characters of which they are components. Sichuan officials also told us the 1,500-character criterion was determined by research, but did not describe its nature. By whatever method the number was initially set, it may receive continuing validation (or invalidation) through the examination program conducted in spare-time literacy courses. Inspection groups (it is not clear from my notes which administrative unit they represent) administer three exams to students as tests of basic literacy proficiency: (*a*) character recognition (the worker-student must know 85% of 2,000); (*b*) reading a passage from a newspaper; (*c*) writing some letters. Correlations among scores might be used to determine relationships among character knowledge and comprehension and production of written material, but we were given no indication that this kind of analysis was or is being carried out.

Literacy education programs

Literacy education is conducted under guidelines set by the Central Ministry of Education, but textbooks are compiled by each province. In Sichuan, consideration is "given to the needs of production" in determining textbook content. Yet the same textbooks are used in all classes, whatever the auspices. In the countryside, many education departments are involved, paralleling organizational levels of production (commune, brigade, and team). In the city, management and union-sponsored courses are given in factories and offices; block committees in large cities such as Beijing organize reading and writing classes; and many other settings and organizational units also seem to be involved.

Some basic literacy programs are offered on a full-time basis, with estimated time needed to reach criterion variously reported as 2 to 3 months (Chengdu municipal education official) and 4 months (education director of #1 Cotton Mill). As is true of all mass literacy campaigns, the bulk of the work is carried out through spare-time classes. These are held two to three times a week as group sessions with a teacher. In #1 Cotton Mill in Chengdu, literacy classes meet twice a week after the work shift for one-and-a-half-hour sessions; members of the Communist Youth League also give individualized coaching there. In our Chengdu meeting we were told that it takes spare-time students about one year to learn the required 1,500 characters. Translated into hours (assuming twice-a-week classes and one and a half hours per class), approximately 150 hours of classroom instruction are required for attainment of minimal literacy.

(Evaluations of literacy programs conducted under UNESCO's Experimental Worldwide Literacy Program [*World of Literacy*, 1979] have found that, on the average, adults master basic skills taught in primary schools in 200 hours. Nevertheless, the concept "basic skills taught in primary schools" is too ambiguous to help us place the Chinese experience in proper international perspective. Our ignorance of the actual content of "basic literacy" in China, or elsewhere for that matter, further complicates an attempt to appraise the efficacy of instruction. One informative comparison is with reported literacy acquisition rates among primary school children in China. Under the concentrated reading method that involves both learning of characters and reading with comprehension, and daily lessons, children are said to be able to master 500 script characters the first half year and 700–800 the following semester. This is a considerably slower rate than demonstrated by adults in spare-time classes.)

Mr. Lung Kuiyun of Chengdu Municipal Education Bureau talked at some length about how adult literacy teaching differs from primary school teaching, and how adults learn faster than children. "Adults have more life experience and children cannot compare with them. For example, adults use many words in conversations and know their meanings before they start to read." (Mr. Kuiyun's example was the word *discussion*.) He claimed that the concentrated reading method, which combines memorization of characters with reading, was invented in adult education programs (another source said it was first introduced in army literacy courses), and that it is more effective with adults than with children. According to Mr. Kuiyun, the major national problem is not learning but "consolidation." The retention problem is particularly acute in the country: "Because farmers are busy in work and have less time to review lessons," follow-up is needed to ensure consolidation of learning. This problem seems to be attacked largely by encouraging continuing classroom education. Literacy learning is seen as only the first link in a comprehensive program of worker and peasant education that includes spare-time, and some full-time courses covering the primary and middle school curricular technical training, and TV university courses. As we pointed out earlier, continuing education is now predominant among factory workers in Chengdu. The same range of courses is provided in the countryside but the basic literacy/continuing education ratio is the opposite of that reported for the industrial population. The following are enrollment figures for Sichuan Province farmers:

Peasant enrollment in Sichuan Province, 1980

Basic literacy	330,000
Short technical courses	100,000
Primary school	28,000
Middle school	30,000

Some observations

China's commitment to universal literacy seems unquestionable and its progress toward this goal impressive. As in other socialist countries that have been acclaimed for their literacy achievements (USSR, Cuba, to some extent Tanzania; see *World of Literacy*) socialist philosophy on human development, combined with planning and organizational resources, has led to achievements in mass education that often elude other basically agrarian societies. At the present time, China's commitment to worker and peasant education is also undergirded by its modernization aims. Education ministry personnel spoke emphatically on China's need to raise the technical level of its production force, especially in industry; this is now one of the principal objectives of adult education. This emphasis, of course, may impose a new set of priorities on literacy education; and this brings us to questions that require further attention.

One such question is the extent of literacy today. It is somewhat difficult to square the officially cited 14% illiteracy figure nationwide with the detailed picture we secured in Sichuan Province and with the information that an 80% literacy rate still remains to be achieved among the peasantry there. All indications suggest that popular literacy has been achieved in urban areas, but substantial segments of the adult rural population still lack functional literacy skills. How "substantial" is a question we cannot address.

Several strands of evidence point to the unfinished nature of China's mass literacy efforts. Officials of the Central Educational Research Institute acknowledged concern with the continuing problem of illiteracy. Three groups make up the nonliterate sector: adults not yet reached by literacy programs; "newly emerging illiterates" among children who either do not enter school or leave without attaining minimal skills; and once-literate adults who "forgot the characters." Special problems presented by these latter groups are recognized. Institute representatives listed as one of their major educational problems the fact that completion of primary school is not universal: The ranks of nonliterate children and youth will continue to swell. They also felt the quality of spare-time worker and peasant education is low. Sichuan officials stressed the gravity of the retention problem. China is not alone in finding that adult minimal literacy is often a transitory accomplishment. But we know that retention rates are very much affected by whether or not a "critical level" of adult literacy has been achieved, sufficient to sustain a popular climate of literacy and individual skills. (The critical level is estimated at 60%–70% of a nation's adult population; *World of Literacy*. I have not seen any estimates for regions or communities.) I interpret China's consolidation problem as indicating, at least in part, that literacy has not yet penetrated certain areas of the countryside in that reading and writing activities are naturally encountered, or required, in the daily practice of farming or in social and recreational pursuits.

Although China's literacy programs represent a tremendous mobilization of national resources, it seems that even in early stages they followed a priority policy. It will be interesting to see whether the present emphasis on building a more skilled work force will drain resources from rural areas or whether efforts will continue, or intensify, to complete the "literacization" of the peasantry.

We had no way of judging the efficiency of literacy programs. Some educators we met expressed the opinion that literacy acquisition would be accelerated if the script were simplified or alphabetized, but this sentiment was not expressed by Sichuan adult education people. The necessity of memorizing a large number of characters before reading can begin may account for the top-down, didactic nature of the literacy instruction described to us and for the use of uniform textbooks. This approach stands in contrast to the "inductive, participatory" approach that international literacy analysts report as most effective in other industrializing nations (see *World of Literacy*).

We had no opportunity to see literacy instruction in progress, and educational interactions may be richer and more varied, and involve more local participation in curriculum, than our report suggests. On the other hand, it may be that China's experience is instructive as a caution against overemphasis on the search for a "one best technique."

In one aspect, China's adult literacy activities are much like ours and those of other countries: Research is not an integral component. It is true that research was credited with establishing the functional literacy criterion of 1,500 characters. But basic research in adult education was not mentioned as an ongoing or planned-for activity by any group – education ministry officials, psychologists, or university personnel. The Central Research Institute has a research section on early childhood education but none on adult education. Developmental psychology models go only as far as Piaget's adolescent period. The Institute of Psychology is stressing research and pedagogy for preschool children. Although the concentrated reading method was reported as effective with adults, evaluative studies on this method seem to be restricted to child populations. We heard of no studies specifically directed at the consolidation problem of adult learners. Given the importance attached to worker and peasant education in China, and insights shared with us as to the special needs and learning competencies of adults, it would seem that research might serve a useful function in this domain as well as make a contribution to scientific knowledge in general.

On a less grandiose scale, detailed descriptive reports and documentations of literacy programs would be most helpful to other nations, including our own, which are still seeking to break down age-old barriers in access to the written word.

Notes

1. To put the account of China's literacy programs in some comparative context, I have used as a major reference work an analysis of world literacy programs that draws on authoritative UN and scholarly sources:

International Council for Adult Education. M. Gayter; B. Hall; J. R. Kidd; & V. Shrivasrava. *The World of Literacy: Policy, Research and Action.* Toronto: International Development Centre, 1979. (Cited as *World of Literacy*).

2. Our primary source of information was an evening meeting in Chengdu held October 15, 1980. Participating for the U.S. delegation were Michael Timpane, Director of the National Institute of Education, and myself.

   Chinese representatives were:

   Mr. Lung Kuiyun
   The Research Group on Education of Workers and Peasants
   Chengdu Municipal Education Bureau
   Sichuan

   Mr. Gong Ghenhen
   Section of Education of Workers and Peasants
   Sichuan Administration Bureau of Education
   Chengdu, Sichuan

   I am also drawing here on comments on literacy made in the following meetings: delegation meeting with representatives of the Central Institute for Educational Research and Editorial Department of *Education Research* magazine, held October 3rd in Beijing; meeting with the Director of the Political Department, Director of Education, and numerous other personnel of the #1 Cotton Mill of Sichuan Province, October 14th. Other meetings and conversations contributed background information.

18   Studying literacy at work: Bringing the laboratory to the field

In the last months, my colleagues and I have driven around town on a 3 A.M. milk route, helped cashiers total their receipts and watched machine operators logging in their production for the day. On these and other occasions, we made detailed records of how people were going about performing their jobs. We collected copies of all written materials they read or produced – everything from notes scribbled on brown paper bags to computer print-outs. We photographed devices in their working environment that required them to process other types of symbolic information – thermometers, gauges, scales, measuring instruments of all kinds.

We undertook these activities as part of the research study described here as naturalistic observations of industrial literacy. What is their purpose? What kind of evidence will they yield and what bearing will such evidence have on the educational objectives with which this conference is concerned – enabling all people to achieve a level of mastery of basic skills that will enhance their effective participation in society?

We can begin with the first part of the question – our objectives. These dictated our research strategy and set us off on our efforts to combine anthropological field work techniques with techniques of task analysis developed in psychology laboratories. Ours is a multi-method study and I will describe briefly how we are trying to integrate field work and lab work. We are still at the midway point of our study and I have no firm conclusions to report; but to illustrate our procedures and foreshadow likely outcomes, I will describe two work tasks involving literacy that we have analyzed in some detail and that display features that seem to be widely shared in what I refer to as *practical*

This is an incomplete draft of an oral presentation at the NIE Conference on Basic Skills for Productivity and Participation held May 22–23, 1980. Scribner wrote a more formal version entitled "Naturalistic Observation of Basic Skills at Work" to be included in a final report of the Conference, in 1981, entitled "Basic Skills and Employability."

223

literacy. With this information before us, I will speculate on the contribution our own and similar studies might make to equity objectives in education and employment. As with every line of research, these contributions can be expected to be partial and modest.

Purpose

One obvious reason we have been observing how people use literacy on their jobs is to document the role of symbolic information in the workaday world. But this is not our central aim. Our central aim is to develop methods for analyzing the specific cognitive and linguistic operations that are involved in on-the-job literacy activities. Traditionally, the type of analysis that seeks to identify underlying processes involved in reading and writing has been characterized as basic research; it has been carried out primarily in psychology laboratories, and recently extended to classroom settings as well.

This research has been valuable in providing a sounder foundation for instructional practices, but we believe that it needs to be supplemented by analytic studies of reading, writing and arithmetic in non-academic, non-laboratory settings. We make this claim because there are grounds to believe that what we loosely call "basic skills" may in fact be quite different when they are applied in different settings, even if they look the same on the surface. Common sense has it that counting is counting and reading is reading. Yes, but – the particular operations comprising these complex activities may be quite varied – we can reach a proper sum counting by sixes as well as by ones (using six as a unit of count is characteristic of one of the occupations we studied). And recent research has shown such variability to be common in reading as well as math. Since much of this paper will be devoted to supporting this claim from our own research, I want to lay out the logical line of argument which leads from the notion of variation in basic skills to the strategy of conducting observational studies in the workplace.

1. We start with the fact that one important source of variability is the goal or purpose for which reading, writing or arithmetic activities are carried out. Sticht, Frase, Rothkopf and others have shown, for example, that how a reader interprets information may be highly sensitive to the requirements of the particular reading task at hand.

2. On the basis of common knowledge, we expect that tasks involving literacy and math outside of school settings may differ in certain significant respects from tasks encountered in school. Here is one obvious difference. In school, reading and arithmetic tasks are often ends in themselves. When a student reads a passage, her task is to demonstrate that she has read that passage with comprehension; when given an arithmetic problem, her task is to show that she has learned certain rules of arithmetic. Research on literacy and basic skills has been almost exclusively devoted to analysis of these school-type tasks. But our

very first observations in the workplace revealed that literacy and math activities here – especially in the blue collar operations – have quite a different structure. When we approach a mechanic or a truck driver studying a piece of paper and ask him: "What are you doing?" – we never get the answer, "I am reading." Instead, we get replies of this sort: "I'm fixing this engine. I'm planning how to load these products on my truck." (See Sticht's distinction between reading to learn and reading to do.) Reading in these examples – and writing and math in others – are instrumental activities; that is, they are embedded in other larger systems of activity and serve to accomplish definite behavioral goals. We would thus expect that the way they are actually carried out will be affected by the conditions and requirements of these larger job tasks. That is our second starting point.

3. The third starting point is this: if the knowledge and skills involved in various literacy activities are affected by the tasks they are used to carry out, we need to be cautious in generalizing from performance in one setting to performance in another. We need especially to be cautious about the conclusions we draw about individual competencies on the basis of samples of literacy behavior that are tied to the kinds of tasks that arise in school or tests. Minority and working class youth report to us (this is impressionist evidence only) that they often can pick up math or reading skills they need on the job, while school assignments gave them trouble.

Research needs follow: we need to extend the range of the literacy and math phenomena we study. We have to become naturalists, as it were, and locate different species of tasks requiring literacy and math skills. We need systematic investigation of how these skills vary with the requirements and conditions of job tasks. Are these variations haphazard or are they rule-governed? Can we identify the rules? Can we specify component work-related literacy and math skills with sufficient precision to enable us to develop some typical models of work-based literacy so that we can compare these models to models developed on the basis of laboratory and school tasks?

A tall order – beyond the capacity of one research project. What we undertook to do was to see what would be involved in carrying out such a program. What methods would be useful? Could we secure needed cooperation from employers and workers who are not part of a captive population as school-children and army recruits are? What problems do we face in trying to carry out a functional analysis of actual tasks?

We designed a three-tier approach. Rather than pick scattered industrial occupations here and there, we decided to select a plant whose production system we could get to know well. We would let this knowledge be our guide to the selection of literacy-related tasks that were significant within the system as a whole and were amenable to study. We would begin with an ethnography of the plant, focused on literacy functions within it; our second tier of fact-gathering would be detailed descriptions of selected literacy-related tasks as actually carried out under normal day-to-day working conditions. Our third phase will consist of using these descriptions to generate models of the component processes involved in these tasks and test out these models in laboratory-like experiments and interviews.

We were invited by both management and union to conduct our study in a medium-sized milk processing plant in a nearby city. I'll call it Good Stuff Dairy (its initials are GSD). Good Stuff Dairy, with some 300 employees, was neither too large to be overwhelming nor too small to include a representative array of blue- and white-collar occupations. In fact, GSD has a broad spectrum of jobs – machine operations to engineers and mechanics and office personnel. It runs a fleet of wholesale and retail delivery trucks, operates a garage and a small laboratory, and runs a retail store on the premises.

Two of us spent some eight or nine months conducting our ethnography; we engaged in all the observational, interview and collecting activities I spoke about in my opening remarks. This phase of our research is completed. I can't communicate the results of an ethnography in three minutes, but as I proceed to describe some of the critical literacy-related tasks we identified and have begun to analyze, I think you will readily see the usefulness of the background information we were able to bring to our analysis.

Almost all written materials circulating in Good Stuff Dairy are company-produced forms and most of them take entries requiring some arithmetic computation. By last count, we had collected some 250 different forms in an environment that we would not ordinarily consider literacy-rich. One form – a load out order form – is the life line of the system. Produced in the computer room, in a four-part format, it circulates to inventory men and loaders in the ice box, to wholesale drivers and back through driver supervisors, and cashiers and billing clerks to the computer room. Every occupation engages in different interactions with this form. Wholesale drivers fill out two columns of numbers. One column takes the number of units of each product he expects to need for his route the following day – say 56 gallons of homogenized milk or 896 half-pints of chocolate milk. On the next day, the driver will need to calculate the prices for each of these products – the homogenized milk, the chocolate milk and so on. So, there are two entries –one, we will call a product estimate, the other a product price. Consider the estimate first. Reading the number 56 or the number 896, we might think that filling in the product estimate was extraordinarily simple and mundane. Because we were familiar with all aspects of the production and delivery system and had talked with and made detailed observations of the drivers completing the forms, we knew this simplicity was deceptive. A first complication is that products come loaded on the trucks in standard-sized cases, not units – 9 gallons to the case, 16 quarts to the case, 48 half-pints to the case. Forecasts are based on standard delivery orders and these orders are expressed in cases, or cases and units, not simply units. So, when the driver is making his estimate in unit figures, he is engaged in a set of math processes known in the Dairy as casing out – converting from case quantities to unit quantities. From our observations, much of this casing out is handled in the head, so to speak, without the aid of calculator or paper and pencil. But casing out is only the tip of the iceberg. The information the driver uses about his standard order to arrive at an estimate of units needed for the next day is only one input into the estimation process: perhaps sales have been slow for one supermarket customer and he can't store his usual number of quarts of skim. Cutting that customer's allocation will reduce the total number of quarts of skim the driver has to take out on his truck. But that leaves room for additional quarts of buttermilk, and we have hardly begun to list the considerations and entailments that enter into an experienced driver's forecast of next day's delivery. At one time the Dairy had attempted to have such estimates handled by the computer, but the effort was withdrawn; computer estimates were unsatisfactory. So we have a column of entries that are estimates of units needed. Now, as it turns out, while the processes leading up to this estimate are complex, the figures put down on the forecast sheet are not exactly precise but sometimes have the nature of "ball park figures." Again this is more than anecdotal evidence. Because we had complete access to records in the plant, we could inspect forecast sheets of individual drivers, compare what they said they needed with their delivery tickets which showed what they actually delivered on those days, and with their truck inventories which showed what they had left at the end of the day. This is how we could determine the degree of match or accuracy typically achieved in the estimation task. There is room in the system for a range of satisfactory answers, and, barring serious misjudgment or miscalculation, the driver will suffer no repercussions from an estimate that results in some carry-over to the next day.

Now let's turn to the task we have called pricing out the product. Here the driver must determine and enter on the form the total value of each type of product he is ordering. He has a product price list for this purpose. This list gives prices in units – quarts, pints, gallons – not in cases. This arithmetic seems to be a straightforward multiplication problem: multiply number of units by unit price and use the hand calculator (all drivers now carry them) for the big number problems. Not so straightforward. Of the four drivers we have observed doing pricing out tasks, none went down the list handling all price computations in this manner. We have documented four different solution strategies. Several involve using information on the case conversion factor. Faced with a problem of computing the value of 32 quarts of homogenized milk, one driver consistently converted 32 quarts to 2 cases, plugged in the case price, simplifying the multiplication to a doubling operation. The wholesale driver I rode with had prepared a "crib sheet" – a listing of prices by case for his most frequent products and by multiples of cases on high-volume items. This spontaneous act of literacy would not be captured by a formal analysis of the driver's task or simple inspection of official forms; it was captured in our naturalistic observations. One final comment on the pricing out task: the exactitude of the figures in this column count. Ball-park estimates won't do. The driver is held accountable to the penny for the value of the products he takes out on his truck.

One form that has to be filled out, two tasks involving computations, and heuristic strategies that seem well adapted to the precision requirements that accounting and production needs set for these tasks.

Now what we have been able to do thus far through observation and interview, backed up by an analysis of documents, has been to uncover some of the ways in which drivers transform arithmetic tasks and the different calculational strategies that bring to bear in their solution. We do not yet know whether certain strategies are applied only to a certain class of items; and we don't know whether the driver's frequent practice with case conversions has given him special skills in dividing and multiplying by factors such as 16 or 32 – common unit conversion factors. For such questions we turn away from naturalistic observations to the administration of devised tasks. We are constructing a simulated pricing out task, using a set of critical problems that we devise to help us answer such questions.

My second illustration concerns not math, but reading knowledge.
(Draft ends here.)

Note

1. This research study is funded by a grant from the Ford Foundation. My colleagues are Evelyn Jacob, anthropologist and co-investigator, and Edward Fahrmeier, a psychologist now specializing in reading research.

19   Introduction: *The future of literacy in a changing world*

As we know from experience in many fields, a comparative approach offers an opportunity to tackle basic questions concerning constancy and variety in human affairs that cannot be addressed by concentration on a single setting. In the case of literacy development it is evident that countries can best benefit from each other's experience if comparative research sorts out those aspects of literacy that are constant across cultures ("universals") and those that vary ("culture-specific" features). Universals and differences, of course, are only determinable within a particular theoretical framework and disciplinary perspective. The chapters that follow clearly illustrate this contingency relationship. Brian Street draws on cultural anthropology and evidence from historical and ethnographic case studies to argue that the model of a universal literacy, defined in technical terms, is inconsistent with actual social practices; the functions and meanings of literacy, and its impact on social relationships, vary with the power structure and belief systems in a given society. John Downing distills an extensive body of research, conducted primarily by psychologists, to support the thesis that basic processes of literacy acquisition are universal, although effective educational practices need to take into account the specific features of literacy use and learning in particular communities. Jeanne Chall, on the basis of psychological studies of reading, maintains that an invariant sequence characterizes reading development, not only among children of all societies, but among adults as well.

An interesting feature of these contributions is that analyses conducted primarily from the psychologist's perspective emphasize the universal aspects of

This essay originally appeared in D. A. Wagner, *The Future of Literacy in a Changing World* (Philadelphia: University of Pennsylvania, 1987), pp. 19–24. Reprinted with the permission of the Literacy Research Center, Graduate School of Education, University of Pennsylvania.

literacy, while those contributed by social and historical scientists stress variety and relativity. As several contributors to this volume (e.g., Carraher, Reder, Wagner) observe, there is an unresolved and underlying tension between models of literacy based on studies of psychological processes and models based on social processes at the macro-level. They do not seem to fit well together into a larger picture, and sometimes generate conflicting implications for literacy programs and policies.

This problem of integrating findings generated from psychological and social sciences is not unique to scholars of literacy. It reflects basic theoretical problems of long standing for which over the years various resolutions have been proposed (see Leacock, 1985, for a historical review of efforts in anthropology to provide an integrative frame; Wertsch and Lee, 1984, cite similar efforts in psychology). In these brief notes I want to draw attention to several current theoretical projects which I think offer useful constructs for an integrative framework for social and psychological approaches to literacy research. The two projects concern the clarification of the problem of integrative levels: a problem in the philosophy of science; and the development of an activity approach to theory and research in psychology. I will give a very sketchy presentation of these approaches here, and then consider what kinds of questions they pose for literacy research.

The levels concept

Initially introduced as a way of ordering phenomena in biology (Woodger, 1929; Needham, 1937) the concept of levels of organization has been elaborated as a general methodological approach in many sciences (see Aronson, 1984, for a historical review and analysis). This approach views all material entities and processes as being organized hierarchically in progressively more complex systems or levels of integration. Principal levels are frequently and roughly characterized as the physical level, the biological, the psychological and the social levels, although other and more differentiated schemes have also been proposed. Each level has its own unique properties which cannot be predicted from knowledge of lower-level processes; thus processes on a societal level cannot be explained by reducing them to psychological or physiological processes. At the same time, knowledge of lower-level processes is essential for understanding higher-level processes, since these continue to be operative in the higher-level system. Full understanding of a given phenomenon often hinges on a grasp of the relationship of levels to each other: how do higher levels modify processes at a lower level? How do levels become integrated into more complex systems? Here formidable problems arise. Concretization of the levels approach for a particular inquiry makes enormous demands on still-scant theoretical resources. Some progress, however, has been made in formulating general principles of attack. Tobach (in press) has contributed the critical insight that if these concepts are to be fruitful, levels and their relationships need to be analyzed, not "in general" but with respect to a particular scientific category or question.

Now what does this mean for the present discussion? I think it suggests first, that phenomena in literacy learning and practice cannot be considered as *either* psychological *or* social but as particular integrations of processes operating on both these levels. Second, it suggests that, to examine the integration of these processes, we need to pursue the analysis, not with respect to literacy "in general", but with respect to some particular unit or aspect of literacy. A prior requirement, then, is to conceptualize literacy within some theory which offers applicable units of analysis, around which we can seek to integrate the knowledge gained through social practice and through research in many disciplines. The theory of activity developed by psychologists and philosophers working in the tradition of L. S. Vygotsky is such a foundational theory (see Leont'ev, 1978, 1981; Wertsch and Lee, 1984 for expositions).

Activity theory

Activity theory holds that the integral units of human life – humans interacting with each other and the world – can be conceptualized as *activities* which serve to fulfill distinctive motives. In the course of activities, people engage in goal-directed *actions*, carried out for particular purposes under particular conditions and with particular technical means. The *operations* which compose actions may be, and typically are, both mental and behavioral, and vary with both subjective and objective conditions and means. I emphasize the terms *activities, actions* and *operations* since the theory holds these to be the structural units of human behavior, and, accordingly, units of analysis for the behavioral sciences. These units are non-additive: an activity may be realized by different actions (one can satisfy hunger by catching fish or opening a can of soup), and, conversely, one and the same action may realize different activities (a fisherman may try to land a big fish to feed a family or to win a sportsman's prize). Actions and operations are similarly non-contingent, since various operations are often available to meet the same goal, and the same operations may contribute to attainment of different goals.

Consider literacy in this light (see Scribner and Cole, 1981, for a fuller but somewhat different elaboration of an activity approach to literacy). We may conceptualize literacy as a set of activities satisfying distinctive motives related to the written language: creating distinctive genres of communication, for example, or transmitting information over time and space. Literacy can also be conceptualized as actions, in this case acts of reading or writing carried out for particular purposes. According to our guiding framework, literacy actions may realize literacy activities, but they may also, and more frequently do, realize other activities with a broad array of motivations – educative (getting through school), religious-ideological (becoming a holy person) or political (organizing a social movement). Literacy may also be considered as operations – namely, the set of processes and procedures by which reading and writing actions are executed in a given time and place.

It is immediately evident from this analysis that literacy – considered on all of these scales – is always profoundly and pervasively social in nature. Literacy activities come into being (acquire "motivational" power) through larger political, economic and cultural forces in a given society; neither their structure nor function can be understood outside of their societal context. Literacy actions are similarly profoundly and pervasively social, since the purposes for which people read and write, and the settings in which these actions take place are socially organized and maintained, and the activities whose motives they realize are socially generated. As for operations, these, too, take shape around the particular symbolic systems (language and orthography) in a culture or social setting and the technical means for producing written language available within the community (whether stylus and stone, or terminal key and computer screen).

Where do psychological processes come in? I would maintain that psychological processes are integrated with sociocultural processes throughout all of these structural units. Consider activities. Motivations for literacy activities are acquired by individuals in the course of their own personal life histories as members of a social group. As for actions, it is similarly the case that the purposes and goals of literacy actions (particular acts of reading and writing) must make sense to individuals who undertake, or refrain from undertaking, them (that is, they must be seen to realize some motive). And, patently, individuals must acquire the knowledge and perceptual and intellectual skills (operations) involved in acquiring and using a given culture's means of literacy and modal literacy actions. Note that this framework is a departure from the more common approach of equating the "psychological" with "micro-processes" and the "cultural" with "macro-processes." That equation leads to a separatist view – as though psychological processes could be separated from sociocultural processes and "lead a life on their own."

It is perfectly clear that the complexity of literacy is not about to yield to a schematic application of a theoretical approach, which is itself in an early stage, more valuable for offering constructs than providing testable theories. Still, the perspective raises interesting suggestions about future directions in an integrated approach to literary research.

In attempting to integrate knowledge derived from practice and research in various disciplines, it is useful to sort out the structural units of literacy which are objects of concern and analysis. One source of underlying tension between psychological analyses of literacy, and historical, social and cultural analyses, may be the mismatch between the units of literacy each has traditionally emphasized. Social sciences customarily probe the factors generating and sustaining literacy activities, and examine the social forces regulating their distribution. Ethnographic research, in addition, contributes highly detailed case studies on the organization of literacy actions in various social contexts – the sorts of reading or writing projects members of a cultural system engage in and the purposes these satisfy. In psychological research, investigators have overwhelmingly devoted their energies to analyzing perceptual, linguistic, and cognitive processes implicated in reading and writing, which we have referred to here as operations.

The problem of integrating the great bulk of psychological research into social analyses of literacy – and into direct programs – thus revolves around an assessment of how knowledge about reading and writing operations relates to larger questions about literacy. Clearly it does. For example, if research indicates that the beginning reading process is lengthened by the heavy memorization demands a script such as Chinese imposes on learners, then educators and policy-makers attempting to extend popular literacy may well want to consider some measures of script modification. But useful information on the kind of modification to make, and when and how it might be implemented, will not flow directly from research on reading operations. These questions require attention to social and psychological analyses on literacy activity and action levels as well. How might instructional activities be affected? Will current literacy teachers be motivated to teach a script they may not value? Will script changes restrict the kinds of reading available to new literates? And, if so, how will this affect the purposes for which they chose to learn how to read in the first place? As this line of analysis indicates, an activity frame of reference not only provides some guidelines for piecing together research pieces, but enlarges the realm of research questions which might contribute to literacy programs.

From the vantage point of a psychologist, two arenas of exploration are especially challenging. One has to do with the level of actions. Wagner (Wagner, *et al.*, 1986) and others in this volume (e.g., Street, Bennett and Berry, and Reder) have deepened our understanding of the diversity and modal types of reading actions that are undertaken in various cultural settings. The array of purposes for which people engage in reading in their "indigenous settings" may be more or less compatible with the purposes for which reading actions are undertaken in school. How do the purposes of school-based reading actions come to make sense to students whose everyday activities do not encompass such purposes? What are the processes of goal formation?

Finally, though I have not seen studies of this kind in collections of papers on literacy, social psychological research on such issues as group dynamics, the autonomization of motives, and the formation of ideologies may have much to contribute to our understanding of the origin and history of literacy activities.

References

Aronson, L. R. (1984). Levels of integration and organization: A revaluation of the evolutionary scale. In G. Greenberg and E. Tobach (eds.), *Behavioral evolution and integrative levels*. Hillsdale, N.J.: Lawrence Erlbaum.

Leacock, E. (1985). The individual and society in anthropological theory. In *Dialectical Anthropology*, vol. 9.

Leont'ev, A. N. (1978). *Activity, consciousness, and personating*. Englewood Cliffs, N.J.: Prentice-Hall.

Leont'ev, A. N. (1981). Sign and activity. In J. V. Wertsch (ed.), *The concept of activity in Soviet psychology*. New York: M. E. Sharpe.

Needham, J. (1937). *Integrative levels: A revaluation of the idea of progress*. Oxford: Clarendon Press.

Scribner, S. and Cole, M. (1981). *The psychology of literacy*. Cambridge, Mass: Harvard University Press.

Tobach, E. (in press). Integrative levels in the comparative psychology of cognition, language and consciousness. In G. Greenberg and E. Tobach (eds.), *Cognition, language and consciousness: Integrative levels*. Hillsdale, N.J.: Lawrence Erlbaum.

Wagner, D. A., Messick, B. M. and Spratt, J. (1986). Studying literacy in Morocco. In B. B. Scheiffelin (ed.), *The acquisition of literacy: Ethnographic perspectives*. Norwood, N.J.: Ablex.

Wertsch, J. V. (ed.). (1979). *The concept of activity in Soviet psychology*. New York: M. E. Sharpe.

Wertsch, J. V. and Lee, B. (1984). The multiple levels of analysis in a theory of action. *Human Development*, 27(3–14), 193–6.

Woodger, J. H. (1929). *Biological principles*. London: Routledge & Kegan Paul.

A Complaint
Lev!
Lev Semonovitch!
Where are you?
You've gone off
And left me
Starving here
Between two bales of hay.

A shame!

You took away my dice
And made an ass of me.
That wasn't nice.

But wait, you'll see . . .

I'll be hanging round again
In Leo's famous gambling den

Playing games of chance until
I get the sign.

Who needs a mediator when
Free will
is mine?

Sylvia Scribner

PART IV

Cognitive development: Sociohistorical perspective

Introduction

The papers in this section were written while Scribner was Professor of Developmental Psychology at the City University of New York. Like many of her other writings, these papers are grounded in activity theory as a theoretical perspective, but they specifically focus on developmental questions and examine the theoretical and methodological logic of a sociohistorical approach to the study of mind. In doing so, Scribner's work is embedded within the rich terrain of contemporary discussions of Vygotsky's theory and it brings to them a distinctive emphasis. She explicitly draws on the dialectical-materialist foundation of activity theory, an emphasis continuous with her conceptualization of the societal basis of thinking and work. The works included in this section show how the dialectical basis of Vygotsky's sociohistorical theory is, in Scribner's view, essential for an adequate conceptualization of the genesis of higher mental functions.

"Vygotsky's Uses of History," now a classic, focuses on development in its most fundamental relationships between histories on different levels. Scribner's lucid explication of "the logic of [Vygotsky's] method of theory construction" shows how the general history of humanity, the child's history, and the history of higher psychological functions, as "phenomena in movement," are dialectically related in the theory. Placing the theory itself in the historical context of psychology, she argues that Vygotsky, in contradistinction to others and despite his analogical parallels between the child and primitive societies, is not offering a "recapitulation" theory in which the history of the species would be mirrored in the history of the child. Her analysis counters this common reading of Vygotsky, which she attributes to his lack of precision in using his own concepts. She shows that the theory describes instead a dialectical integration of the history of the species and the history of the culture at the individual level of development. Likewise, she clarifies in her analysis that Vygotsky's formulations of the relation between biology and culture is not simple interactionism. Her discussion enriches the Vygotskyan framework by integratively describing changes in all three systems simultaneously, thus making Vygotsky's formulations more precise.

In the same paper, Scribner extends the historical approach by introducing a fourth level of history, the histories of particular societies, and by stressing their plurality. This, she states, is needed "for purposes of concrete research and for theory development in the present," a theme to which she returns in other writings in this section. General history alone is not sufficient to address questions about the production of higher mental functions in their full social and cultural specificity and the transformations of those functions. As is evident in her writings on literacy and on cross-cultural research and in her research on thinking at work, Scribner envisioned development broadly as encompassing adults as well as children, institutions and cultures as well as individual persons.

237

The theoretical analysis she develops here maps out the broad framework of those lines of research.

While writing this article, Scribner was also preparing to participate in the International Congress of Psychology in 1984 and preparing a paper entitled "Does Ontogeny Recapitulate History? An Examination of Vygotsky's Socio-historical Theory" for delivery at the congress. In the presentation, she discusses these ideas with different critical stresses and points to the need for developmental research to include the sociohistorical background of the child. The paper was actually read by Vera John-Steiner, as Sylvia Scribner stayed at home with her husband during one of his serious episodes of illness. As it was explicitly prepared for oral presentation and because there is some overlap in coverage with the previous paper, we have not included it here.

The methodological consequences of the epistemological stance of Vygotsky's sociohistorical theory are examined in "A Sociocultural Approach to the Study of Mind." Scribner discusses the way cognition is formulated in the theory of activity and distinguishes it from the approach then prevalent in cognitive psychology. The culturally mediated and historically produced nature of mental functioning has methodological implications. "[An] analysis of changing social practices becomes integral to – rather than merely peripheral to – an inquiry into learning and development," hence the necessity of drawing on interdisciplinary procedures when investigating mind. This theme parallels and extends Scribner's earlier call for integrating sociocultural factors into psychological systems (Part 2 of this volume).

With characteristic rigor, she stresses how, in that endeavor, the specification of particular hypotheses and particular mediating mechanisms occupies a central place, above and beyond the general parameters laid out in "grand" theory. She exemplifies this approach in her description of the rationale and methodology of the Vai studies carried out by her and Michael Cole and their colleagues. The research is an illustration of how changes in symbolic mediators and in social practices shape thought, and she discusses it in its historical dimension.

Scribner's important point is that, by embedding humans both in a general species history and in specific activities shaping cognitive functional systems, the sociohistorical view of mind addresses both the universal and the culturally specific aspects of human thought. The dialectic of the universal and the particular was an early and long-standing principle in her thinking, and her discussion of the issue in this and other papers previews current discussions of the relations between the two in a range of disciplines, from philosophy to women's studies to political science.

In the final paper in this section, "Three Developmental Paradigms," Scribner reflects on psychology and development from a metatheoretical perspective. The paper, of which only a draft was found, was delivered to an anthropological audience, and in its historical presentation is both didactic and intellectually provocative in stressing the philosophical underpinnings of empirical science. Says Scribner to this audience of anthropologists: "Psychology investigates how external activity gives rise to internal mental processes, how these processes are functionally related to particular external activities, and how external and internal activities mutually transform each other."

She criticizes Piaget for his nondialectical approach. Piaget, grounded in an individualist paradigm, uses as basic "building blocks" the individual and the environment. His is an "action" theory as contrasted with an "activity" theory, and his "inclusion" of social factors does not alter the individual–environment dichotomy; the theory lacks the tools to address relations between the social and the individual.

In the social interactionist paradigm, exemplified by Mead's sociogenetic concept, the building blocks are the individual and the social. Scribner calls Neo-Piagetian attempts to establish a social account of cognitive development a major event in contemporary psychology but criticizes this paradigm for relying on individual interactions rather than societal interaction, a theme already present in her writings on psychology and society in Part 1 and here applied to cognition: "They cut off cognition from objects and actions in the world of things."

In contrast to those two paradigms, Scribner notes, activity theory integrates the individual's relations with the world of objects and the world of people within the framework of the larger societal system. The individual, the environment, and the societal are integrated to produce the unit of analysis. She stresses the need to account for the historical evolution of human consciousness and its development in ontogeny. Human labor is the primary activity that integrates individual function, social organization, and society as mediated through tools and symbols.

In this paper, as in others, Scribner attempts to involve her audience in addressing these issues. Activities, constituted on the level of social organization, are methodologically prior as units of analysis to an analysis of their psychological constituents. Thus, she insists, complex as this line of study may be, socially defined categories of activity can serve as the organizing domains for comparative psychological research. To this end, she urges a collaboration between anthropology, the study of socially significant modes of activity, and other social sciences.

The theoretical analyses Scribner develops in those essays have ramifications for the study of thinking, literacy, and cultural systems she had recently pursued (discussed in her writings in Parts 2 and 3 of this volume) as well as for the study of thinking at work. Scribner during that time was developing the research program on thinking at work initiated in Baltimore, analyzing cognitive transformations functionally shaped by goal-directed work activities in a variety of technological settings (see Part 5). Characteristically, the theoretical tools she develops in this section would be put to the challenge of articulating concrete research questions with social significance, and fine-grained analyses of mental processes.

Selected Coauthored Works

Cole, M., Scribner, S. (1975). Theorizing about socialization of cognition. *Ethos* 3, 249–67.

Cole, M., John-Steiner, V., Scribner, S., Suberman, E. (1978). *L. S. Vygotsky: mind in society.* Harvard University Press, Cambridge, Mass.

Bartlett, E. J., Scribner, S. (1981). Text and context: an investigation of referential organization in children's written narratives. In: *Writing: the nature, development and teaching of written communication,* vol. 2 (Eds.: Dominic, J., Whiteman, M., Fredericksen, C.). Lawrence Erlbaum Associates, Hillsdale, N.J., 153–67.

Hawkins, J., Pea, R. D., Glick, J., Scribner, S. (1984). Evidence for deductive reasoning by preschoolers. *Developmental Psychology* 20, 4, 584–94.

20   Vygotsky's uses of history

> "History" is not a distinctive subject-matter to be inquired into. It is rather at once a trait of all subject-matters, something to be discovered and understood about each of them; and a distinctive way of inquiring into any subject-matter.
>
> Randall, Jr. (1962, p. 28)

This chapter is a beginning exploration of the question "What is history?" in the psychological theory of L. S. Vygotsky.

Although the uses psychologists make of history is a topic worthy of analysis in its own right (White, 1976), the present inquiry addresses a special concern. Since the early 1970s social scientists have shown heightened interest in the relationship between culture and cognition. In spite of many advances in research methods and findings, however, conceptual difficulties continue to limit the enterprise. Principal among these difficulties is the problem of determining for any given domain of intellectual functioning (e.g., conservation, memory, logical reasoning) which aspects are universal in nature and which are specific to particular social environments. Theories of psychological development are of propaedeutic value here, and among them, Vygotsky's theory would seem to hold special promise for construction of an integrative account of cultural variations in thought. Some of us have attempted to develop this promise and use Vygotsky's framework as a guide to our work (Cole and Scribner, 1977; Scribner and Cole, 1981) but the implications of his theory for comparative studies of cognition have proved ambiguous. One source of ambiguity is that Vygotsky, like other developmental theorists, applies his concepts of development to the careers of both the child and the "primitive." These actors walk

This essay originally appeared in *Culture, Communication, and Cognition*, ed. J. V. Wertsch (New York: Cambridge University Press, 1985), pp. 119–45. Reprinted with the permission of Cambridge University Press.

hand-in-hand through his pages in a relationship we find difficult to define yet impossible to ignore. Are we to infer from these passages that Vygotsky believed that in some cultures characterized as "primitive" adults are "childlike"? If not, are we forced to dismiss Vygotsky's child–primitive comparisons as an unfortunate aberration in an otherwise brilliant and useful approach to the social foundations of thought? More is at stake in these vexing questions than the accomplishment of a balanced appraisal of Vygotsky. Child-primitive comparisons continue to dominate many studies of cultural influences on thought [Hallpike (1979) is a recent anthropological effort using this framework] and continue to arouse controversy and debate (Cole and Scribner, 1977; Lave, 1981). In this context, clarification of Vygotsky's views seems essential; without it, his writings are subject to misuse; with it, we can hope for further constructive development of a sociohistorical theory of mind.

Clarifying Vygotsky's views of primitive thought, however, turns out to be no simple matter. If we want to go beyond a mere restatement of what Vygotsky said, we need to determine the function child-primitive comparisons played in his system as a whole. To conduct this analysis we are forced to shift our starting point. We need to begin, not with "child" or "primitive" but with more inclusive and fundamental categories in Vygotsky's theory. And this brings us to "history," the topic of this chapter. Vygotsky declares that historical analysis is the key to his system. The essence of a dialectical approach, he states, is to study something historically, to study "phenomena in movement"; "the historical research of behavior is not an additional or auxiliary aspect of theoretical study but forms the very basis of the latter" (DHF, p. 105).

Accepting this view, we can examine how Vygotsky worked out his historical research of behavior, anticipating that this analysis might help us understand the significance of his methodology involving child and primitive thought. A complete analysis of Vygotsky's historical approach is, of course, a large undertaking and beyond the scope of this chapter. Here I will offer a series of preliminary observations, concentrating on the "sequences of moving phenomena" to which Vygotsky applied the term "history" and their functional role in his theory. Although certain of Vygotsky's concepts have been superceded or substantially modified by Soviet psychologists (see, for example, Leont'ev and Luria, 1968) I have chosen to conduct this analysis in Vygotsky's own terms. I am interested in following the logic of his method of theory construction rather than in evaluating the status of the theory.

Historical approach: Vygotsky's leading contribution

Of Vygotsky's many contributions to psychological theory, he has perhaps been most widely acclaimed for introducing the historical approach to the development of higher mental processes. Graham (1972) tells us that Soviet historians of science, who hold different assessments of Vygotsky's work, agree in honoring him as the first to explicate the historical formation of the mind. This approach is so central to evaluations of Vygotsky that it has been elevated over other constructs to serve, in various compound forms, as the *name* for the theory as a whole. Soviet psychologists refer to Vygotsky's theory as "cultural *historical* theory" (Davydov, and Radzikhovsky, Chapter 21, this volume) or "social *historical* theory" (Leont'ev and Luria, 1968); and U.S. psychologists often seem to have Vygotsky's position in mind when they speak of the "Soviet *sociohistorical* approach" to mental development (as for example, Wagner and Paris, 1981).

In using the compound term "*sociohistorical*" rather than the simple term "*historical*," commentators appear to be singling out for emphasis one of Vygotsky's uses of history – history as the chronology of events involving humanity as a whole. Vygotsky refers to this series of events as general history and we will follow his usage as we begin our analysis.

General history: The first level of history

Singling out general history as the foundation for the entire theoretical edifice seems consistent with Vygotsky's own view of his enterprise. He begins "The Development of Higher Mental Functions" with a quotation from Engels: "The eternal laws of nature to an ever greater extent are changing into laws of history." Vygotsky invites us to read this work as the unravelling of the mechanisms by which this transformation from the natural to the historical takes place in the phenomena of mental life.

To follow his course, we need to begin with the central questions about mental phenomena that Vygotsky sought to address. As we know, he was absorbed with the problem of the higher forms of behavior or higher psychological functions (we will not concern ourselves with the distinction here). To understand the development of the child, he said, psychology must be able to account for such complex phenomena as acquisition of speech and development of planning and self-control, the outstanding accomplishments of early childhood. But such an account was exactly what the various schools of psychology were unable to construct. Vygotsky devotes more than a fourth of his manuscript to an intricate analysis of the limitations in psychological theory and method responsible for this failure. This critique is not easily epitomized, but it pivoted around two seemingly irreconcilable approaches within psychology to the study of higher behavior. Briefly stated as a reminder of Vygotsky's view of the state of psychology in his day: Empirical psychologists conceived of higher forms of behavior as simply more complicated varieties of elementary processes and, like them, products of biological evolution; accordingly, they tried to explain both classes of phenomena by the same laws (the naturalist or natural science camp). Speculative philosopher-psychologists contended that higher functions are *sui generis*, they are not regulated by biological laws or deterministic laws of any kind, as expressions of "human nature," they are, by nature, inexplicable (the idealist or cultural psychology camp).

Vygotsky's diagnosis of the difficulty was a brilliant penetration beneath the surface of the argument. The limitations of both camps arose from a *common* source: Neither understood the true origin of higher mental processes. These are discontinuous with elementary processes because they do not originate in biological evolution and cannot be explained by "natural" laws (i.e., laws of nature). But they are not lawless. Rather, their roots are to be found on another level of explanation – the regularities of the laws of history. Vygotsky put it this way: "Neither the eternal laws of nature nor the eternal laws of the spirit" but "historical laws" are the key to discovering the development of higher forms of behavior (DHF, p. 20).

What are these historical laws? In his discussion of the current state of psychology, Vygotsky presents and dismisses historical approaches offered by several schools, most notably psychoanalysis and "understanding psychology" (represented by the works of E. Spranger). Vygotsky called these metaphysical, unscientific positions: "It is not enough to formally bring psychology and history closer to one another; it is necessary to ask: what psychology and what history are we dealing with?" (DHF, p. 32).

As we know from his many citations, Vygotsky was, in the first place, dealing with the materialist history of Marx and Engels. One of their kernel ideas was that the human species differs from all others because, through its manipulation of nature, it frees itself from biological determinism and begins to fashion its own nature. Productive activities (generically "labor") change in the course of history as new resources and new forms of society come into being. This history is material because it establishes the material activities of people and their intercourse with one another as the source of ideas and mental life (Marx and Engels, 1846).

In adopting this outlook, Vygotsky committed himself to two propositions that it entails: (1) Because socially organized activities change in history, the human nature they produce is not a fixed category that can be described once and for all; it is a changing category. Questions about what human nature is, or more appropriately to Vygotsky's enterprise, what human mental life (the "psyche") is, cannot be separated from questions about how human mental life becomes what it is. Questions of genesis thus move to the forefront of the scientific enterprise; psychological study of human nature (thought and behavior) must concern itself with the processes of formation of human nature. (2) Changes in social activities that occur in history have a directionality: hand-powered tools precede machines; number systems come into use before algebra. This movement is expressed in the concept of historic *development* in contrast to the generic concept of historic *change,* and its reflection in human mental life is expressed as mental *development.*

Here is a passage in the opening chapter of "*The Development of Higher Mental Functions*" in which Vygotsky introduces some of these concepts. He has been laying out the deficiencies in the two camps of psychology and he summarizes them in this manner:

> The higher forms of behaviour originated by mankind's *higher development*, are either placed alongside the physiological, organic processes . . . or are totally set apart from all that is material and begin a new and this time eternal life in the realm of ideas . . . Either one or the other. Physiology or mathematics of the spirit, but under no circumstances the *history of human behavior* as a part of *mankind's general history*. (DHF, p. 20; emphasis added)

Vygotsky expresses his main conclusion – the need to search for specifically human behavior in history rather than biology – in this way:

> Human behavior differs from animal behavior in the same qualitative manner as the entire type of adaptability and historical development of man differs from the adaptability and development of animals, because the process of man's *mental development* is part of the *general historic development of mankind.* (DHF, pp. 95, 96; emphasis added)

Many years later, Leont'ev and Luria (1968), in a retrospective assessment, credited Vygotsky's theory of "the sociohistorical formation of higher mental processes" as the key to his solution of the crisis in psychology (p. 341). One might say that Vygotsky used the category of "general history" to achieve a synthesis in psychology between "nature" and "culture" (see Toulmin, 1978).

All aspects of the historical progress of humankind were not of equal importance to Vygotsky. He was concerned with those forms of social life that have the most profound consequences for mental life. As we know, he thought these to lie primarily in the symbolic-communicative spheres of activity in which humans collectively produce new means for regulating their behavior. Vygotsky called these means "cultural" and the new forms of behavior "specifically cultural forms" (DHF, p. 46). Historical laws of development, as they apply to human mental life, are therefore laws of development of cultural forms of behavior, and the other way around: Cultural forms appear slowly, each new stage building on a preceding one, so that everything cultural is "in its very nature, an historic phenomenon" (DHF, p. 21). Thus, we find Vygotsky introducing the term "cultural development" in his discussion of the origins of higher psychological functions and in some contexts using it interchangeably with "historical development".[2]

By situating the origin and motor force of the higher mental processes in human cultural history, Vygotsky at the same time redefined the nature of psychological explanation. Insofar as its object of inquiry is regulated by historical rather than biological processes, psychology's search for laws of development (formation of human nature) must be conducted on the sociocultural level of reality, and it must devise a methodology appropriate to this enterprise.

For Vygotsky, then, the transformation of phylogeny (biological evolution) into general history (historical development) is more than a backdrop for a

Marxist psychology; it is a first building block in the construction of this science, setting before it the task of explaining the genesis and development of cultural forms of behavior and developing a method for this purpose.

Ontogeny: The second level of history

The second level of history that enters into Vygotsky's system is the "subject's individual history" (T&S, p. 27) or the "history of the child" (T&S, p. 63). Although Vygotsky's concern with the course of human history distinguishes him from other developmental psychologists, his attention to individual growth and change seems to require no theoretical prolegomenon. Individual history appears to many U.S. psychologists to be the natural subject of Vygotsky's psychology or, more conservatively, the domain in which Vygotsky's psychology coincides with the field of developmental psychology as it is customarily defined.

Vygotsky's analysis of child history centers on the same topic as his analysis of general history: the characterization of "uniquely human aspects of behavior" (Vygotsky, 1978; p. 19). Just as Vygotsky rejected the notion that biological laws can explain the emergence of higher forms of behavior in general history, he rejected their explanatory value for these behaviors in child history as well. He claimed that on the individual level of organization, as well as on the species level, two lines of development must be distinguished – the biological (sometimes referred to as natural; see note 2) and the cultural. Natural processes regulate the growth of elementary psychological functions in the child – forms of memory, perception, and practical tool-using intelligence, for example, that are continuous with the mental life of apes and other species. Social and cultural processes regulate the child's acquisition of speech and other sign systems, and the development of "special higher psychological functions" such as voluntary attention and logical memory (DHF, p. 35). These acquisition processes constitute the cultural development of the child, or what Vygotsky claims is the same statement (we will return to this equivalency later), the cultural development of behavior (DHF, p. 17). The cultural line of development is closely linked to the child's "social history," the particular societal and cultural medium in which he or she grows up (T&S, p. 27). It proceeds by the child's mastery of the means and forms of behavior "elaborated in the course of the historical development of human society" (El'konin, 1967, p. 85).

Although most of Vygotsky's work is a sustained argument for psychology's recognition of a separate cultural line of development in the child, he tends to retain the biologically derived term "ontogeny" as a generic term to refer to *all* processes of child development (see note 2). Vygotsky makes a crucial distinction between ontogeny and phylogeny, however. In contrast to phylogenesis, in which the line of historical-cultural development *displaces* the biological, in ontogenesis both lines of development co-occur and are fused. As children grow in size and gain control over locomotion (biological development), they are also acquiring use of tools and speech (cultural development).

We now have two series of changes, each of which involves a line of cultural development, one taking place on the level of general world history and the other on the level of individual history. On both levels specifically human aspects of human nature are in the process of formation.

How do these two series of cultural development relate to each other? Before we try to work out the answer to this question, it seems necessary to justify why it should be raised in the first place. We might take Vygotsky's discussion of the historical development of human nature as an independent topic in its own right. It clearly served the theoretical function of carrying the critique against dualist positions in psychology and establishing the main directions for a new science of behavior. Having served these functions, the concept of general history might silently leave the scene. Adoption of this position would imply that the sociohistorical aspect of Vygotsky's theory plays no significant functional role in his systematic study of higher mental processes in child development.

Vygotsky's writings, however, do not readily lend themselves to such an interpretation. He not only engages in general theoretical discussion on cultural development, but he laces his texts with detailed descriptive material on human behavior in early history and primitive cultures – material culled from the writings of ethnologists, the French sociological school and the field of "ethnic psychology." (Levy Brühl and Wundt are two well-quoted sources in the latter fields.) This material always involves "primitive man," a term variously referring to the prehistoric species at the threshold of humanity, to *Homo sapiens* in the earliest historical epochs, or to "the most primitive man of the now living tribes" (Vygotsky, 1966, p. 18). Vygotsky insists that the data of ethnic psychology need to be taken into account in child psychology if effective approaches are to be worked out for the study of higher processes. And to emphasize the point, as it were, he follows a practice of interweaving material from both these fields in discussions of substantive topics and he does so within an avowedly comparative framework. Thus, Vygotsky seems to be saying that it is not merely history in the abstract but some actual stuff of history that is critically important to theory and research on child development. Let us consider the kind of information he uses from history and anthropology and the contexts in which he considers such material relevant.

Child and primitive

I have selected illustrative material dealing with the two classes of phenomena Vygotsky defined as branches of the development of higher functions – organization of functional systems and acquisitions of sign systems. (Unless otherwise indicated, all emphasis in quotations is mine.)

EXAMPLE 1: MEMORY. In the essays in "Tool and Symbol," Vygotsky undertakes an analysis of sign operations in the child, focusing on their role in integrating elementary processes into higher systems. He elects to begin with the "history of child memory" since memory is an "exceptionally advantageous subject" for a "comparison of elementary and higher functions" (p. 83). But he immediately introduces material from general history. "The *phylogenetic* investigation of human memory shows that, even at the most primitive stages of psychological development, we can clearly see two, principally different types of memory functions" (p. 85). When he completes the description of stages of memory in early history, Vygotsky presents a series of studies he and his colleagues conducted on the development of memory operations in *children*.

EXAMPLE 2: COUNTING. In "Development of Higher Mental Functions," Vygotsky includes an important theoretical section analyzing the first forms of sign-mediated activities. He describes as one such activity finger-counting systems among the Papuans of New Guinea: "Counting fingers was once an important cultural triumph of mankind. It served as a bridge over which man passed from natural arithmetic to cultural. . . . Finger counting underlies many scales of notation. It is widely represented to this very day *among primitive tribes*" (p. 28). "Studying these primitive counting systems, we may observe in developed and active form the same process that is present in rudimentary form during the *development of a child's arithmetic reasoning,* and, in certain cases in the behavior of grown-ups" (p. 129).

EXAMPLE 3: PREHISTORY OF WRITING. This discussion (Vygotsky, 1978) presents a clear revelation of the movement of Vygotsky's thought from child to human history to the history of writing to the writing of a traditional people and back to the child. (The passage is continuous but several sentences are omitted for condensation purposes.)

The gesture is the initial visual sign which contains the *child's* future *writing* as an acorn contains a future oak.
. . . Wurth pointed out the link between pictorial or pictographic writing and gesture in discussing the *development of writing in human history*. He showed that figurative gestures often simply denote the reproduction of a graphic sign; on the other hand, signs are often the fixation of gestures. For example, the *pictorial writing of Indians* represents a line connecting points by one that indicates motion of the hand or index finger.
. . . Now we will point out two other domains in which gestures are linked to the *origin of written signs*. The first concerns *children's scribbles*." [And the second, Vygotsky goes on to say, concerns children's play]. (Vygotsky, 1978, p. 107).

Does ontogeny recapitulate general history?

Reading these passages, we hear echoes of many other comparisons between primitive and child mentality in the history of psychology. Developmental psychology, in particular, has rarely escaped such comparisons. Implicitly or explicitly they are present in the major theories and were certainly a prominent feature of the genetic psychology movement of Vygotsky's day. Most of these comparisons take the form of parallelism, a framework developed in biology that proposes that stages of ontogeny correspond to sequences of life forms in phylogeny. The most conspicuous version of parallelism attempted to account for these correspondences through a biological law of repetition (the biogenetic law) whose workings are inscribed in memory in the famous aphorism that "ontogeny recapitulates phylogeny."

One particular feature of recapitulation theory is of special interest to our present inquiry. Whereas all species have always consisted of both immature and mature members, evolutionary history has been conventionally depicted as a sequence of successive adult stages; and whereas ontogeny is, properly speaking, the entire life history of an individual, conventionally it has been studied with respect to stages of development up to the point of maturity or adulthood (Gould, 1977, p. 484). Accordingly, most ontogeny–phylogeny comparisons take the form of finding resemblances between immature members of higher species and mature members of lower species. When Hall and other genetic psychologists at the turn of the century extended recapitulation theory from anatomy to behavior, they left this form of comparison intact; they proposed that the biogenetic law reproduces forms of thought and behavior in ontogeny that correspond to various stages of cultural evolution. According to the theory, the white Western child passes through all earlier and lower stages to arrive at "civilization"; individuals in traditional societies, however, retrace only part of this ancestral cultural history and remain arrested at one of the lower levels. In this scheme, the term "primitive" applied to early humans of all ages, adults in contemporary traditional societies, and children in industrial societies. [See Grinder (1967) for readings of genetic psychology and Hallowell (1967) and Gould (1977) for critiques.]

As Gould (1977) documents, recapitulation theory supported racist ideology and practices and persisted in psychology long after its repudiation in biology as scientifically worthless.

With this historical background, it is understandable that questions have arisen on the meaning of child–primitive comparisons by Vygotsky's work. Vygotsky's view of higher mental functions as having social-historical, rather than biological, origins sets his theory apart from others and certainly distinguishes it from the thinking of the genetic psychology movement. Still, without diminishing the significance of his theoretical break with biologically oriented psychologies, we need to consider the following possibility: In displacing the biological concept of phylogeny with the social concept of history, did Vygotsky nonetheless leave the structure of the older theories intact? Does ontogeny recapitulate history? Or, in the weaker version, does the child parallel stages of culture on its way to mature intellectual functioning?

These questions are not idle: A biological orientation to intellectual development is not logically necessary to a recapitulationist or parallelist view. And several surface features of Vygotsky's comparative remarks resemble those of classic parallelist theories. For one thing, Vygotsky frequently compares characteristics of the modern child to those of the primitive adult; or, to put it the other way around – for it is in this version that the "shoe pinches" – he compares the primitive adult to the modern child. A second resemblance, as we have pointed out, is that Vygotsky adopts the tradition of using the term "primitive" to refer not only to ancient forebears but to living men and women in contemporary societies whose technological means are primitive.

As an example of the interpretive problems Vygotsky's comparisons pose, consider Luria's (1976) cross-cultural research and the controversy it aroused. In the early 1930s, Luria undertook to test the sociohistorical aspects of Vygotsky's theory in a remote area of the Soviet Union that was undergoing rapid changes in modes of production and social life. In a series of studies among adults, he found conceptual and reasoning differences between nonliterate peasants and others who had participated in agricultural collectives or in literacy and training experiences. These differences were similar to age-related changes psychologists had identified in ontogeny, and Luria tended to interpret them within a development perspective. For example, he considered the grouping of objects by perceptual-functional attributes (common among his nonliterate respondents and young children in other studies) developmentally lower than grouping by taxonomic class membership (the preferred mode of literate, schooled respondents and other children). Luria presented these findings as confirmation of Vygotsky's thesis that the higher psychological processes change as a function of sociohistorical changes. But did this work and its interpretation imply that the "unchanged" Uzbekistanian peasants were childlike? Some critics apparently thought so. Cole (1976, p. xiv) points out that Luria's research received a mixed reception when it was first reported; some believed it insulting to ethnic minorities in the Soviet Union; other commentators faulted not merely this piece of research, but the general theory for its imputation that certain classes and sections of the population who were carrying out Soviet policy were not capable of abstract thought (cited in Cole and Griffin, 1980).[3]

Disagreements as to the implications of Vygotsky's sociohistorical views are not confined to the Soviet Union or the past (see Cole and Griffin, 1980). As I hope my presentation has shown, Vygotsky's writings in the context of the history of developmental psychology provide grist for controversy.

If ambiguities are present in Vygotsky's work, it is not the function of interpretation to "get rid" of them. What I want to show is that some, if not all, of the sources of controversy disappear when we go beneath the surface and examine the functional role of ontogeny–history comparisons in Vygotsky's theory. Before doing that, however, I think it useful to draw attention briefly to material that refutes a recapitulationist position and cautions against an assimilation of

Vygotsky's views to classical parallelist positions as well [for descriptions of these theories, see Gould (1977)].

I will confine my remarks to four points.

1. First, Vygotsky vigorously denies that his is either a recapitulationist or a parallelist position. He was quite aware of the possibility that his citation of ethnopsychological material might be interpreted as supporting such positions and he was concerned to set the record right. One passage (others might be cited, viz. T&S, p. 129) illustrates the tone of his argument:

> In the child's development, we find represented (but not repeated) both types of psychological development which we find in phylogenesis in isolated form: the biological and the historic. In ontogenesis both processes have their analogies (not parallels). This is a fundamental and central fact. . . . By this we certainly do not wish to say that ontogenesis in any form or degree repeats or reproduces phylogenesis or runs parallel to it. (DHF, p. 47)

2. A recapitulationist position requires that the same processes operate on both the individual and species level; in biological theories this requirement was met by postulating a biogenetic law of repetition. Vygotsky, however, repeatedly points out that the child's acquisition of tool and sign use does not follow that of primitive man (e.g., DHF, p. 49). He judged Spranger's cultural psychology deficient, in part, because it tried to equate "such different life processes as the historical development of mankind and the child's psychological development" (DHF, p. 32). Equation of these life processes is precluded by the distinctive characteristics of child and general history: The child is an assimilator of sign systems and develops higher functions through processes of internalization. Adults in the course of history are the inventors and elaborators of sign systems, as well as users. Assimilative and creative processes are not psychologically the same. The contrast is well illustrated in Vygotsky's discussion of the development of cultural forms of memory. Children of a certain age learn to use external aids for remembering. In the history of society we also find a stage in which adults rely on external memory aids (notched sticks, knotted ropes). Vygotsky recalls an anecdote related by Levy-Brühl: A missionary observed a man in a preliterate culture carving figures in a piece of wood to help him remember a sermon that impressed him. Vygotsky says that Levy-Brühl saw this as an example of the way primitive man relies on memory instead of thought, but "we are prone to see the contrary in this example, how man's intellect leads to the formation of new forms of memory . . . how much thought must have been necessary to inscribe a speech by carving figures on a piece of wood" (DHF, p. 125). What is memory to a child (use of an aid to remember) is thought for the adult (preparation of an aid to remember).

3. Turning to parallelism: Classical positions set up correspondences in the *content* of child behavior and the *content* of adult behavior in earlier epochs. In the genetic psychology movement, fears, ideas, and beliefs about the world were

the material proof of the affinity of child and cultural developments. [See Gould (1977) for some startling examples. Grinder (167) reports that Hall, a founder of genetic psychology in the United States, launched his work with a volume on *The Content of Children's Minds*.] Vygotsky makes no claim for phenotypic similarities and severely criticizes psychologists who do. "It goes without saying," he points out, that "to base oneself on ethnopsychological data does not mean to transpose them directly to the doctrine of ontogenesis" (DHF, p. 38) nor does it mean there is a correspondence between actual phenomena of cultural development in the child and in history. Vygotsky's refusal to assume likenesses in mental content across time and place is consistent with his view of sociohistorical shaping of mind: Ontogenetic development is influenced by its particular sociocultural milieu; not only are modern children unlike primitive adults in "real life" but they are unlike children in other times and places. In an obvious reference to Piaget's early work, Vygotsky protests that, in certain psychological research

the world outlook and causal concept of the contemporary European child of intellectual background and the same outlook and concept of a child coming from some primitive tribe, the outlook of a child from the Stone Age, that of the Middle Ages, and that of the XX century – these are all conceived as being basically identical; one and the same in principle, always equal one to the other (DHF, p. 22, 23)

4. Finally Vygotsky's position lacks a principal feature of classical parallelist theories – a "stage theory" of culture that can be brought into correspondence with stages in ontogeny. I find no evidence that Vygotsky incorporated a Spencerian (1888) or other doctrine of cultural stages in his theory. According to Spencer, societies develop over history, becoming increasingly complex and more highly organized, each marked by more advanced forms of thought. According to Vygotsky, the decisive moment in history is marked by the *advent* of culture – more exactly, the invention of cultural means for regulating behavior. The transition from nature to culture is the lever for movement from lower to higher forms of thought. In a generic sense, all cultures exhibit some higher forms of behavior and thought; indeed these define the human species. For what makes an individual a primitive human rather than an animal is the fact that he or she uses tools and signs to mediate interactions with nature and with others. All humans participate in the most powerful, most basic of all sign systems, speech. Because every language incorporates a system of socially created significances, all human adults who have mastered this system will have a human, that is, semantic, consciousness. And because all human societies known to us engage in processes of dialogue and communication, we must make the assumption that in childhood, speech has gone inward and has reorganized some forms of psychological functioning in at least some domains. Vygotsky says just that "should it be exposed ethnologically, we would witness an all-encompassing stage of culture which has been reached during different epochs and in differing forms by all nations" (DHF, p. 108). Such a framework –

holding that adults in all cultures have higher sign-mediated systems of some kind – imposes a substantial constraint on developmental interpretations of cognitive differences among adult populations. Over and beyond the "all-encompassing stage of culture," differences will be located in the particular characteristics of higher systems and the functions they serve, not in the absence or presence of "higher thought." Because cultural means have developed over history, and will continue to develop, we expect to find continual changes in the structure and form of higher systems.

It would be possible, of course, to order higher systems in a progression according to their different characteristics, assigning one level to a certain historical period and another more advanced level to a nearer point in time. But just as Vygotsky does not offer a "progression of cultural stages," he does not offer a stagelike progression of higher forms of behavior. One reason, I believe, is that he does not represent higher systems as general modes of thought or as general structures of intelligence in a Piagetian sense. Vygotsky addressed the question of general processes of formation of particular functional systems, a project quite at variance from one aimed at delineating a particular sequence of general functional systems. In the passages quoted above, we note that Vygotsky's comparisons are always made with respect to some particular system of sign-mediated behavior – memory, counting, writing. As we will see, each of these systems has its own course of development; all of them ("higher" or "cultural" by definition) advance from rudimentary to more advanced forms. But there is no *necessity* in theory for all functional systems characterizing the behavior of an individual, or behaviors in a given social group, to be at the same level. Vygotsky's theory allows for the possibility, for example, that highly developed forms of memory or planned behavior will coincide with the use of primitive counting systems, or the other way around. Various combinations are theoretically conceivable. In actuality, because cultural means have a single line of historical development according to Vygotsky, all combinations are not likely to be realized: looking backward at early human societies, we find no examples of highly advanced mathematical systems in the absence of written notational systems. Thus Vygotsky sometimes refers globally to the "psychology of primitive man" (DHF, p. 41) and contrasts it, in dichotomous fashion, to the "higher psychology of modern man." His theoretical scheme, however, does not itself impose such global comparisons. Since his child–primitive comparisons are made with respect to particular functional systems, it is in Vygotsky's studies of the formation of these systems that we expect to locate their functional significance.

Higher psychological functions: A third line of history

Higher psychological functions have their own genesis and stages of development, – in the broadest sense, a history. This history, is, of course, embedded in the history of real people and is therefore realized on the two planes of phenomena we have already examined – general history and child history: "These functions, which from the point of view of phylogenesis are [products of] the historical development of the human personality possess also from the point of view of ontogenesis, their own particular history of development" (T&S, p. 64).

As compared to the history of humanity or child history, the history of the development of the higher psychological functions (this is Vygotsky's terminology) is "an absolutely unexplored field of psychology" (DHF, p. 1). Yet, Vygotsky argues, to understand the cultural development of the child, we need to know the specific features of structure and function that characterize higher systems, their origin and development to "full maturity and death" (DHF, p. 6), and the laws to which they are subject. The title of Vygotsky's "Development of Higher Mental Functions" now becomes clear. He proposes to accomplish psychology's mission – achieving an understanding of the formation of human nature (see the discussion under the heading "General history . . .") through studies of the origin and development of higher psychological functions *as such*. This is a radical enterprise for it amounts to nothing less than constructing a new object of scientific investigation. In the essays collected in "Tool and Symbol," Vygotsky set his exposition in the framework of approaches to child psychology and made it clear that his topic was human ontogeny. But in the later work, he equally clearly distinguishes his inquiry from the study of the child as a whole (DHF, p. 3). For purposes of theory construction, he takes as his conceptual object "higher psychological systems" and separates it from the natural object, the "child." [Glick (1983) makes this distinction between conceptual and natural objects in a penetrating analysis of Piaget's theory of development.]

Since Vygotsky took a new object for investigation, he needed a new method for this task: "The study of any new field must always begin by a search for and elaboration of method . . . the object and the method of study emerge as closely linked to each other" (DHF, p. 68).

How to begin? The psychologies of Vygotsky's day offered few leads. Cultural psychology was concerned with the products, not the processes, of cultural development. Traditional approaches in child psychology, including experimental psychology, did not recognize the separate status of cultural forms of behavior and offered neither concepts for thinking about them nor techniques for their investigation. It seemed necessary to begin at the beginning, with information about actual forms of cultural behavior. Where could one turn to find such material? Because the history of higher functions appears twice, once in child history and once in general history, it might appear that information derived from either of these two sources would serve as a suitable point of departure. Not so, says Vygotsky. We cannot follow the obvious path of sifting through the thousands of accumulated facts on child behavior, because this behavior is the product of two lines of development, the natural and the cultural, fused into a "common although complex process" (DHF, p. 37). The two can be disentangled through a process of abstraction, but such a process empties child development of the concrete content the theory builder needs. The way out of the difficulty is to turn to facts of behavior that are the product of the cultural line of development exclusively; these are to be found in the data of ethnic psychology, where higher psychological functions appear before our eyes in clear outline (DHF, p. 44). In phylogenesis,

> both these processes – that of the biological and cultural development of behavior – are represented as independent and self-sufficient lines of development. . . . Therefore we must turn to phylogenesis which shows no such unification and fusing of both lines so as to untie the complicated knot inherent in child psychology (DHF, p. 36, 37).

As this passage reveals, it was not only to demonstrate the validity of a historical materialist approach that Vygotsky ventured into folk psychology. His excursion was obligatory for methodological reasons: "For the clarification of the basic concepts . . . must by necessity, considering the present level of our knowledge of this issue, base itself on an analysis of how man's psyche developed during consecutive stages of historical development" (DHF, pp. 37, 38).

We now have an additional answer to the question that motivated this exploration of Vygotsky's approach: Why does Vygotsky place such emphasis on the facts of primitive life as the ethnopsychology of his day revealed them? They were the only available source of evidence about changing human behavior that could be used for a psychological analysis of the cultural development of behavior, or, what to Vygotsky was the same thing, the development of cultural forms of behavior. Ethnopsychological material was the only available source because Vygotsky's ideas about two lines of development in ontogeny precluded his use of facts of child behavior for this purpose until they were refracted through the evidence of general history.

This is a broad answer. But we can be more precise in Vygotsky's uses of historical data. He turned to ethnopsychology for discovery purposes and, if we follow his account, we can determine what discovery he made there. What follows is my logical reconstruction of Vygotsky's steps in building a method for the study of formation of cultural behavior. (We have no way of knowing, of course, whether or not the logical order coincided with the chronological order in which he actually carried out the work and developed his ideas.)

Constructing a model: General history as the middle link

Beginning with Vygotsky's stated goal of achieving a complete dynamic analysis of higher psychological systems, encompassing their genesis, structure, and function, we can identify four moments in his theory-building procedure. The first concerns the discovery of the structure of higher psychological systems. Although Vygotsky tells us he must turn to ethnic psychology to untie the knot in child psychology, in fact he begins to untie the knot with observations about the behavior of *contemporary*, not primitive, adults! As Vygotsky presents it, his starting points were little noticed, but everyday cultural forms of behavior. Certain phenomena, trivial in themselves, are significant to the psychologist for revealing in pure form the defining properties of all higher systems of behavior. Vygotsky called these phenomena "rudimentary forms" – vestiges of behavior developed early in cultural history, now functioning as "living fossils" removed from the contexts that gave them social meaning but valuable as prototypes or blueprints for study. Vygotsky singled out three such rudimentary cultural forms for analysis: casting lots, tying knots, and counting fingers. Each reveals the tripartite structure of cultural forms of behavior consisting of environmental stimulus and response and a human-created symbolic stimulus mediating between the two. Casting lots represents a situation in which a person creates an artificial stimulus to determine her choices in a situation in which a response is blocked by two equipotent and opposing stimuli; tying knots exemplifies the invention of a stimulus to ensure retrieval of information when it is needed; finger counting is the adaptation of always available objects to support intellectual procedures with a high potential for inaccuracy. Each form reveals the "key to higher behavior" (DHF, p. 129) – the transition point in which the species became human by creating symbolic means to master its own activity.

These rudimentary forms, however, have been superseded in modern societies by different forms of symbolic mediation. Although they are useful in helping the psychologist identify the structural components of higher systems and the primary instrumental function of signs, they cannot reveal their own future. To determine how rudimentary forms change to new forms requires a shift away from observations of everyday contemporary behavior to another domain of behavior. It is at this point, the second moment of theory building concerned with the transformation of structures, that the stuff of general history plays a critical role. At least with respect to some psychological functions, sufficient information is on hand to permit reconstruction of the phases of transformation through which rudimentary forms pass on the way to becoming higher systems. Examining the evidence from ethnopsychology, Vygotsky found that the history of transformation appears similar for various systems of higher behavior. External means of regulation of behavior (e.g., knots) "go inward," passing through a series of stages until symbolic regulation has an entirely intrapsychological form. In this sequence of interiorization, Vygotsky believed he had found a model of the formation of higher psychological functions that might apply to the cultural line of development in ontogeny as well as history. Such a model, of course, was hypothetical, since it was derived by the interpretative mode from documentary evidence. To be established as a scientific scheme, it required testing and elaboration. Observation of child behavior was not the optimal method of test for the reasons that limited the usefulness of facts of child behavior as a method of discovery in the first place. The fusion of two lines of development in child behavior conceals the pure form of cultural development.

Vygotsky's genius now takes hold – the historical sequence can serve as a model for an artificially evoked process of change in children, a process evoked through experimental means. If children of different ages are used as subjects and the experiment is appropriately set up [see chapter 5 in Vygotsky (1978)], the investigator will be able to follow the way in which children make the transition from rudimentary to higher psychological forms. The experiment will reveal in "pure and abstract form" (DHF, p. 130) how cultural development proceeds in ontogeny.[4] In the terms in which we have been laying out the logic of Vygotsky's procedure, the experimental-genetic method constitutes the third moment of theory building and the source, Vygotsky claimed, of the richest and most vital evidence. The experiment reveals the very essence of the genetic process. By its means, we can witness the drama of the formation of human nature unfolding according to its own laws of development.

Leont'ev's (1964) research on memory development is an especially clear example of the movement from ethnopsychological to experimental data that we have just described. His introduction to that research begins with a review of the phylogenetic history of human memory that traces the creation and elaboration of external signs as memory aids in history and their replacement by self-generated signs or behaviors that are solely internal. He presents this progression as conjectural. It serves only as a "hypothesis" for experimental investigations, whose task is to reproduce artificially under laboratory conditions the process of development of memory (Leont'ev, 1964).

At this juncture, material on the behavior of primitive humans does not represent as great a leap from descriptions of child behavior as the passages quoted so far first suggested. From a systematic point of view, primitive history comes into play to supplement knowledge of certain forms of behavior among contemporary adults with information about adults in earlier times. Ethnopsychology is thus related to child psychology only indirectly through the scheme it presents of how rudimentary cultural forms develop into higher forms.

The rudimentary functions . . . furnish us with a fulcrum for the historical approach to the higher psychological functions and for establishing a link between the psychology of primitive man and that of man's higher psychology. At the same time they furnish the scale by which we may transpose the data of ethnic psychology to experimental psychological research. (DHF, p. 104)

In the present interpretation, the stuff of general history prepares the way for experimental modeling of higher psychological systems. What about the stuff of child history? Observations about the actual developmental progress of contemporary children constitute the fourth moment of theory building. Vygotsky believed that models emerging from experimental studies are, of necessity, schematic and simplified (DHF, p. 221). The experiment fails to inform us about how higher systems are actually realized by the child; an experimentally induced process never mirrors genetic development as it occurs in life (Vygotsky, 1962, p. 69). Nor do experiments capture the rich variety of child behavior in the many settings in which children grow up and acquire culturally elaborated means made available to them in their particular social milieus. Although the experiment models the process, concrete research is required to bring the observations made there into harmony with observations of naturally occurring behavior. Child history provides the material to corroborate or correct the model and reveal how higher processes are formed in everyday activities (DHF, p. 222). Thus Vygotsky begins with and returns to observations of behavior in daily life to devise and test models of the history of higher systems. Starting from behavioral observations of contemporary adults, he moves to observations of primitive adults documented in ethnopsychological records and then, by way of experiment, to behavioral observations of children in modern times.

Vygotsky's sociohistorical approach turns out on analysis to be not only the foundation of his theory of development but a crucial element in his methodology as well. With this in mind, we can understand his somewhat scornful comment that only "sloth" (DHF, p. 48) would assimilate his theory to recapitulationist on parallelist positions. A final verdict is not yet in. But whatever ambiguities his works present, it is clear that he used ethnopsychological material principally for heuristic purposes. Vygotsky was advancing a complicated proposition for psychologists to consider: Look to cultural history for hypotheses about the origin and transformation of higher functional systems. His work may be read as an attempt to weave three strands of history – general history, child history, and the history of mental functions – into one explanatory account of the formation of specifically human aspects of human nature.

Conclusions: Extending the historical approach

Our analysis of Vygotsky's historical approach was motivated by current concerns in research on cultural variations in thought. Sociocultural changes are not a matter of past history but constitute a major condition of life in our times. Whereas investigators of cultural influences on thought have tended to concentrate their studies in traditional societies, new cultural means are being elaborated at an accelerating rate in industrialized nations as well. Hardly have we approached the problem of understanding the intellectual impact of the printing press (Eisenstein, 1979) than we are urged to confront the psychological implications of computerization (Tikhomirov, 1981). Technological and social changes occurring in all societies create a need for comprehensive theories of learning and development; at the same time they provide the context for fundamental research that can contribute to those theories and to more effective programs of education.

For these reasons, it would seem shortsighted to look upon Vygotsky's socio-historical approach as past achievement rather than as guide to the present. In what ways might we enhance the usefulness of this framework for contemporary cognitive science? One step is to arrive at a more balanced interpretation of Vygotsky's views on cultural differences in thought and a better appreciation of his methodology. Most of this chapter has been directed to that end. However, our analysis also points to certain inadequacies in Vygotsky's historical approach that may limit its current application. We might more accurately described these as "incompletenesses." Some of the theoretical ambiguities we have noted seem paradoxically to result from Vygotsky's failure to use the historical approach to the fullest: He did not encompass the full range of "phenomena in movement" on the level of either general history or individual history.

Consider general history. In Vygotsky's theory, this history appears as a single unidirectional course of sociocultural change. It is a world process that informs us of the genesis of specifically human forms of behavior and their changing structures and functions in the past. For Vygotsky's model-building purposes, it might have been sufficient to look back at history and view it in this way as one stream of development. But for purposes of concrete research, and for theory development in the present, such a view seems inadequate. Societies and cultural groups participate in world history at different tempos and in different ways. Each has its own past history influencing the nature of current change. Particular societies, for example, may adopt the "same" cultural means (e.g., writing system) but, as a result of their individual histories, its cognitive implications may differ widely from one society to the other. Saxe (1982) provides a dramatic example in his studies of the Oksapmin people of Papua New Guinea. Until recently, this aboriginal group relied exclusively on a rudimentary number system based on body parts to carry out simple quantitative operations needed in daily life. Saxe documents how the organization of the system is changing as a result of new occupational and trading activities. At the same time that this ancient system is undergoing modifications, indications are that the Oksapmin will soon be learning to use hand-held calculators to keep accounts in the number of trade stores in the country (Edwards, 1981). Americans are also learning to use hand-held calculators that are displacing highly routinized paper-and-pencil calculations that have long dominated arithmetic practice in school and personal life. In world history, written arithmetic precedes electronic arithmetic, and there is only this one course of cultural development. This sequence, however, is realized in United States history but not in Oksapmin history. Would we expect psychological implications of computer use to be equivalent in the two societies? Could this question be appropriately addressed in empirical research based on the world history model alone?

Many such discontinuities come to mind, but the import of this single comparison is clear. Individual societal histories are not independent of the world process, but neither are they reducible to it. To take account of this plurality, the Vygotskyian framework needs to be expanded to incorporate a "fourth level" of history – the history of individual societies. [For a discussion on issues in integrating the history of human society in general with the history of individual societies, see Semenov (1980).]

This expansion of the scheme would have the added advantage of firmly anchoring all studies of social and psychological change in the present. "The most primitive of now living tribes" is a member of a live culture and not a past one. This means that hypotheses about psychological change need to be informed by knowledge of conditions in cultures here and now, and not derived solely from historical reconstructions.

Now let us turn to the level of individual history. In Vygotsky, as in other classic developmental theories, ontogeny stops with the attainment of adolescence. Biological theories of parallelism, as we have pointed out, also work with this truncated ontogenetic sequence; perhaps there is some justification for this practice in biology inasmuch as maturational processes are most marked in early life stages. But what is the justification for a restricted individual biography in a psychological theory emphasizing the "cultural line of development"? Vygotsky himself said that it is not until adolescence that the "problems of cultural psychology" clearly emerge (DHF, p. 26). Whatever one's views about the nature of maturational processes in childhood, it is certain that in youth and adulthood normal psychological change is not attributable to these processes. Flavell (1970) described adulthood as a pure experiment in nature of the effect of experience, and Vygotsky acted on that concept when he resorted to observations of adult behavior to develop his experimental schemes. It is fascinating to consider why Vygotsky's group did not follow through on the logic of the method – why, with the exception of Luria's cross-cultural studies, adults dropped out of the research program. Whatever the reasons, opportunities are now present to fill in the missing link of adult cognitive change.

Basic theoretical questions are at issue. Do adults acquire new sign-systems and new sign-mediated functions in the same way as children? For example, is the learning-to-read process the same for adults with fully developed language competencies as for children? (Weber, 1977). Will Oksapmin adults and children assimilate calculators into their problem-solving routines differently? Does cognitive change in adults proceed in all cases, as with children, from the social interpsychological to the intrapsychological plane? Opportunities to investigate such questions are multiplying and, compatibly, so are the interests of developmental psychologists and educators in extending research to encompass the entire life span. It seems desirable, therefore, to enlarge Vygotsky's framework by replacing "child history" with "life history."

When we incorporate these revisions into Vygotsky's scheme, we have a historical framework consisting of four levels of "culture development" (depicted in Figure 20.1) in which to locate particular theoretical and research questions. It is customary for investigators concerned with culture and thought to single out for emphasis one or another level of change as seems suitable for the

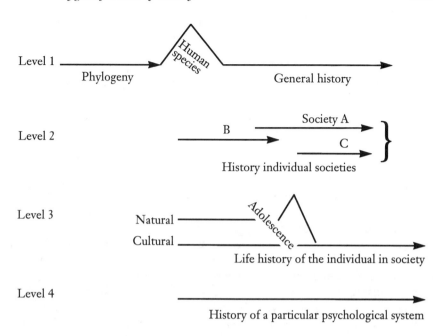

Figure 20.1. Vygotsky's levels of history – a modified scheme. (As explained in the text, we have modified the scheme to include level 2 and to extend level 3 to encompass adulthood.)

inquiry at hand. Psychologists, for example, tend to conceive of the individual as a dynamic system while assuming in their research designs that history on the societal level is static; anthropologists often make the reverse assumption. When Vygotsky turned his attention to specific topics of child development [e.g., play (Vygotsky, 1978)], he also followed the practice of assuming that only child history was in movement and other lines of cultural development remained constant. Extracting one process of change for study in this manner is a useful and often necessary technique. But Vygotsky's work in its totality makes clear the levels of cultural development are interrelated, that they are proceeding concurrently and mutually influencing each other. His framework is thus a useful guide for researchers who, increasingly today, confront the need to deal simultaneously with more than one level of change. Life-span developmental psychologists, for example, are challenging the dominant view that individual change can be studied independently of sociocultural change. Over a long period of time, the assumption of social stasis is untenable; an eighth-grade education may have been the national norm of half-century ago, but a high school education is the norm today. In this new field, investigators are devising and testing new techniques for studying concurrent changes in individual and social histories (see Schaie, Labouvie, and Buech, 1973).

Cross-cultural researchers are also discovering that presuppositions about the independence of individual and cultural change may need scrutiny. The typical paradigm for studying cognitive development cross-culturally assumes that in each society some stock of cultural means – language, number systems, and the like – is in place and has been mastered by adults who then, informally or formally, help children achieve competency in these systems. As our earlier discussion of Oksapmin society indicated, such assumptions may be unwarranted. We reported that in this aboriginal culture, three arithmetic systems may be competing with one another in the near future – the indigenous body-parts number system (itself undergoing change), paper-and-pencil school arithmetic, and calculator arithmetic. Parents may be shifting over from one or another system or devising inventive combinations of several systems at the very time their children are acquiring their first number concepts. A simple transmission model with arrows running from adult to child seems insufficient here. Novel questions arise. One might ask how adult–child dyadic learning relationships are affected when both members of the dyad are novices and are acquiring new number facts and computational skills together. Or we might want to inquire into the development of "binumeracy" (drawing an analogy with bi-literacy) among adults and children and investigate how uses of one or another number system are influenced by the characteristics of the particular arithmetic tasks that Oksapmin now encounter in their communities. We might be concerned to document whether social pressures are being generated for conversion to a modern number system at a faster rate than some adults are prepared to accept and what consequences such a situation might have for their children's learning progress.

These are among the intriguing questions posed by a consideration of Vygotsky's uses of history. Vygotsky presents us with a mode of theory-building that calls for the integration of all levels of history into one explanatory account of the sociohistorical formation of mind. Few may be ready to concern themselves with such a grand design, but whatever our disciplinary backgrounds, many of us will find it profitable to follow Vygotsky's invitation and explore new ways of bringing an historical perspective to the study of human nature.

Notes

1. My major sources were English translations of unpublished manuscripts by Vygotsky. One is a collection of essays under the title "Tool and Symbol in the Development of the Child" (referred to as T&S), and the second is the book-length manuscript "The Development of Higher Mental Functions" (referred to as DHF). Most of "Tool and Symbol" and some sections of "The Development of Higher Mental Functions" are available in published form in Vygotsky (1978). An abridged version of "The Development of Higher Mental Functions" is included in Leont'ev, Luria, and Smirnov (1966); Wertsch (1981) has a complete text of Vygotsky's chapter 5. The views I have credited to Vygotsky are all expressed in these published works, but I have followed

the practice of citing the manuscripts because these contained his fullest discussion of methodological choices.

In preparing this chapter I found that Vygotsky's essays in *Thought and Language* [published in English as Vygotsky (1962)] could not easily be integrated with material in the other manuscripts. *Thought and Language* contains Vygotsky's writings on generalization and the semantic structure of consciousness; in these essays, he presents *word meaning* as a crucial unit of analysis for the psychology of thought. In "Tool and Symbol" and "The Development of Higher Mental Functions," on the other hand, Vygotsky deals with the role of speech and other sign systems in intellectual operations and treats higher psychological systems as a unit of analysis for developmental psychology. Piaget's distinction between figurative and operative aspects of thought comes to mind, though I do not mean to imply that this classification is appropriate for Vygotsky's work. As additional writings become available, Vygotsky scholars may achieve a better integration of these approaches. For my purposes, I thought it best to confine my account to the two works on higher mental systems because it is in these that Vygotsky engages in the most extensive discussion of methodology.

Because of these limitations in source material, the interpretation I present here has to be considered incomplete.

2. Vygotsky's terminology presents a number of problems, some of which I have flagged in the text. He uses the terms "historical development" and "cultural development" interchangeably. On some occasions he uses the term "phylogeny" to refer to the biological evolution of species and distinguishes this sequence of development from general history. But, on other occasions, he uses "phylogeny" in a superordinate sense to encompass both biological and historical development. In discussing child development, Vygotsky sometimes contrasts the *biological* and cultural lines of change, and at other times draws the contrast between *natural* and cultural lines. Wertsch (pers. commu.) believes that Vygotsky was not consistent in his use of the term "natural": "Sometimes he equated it with biological phenomena, but sometimes it also seems to have included elements of what Piaget would later call sensorimotor intelligence."

3. Luria's studies appear to have been inspired principally by Vygotsky's work on concept formation and generalization, as reported in *Thought and Language,* rather than by the work on higher mental functions [see account in Luria (1971)]. Vygotsky's treatment of concept formation seems to imply a stronger developmental approach to sociohistorical changes in thought than do his other writings, but further analysis is needed.

4. The account given here of the methodological significance of Vygotsky's experimental-genetic studies is substantially the same as that presented by El'konin (1967). He asserts that the aim of Vygotsky's research was modeling, rather than empirically studying, developmental processes. But he also observes that this interpretation has not been widely recognized.

References

Cole, M. 1976. Introduction. In A. R. Luria, *Cognitive development: Its cultural and social foundations.* Cambridge: Harvard University Press.

Cole, M., and Griffin, P. 1980. Cultural amplifiers reconsidered. In D. R. Olson (Ed.), *The social foundations of language and thought.* New York: Norton.

Cole, M., and Scribner, S. 1977. Developmental theories applied to cross-cultural cognitive research. *Annals of the New York Academy of Sciences, 285,* 366–373.

Cole, M., and Scribner, S. 1978. Introduction. In L. S. Vygotsky, *Mind in society.* Cambridge: Harvard University Press.

Edwards, A. 1981. Papua New Guinea: Calculating the way to numeracy. *Bulletin 12.* Reading, England: University of Reading Agricultural Extension and Rural Development Center. May, pp. 20–21.

Eisenstein, E. L. 1979. *The printing press as an agent of change.* New York: Cambridge University Press.

El'konin, D. B. 1967. The problem of instruction and development in the works of L. S. Vygotsky. *Soviet Psychology, 5*(3), 34–41.

Flavell, J. H. 1970. Cognitive changes in adulthood. In P. Baltes and L. R. Goulet (Eds.), *Life-span developmental psychology.* New York: Academic Press, pp. 247–253.

Glick, J. 1983. Piaget, Vygotsky and Werner. In S. Wapner and B. Kaplan (Eds.), *Towards a holistic developmental psychology.* Hillsdale, N.J.: Erlbaum.

Gould, S. J. 1977. *Ontogeny and phylogeny.* Cambridge: Harvard University Press.

Graham, L. R. 1972. *Science and philosophy in the Soviet Union.* New York: Knopf.

Grinder, R. E. 1967. *A history of genetic psychology, the first science of human development.* New York: Wiley.

Hallowell, A. I. 1967. The recapitulation theory and culture. In A. I. Hallowell, *Culture and experience.* New York: Schocken.

Hallpike, C. R. 1979. *The foundations of primitive thought.* New York: Oxford University Press.

Lave, J. 1981. Review of *The foundations of primitive thought* by C. R. Hallpike. *Contemporary Psychology, 26,* 788–790.

Leont'ev, A. N., and Luria, A. R. 1968. The psychological ideas of L. S. Vygotsky. In B. B. Wolman (Ed.), *Historical roots of contemporary psychology.* New York: Harper & Row.

Leont'ev, A. N., Luria, A., and Smirnov, A. (Eds.) 1966. *Psychological research in the U.S.S.R.* (Vol. 1). Moscow: Progress Publishers.

Leont'ev, A. N. 1964. *Problems of mental development.* Washington, D.C.: U.S. Joint Publications Research Service.

Luria, A. R. 1971. Towards the problem of the historical nature of psychological processes. *International Journal of Psychology, 6,* 259–272.

Luria, A. R., 1976. *Cognitive development: Its cultural and social foundations.* Cambridge: Harvard University Press.

Marx, K., and Engels, F. 1846. *The German ideology* (reprint. ed.). New York: International Publishers, 1970.

Randall, Jr., J. H. 1962. *Nature and historical experience: Essays in naturalism and in the theory of history.* New York: Columbia University Press.

Saxe, G. B. 1982. Developing forms of arithmetic thought among the Oksapmin of Papua New Guinea. *Developmental Psychology 18,* 583–594.

Schaie, K. W., Labouvie, G. V., and Buech, B. U. 1973. Generational and cohort-specific differences in adult cognitive functioning. *Developmental Psychology, 9,* 151–166.

Scribner, S., and Cole, M. 1981. *The psychology of literacy*. Cambridge: Harvard University Press.

Semenov, Y. I. 1980. The theory of socioeconomic formations and world history. In E. Gellner (Ed.), *Soviet and Western anthropology*. New York: Columbia University Press.

Spencer, H. 1888. *The principles of sociology* (Vol. 1) (3rd ed.) New York: Appleton.

Tikhomirov, O. K. 1981. The psychological consequences of computerization. In J. V. Wertsch (Ed.), *The concept of activity in Soviet psychology*. Armonk, N.Y.: Sharpe.

Toulmin, S. 1978. The Mozart of psychology. *New York Review of Books*, Sept. 28.

Vygotsky, L. S. 1962. *Thought and language*. Cambridge: MIT Press.

Vygotsky, L. S. 1966. Development of the higher mental functions (abridged). In *Psychological research in the U.S.S.R.* (Vol. 1). Moscow: Progress Publishers.

Vygotsky, L. S. 1978. *Mind in society: The development of higher mental processes*. Cambridge: Harvard University Press.

Vygotsky, L. S. 1981. The genesis of higher mental functions. In J. V. Wertsch (Ed.), *The concept of activity in Soviet psychology*. Armonk, N. Y.: Sharpe.

Wagner, D. A., and Paris, S. G., 1981. Problems and prospects in comparative studies of memory. *Human Development*, 24: 412–424.

Weber, R. 1977. Learning to read: The linguistic dimension for adults. In T. P. Gorman (Ed.), *Language and literacy: Current issues and research*. Teheran: International Institute for Adult Literacy Methods.

Wertsch, J. V. (Ed.) 1981. *The concept of activity in Soviet psychology*. Armonk, N.Y.: Sharpe.

White, S. H. 1976. Developmental psychology and Vico's concept of universal history. *Social Research*, 43, 659–671.

21   A sociocultural approach
       to the study of mind

This chapter examines the contribution of the sociohistorical school of psychology to the construction of a scientific methodology of mind. What are the philosophical premises and guiding constructs of this school, and how does it frame research questions about the origin and development of mind? After a brief theoretical exposition, I describe and analyze a series of studies designed to test a particular hypothesis about cognitive change derived from this theory. In this account, I "descend" to a level of description involving particulars of research design and interpretation not often included in a treatment of epistemological issues. I have two justifications for this approach. First, a scientific epistemology, as distinct from one based on metaphysical speculation, is grounded on knowledge gained through the empirical procedures of the various disciplines investigating mind. We need to concern ourselves, then, with the logic, possibilities, and limitations of the research methods now on hand in these disciplines and the questions they most suitably address. A second reason is pragmatic. Exemplifying a theoretical approach enhances its graspability. Because the social-historical school of psychology is only now becoming widely known, I want to bring both example and principle to bear in considering its contribution to the epistemic enterprise.

One other introductory observation is in order. As our discussion here demonstrates, the terms *mind, cognition, knowing,* and *knowledge* tend to acquire different content as they move from one discourse or scientific frame of reference to another. Or, more troublesome still, they seem at times to lose concrete content altogether, blending into general abstract concepts that are not amenable to any particular methodology or disciplinary attack. Let me put my enter-

This essay originally appeared in *Theories of the Evolution of Knowing,* ed. G. Greenberg and E. Tobach (Hillsdale, N.J.: Lawrence Erlbaum Associates, 1990). Reprinted with the permission of Lawrence Erlbaum Associates.

prise into perspective then, by taking the general concept of cognition and giving it specific content as an object of inquiry in theory and research.

As a cognitive developmental psychologist, my interest is centered on human cognition, and my research is addressed to questions about the structure, function, and mode of development of human cognition. More specifically, I have been concerned with understanding those aspects of human cognition that early psychologists (Wundt, 1916, for example, and see discussion on Vygotsky following) referred to as the "higher psychological functions." They subsumed under this term such complex processes as logical reasoning, intentional memory, planning, and decision making, among others. Although the term has fallen out of favor, the new cognitive sciences, especially those employing information-processing and artificial intelligence models (e.g., Newell & Simon, 1972, on problem solving; Johnson-Laird, 1983, on syllogistic reasoning; Gentner & Gentner, 1983, on mental models, among others) and much of developmental psychology (Brown, 1978; Brown, Bransford, Ferrara & Campione, 1983, on metacognition; Piaget & Inhelder, 1958, on propositional reasoning: Joffe-Falmagne, 1980, on deductive inference) continue to devote major resources to conceptualizing and studying these complex mental phenomena.

Tobach (1987) holds that a scientific understanding of changing (developing) phenomena rests on an identification of both continuities and discontinuities in underlying processes. This principle would certainly seem to carry special force in an inquiry into the grounds of knowing. However, as a number of contributions to this volume attest, the deployment of neo-Darwinian concepts and mechanisms to epistemological objects maintains a one-sided focus on cross-species continuities in cognition. Missing from theories involving biological mechanisms (e.g., blind variation; Campbell, 1960) as primary means of knowledge acquisition throughout the phylogenetic scale is any considered treatment of discontinuities – in particular, the special modes of knowing that arise in human society and bring into being those qualitatively distinct, "higher" intellectual functions that generations of psychologists have sought to understand and that remain the central concern of philosophical epistemology. It is the leading achievement of the sociohistorical school of psychology that it puts forward an account of these functions that resorts to neither vitalism nor reductionism (Vygotsky, 1981); this account, therefore, offers important theoretical resources for the construction of a scientific epistemology.

Sociohistorical theory and cognitive psychology

L. S. Vygotsky (1896–1934) is the founder of a dialectical materialist approach to psychological theory that has been variously characterized as a "sociocultural" or "sociohistorical" framework. His students and colleagues – A. R. Luria and A. N. Leont'ev are among the better known – together with other psychologists and philosophers in the Soviet Union elaborated and sys-

BASIC ATTRIBUTES OF HUMAN COGNITION
(Higher Psychological Functions)

STRUCTURE	Mediated (tools/signs)
FUNCTION	In goal-directed activities
MODE OF DEVELOPMENT	Historical/Social

Figure 21.1. Sociohistorical Theory of Mind.

tematized this framework, which, in recent years, has become internationalized (Engestrom, 1987; Hildebrand-Nilshon & Ruckriem, 1988; Wertsch, 1981). Now identified as "activity theory," this project may be more accurately characterized on the level of *meta*theory. Seeking to overcome Cartesian dualities, it lays out new analytic categories for the construction of domain-level theories within the respective subfields of epistemology (Lektorsky, 1980) and psychology (Leont'ev, 1978, 1979). Within psychology, various schools of thought (Brushlinskii, 1987; Kozulin, 1986; Laboratory for Comparative Human Cognition, 1983; Wertsch, 1985) offer alternative views of how these basic level categories can best be brought to bear in investigating and explaining processes of learning and development. In spite of these divergences, most scholars accept Vygotsky's (1978; 1986) main ideas as essential building blocks.

I present here (Fig. 21.1) a simplified and schematic sketch of these building blocks as they bear on the topic at hand: human cognition.[1]

Three terms capture the principal features distinguishing human knowing from that of other species: Human cognition is *culturally mediated;* it is founded on *purposive activity;* and it is *historically developing.* These are three interconnected constructs, and although I consider them individually, we will see how they work together.

A defining characteristic of human behavior generally and of human cognition in particular that sets it apart from the behavior of other species is that humans do not interact directly with the environment (Vygotsky, 1978; 1981). Rather, they regulate their interactions with each other and with the environment through systems of "objects." These objects stand in-between, or "mediate" human actions in the world. The classic case of human activity mediated by objects is labor; and Marx's (1967) description of the role of tools or instruments in this process served Vygotsky as a prototype of all human actions: "The elementary factors of the labour-process are 1) the personal activity of man, i.e., work itself, 2) the subject of that work, and 3) its instruments. . . . An instrument of labour is a thing, or a complex of things, which the labourer interposes between himself and the subject of his labour, and which serves as the conductor of his activity" (p. 174).

Vygotsky extended this notion of mediating instruments to human intellectual as well as behavioral functions. Human thinking, he said, is mediated by signs, just as human behavior in the world – practical behavior – is mediated by tools. Incorporation of cultural sign systems into human mental activity is the decisive moment in evolutionary history, transforming "elementary" cognitive processes into the complex functional systems ("higher" functions) that characterize mature thought in all human societies. (See Leont'ev & Luria, 1968, for later criticism of this view.)

A rudimentary illustration of sign-mediated cognition is remembering with the aid of external cues. The practice of cutting notches in sticks is an early example of human use of objects as "conductors" of mental activity. Instead of relying on the spontaneous appearance of cues for recall, humans introduce changes in the world that help them regulate and control their own memory processes. The notched stick has no significance as a physical object; it is what the notch stands for – its meaning – that affects the remembering process. In human consciousness, significant mediating "signs" are not simply isolated things of this kind, but complex symbolic systems. Language is the principal and universal sign system, which functions not only as the prime vehicle of species communication but as the means through which humans acquire conceptual thought. Significant mediators include number, writing, and other notational systems, and more broadly, all artifactual and ideational (knowledge, theories) systems through which and by means of which humans cognize the world. As is clear, "symbols" or signs in this theory are not the meaningless strings of manipulable elements that feature in computer models of mind; they are semantic objects. Mediators are cultural, therefore, in the most profound sense: All meaning-systems whether in the form of beliefs, knowledge, or scientific theories are products of human culture; and they are invented and transmitted through the social processes and institutions by which succeeding generations reproduce and change their cultural heritage.

The concept that human activity, including its cognitive aspects, has a tripartite structure has profound theoretical implications. Psychological theories have historically attempted to account for behavioral and mental development through two terms: *organism* and *environment*. Theories are distinguished from one another by the way in which they combine these terms; "environmental determinists" stress the primacy of one term; "nativists" or "organicists" stress the primacy of the other; and "interactionists" stress the reciprocal effects of both. A tripartite scheme – *organism*, *environment*, and *cultural mediator* – radically changes the structure of explanation of human behavior and cognition (Davydov & Radzikhovsky, 1985), and provides a new foundation for epistemological endeavors. (Lektorsky, 1980, develops these implications from a philosophical standpoint.)

We move now to the second term: *purposive activity*. In the view of the sociohistorical school, mental and behavioral processes are aspects of a unitary system of human action-in-the-world. Planning, remembering, reasoning, and problem solving — cognitive acts in general – are not undertaken as isolated acts or ends in themselves; they are not functions of a mind cut off from a body. Rather they are indissolubly tied to behavioral actions, with both embedded in larger systems of activity whose purposes they serve. Cognition functions as an integral aspect of purposive activities. In every human society, socially patterned systems of activities (sometimes referred to as social practices) arise to satisfy human needs and aspirations: We play, we work, we praise the gods, we conduct experiments, we go to school. These larger, motivationally driven activities provide what is loosely called the "context" of cognition. Such activities may be primarily directed toward practical ends (productive labor is the prototype here) or they may serve aesthetic, ideational or affective ends; all are directed at satisfying motives that are socially generated, and all are carried out through social means and modes of action. As individuals participate in these socially patterned activities, they acquire the cultural forms of acting and thinking incorporated in them; reciprocally, they contribute to changing these activities and to inventing new modes of action and thought. In the contemporary form of the sociohistorical school (activity theory), this category of purposive activity has become the central explanatory construct for understanding behavioral and mental development. For cognitive inquiry, the theoretical implication is that empirical sciences such as developmental psychology need to shift away from preoccupation with the "individual human mind" as the sole or principal unit of analysis for understanding modes of thought (as in Piagetian theory) to a consideration of the systems of socially constituted activity in which human consciousness and behavior develop.

Finally we come to *mode of development.* It follows from the culturally mediated nature of human psychological systems and their functional role in social practices that changes in the sociocultural level of organization will have major implications for changes in psychological organization. Social practices and activities change over time, and so do symbolic mediational means. Such transformations are to be understood as constructed historically through human action, rather than resulting from changes in the biological constitution of the human organism. Although evolutionary mechanisms account for the origins of elementary mental processes, their organization into functional, sign-mediated systems comes about through historical processes: History, rather than phylogeny, becomes the dominant motor of cognitive change. Vygotsky expressed this conclusion in the following way (cited in Scribner, 1985): "Human behavior differs from animal behavior in the same qualitative manner as the entire type of adaptability and historical development of man differs from the adaptability and development of animals, because the process of man's *mental development* is part of *the general historic development of mankind* [emphasis added]" (p. 123).

Note that this view accounts for both universal and culturally specific features of human thought. All humans participate in a general species history in which human activities became organized around symbolic-communicative and technical means; thus all exhibit "higher mental functions." But because activities and means vary over time and space, these cognitive functional systems will also reflect such differences. (For a fuller exposition of Vygotsky's historical methodology, see Scribner, 1985.)

("Evolutionary epistemology" in this view serves as only one leg on which a scientific methodology of mind can stand: "historical epistemology" is the other, Wartofsky, 1982).

The distinctive contribution of sociohistorical theory of cognition is also highlighted when it is contrasted to another contemporary epistemologic enterprise that seeks empirical grounding—the effort by certain analytic philosophers to formalize relations between philosophy's classic concern with the grounds for "true and justified belief" and the knowledge psychology provides about cognitive processes. Goldman's (1986) attempt at synthesis is of special interest here, for he makes clear that he looks to cognitive science to provide knowledge about the *human* mind because the human mind's "belief-forming processes" are relevant to epistemology. Goldman's human mind, however, is timeless. It has an "architecture" or "intrinsic properties" that Goldman looks to psychology to identify and describe; epistemology is concern with "native cognitive mechanisms" whose strength and weaknesses epistemology assesses. Thus, on the other hand, we confront theories (e.g., Campbell) that focus on evolutionary mechanisms of change in mental processes but that fail to account for the special characteristics of human mind; on the other, we have theories (e.g., Goldman) that take the distinctive characteristics of human mind as the object of inquiry but that fail to account for its origin in evolution or change over historical time. Vygotsky's sociohistorical theory contributes a perspective for overcoming this opposition.

Methodology

Certain methodological principles are implicated in this approach. The theory suggests that changes on the sociocultural level – changes in activities and mediational means – will afford possibilities for changes in individual cognition. Accordingly, an analysis of changing social practices becomes integral to – rather than merely peripheral to – an inquiry into learning and development. This framework also places a premium on the comparative method, one that searches for commonalities and differences among social practices within or between cultures. In certain domains of investigation, the accumulated research base and conceptual framework may be adequate for the formulation of specific hypotheses about the way in which changes in social activities articulate with cognitive change. However, as is the case with other "grand" or metatheories, activity theory provides no formula for a search for specific mediating mechanisms. Working from the level of general theory to the generation of particular hypotheses requires the usual mix of knowledge, example, and intuition. Fortunately, examples of useful empirical investigations within the socio-historical theoretical approach are accumulating (Engestrom & Engestrom, 1984; Hacker, 1982; Saxe, 1982; Scribner, 1984; Tulviste, 1979), providing grist for further theory development.

I describe one such investigation, drawing on my own experience, to illustrate both the problems and possibilities of this approach. The research question stemmed directly from Vygotsky's hypothesis about symbolic mediators and their cognitive implications: Specifically, we attempted to test empirically whether mastery of a written language systems fosters special modes of memory and thinking.

Speculations on literacy and thought

The choice of literacy as a domain for testing a sociocultural approach to cognition had certain obvious advantages. We cannot doubt that writing systems are a human invention whose origins lies in history rather than in biological evolution. Characteristics and uses of earliest known scripts have been shown to change over time in consonance with changing social practices – expansion of trade, for example (Schmandt-Besserat, 1978) or changes in modes or religious education (Resnick & Resnick, 1988). And, a great deal of evidence, drawn from various historical epochs, indicates that the introduction of writing systems often went hand-in-hand with the accumulation of knowl-edge and changes in intellectual practices (Goody, 1968). Most challenging was the fact that, although speculations about the relationship between "writing" and "mind" stretch back to antiquity, great thinkers failed to reach consensus about the nature of that relationship. Contrary responses of Greek philosophers to the spread of literacy among them characterize this age-old debate. Rational analysis suggested to Socrates that writing would diminish human powers by leading to forgetfulness and a propensity to confuse "words" and "ideas." Rational analysis suggested to Plato, however, that writing would strengthen human reason by freeing it from the emotional connotations that inhere in language in the oral mode.

Since the last century, comparative scholars in such fields as history, anthro-pology, and linguistics have sought to bring philosophical speculation into con-tact with evidence derived from field work studies and documentary analyses. Goody (1977, 1987), a leading scholar in this field, has concluded that the weight of this evidence strongly supports an "enhancement" position: Literacy (especially alphabetic literacy) fosters abstract reasoning, logical inference, hier-archical classification, and other higher cognitive functions.

Significant as these analyses are for informing us of the intricate pattern of relationships among literacy activities and other cultural practices, they fall short of providing critical evidence for generalizations about cognitive change in individuals. Social science scholars have assumed that these relationships – for example, the relationships between alphabetic literacy in Greece and Aristotle's invention of the syllogism – are mediated by changed modes of thinking in individuals, but they offer no direct evidence that this is the case. Historically, the kinds of observations that substantiate claims about individual thought processes have been the province of psychology and a product of its theories and investigative methods. To support the thesis that literacy makes a difference in mental processes, psychological analysis has to be joined with cultural analysis. Vygotsky recognized this necessity, and it is not accidental that he was the first to organize *experimental* research into the consequences of schooling and literacy (Luria, 1976; for an appraisal of this research, see Cole, 1988).

A project for identifying literacy as a mediator of cognitive change puts stringent demands on research design. Prospective longitudinal studies require more control over literacy education programs for a longer period of time with a larger group of people than most researchers can achieve. Cross-sectional comparisons of literate and nonliterate individuals appear more feasible but these must meet many constraints:

- To sustain inferences that literacy is the crucial mediating mechanism requires comparisons among literate and nonliterate people living in the same social milieu, speaking the same language, and experiencing life circumstances that do not differ in any systematic way. Precluded, therefore, are such ready-to-hand comparisons as those between affluent literates and poor nonliterates, or between literates who speak and write English and nonliterates who speak Spanish.
- It requires that literacy be disentangled from other educative experiences such as knowledge acquisition, which co-occur with literacy instruction in school.
- Finally, it requires that we distinguish cognitive changes that may be associated with literacy from general developmental changes in intellectual function, such as those posited by Piaget for the period up to and including adolescence. Precluded, therefore, is any research design in which increasing mastery of literacy covaries with increasing age.

Such constraints argue for a within-culture comparison of "like" adults among whom some form of literacy is achieved outside of schooling – a prescriptive model that forces researchers to seek specialized sites for their inquiry and forces psychologists out of the laboratory into the field.

Literacy in Vai land

We were fortunate in finding a site among the Vai people in West Africa that satisfied many of these constraints. The Vai are a Mande-speaking people who, like their neighbors, practice slash-and-burn rice farming using simple iron tools, but they have attained a special place in world history as one of the few cultures to have independently invented a phonetic writing system (Dalby, 1967; Gelb, 1952; Koelle, 1854). The Vai script is a syllabary of some 200 characters and has been in active use within the context of traditional rural life for almost 2 centuries. Widely available to all members of the society (although in practice restricted to men), Vai script is passed on from one individual to another, much as are other specialized skills such as weaving or tailoring; schooling is not involved nor is there any institutionalized profession for teaching the script. Moreover, Vai script coexists with two universalistic and institutionally powerful scripts – the Arabic and English alphabets – which are also used by some Vai people in the village setting. Arabic literacy is acquired through instruction in the Qu'ran (relying primarily on recitation and memorization), and English literacy is acquired through attendance in Western-type schools. These circumstances established conditions for a "natural experiment," as it were, in which we could compare unschooled literacies (Vai script and Arabic) with literacy-cum-schooling (English), and the two nonschooled literacies with each other. (For a full description of the Vai literacy research program, see Scribner & Cole, 1981.)

An interdisciplinary approach

We assembled an interdisciplinary team including anthropologists (one of whom was a Vai man), experts in the Vai script, and cognitive psychologists. The first phase of the research consisted of a sociocultural analysis of literacy practices in each of the scripts. Through ethnographic observations and systematic survey interviews, we sought to determine the larger activities in which reading and writing tasks were embedded. How were the scripts used in ritual, trade, and craft, in family relations, in government administration? We sought, too, to outline principal characteristics of the instructional settings in which each script was learned, a project that led us to conduct on-site field studies of Qu'ranic learning in the villages and to document various forms of tutorial instruction in the Vai script. Not surprisingly, we found great diversity of practices associated with each script: Each literacy had its own distinguishing features, mode of instruction, specialized social functions, cultural meaning, and symbolic significance. There was no "literacy in general" among the Vai.

We are now in a position to undertake psychological studies focusing on literacy as a mechanisms of cognitive change. In our first experimental assay, we used standard experimental paradigms that were initially designed to serve as indices of developmental status among Western-schooled children and adults, but which had also been widely used in cross-cultural research. These included classification and word memory tasks, syllogistic reasoning problems, similarity judgments, and the like. A principal outcome of these studies was a "school effect": Only those Vai people who had attended Western-type schools consistently performed in accordance with Western norms. Because schooled people were also the only participants with prior practice in tasks of this kind (most standard experimental tasks involve skills implicated in school performance), this outcome was basically uninterpretable as well as unilluminating with respect to our literacy hypotheses.

With this experience on hand, we reevaluated the methodological implications of our theoretical framework. This framework emphasizes the specificity of mediational systems and the varying as well as the common aspects of social practices. It appears that, if we want to use experiments to investigate the relationship between some aspect of social practice and cognition, we need to construct tasks that bear a closer relationship to the practices of interest than standard laboratory paradigms. We turned again to observational procedures, this time for a more fine-grained analysis of the modal reading and writing tasks required in literacy practices involving the different scripts. After identifying such tasks, we analyzed their component cognitive skills and devised experimental tasks embodying them. Rather than function as general instruments of assessment, our tasks served as models of those arising in naturally occurring activities. We used them to test a generalization question: Did the skills we had identified in everyday literacy activities generalize to cognitive tasks encountered outside the context of the original practice? Here by way of illustration is a description of one line of investigation involving hypothesized skills in Vai script literacy.

Illustrative experiment

Reading hand-written letters from friends and kin was one of the most common functions of Vai script literacy, and our observations indicated that it was a cognitively demanding one. Graphic signs in the Vai script represent syllables in the spoken language, but there is not a perfect correspondence between them. Vowel tone and vowel length, two semantically crucial features for understanding spoken Vai, are not represented in the script and need to be inferred from context. Writing conventions, as in ancient Greece, do not segment lines of text into words or other semantic or syntactic units. Each syllable stands alone with space surrounding it. Because Vai words may consist of more than one syllable, readers must find a way of integrating individual syllables on the sheet of paper into meaningful chunks of language. A common solution to these problems is reading aloud – grouping and regrouping strings of syllables that are problematic and varying their pronunciation until they are organized into such meaningful chunks. In this recycling process, readers must keep separate syllables in mind until they can be integrated into words or phrases. We supposed that this experience might foster skills in integration of linguistic units, and that these skills might be available for language processing in contexts that did not involve the script.

Table 21.1. *Means scores on auditory task, integration survey*

Literacy Group	Word sentences Perfectly recalled (max 5)	Syllable sentences Perfectly recalled (max 5)
Nonliterate men	1.45	.90
Arabic literates		
Qur'anic only	2.50	1.00
Arabic language	2.60	1.10
Beginning Vai script literates	2.80	1.10
Advanced Vai script literates	2.85	2.40

Note: Adapted from Scribner & Cole (1981).

To test this idea, we developed an oral comprehension and recall task. We asked nonliterates and members of the various literacy groups to listen to tape recordings of a native Vai speaker. The speaker presented meaningful Vai sentences one at a time without tonal variations, mimicking their representation in the script. Each informant received two sets of sentences; sentences in one set were segmented into nine syllable units separated by a 2-second pause; sentences in the other set were segmented into an equal number of word units. Word unit sentences served as a baseline control for possible individual or group differences in hearing or memory. Informants were asked to repeat each sentence immediately after hearing it, and to answer a comprehension question about it.

We conducted a number of studies with various population groups, replicating basic results. Table 21.1 displays the general pattern of our findings – namely, a striking interaction between population group and task materials.

There were no distinguishable differences among literacy groups in recall comprehension ("perfect recall") of sentences segmented into words, and all literacy groups were superior in performance to nonliterates. But recall dropped precipitously on syllable unit sentences for all groups except those classified as Advanced Vai script readers based on reading test scores. Proficient Vai script readers had comparable performances on words and syllables, whereas readers of other scripts dropped to the level of nonliterates when syllables were substituted for words. Regression analysis confirmed the contribution of Vai script reading score to syllable recall measures. We performed an even more stringent test: We entered each person's recall score for word sentences as a control in equations predicting syllable recall scores. We wanted to determine whether additional factors, over and above those contributing to word sentence recall, facilitated integration and interpretation of syllables. Of 20 background factors examined, only one affected performance – advanced reading scores in Vai script. This outcome provides the most compelling evidence that ability to understand, remember, and reproduce sentences parsed into syllables reflects expertise in reading Vai script – no other literacy or experimental factors examined in our analyses offered an alternative route to these skills. Moreover, these analyses indicated that it was not merely exposure to Vai script literacy but level of mastery attained that was critical to performance; the fact that different levels of proficiency within a single literacy group made a difference strengthens the argument that the skills involved in the experimental tasks were indeed literacy related. We went one step further in unpackaging "Advanced Vai Script" proficiency. We compared individuals classified in the Beginning and Advanced Vai script groups and found them similar in demographic characteristics such as age, knowledge of languages, and the like but quite different in the quantity and quality of their literacy activities. Advanced Vai script informants had known the script twice as long as Beginning Vai informants; they reported using it more often and for more diversified purposes; all had taught the script to someone else whereas only a minority of Beginning Vai had ever taught it.

These experimental studies suggest that practice in reading may promote the acquisition of specialized skills for linguistic analysis in the auditory mode: Reading may improve listening comprehension. This result is neither trivial nor self-evident. Recall that all Vai people in these studies were native speakers; no group had more or less experience listening to naturally spoken Vai than any other. Vai script readers, however, were also required to hear and make sense of segmented Vai, a form of linguistic analysis not demanded in situations of oral communication. Because our observational and experimental evidence implicate the same set of skills, we can present a strong case for the formative role of literacy practice.

In other experiments designed on the same lines, we demonstrated literacy effects on higher order cognitive skills. Vai script literates engage in discussion and criticism of modes of expression in written communication – a practice that enhanced their ability to detect and explain syntactical deviations in spoken Vai. These literacies, with extensive experience in letter writing, were also superior to others in a variety of oral instructional tasks that required the transmission of explicit information in a well-structured form. As for Arabic literates, we found that a memory strategy used for rote learning of Qu'ranic verses was generalized to an experimental recall tasks in which it was an efficient means of accurate information retrieval. Moreover, the strategy was more effectively used by those with longer periods of Qu'ranic study than by novice students.

The skills associated with literacy in Vai country are not necessarily associated with everyday literacy in other societies, nor do literacy activities here represent the full range of practical and intellectual functions of literacy in other parts of the world. The general significance of the research, therefore, lies not so much in its specific findings as in the methodology it developed for analyzing how changes in symbolic mediators (e.g., new writing systems) and in social practices (e.g., communication by letter instead of messenger) affect changes in individual cognition. The methodology is time consuming, labor intensive, and dependent on the organization of knowledge and techniques from a number of disciplines. The information it yields is detailed and local, and it speaks to theory in a cumulative fashion, an incremental manner; it neither upholds nor disconfirms grand theories. But we hope that small gains made by many investigators will, in time, contribute to a more systematic theory of the sociohistorical development of human thought and the working out of an integrative framework in which human thought takes its place in the evolutionary scheme.

Note

1. Leont'ev (1981) provides a comprehensive and creative account of the origin and development of mind across the entire phylogentic spectrum from an activity theory perspective. His account, with contributions dating from the early 1940s, serves as an early model of an empirically based epistemology.

References

Brown, A. L. (1978). Knowing when, where and how to remember: A problem of metacognition. In R. Glaser (Ed.), *Advances in instructional psychology* (Vol. 1). Hillsdale, NJ: Lawrence Erlbaum Associates.

Brown, A. L., Bransford, J., Ferrara, R., & Campione, J. (1983). Learning, remembering and understanding. In P. H. Mussen (Ed.), *Handbook of child psychology* (Vol. 1). New York: Wiley.

Brushlinskii, A. V. (1987). Activity, action and mind as process. *Soviet Psychology, 25*, 59–81.

Campbell, D. T. (1960). Blind variation and selective retention in creative thought as in other knowledge processes. *Psychological Review, 67*, 380–400.

Cole, M. (1988). Cross-cultural research in the sociohistorical tradition. In M. Hildebrand-Nilshon & George Ruckriem (Eds.), *Proceedings of the 1st international congress on activity theory* (Vol. 1). Berlin: Druck & Verlag System Druck, 65–86.

Dalby, D. (1967). Further indigenous scripts of West Africa: Mandingo, Wolof and Fula alphabets and Yoruba "holy" writing. *African Language Studies, 8*, 1–51.

Davydov, V. V., & Radzikhovsky, L. A. (1985). Vygotsky's theory and the activity-oriented approach in psychology. In J. V. Wertsch (Ed.), *Culture, communication and cognition*. New York: Cambridge University Press.

Engestrom, Y. (1987). *Learning key expanding*. Helskinki: Poinette Gummerus Org.

Engestrom, Y., & Engestrom, R. (1985). Developmental work research: The approach and an application in cleaning work. *Nordisk Pedagogik, 6*, 2–15.

Gelb, I. J. (1952). *A study of writing*. Chicago: The University of Chicago Press.

Gentner, D., & Gentner, A. (Eds.). (1983). *Mental models*. Hillsdale, NJ: Lawrence Erlbaum Associates.

Goldman, A. I. (1986). *Epistemology and cognition.* Cambridge, MA: Harvard University Press.

Goody, J. (Ed.) (1968). *Literacy in traditional societies.* Cambridge: Cambridge University Press.

Goody, J. (1977). *The domestication of the savage mind.* Cambridge: Cambridge University Press.

Goody, J. (1987). *The interface between the written and the oral.* Cambridge: Cambridge University Press.

Hacker, W. (1982). Objective and subjective organization of work activities. In M. von Cranach & R. Harre (Eds.), *The analysis of action.* New York: Cambridge University Press.

Hildebrand-Nilshon, M., & George Ruckriem (Eds.). (1988). *Proceedings of the 1st international congress on activity theory* (Vol. 1, pp. 65–86). Berlin: Druck & Verlag System Druck.

Joffe-Falmagne, R. (1980). The development of logical competence: A psycholinguistic perspective. In R. Kluwve & H. Spada (Eds.), *Developmental models of thinking.* New York: Academic Press.

Johnson-Laird, P. N. (1983). *Mental models.* Cambridge, MA: Harvard University Press.

Koelle, S. W. (1854). *Outlines of a grammar of the Vai language.* London: Church Missionary House.

Kozulin, A. (1986). The concept of activity in Soviet psychology. *American Psychologist, 41,* 264–274.

Laboratory for Comparative Human Cognition (1983). Culture and cognitive development. In P. H. Mussen (Ed.), *Handbook of child psychology* (Vol. 1). New York: Wiley.

Lektorsky, V. A. (1980). *Subject object cognition.* Moscow: Progress Publishers.

Leont'ev, A. N. (1978). *Activity, consciousness and personality.* Englewood Cliffs, NJ: Prentice-Hall.

Leont'ev, A. N. (1979). The problem of activity in psychology. In J. V. Wertsch (Ed.), *The concept of activity in Soviet psychology.* White Plains, NY: M. E. Sharpe.

Leont'ev, A. N. (1981). *Problems of the development of mind.* Moscow: Progress Publishers.

Leont'ev, A. N., & Luria, A. R. (1968). The psychological ideas of L. S. Vygotsky. In B. B. Wolman (Ed.), *Historical roots of contemporary psychology.* New York: Harper & Row.

Luria, A. R. (1976). *Cognitive development: Its cultural and social foundations.* Cambridge, MA: Harvard University Press.

Marx, K. (1967). *Capital* (Vol. 1). New York: International Publishers.

Newell, A., & Simon, H. A. (1972). *Human problem-solving.* Englewood Cliffs, NJ: Prentice-Hall.

Piaget, J., & Inhelder, B. (1958). *The growth of logical thinking from childhood to adolescence.* New York: Basic Books.

Resnick, D. P., & Resnick, L. B. (1988). The nature of literacy. In E. R. Kintgen, B. M. Kroll, & M. Rose (Eds.), *Perspectives on literacy.* Carbondale: Southern Illinois University Press.

Saxe, G. B. (1982). Developing forms of arithmetic thought among the Oksapmin of Papua New Guinea. *Developmental Psychology, 18,* 583–594.

Schmandt-Besserat, D. (1978). The earliest precursor of writing. *Scientific American,* *238,* 38–47.

Scribner, S. (1984). Studying working intelligence. In B. Rogoff & J. Lave (Eds.), *Everyday cognition: Its development in social context.* New York: Cambridge University Press.

Scribner, S. (1985). Vygotsky's uses of history. In J. V. Wertsch (Ed.), *Culture, communication and cognition.* New York: Cambridge University Press.

Scribner, S. & Cole, M. (1981). *The psychology of literacy.* Cambridge, MA: Harvard University Press.

Tobach, E. (1987). Integrative levels in the comparative psychology of cognition, language and consciousness. In G. Greenberg & E. Tobach (Eds.), *Cognition, language and consciousness: Integrative levels. Proceedings of the 2nd T. C. Schneirla Conference.* Hillsdale, NJ: Lawrence Erlbaum Associates.

Tulviste, P. (1979). On the origins of theoretic syllogistic reasoning in culture and the child. *The Quarterly Newsletter of the Laboratory of Comparative Human Cognition, 1,* 73–80.

Vygotsky, L. S. (1978). *Mind in society.* M. Cole, V. John-Steiner, S. Scribner, & E. Souberman (Eds.). Cambridge, MA: Harvard University Press.

Vygotsky, L. S. (1981). The genesis of higher mental functions. In J. V. Wertsch (Ed.), *The concept of activity in Soviet psychology.* Armonk, NY: M. E. Sharpe.

Vygotsky, L. S. (1986). *Problems of general psychology. Vol. 1 Thinking and speech.* New York: Plenum Press.

Wartofsky, M. (1982). From genetic epistemology to historical epistemology: Kant, Marx, and Piaget. In L. S. Liben (Ed.), *Piaget and the foundations of knowledge* (pp. 1–17). Hillsdale, NJ: Lawrence Erlbaum Associates.

Wertsch, J. V. (1985). *Vygotsky and the social formation of mind.* Cambridge, MA: Harvard University Press.

Wundt, W. (1916). *Elements of folk psychology.* London: Allen & Unwin.

22 Three developmental paradigms

In this symposium, I want to consider Soviet activity theory from the point of view of cognitive developmental psychology – the branch of my discipline concerned with the history and ontogeny of the intellect. We look to developmental theories to furnish a double-sided account of cognition: to illuminate how children growing up in all cultures acquire certain basic and universal competencies, and to specify how children also acquire those specific modes of thinking that are valued and functional in their particular cultures. Activity theory has, I think, a distinctive contribution to make to this endeavor. It offers a unit of analysis – activity – which integrates three constructs that psychology has historically paired off in partial and conceptually limited relationships. These constructs are: *the individual, the environment or world, the social unit.* Because activities occur within culture and not as abstractions from it, their study offers a new basis for a truly comparative, developmental psychology.

That is my argument – and of course I cannot develop it fully here. What I will try to do is to bring out the distinctiveness of activity theory's premises by setting it in contrast to the models dominating developmental psychology. My remarks will center on Piaget's theory of intelligence which has inspired so much research here and abroad in recent decades.

The individualist paradigm

If there is any major motif in developmental psychology, it is one of epistemological individualism – a commitment to the notion that mind is the outcome of processes set in motion by the individual organism. Most paradigms invoke the two terms – *individual* and *environment* or *world* – as basic categories

This paper was originally presented at the annual meeting of the American Anthropological Association, Washington, D.C., December 7, 1985.

for explaining the origin and nature of intelligence. Differences arise over the content of these categories and the specific form of their relationship, but a wide range of schools from behaviorism to cognitivism take for granted the adequacy of these two building blocks.

Piaget's theory of intelligence, in the form in which it has had its greatest impact, fits this *individual-world* model. In his treatment, both *individual* and *world* function as natural systems: the biological individual constructs intelligence initially through actions on objects in the physical world. These actions become internalized and are gradually coordinated into increasingly powerful structures of thought which can be described by logical models. An example favored by Piaget (1972) nicely captures this naturalistic action-theory view of the origins of logic. A small child sits on the ground counting pebbles. She puts them in a row and counts up to ten; then she counts from the other direction and once again finds ten. Intrigued, the child arranges the pebbles in a circle, counts them and finds ten once more. In this way, says Piaget, the child discovers that the sum of elements is independent of their order. By abstracting this property of enumerative action and transposing it to the symbolic plane, the child creates a basis for later mathematical deduction. Into this basic scheme Piaget (1966) added social factors. He thought that processes of social coordination and cultural transmission might facilitate or retard development, and influence the specific content of knowledge. But the inclusion of social factors in this form does not, in my opinion and that of others, (e.g., Glick, 1983) alter the basic two-component structure of his system and its naturalistic bias.

Social interactionist paradigms

The individualist paradigm has not been without its critics. Influential psychologists and social philosophers – the name of George Henry Mead comes to mind – have sought to displace the theory of individual genesis of intellect with what has been called a sociogenetic account. In these frameworks, the two fundamental categories are no longer *individual* and the *world* – but *individual* and *social*. A recent landmark book by two Genevan psychologists, Willem Doise and Gabriel Mugny (1984), commands attention because it is a bold attempt to shift Piaget's central paradigm to a sociogenetic model. (The book by the way has a title reminiscent of the title of this symposium: *The social development of the intellect*.)

Doise and Mugny set out to demonstrate through research the ways in which social processes generate – they use the term cause – the cognitive abilities analyzed by Piaget. And, in an interesting turn of history, they find inspiration in the young Piaget. In the 1920's and 30's, Piaget (1928) by his own account, chose to use the language of sociology, in preference to biology, to describe the development of thought. In this language he speculated that children overcome the limitations of egocentric, a-logical thinking by participating in cooperative endeavors with others which force them to take account of different perspectives. Extending this notion, Doise and Mugny propose a specific mechanism of social causation: The source of logic, they suggest, is coordination among individuals in social interactions:

"It is in the very coordination of his actions with those of others that the individual acquires mastery of systems of coordinations which are later individualized and internalized – coordinations *between* individuals are the sources of individual [mental] coordinations and . . . the former precede and produce the latter (p. 23)."

In their experimental situations two children or child-adult pairs have to accomplish tasks or make judgments requiring the coordination of different perspectives. The child is no longer sitting alone counting pebbles. Now she is, for example, sitting at a table opposite another child judging whether two sticks whose ends do not meet are equal or unequal in length. The sticks are equal, but to Suzy on one side of the table, stick A appears longer, whereas stick B appears longer to Ken on the other side. The children make and compare their judgments and discussion ensues.

On this and other tasks, 7 and 8 year old children, who had not yet mastered certain concepts of concrete logical thinking (conservation of length, for example), were able to acquire (or display) these concepts in the social interactional situations. They maintained these concepts for a period of time and generalized them to new contents in other experiments. Interpreting their results, Doise & Mugny claim that sociocognitive conflict – the existence of different points of view and the need to resolve them – is the critical element within social interaction that generates cognitive development.

I cannot do justice to or properly evaluate this significant line of research here. I have singled it out for attention as a major move in contemporary psychology to establish a social account of cognitive development. For our purposes, two features are theoretically important:

First, this attempt to socialize mind takes the form, as it has classically in psychology, of locating critical social processes at the level of interactions among individuals. Macrolevel or societal processes have no part in the scheme. Sociogenesis, in Doise & Mugny's words, refers to the formative effects of "interindividual relations established within specific social situations (p. 13)." With this interpretation of the social, it is understandable that these psychologists announce a kinship between their position, George Herbert Mead's, and Vygotsky's account of the genesis of higher mental functions.

Second, in adopting a social interactionist perspective, Doise and Mugny lose the world. They cut off cognition from objects and actions in the world of things. Although they characterize themselves as both social interactionists and constructivists in the classic Piagetian tradition, their theoretical account at this point fails to integrate the two paradigms. Summing up their work, they conclude that cognitive development can be understood as a spiral of causality in which various cognitive preconditions in the child, which are themselves based on previous social interactions, allow the child to participate in more complex social interactions, ensuring the elaboration of more complex cognitive instruments, and so on. Put simplistically: social interaction begets cognition which begets social interaction in ever-increasing complexity.

I do not intend in this whirlwind tour to detract from the outstanding achievements of Piagetian theory, either in its naturalistic or social interactionist forms, or from the pioneering work (and it is) of Doise and Mugny. My intention has been to dramatize the bifurcated picture of human development which these contrasting approaches offer. Each approach identifies a certain system of interaction – person-world of objects, or person-person – which demonstrably plays a role in the formation of intellect. Each, however, minimizes the role of the other system and seats them in opposition. Both entirely ignore the larger systems of social relationships and practices which constitute society and culture, and make individual transactions possible and meaningful.

The psychological theory of activity, in contrast, attempts to achieve an integration of the individual's relations with the world of objects and the world of people, and to do so within the framework of the larger social system.

Such an integration, of course, is accomplished on the philosophical plane, rather than on the plane of empirical science. The content of activity, as a general philosophical category, represents the working out of an epistemology – a theory of cognition – within the dialectical materialist world view elaborated by Soviet philosophers. A central question within this world view is to account for the historical evolution of human consciousness and its development in ontogeny.

According to A. N. Leont'ev (1978), a Vygotsky student and an architect of activity theory, the pursuit of this question requires a new starting point. We must start, he said, not from the features of the subject's organization taken by itself, and not from the reality surrounding her, taken by itself, but from an analysis of life processes that really link these two together. The concept of activity applies to and encompasses all those processes that, by linking humans to the world, meet specific human needs.

The integrated nature of human activity finds its first expression in the labor process, the archetypal form of human activity. The two fundamental features of labor, which later become characteristic of human activity in general, are its mediated structure and its collective social organization. And these turn out to have important psychological implications. Humans do not work on the world directly but through tools or instruments, using this term in the broad sense to include symbolic means. And since labor is performed in conditions of social organization, the individual functions in this process not only in a certain relationship with nature but also with other people, members of a given society. The *individual, the world of objects* – and *society* – are unified in this construct of activity and together are constitutive of it.

Moving down from this most abstract level of general activity, the human sciences must deal with actual activities that occur in particular, historically situated cultures, use specific technical and symbolic means and accomplish purposes valued in those cultures. These activities also generate certain forms of social interaction, and culture-specific as well as universal systems of mental skills. Activities are suitable objects[1] of empirical inquiry for a variety of disciplines, but each will pose questions reflecting its own theoretical concerns.

Psychology's mission is to study the psychological content of various activities. From a developmental point of view, psychology investigates how external activity gives rise to internal mental processes, how these processes are functionally related to particular external activities and how external and internal activities mutually transform each other.

So much for capsule exposition. Let us come back to the child. In this perspective, the child will be seen as part of the life of the whole society from the very beginning. She acquires speech and cognitive abilities through participating with others in purposive activities involving social objects and means. Leont'ev gives this example, and this is our third child. A toddler at mealtime in a Russian home is playing with a spoon. Left to her own devices, she might bang it, lick it, or throw it on the floor – but she will only manipulate it to carry cereal to her mouth under the guidance or example of others. In learning how to use a spoon, the child is also learning about the social significance of eating and how a good Russian child is "supposed" to eat.

D. B. El'konin (1977) a developmental psychologist in the Vygotsky-Leont'ev tradition, generalizes this scene. In acting with objects, he says, the child is not merely learning the physical properties of things but mastering the social modes of acting with those things. These socially evolved modes of action are not inscribed in the objects themselves and cannot be discovered independently by the child from their physical properties – they must be learned through a socially mediated process. (Note that this position is capable of incorporating Piaget's notions that there are universal concepts and logics of action arising by virtue of the biological properties of individuals and the physical properties of things.)

Consider, too, the child's interactions with adults. These are also mediated relations. In embryonic form, the infant's relationship with others is mediated through objects – a bottle, a hand, a spoon in the example I just gave. As the child acquires and internalizes speech, social interaction is mediated by powerful systems of symbolic communication which are capable of liberating activities from the restrictions of the setting in the here and now. The central point is that both child-object and child-other interactions are part of a unitary process of activity for some purpose.

How does this concept contribute to a psychological theory of development? El'konin submits an interesting proposition. While children, like adults, engage in multiple, often co-occurring activities, El'konin suggests that one particular activity assumes primary psychological significance for the child at different stages of her life. These leading activities alternate between those in which relations with others dominate and those in which relations with things dominate. The neonate and infant is involved in activity of an emotional nature to produce contact with adults. The toddler's primary activity is object manipulation and interactions with others are subordinated to this purpose. Preschoolers' dominant activity is play, especially in the form of role-playing in which the child assumes the functions of the adult. Object-oriented activity becomes dominant again in school years with the child now engaged in mastering knowledge and new symbol systems. In adolescence, the leading activity again becomes one of social contact and the building of personal relations, and this period leads to full engagement in the world of work or continuing education.

The sketch offered by El'konin highlights both the possibilities and problems of an activity approach to comparative studies of development. I will conclude by considering one possibility close to our common interests and that will bring us to problems.

As for the possibility: If the child's intellectual operations and personality development arise in systems of activity, an analysis of the psychological content of those activities, including their characteristic forms of social interaction, might provide the basis for a truly comparative developmental psychology. This requires that psychologists make activities themselves an object of study and that children-in-activity become the topic of inquiry in developmental research. What do children do in various societies? By what means, for what purpose, and what is the social meaning of these undertakings?

And now the problem. Where do we begin the inquiry? We cannot begin with the general abstract philosophical notion of activity – it does not connect with actual life. Yet we cannot begin with the myriad concrete activities in which real children (or adults) engage. These are potentially beyond count and to complicate matters an individual is likely to engage in more than one activity at a time. Nor does the theory specify, as far as I now, a principled way of assigning observed actions to one or another activity. Leont'ev (1982) for example describes the case of a child doing homework. Initially, she may be studying simply to avoid parental reprimand, and her action is thus to be analyzed as part of a socialization activity. Later the child may undertake homework to satisfy her own intellectual curiosity, in which case the homework may be considered part of a learning activity. Leont'ev's writings offer a variety of human endeavors on many levels of generality or specificity as examples of a unit called "activity." This practice appears theoretically motivated rather than accidental; activities are conceptualized on a psychological level as dynamic, and as changing in relation to the shifting motivations which an individual actor or group of actors seeks to satisfy through them. This approach renders the specification of activity problematic within a culture, and the project of identifying and studying comparable activities across cultures formidable indeed.

A heuristic strategy is available to activity theory, however, for approaching the question of comparable units of study. In the Soviet account, activities are constituted on the level of social organization and are amenable to analysis on this level. Indeed, a social analysis of activities is methodologically prior to an analysis of their psychological content. What this suggests is that we need to turn to the social sciences for a theory and typology of activities. Have the social sciences identified common spheres of activity in which social life is organized in various societies and in terms of which members of a society conceptualize their purposes? If so, these common spheres – call them social practices if you prefer – can serve as the middle links between abstract activity on the one hand and the teeming variety of everyday pursuits on the other. Socially defined categories of activity can serve as the organizing domains for comparative psychological research.

Here we make contact with what I take to be one of the classic missions of anthropology – the study of socially significant modes of activity. Historical and ethnographic studies have already yielded evidence for activities of universal human significance (play, for example) as well as activities of a culture-relative nature (magic or science, for example). Such anthropological material provides a more suitable starting point for research and theory than El'konin's regrettably culture-biased list. In suggesting a specification of "kinds" of activity, I do not intend to imply that a desirable or attainable objective is a neatly ordered hierarchical list of non-overlapping activity genres. But I think it not unreasonable to expect some consensus on the modal activities in social life that are significant from a developmental perspective.

Implicit theories of basic activity-kinds already motivate anthropological research on child development and cognition. Research using such ready-to-hand categories of activity can accompany the long-term and thorny theoretical problem of working out a conceptually sound approach to activity-kinds. It is to be hoped that in the coming years, as activity theory becomes internationalized, it will be elaborated into a framework that overcomes the old oppositions between the natural and the social worlds, and achieves an integrated view of human ontogeny capable of assimilating empirical findings and raising new questions for developmental research.

Note

1. The term "object" here does not refer exclusively to physical things, but encompasses conceptual and symbolic objects.

References

Doise, W., & Mugny, G. (1984). *The social development of the intellect.* Oxford: Pergamon Press.

El'konin, D. B. (1977). Toward the problem of stages in the mental development of the child. In M. Cole (Ed.), *Soviet developmental psychology*. White Plains, N.Y.: M. E. Sharpe, Inc., pp. 538–563.

Glick, J. (1983) Piaget, Vygotsky and Werner. In *Toward a wholistic developmental psychology*. S. Wapner & B. Kaplan (Eds.), Hillsdale, N.J.: Erlbaum.

Leont'ev, A. N. (1978). *Activity, consciousness, and personality*. Englewood Cliffs, N.J.: Prentice-Hall.

Leont'ev, A. N. (1982). *Problems in the development of mind*. Moscow: Progress Publishers.

Piaget, J. (1959). *Judgement and reasoning in the child*. Paterson, N.J.: Littlefield Adams, & Co.

Piaget, J. (1966). Need and significance of cross-cultural studies in genetic psychology. *International Journal of Psychology*, 1: 3–13.

Piaget, J. (1972). Development and learning. In R. E. Ripple & V. N. Rockcastle (Eds.), *Piaget rediscovered*. Ithaca: Cornell Press.

Activity Theory

If I were doing a piece
To be counted
I'd speak
Of means
And mediators
Triangles
And agents
Aging
In actions
Of negative spin.

Sylvia Scribner

PART V

Thinking at work

Introduction

Thinking at Work was the title of the book that Sylvia Scribner was planning to write, and that would have synthesized a number of themes derived from twelve years of research on thinking in the workplace. Her approach was grounded in an activity theory framework. Scribner, however, took activity theory to be not a theory but a metatheory for cognition. As she lucidly states in "Head and Hand" at the end of this section, it provides investigators with a general framework for studying cognition. Her work aimed to "concretize and elaborate activity theory constructs." Her book would have contributed experimental, qualitative, and theoretical analyses to the further development of activity theory.

Scribner's research program focused on practical thinking, a "natural kind" of thinking, and analyzed mental processes and cognitive transformations functionally grounded in goal-directed work activities. The research program began with Scribner's studies of cognitive activities of dairy workers, carried out in Maryland in collaboration with Ed Fahrmeier and Evelyn Jacob while she was at the Center for Applied Linguistics. When Scribner subsequently joined the faculty of the City University of New York, her ideas and agenda quickly generated considerable student interest. She soon formed the Laboratory for Cognitive Studies of Work in which she worked with a number of graduate students and staff on practical thinking and its development in a wide variety of everyday settings, in particular, on the transformations in practices and in thinking when new technologies are introduced into the workplace. Members of the laboratory included King Beach, Lia di Bello, Michael Cohen, Emily Filardo, Farida Kahn, Jesse Kindred, Edith Laufer, Laura Martin, Patricia Sachs, Rosalie Schwartz, Joy Stevens, and Elena Zazanis.

Others joined the regular laboratory meetings, including Dalton Miller-Jones of the faculty of the Developmental Psychology Graduate Program, Kimberly Kinsler of Hunter College, and visiting scholars from many different countries. It was an interdisciplinary group whose discussions tackled issues such as Vygotsky's theory of scientific concept development in comparison with current theories; methodological questions, such as the questions of anthropology and the nature of the analysis they permit; or critiques from Europe and the United States of postmodern capitalist views of changes in the workforce due to the introduction of new technologies. During those years, Scribner was also engaged in a study of Hegel's dialectics and of Ilyenkov's dialectical logic, and was reading widely in philosophy of science, science studies, and other fields, including the works of comparative psychologist T. C. Schneirla and anthropologist Eleanor Leacock. The broad array of tools and viewpoints that Scribner introduced into her laboratory, along with her own analytic insights, gave the work a depth and credibility that proved compelling to other researchers, policy makers, and funders.

291

Scribner's choice of the industrial environment as the setting for her research on practical thinking is significant. Her focus on industrial workers was based on her own experience in the labor movement, which she had recognized as a critical segment of society even while in high school when she chose to work in a lace factory during one summer's vacation. She also saw that an industrial production system would epitomize the interconnections of individual, societal, and historical processes.

In addition, in this setting, while the components of accomplishing tasks and goals could be operationalized in a clear way for study, these activities would be valid as units of analysis because they were considered first in the context of their occurrence, which included the influences of social as well as cognitive organizers. Scribner was able thus to translate theoretical questions about the nature of activity and the development of mind into research methods that were congruent with the questions asked. In several of the papers included here, she elegantly discusses the logic of her approach, its methodological implications, and the method she developed.

Scribner also experimented ingeniously with different interview methods and protocols to capture transformations in people's cognitive processes in workplace settings while respecting their experiences, work histories, and responses to participating in a study. Her ethical commitments to her informants were clear. In every site in which she worked, she made a point of developing a dialogue about her research program with the local union members, of obtaining their consent for the study to take place, separately from that of the employer, and of ensuring that they remained fully informed.

One of her earliest writings, an invited address at the biennial meeting of the Society for Research in Child Development, "Mind in Action: A Functional Approach to Thinking," describes a practice framework for cognition, an elaboration of the practice framework for literacy she developed at the conclusion of the Vai research. She draws the methodological consequences from that framework, and applies them to interpret the findings from her study of a product-assembly task, in particular, the development of work-related skill systems (her equivalent of the "novice–expert" shift).

In "Knowledge at Work," Scribner stresses the importance of understanding the relation between knowing and doing, and points out the inadequacies of the Cartesian dualism on which mainstream psychology is predicated for examining this relation. In contrast, Scribner's approach, and activity theory generally, "represents knowledge as an integral component of activities, along with technologies (tools and sign systems) and functional skill systems" (p. 309) The dairy work is then discussed from that perspective.

The next paper, "Thinking in Action: Some Characteristics of Practical Thought," discusses the status of practical thinking within the overall organization of thought and differing perspectives on this issue.[1] In particular, Scribner challenges the traditional dichotomy between practical and theoretical thinking present in mainstream cognitive science. Scribner proposes to consider practical thinking as a "natural kind." Doing so may provide a "coherent structure of explanation," capable of addressing task-related variations without being driven to particularism, by identifying common characteristics of practical thinking across contexts and situations. Scribner develops a model of practical thinking in which operations are organized as a purposive system; skilled practical thinking is characterized by adaptive flexibility and by economical modes of solution.

In the same paper, she critiques contextualism and introduces the important idea that the environment is incorporated *into* the problem-solving system and is actively exploited by it: "The characteristic we claim for practical thinking goes beyond the contextualist position. It emphasizes the inextricability of task from environment, and the continual interplay between internal representations and operations and external reality throughout the course of the problem-solving process – an interplay expressed in activity theory (Leont'ev, 1979) as the mutual constitution of subject and object."

In "Studying Working Intelligence," Scribner analyzes the specific relation between practical and theoretical thought. While practical thought is distinguished by its greater reliance on concrete forms of knowledge, Scribner stresses that this distinction is functional rather than mentalistic: it is the purpose of thinking rather than the nature of the mental representations per se that distinguishes practical from theoretical thinking. She contrasts this functional distinction with Aristotle's categories of thought and with contemporary distinctions that imply superiority of the theoretical over the practical. In fact, Scribner suggests, the difference between practical and formal problem solving is not a fundamental one; those settings are, after all, particular situations in the network of social structures and cultural practices.

In her discussion of a functional approach to the study of thinking, she analyzes empirical observations in the product-assembly task to detail sign-creating activities (pricing) through which a material object (the milk case) yields a symbol and thus "begins to serve a sign function and becomes incorporated in mental operations" (p. 354). She thus lays the ground for the functional equivalence of the mental and the manual, a notion she would elaborate in later papers.

In "Mental and Manual Work: An Activity Theory Orientation," Scribner introduces the important construct of a functional action system, extending Luria's (1973) notion of functional system to include "the action unit as a whole, including not only the inner and outer operations but the object to which these are directed," a notion that resonates with her insistence, in "Thinking in Action," that the environment is incorporated into the problem-solving system. Mental and manual work are functionally equivalent in such a functional action system, as are inner processes and outer operations.

In 1984 Sylvia Scribner was asked to be guest editor of a special issue of the LCHC quarterly newsletter devoted to the research of her Laboratory of Cognitive Studies of Work. The issue mainly includes studies by Scribner and her collaborators of specific activities in the dairy work project as one example of cognitive studies of work, and a few works in progress by members of her laboratory extending the approach to different worksites.

In "Toward a Model of Practical Thinking at Work," Scribner presents the important idea, derived from her empirical research, that skill acquisition at work involves mastery of the concrete (pp. 380–381). The relation between the abstract and the concrete was of great interest to her and she saw these as reciprocal rather than as dichotomous. "Mastery of the concrete, of course, does not imply the absence of a reciprocal process of abstraction. . . . Without minimizing the abstract processes involved, it seems appropriate to describe the primary course of attainment of problem-solving skills at work as a process of 'concretization' " (p. 381).

"Head and Hand" is a paper that articulated and brought together the many constructs and threads of Sylvia Scribner's theorizing about thinking at work. Pursuing themes introduced earlier, she discusses thinking and doing as integrated, and thinking as linked to action in the world. The operations of head and hand are functionally equivalent and often can substitute for one another. Thinking is an aspect of concrete activities. Both are shaped by and participate in the system of social life, and Scribner discusses the methodology that results from this view.

She returns to considering the relations between the particular and the general and how they contribute to knowledge, a question discussed in her earlier writings on thinking and cultural systems, and which she addresses here with reference to the kind of knowledge that can be gained from studying specific operations deployed in a specific task. In stating her overall research strategy, she writes: "We are interested, not in whether *particulars* about practical tasks generalize, but whether we can find *general* characteristics across a wide range of *particular* tasks" (p. 397).

Scribner's theorizing and methodology, in this research on thinking at work as well as in her other lines of research, are committed to preserving the integrity of the phenomenon while describing it with precision. While she rejected the metaphysics and methodology of mainstream cognitive science, she selectively utilized some of its tools, adapted to the needs of her project. Her analysis of thought is fine-grained, but it always examines thinking as a purposive action embedded in a system of societal and material structures and culturally defined practices.

The research on activities in the workplace brings together the theoretical inquiries and commitments that guided Sylvia Scribner's work on development, on literacy, on thinking and cultural systems, and on psychology and society.

Note

1. We omit the description of the method, well-covered elsewhere.

Selected coauthored works

Scribner, S.; Fahrmeier, E. (1983): *Practical and theoretical arithmetic.* Working Paper no. 3. Industrial Literacy Project, City University of New York.

Scribner, S.; Sachs, P. (1990): On the job training: a case study. *NCEE Brief* no. 9, August.

Martin, L. M. W.; Scribner, S. (1991): Laboratory for cognitive studies of work: a case study of the intellectual implications of a new technology. *Teachers College Record* 92, 4, 582–602.

Scribner, S.; Sachs, P.; with DiBello, L.; Kindred, J. (1991): Knowledge acquisition at work. *NCEE Technical Paper* no. 22.

Scribner, S.; Beach, K. (1993): An activity theory approach to memory. *Applied Cognitive Psychology* 7, 185–90.

23   Mind in action:
A functional approach to thinking

I welcome this chance to talk to you. What I have decided to do is spend the time, not summing up past work, but introducing a new line of research that I undertook several years ago and that I think has important implications for adult learning and development

I will introduce this research by asking you to imagine the following scene. My colleague and I are standing between stacks of milk cases in the refrigerated warehouse of a dairy. (My colleague's name, by the way, is Edward Fahrmeier and he is an important contributor to the research I will be telling you about.) Ed is armed with a sketch pad and pencil which he manipulates somewhat clumsily because he is wearing mittens. I am clutching a microphone and a tape recorder, having trouble holding on to them because I was not clever enough to *wear* mittens. We are watching a man called a preloader assemble just the right number of cartons of milk to fill a driver's order, and we are diagramming on paper and describing into the tape recorder exactly how he does this. Every now and then, when our hands and voices shake with cold, we run outside to sit on the factory steps. The 38 degree warehouse temperature collides with the 98 degree temperature of an August evening in Baltimore. Thawed, we return for more data collection.

In spite of the hazards of naturalistic observation portrayed in this episode, observation is an important component of the research project my title refers to – studying mind in action. What I am trying to do is analyze the characteristics of memory and thought, not as they appear in isolated mental tasks, but as they function in the larger, purposive life activities in which we engage. This approach contrasts with the dominant view in cognitive science today. The prevailing perspective views mind as a system of symbolic representations and

This paper was originally presented at the biennial meeting of the Society for Research in Child Development, April 24, 1983.

operations that can be understood in and of itself, in isolation from other systems of activity. Accordingly, most researchers studying mental operations proceed by giving people isolated mental tasks to accomplish. If we study memory, we ask people to remember some information or event; if we study problem-solving, we ask people to talk aloud while solving problems. In these tasks, remembering and problem-solving are goals in themselves. When research is well developed, it is sometimes possible to specify the component operations in a task with sufficient precision to program them on a computer – a computer which sits in a room having no transactions with the external environment, a computer that is, so to speak, lost in thought.

This approach to cognition has many important achievements. Without minimizing them, it is fair to say that the metaphor "mind as computer" fails to capture significant aspects of human mental functioning. Memory and thinking in daily life are not separate from, but are part of, doing. We understand cognitive tasks, not merely as ends in themselves but as means for achieving larger objectives and goals; and we carry out these tasks in constant interaction with social and material resources and constraints. Unlike computers that *only* sit and think, people think while playing, working, creating art and talking with one another. How does thought embedded in these on-going activities compare with thought processes on isolated mental tasks? In recent years, as a result of the penetrating critiques of Cole, Bronfenbrenner, Neisser and others, we can no longer take for granted the optimistic assumption that laboratory-type tasks capture the critical characteristics of mental processes embedded in life activities. To discover the functional properties of thought in action requires that we take a look at the actual phenomena under natural conditions.

That is what my enterprise is about. I am attempting to place the study of naturally-occurring activities at the center of *cognitive* inquiry. As my opening anecdote illustrates, I am grounding this enterprise in the study of activities which are of exceptional importance to youth and adults in our society – activities which we call work. In the workplace, tasks must be accomplished which require selection and retention of information, accumulation of knowledge, mastery of new symbol systems and on-line problem-solving – all in the service of getting other things done. How do adults cope with these demands? how, without formal instruction, do new workers acquire the intellectual skills these pursuits entail? and most importantly, how do cognitive skills in the workplace compare with those nurtured and demanded in academic settings? I went to the milk-processing plant in Baltimore to begin an exploration of these questions.

This is a preview of my research and my thesis. Before I take you back to the Dairy to tell you what we did and learned, I want to provide a brief account of how I came to this venture, the developmental questions it addresses and the theoretical framework which guides it.

My interest in studying intellectual aspects of practical activities grows out of earlier attempts to understand the formative role of culture in cognitive development. In spite of the ambiguities that plague the field, cross-cultural research has revealed that the human intellect is not only universal in its *capacities* but diverse in its ways of *functioning*. After years of probing, psychologists and anthropologists have discerned some patterns in this diversity – patterns that reflect the impact of particular social institutions and practices. Most prominent in this line of work is the well-demonstrated association between Western-style schooling and features of performance on cognitive tasks.

While the interpretation of school-related cognitive skills is controversial, their very existence is a challenge to our theories. Even if we view such skills as specific rather than general in nature (and this view has been convincingly argued) we still confront a remarkable fact: an historically evolved and culturally rooted institution – school – fosters intellectual achievements that developmentalists, until recently, attributed solely to age.

Nor is school unique in its formative effects. New studies in Africa, the South Pacific, Pakistan have been documenting, sometimes with fine precision, the cognitive impact of other educative institutions – such as apprentice training and tutorial instruction in crafts and trades. This research has focused on the specialized knowledge and specific abilities that individuals acquire through participation in indigenous pursuits.

My own research among the Vai with Michael Cole has shown that literacy, too, has cognitive consequences of a specialized kind. The Vai people practice literacy in three scripts – two handed down without schooling and English acquired in government schools. We went to Vailand hoping to prove that literacy, with or without schooling, promoted higher mental abilities that humanists have long supposed it to do. Our expectations were dashed. Nonschooled literacies among the Vai were not like schooled literacy. We found no *general* effects of literacy as such and no higher skills common to all three literacies.

But we did find particular effects of particular literacies – memory skills associated with one, communication skills with another. In each case the specific skills linked to a given script closely paralleled the uses of that script in Vai society.

This outcome suggested to us the need to rethink the nature of literacy. Instead of conceiving of literacy as involvement with written language that is the same everywhere and involves some fixed inventory of capacities, we began to think of literacy as a term applying to a varied and open set of activities with written language. These activities might range from simple letter-writing to the composition of historical chronicles. In this view the cognitive skills that literacy fosters will also vary – with the kind of activities with writing that particular cultures develop and individuals within a culture are motivated to undertake.

At the conclusion of the Vai research, I put forward a conceptual framework to integrate these cross-cultural studies and guide future research on culture-based skill systems. I call this a practice framework of cognition. You may recognize it as bearing some resemblance to activity theory in Soviet psychology. My version is not a formal theory but a set of coherent constructs which may be helpful in re-thinking the relationship between mental skills and culturally-organized activities.

Let me give you some unelaborated definitions and allow later descriptions to flesh out their meaning. By a practice, I refer to a socially-constructed activity organized around some common objects. A practice involves bounded knowledge domains and determinate technologies, including symbol systems. A practice is comprised of recurrent and interrelated goal-directed actions. Participants in a practice master its knowledge and technology and acquire the mental and manual skills needed to apply them to the accomplishment of actions goals. Navigation is a practice; so is letter-writing; and I will shortly point to others.

This practice framework implies a methodological principle. If skill systems are activity or practice-dependent, one way to determine their characteristics and course of acquisition is to study them as they function in these practices. To put it somewhat differently, the practices themselves need to become the objects of study. Observational methods are necessary to determine what tasks are involved in certain practices and to describe their characteristics. Experimental methods are needed to refine these descriptions and analyze the component knowledge and cognitive skills involved in task accomplishment. In a rudimentary way, we attempted to carry out this progression from observation to experiment in the Vai research but were hampered by conditions of work in an unfamiliar culture. I came home, convinced I needed to be a native to undertake a research program that could test this methodology and elaborate the conceptual framework.

What practices should be selected for initial studies? I chose work for reasons of significance and strategy. Significance is apparent. Just as play represents the dominant activity of preschoolers, and school a dominant activity for children and youth, work is a principal activity for adults. Work occupies the bulk of our time. We tend to identify ourselves through our work: you are a psychologist, she is a surgeon. Work offers us many occasions for acquiring knowledge and developing expertise. While we are certainly not wholly defined through our participation in society's labor, it is unlikely we can fully understand the life cycle of development without examining what adults do when they work.

Considerations of research strategy pointed in the same direction and led me to concentrate my first effort in a single industrial plant. In developing methods for studying thought in activity, we benefit from an environment that imposes tight constraints on performance. A factory is such an environment. Its production system shapes occupational activities in both their social and technical aspects. Goals are predetermined and explicit. In choosing to study factory work we can bypass the need to proceed from fully explicit definitions of "practice" and "goal-directed actions". We can take advantage of natural categories available in the industrial environment, allowing *occupations* to represent *practices* and *work tasks* to represent *goal-directed actions*.

Finally, in many factory occupations, work is embedded in larger manual activities which have observable behavioral outcomes. Thought is related to action in ways that facilitate psychological reconstruction of the knowledge and operations brought to bear in accomplishment of a task. If we can achieve some rigorous analysis of tasks involving external operations, we might then go on to consider how such analyses might function as models for understanding cognitive tasks whose operations are primarily internal.

And so, through this detour, we arrive at the Dairy in Baltimore. We spent six months becoming acquainted with its operations, and, quite unfairly, you have to rely on a short segment of a videotape to give you a bit of background knowledge. I will be illustrating our research with a detailed case history of one job – and even a brief glimpse of what a milk-processing plant looks like will help you follow the description. The concrete details will tell you more about the intellectual intricacies of work tasks than sentences of glittering generalities.

(Tape)

Here is our research design in a nutshell. We selected three occupations and four work tasks for cognitive analysis. Two tasks involved physical objects – product assembly carried out by preloaders, and counting stock, an inventory job. Two tasks involved symbolic manipulations – pricing delivery tickets and forecasting the next day's orders, both the work of wholesale delivery drivers. In each instance, we began with observations of the job as it occurred under normal working conditions. We then constructed a model and simulated the task in experimental sessions. To explore the effects of job experience, we gave all job simulations to individuals from all occupations. Each occupation served as expert on its own task and novice on the others. We also included two distinct novice groups – office workers in the Dairy and 9th grade students in a nearby junior high school.

I have selected product assembly for discussion. This job, considered one of the most unskilled in the Dairy, is carried out in the refrigerated warehouse which was the opening scene of my talk. Preloaders arrive at 6 P.M. to find awaiting them a sheaf of delivery orders called load-out order forms. Each form lists the products and their amounts that a wholesale driver has ordered for his next day's delivery. The preloader reads the form, locates the products and transports them to a common assembly area near a moving track which carries them past a checkpoint out to the loading platform. Speed counts – the preloader's shift lasts until all load out order forms are processed and all trucks filled. Accuracy counts – the checker sends incorrect orders back to the preloader for re-assembly.

An interesting feature of this job involves the symbol system used on the load-out order form to express quantities. Drivers place their orders for products in terms of the number of *units* needed – how many *half-pints* of chocolate milk they need or *quarts* of skim milk. Fluid products are not handled by unit within the plant, however, but by case. Since cases are standard size, the number of units they hold varies with the type of container – one case holds 4 gallons, 9 half-gallons, 16 quarts and so on.

When load-out order forms are produced, the computer cases out the drivers' orders by converting units into case equivalencies. If the required number of units does not amount to an even number of cases, the left-over amount is expressed in units. Rules of conversion result in some mixed orders being expressed as cases *plus* units, for example 1 + 6, and other orders as cases *minus* units, for example 2 − 7.

Thus preloaders confront mixed numbers on the load-out order form, numbers drawn from different base systems depending on the container size they qualify. How do they handle these? Do they always fill them as written – that is, do they always add units to an empty case when the order calls for a case plus units – as in 1 + 6 – or remove units from a full case when the order calls for that as in 1 − 6? Informal observations suggested that preloaders had worked out interpretive procedures for the number representations and often departed from literal instructions.

We planned a night of organized observation to obtain more systematic information, and two of us took up posts at a spot near milk products which had the greatest number of mixed case and unit orders. I have already described our procedures. Our diagrams and transcriptions permitted us to reconstruct for each order the exact array the preloader found on arrival, the moves he made, and the final state of the array. With these classes of evidence on hand, we analyzed the product assembly task as an example of problem-solving within the tradition of laboratory-based research.

The first thing we learned from our systematic observations is that preloaders had a large repertoire of solution strategies for what looked like the "same problem." One order – 1 − 6 quarts – occurred six times while we were in the icebox. Remember there are 16 quarts in a case so that 10 were needed. On two occasions, this order received literal solutions: the preloader removed six quarts from a full case. But on four occasions, the order was rewritten behaviorally. All of these transformations took advantage of partially full cases to reduce the number of units that had to be moved to satisfy the order. In some the *take-away* (1 − 6) problem was changed to an add-to problem: 2 units were added to 8 in one instance and 4 units to 6 in another.

Nonliteral solutions such as these require that the assembler transform the original information into some representation that can be mapped onto quantitative properties of different arrays. We may infer that such solutions involve mental processing, or broadly speaking, mental work, over and beyond retention in short-term memory of the quantity given on the load-out order sheet (which literal solutions also require). When does a preloader elect to engage in such additional mental work? Are nonliteral solutions haphazard or rule-governed? We postulated a "law of mental effort": "In product assembly, mental work will be expended to save physical work." We tested this possibility against our observational records. These records provided us with a precise metric for scaling physical effort – the number of units an assembler moved in completing an order. By comparing various modes of solution in terms of the number of moves they required, we could determine which strategy represented a "least-physical-effort solution" under a given set of circumstances. We refer to these as optimal solutions.

Applying this definition to our observational records, we found that preloaders used literal strategies 30 times and 25 of these were least-physical effort strategies. Nonliteral strategies were adopted 23 times; on every occasion such strategies represented a least-physical effort solution. The evidence overwhelmingly favored the postulated relationship between mental and manual effort on this task.

At this point we moved to task simulation in our lab at the Dairy to further the analysis. We prepared fascimiles of load-out order sheets, restricting orders to quantities of less than a case. The informant, after reading the order, proceeded to an assembly area where we had set up an array consisting of a full case, an empty case and a partial case. The number of units in the partial case varied from trial to trial to fulfill parameters of the problem list.

Over two administrations and some 100 problems, preloaders distinguished themselves from all other groups. They selected optimal nonliteral strategies over 70% of the time – even under the artificial circumstances of our task. Rankings of other groups also highlight the role of experience. Inventory men and drivers who occasionally did product assembly were not far behind preloaders. Office workers with no experience in the task but familiarity with the Dairy used optimal, nonliteral solutions in less than half the instances in which they were strategies of choice. As for students, complete novices, they were with few exceptions single algorithm problem-solvers. Instead of adapting solution strategies to the least-effort principle, they carried out literal instructions on almost all the problems.

Even when novices selected an optimal strategy, they carried it out quite differently from preloaders. Audio and video records indicate they relied heavily on numerical solutions and counting operations, especially on early trials. Here is an example from an office worker's protocol. The order is 1 − 6 quarts (one case of 16 less six). She begins to fill the order and says:

"It was one case minus six, so there's two, four, six, eight, ten, sixteen (determines how many in a case; points finger as she counts). So there should be ten in here. Two, four, six, ten (counts units as she moves them from full to empty). One case minus six would be ten."

In contrast, preloaders often appeared to shortcut the arithmetic and work directly from the visual display. A preloader is discussing how he filled an order for 1 case − 8 quarts: (order of eight)

"I walked over and I visualized. I knew the case I was looking at had ten out of it, and I only wanted eight so I just added two to it . . . I don't never count when I'm making the order, I do it visual, a visual thing you know."

We have still additional evidence that different processes of comparison and solution characterize expert and novice assemblers. A particularly crucial phase of the assembly is the premovement period – the interval between a person's arrival at the array and execution of the first movement. All office workers on some occasion counted out loud during this phase, preloaders never did. We also measured the duration of the premovement period for all 90 problems which had optimal solutions. Decision time averaged 1.4 seconds per problem for preloaders, 3.2 seconds for office workers. This time differential supports the interpretation that preloaders were using perceptual information from the array to determine quantity while clerks used slower, enumerative techniques.

How does a product assembler become a skilled optimizer? No formal instruction is involved, although tips are undoubtedly passed on from old hands to newcomers. In studies now underway in our CUNY Graduate School laboratories, we find that most high school students switch from literal to optimizing strategies on their own as they gain experience with the task; they learn through doing. These studies are also providing a nice confirmation of our hypothesis that optimizing in its initial stages involves expenditure of mental effort to save physical effort. We systematically varied the solution complexity of problems and found that those requiring fewer mental steps were among the first to be solved optimally. More intellectually demanding problems received literal solutions longer, and with some student apprentices, never became fully optimized.

I do not have time to describe problem-solving skills on all the other jobs we studied. But I will tell you a bit about our analysis of the delivery ticket pricing task to demonstrate that, in spite of marked surface differences across tasks, we are discovering some common, perhaps very general, characteristics of problem-solving on the job.

Pricing delivery tickets is all symbolic work. Wholesale drivers are responsible for determining the cost of their daily deliveries to customers. For this purpose, they use standard delivery tickets, preprinted with the customer's name and the products usually purchased. When a driver completes a delivery, he enters the amount of each product on the ticket, expressing this amount in units – 70 quarts of skim, 200 half-pints of chocolate. He then calculates the price for each line item and totals the dollar value of the entire delivery. Accuracy counts. Each driver is responsible for the exact value of products he takes out of the Dairy. Speed counts, too, for the driver's day begins at 3 A.M. and does not end till 1 or 2 in the afternoon. To help the driver price out, the company provides a mimeographed wholesale price list for all major products. All prices are expressed in units on this list because the price structure consists wholly of unit prices. Since the size of each product order is recorded on the delivery ticket in units, and prices are in units, the computation task seems straightforward: take the unit price from the price list or memory, multiply it by the number of units delivered and enter the result in the appropriate column.

Informal observations revealed that drivers, no less than preloaders, frequently departed from this literal format. Mr. B, a driver I rode out with, provided one of the first instances of an alternate pricing strategy. He read the item "32 quarts lowfat" on his delivery ticket, found a price on a crib sheet in his pocket, doubled it and entered the answer. He had read "32 quarts" as "2 cases" and used a case price in his solution.

The milk case played an instrumental role in the product assembly task, both in its physical aspects as a container, and in its symbolic aspects – as a variable that could take certain number values. Pricing out is an activity occurring wholly in the symbolic mode. As a material object the case is without significance for this activity. Yet it appears here, too, as a variable in arithmetic operations. Unremarkable as this may first appear, one can think of the case price as a prototype of human sign-creating activities that play such an important role in theories of higher mental functions. An object which first possesses instrumental value in physical activity begins to serve a sign function and become incorporated in mental operations.

Through a series of simulations, proceeding in the manner described for product assembly, we learned that the use of case price techniques marked the performance of all experienced drivers. When unit quantities were evenly divisible into cases, they used case prices alone. On other occasions, they factored unit quantities into cases and units, and used both prices in various combinations. The versatility of some drivers was impressive. One man, about to retire after 37 years of service, was a mental math virtuoso: he used *25* different case and unit calculation strategies to solve pricing problems that had the identical units-times-unit-price format.

A problem by problem analysis of solution strategies showed that the case price technique functioned as an effort saver in a manner analagous to the nonliteral optimal solutions in the product assembly task – with an important difference. The effort saved here was *mental*, not physical. Use of case price either eliminated computation altogether or simplified it. This effort-saving interpretation is supported by our studies which mapped case price knowledge of individual drivers against their solution strategies. Drivers only used case prices when they knew them or had them readily available on personal crib sheets; no driver computed a case price on the way to a solution.

Our final observation is that drivers were not locked into a case price strategy any more than they were to a unit price strategy. In one experiment we prepared delivery tickets on which some problems could be simplified by use of *unit* prices – 101 quarts for example which can easily be solved as 100 plus one. Other problems lent themselves to *case* price solutions. Drivers were flexible problem-solvers, using the arithmetically simpler strategy in accordance with the problem's numerical properties. Students were inflexible problem-solvers. Most clung to a literal unit price strategy throughout. When some adopted a case price strategy, they used *it* for all problems, covering scratch sheets with long divisions to find a fraction of a case. White collar and warehouse workers fell between the two groups.

Some concluding remarks

Let me now try to establish ties with the broader questions that motivated these studies of practical thinking at work.

One motivation was a test of method. We wanted to determine if we could bring some rigor to the study of naturally-occurring activities. Our entry into the real world was guided by a practice approach to cognition which helped us carve out units of behavior which we could subject to cognitive analysis. These units were work tasks within occupations. Using a research strategy that moved from observation to experiment, we succeeded in achieving a fine-grained specification of the knowledge and skill components of several tasks. My students and I – King Beach, Joy Stevens, and others – are now trying to extend the framework to new settings, different occupations and different kinds of cognitive skills, such as memory and spatial reasoning.

We cannot yet offer an assessment of how far we may travel with the approach we have taken but we have gained some confidence in the analyzability of intellectual components of work. As we proceed, certain old dichotomies that have impeded the adoption of an action-oriented approach to thought become increasingly irrelevant. Observation is not opposed to experiment, but may be the forerunner of it. Description is not opposed to explanation but may function as a first approximation to it.

A second purpose of this research was to examine the formative role of practical activities. We began with a theoretical orientation holding that cognitive skills take shape in the course of participation in socially organized practices. We elected to examine practices that involve neither esoteric bodies of knowledge nor high technologies. Yet the experience-based nature of skilled problem-solving was evident in all the tasks we analysed. In every group comparison, the occupation with on-the-job experience provided the greatest number of experts. The job-related nature of cognitive skills was most readily discernible in contrasts between Dairy workers as a group and students as a group. The claim we make goes beyond the commonsense observation that "practice makes perfect". We have not been concerned, nor have we offered facts here, about *accuracy* or *speed* of performance. The changes we have documented are *qualitative*, not *quantitative*. Our analyses demonstrated that modes of solution change with experience. Practice makes for difference – the problem-solving process is restructured by the knowledge and strategy repertoire available to the expert in comparison to the novice. Other studies have shown such qualitative changes in pursuits such as physics and music. Our research suggests that a pattern of development from novice to expert performance may not be restricted to such demanding activities but may represent the course of adult skill acquisition in the mundane pursuits we commonly think of as "unskilled". The human implications of an approach to work which recognizes it as formative – as educative in the broadest sense of that term – are both exhilarating and sobering – exhilarating in terms of future possibilities and sobering in terms of many present-day realities.

A third purpose of this research was to increase our knowledge about the nature of this phenomenon that I call thinking-in-action, or practical thinking. Although we have examined only a half-dozen tasks, they share common features which offer interesting suggestions for a general theory of practical thinking at work.

One feature of skilled problem-solving is the dependency of problem-solving strategies on knowledge about the workplace. The industrial world as we found it was not only made up of things but of symbols that were in significant respects peculiar to that setting. Mastery of both knowledge and symbol systems was a precondition for skilled problem-solving. A preloader could only depart form a literal solution to an order when he understood the symbol "1 − 6" and knew its numeric value. A driver could only regroup 33 quarts into 32 and one for pricing purposes when he saw the cases in the numbers. Skill in the Dairy was not content-free.

Variability was an outstanding feature of skilled performance on all tasks. On first inspection, product assembly and pricing out appear as prototypical examples of repetitive industrial work. They both present the worker with recurring problems of the same kind, often of an identical kind. Yet workers brought a diversity of problem-solving operations to these same-problem formats. This problem-to-problem variability was not foreshadowed in laboratory research nor accounted for in formal models of problem-solving. Variability is often treated as a perturbation in an otherwise orderly system.

Bartlett's classic studies of thinking are an exception. He considered problem-solving to have the same characteristics of skilled performance in other modalities, and he held that a defining attribute of skill is variability. Moreover, skilled variability is rule-governed. He said:

". . . all forms of skill expertly carried out possess an outstanding characteristic of rapid adaptation . . . so what is called the same operation is done now in one way and now in another, but each way is, as we say, 'fitted to the occasion.'"

This is a fitting description of the kind of thinking we have seen in action at the dairy and other work sites. Following Bartlett, we might consider these regularities as forms of adaptation and put to future studies the following proposition: skilled practical thinking at work is goal-directed and varies adaptively with the changing properties of problems and changing conditions in the task environment.

Must we leave the concept of adaptive thinking on an analogical level? Our research raises a line of speculation that may be worth pursuing: practical thinking at work becomes adaptive when it serves the interests of economy of effort. Product assembly provided a vivid example of thinking saving manual effort; pricing out a parallel demonstration of thinking saving mental effort. Labor psychology laboratories in Paris and Dresden report that working people in those countries, too, evaluate their actions on the basis of an effectiveness criterion – a ratio of effort to result. This search for the economical, optimal solution appears to regulate many mental and manual activities in the workplace, spawning variation. Optimizing thinking stands in sharp contrast to the kind of thinking exemplified in the use of a single algorithm to solve all problems of a given type. Algorithms describe how *computers* solve problems. Variability and flexibility describe how *skilled* workers solve problems. Here we have a basic structural difference between formal, academic thinking and practical thinking at work.

These observations allow us to generate a speculative but intriguing model of the course of development of work-related skill systems. In contrast to the conventional psychological model of learning which assumes a progression from the particular and concrete to the general and abstract, skill acquisition at work seems to move in the direction of mastery of the concrete. The novice enters the workplace with a stock of knowledge, some school-based and some experience-based. Learning at work consists of adapting this prior knowledge to the accomplishment of the tasks at hand. Such adaptation proceeds by the assimilation of *specific* knowledge about the *objects* and *symbols* the setting affords, and the *actions* the work tasks require. Domain-specific knowledge reveals relationships that can be used to shortcut those stipulated in all-purpose algorithms. With domain-specific knowledge, expert workers have greater opportunity to free themselves from rules, and to invent flexible strategies. Skill in this model implies not only knowledge and know-how but creativity – an attribute of the work group as a social entity if not of each individual within it.

Work activities have certain peculiarities and cannot be considered representative of all practical thinking in action. Cognitive studies of work are only beginning, our models are tentative and our findings preliminary. But I hope that they suggest the theoretical and practical importance of studying the role of work in the developmental process. I hope, too, they convey a conception of mind which is not hostage to the traditional cleavage between the mind and the hand, the mental and the manual.

At the end of one interview, a seasoned delivery driver described to me the public's image of a milk man. He said, "Most people believe you only need a strong back to be a milk man. But, come to think of it, there is a lot of brain work involved." I think he is right.

24   Knowledge at work

The enterprise before us – understanding the functional role of knowledge in the everyday world – is haunted by a metaphysical spectre. The spectre goes by the familiar name of Cartesian dualism, which, in spite of its age, continues to cast a shadow over inquiries into the nature of human nature. Cartesianism conceives of mind and behavior as two distinctly different modes of life, each requiring its own terms for description and explanation, each demanding its own method of investigation. Within this philosophical framework, questions about knowledge are referred to specialists of the mind, not to students of behavior.

Most investigations of knowledge carried out in the cognitive sciences today reflect this mentalistic approach to the study of knowledge. Many researchers worry about what it is that people of a particular culture know and how such knowledge is represented in the mind. There is debate whether knowledge is best represented as a semantic network (Anderson 1976), a script (Schank and Abelson 1977), or a categorical structure (Rosch 1975). Other researchers study how knowledge is used in intellectual tasks; for example, in speech understanding (Reddy and Newell 1974) or story comprehension (Stein and Glenn 1979). Still others try to characterize the mental models underlying complex behavior, such as in navigation (Hutchins 1980) and chess-playing (Chase and Simon 1973). These approaches to the study of knowledge have many accomplishments to their credit. But the dominant image they present of the human knower resembles closely that of a computer: This knower is an intelligent system with a storehouse of knowledge and a set of programs, performing tasks in isolation. The knower neither interacts with other people nor engages in transactions with the environment. The question we are addressing

This essay originally appeared in *Anthropology and Education Quarterly* 16, no. 3 (1985): 199–231. Reprinted with permission of the American Anthropological Association.

308

here – how knowers use their knowledge to get about the world and accomplish things – fails to arise as a central theoretical question.

It is clear that to address the relationship between knowing and doing we need another conceptual apparatus – one that offers a monistic framework in which to pose our questions. My work on the social organization of cognition has been guided by one such framework, known as activity theory (Leont'ev 1979). Activity theory was launched 50 years ago by the Soviet psychologist Lev S. Vygotsky and developed by his successors in psychology and philosophy. This theory holds that neither mind as such, nor behavior as such, can be taken as the principal category of analysis in the social and psychological sciences. Rather, the theory proposes that the starting point and primary unit of analysis should be culturally organized human activities. Activities are enduring, intellectually planned sequences of behavior, undertaken in the service of dominant motives and directed toward specific objects. They represent a synthesis of mental and behavioral processes. They can be analyzed on a molar level – as, for example, artistic activities, work activities, play activities – and they also can be analyzed in terms of their lower levels – the goal-directed actions that comprise them or the specific operations by which actions are carried out.

This is not the place for a full exposition of activity theory nor of how knowledge can be conceptualized with it. The approach I have taken represents knowledge as an integral component of activities, along with technologies (tools and sign systems) and functional skills systems. Knowledge and action have a reciprocal relationship. Goal-directed action guides the selection of information from the environment and its organization for the task at hand. Organized knowledge in turn guides goal-directed action. In any segment of action, these two processes occur in parallel, but they can be separated analytically into moments when one or the other dominates.

To make these notions more concrete, I will draw on some of my recent research on work (Scribner 1984) for examples of knowledge-action relationships. The studies I describe are modest and are meant to serve primarily as illustrations of some propositions I want to advance.

The field site for this research was a milk processing plant – a dairy – employing some 300 people. For present purposes, we can think of this dairy as a bounded social system within American society as a whole. The various occupations employed in the dairy may be considered socially organized and culturally shaped activities. Specific work tasks required in these occupations are goal-directed actions. Our overall research aim was to analyze the relationship between cognitive operations and behaviors in some of the principal work tasks in the dairy, and to do so within an activity theory framework.

We conducted several studies, addressing specifically the question of how action guides the acquisition and organization of knowledge. Just as many anthropologists choose to investigate folk knowledge of things in the environment that seem important to cultural activities – for example, plants, or stars –

we chose to investigate a domain of things central to the dairy's activities – the domain of dairy products. All of us, as members of a consumer culture and as supermarket shoppers, know what dairy products are and the names of a great many of them. It comes as a surprise to learn, though, that the dairy that functioned as our research site produces and/or distributes more than 220 items under this general category.

The dairy uses order forms listing these items. Products are divided into kinds – fluid milk, cheese, fruit drinks, and so on. Items within these kinds vary by size and by qualitative characteristics such as flavor or fat content.

We examined dairy knowledge comparatively across five groups. Two groups represented consumers – employees of a language research institute and students from a public junior high school. Three groups represented major occupations in the dairy, selected for study because their work involves them in different kinds of actions with dairy products. Office workers comprised one group; they fill out, compute, or file company forms that require them to read or write product names; they do not handle the actual products. Warehouse assemblers read order forms listing certain products, locate these products in the warehouse, and send them out to be loaded on delivery trucks. Drivers handle the products on their trucks and distribute them to customers; in addition, they check the products against order forms and truck inventories and prepare delivery tickets carrying product names. In short, office workers act only with symbolic representations of dairy products; warehouse assemblers and drivers interact with products in both their symbolic and material forms, but they do so for different purposes and in different settings.

Our first assay at product knowledge took the form of a simple recall task.[1] We asked each dairy worker to name the products the dairy sold, just as they came to mind; and we asked consumers to name as many dairy products as they could recall. As one might imagine, although we pressed each person to name at least 25 items and placed no upper limit, dairy employees retrieved the names of many more dairy products than consumers. But let us concentrate here on a less predictable aspect of product knowledge: How do people with different backgrounds relate one dairy product to another?

The universe of products in the dairy is rich with properties; the warehouse is a panoply of colors, sizes, shapes, and substances. Goods can be linked to each other in multiple ways. Consider a paper quart of chocolate milk. It may be associated with skim *milk* as a member of a common kind category. Or it may be associated with *chocolate* drink by shared qualities of flavor and color; or linked with a *quart* of orange juice through size; or with a *paper* half pint of yogurt by the material of its container. This by no means exhausts the possibilities. Do these objective properties of the dairy product universe impose common organizing principles on everyone who uses or works with dairy products? We thought not. If the actions we engage in with objects influence how we organize knowledge about them, we would expect to find different populations using

Table 24.1. *Recall organization by product attribute*

	Consumers		Dairy occupations		
	Students	Institute employees	Office	Drivers	Warehouse
Mean number of different or compound attributes	4	3	8	8	12
Percent associative links or principal attributes					
Kind (e.g. milk)	92	95	42	26	23
Quality (e.g. chocolate)	0	2	1	0	1
Size (e.g. quart)	0	0	5	7	9
Container (e.g. carton)	1	0	0	0	1
Compound (e.g. chocolate milk)	7	3	52	67	66
TOTAL (percent)	100	100	100	100	100

different properties to organize their recall. To test this possibility we analyzed each person's recall list, using our knowledge of the dairy products to identify associative links between successive items. Were two adjacent items linked together by kind, quality, size, or a combination of these or other attributes?

Consider first the diversity of attributes that individuals used to link one dairy product with another (Table 24.1, top portion). The greatest difference arises in the performance of consumers as compared with dairy workers. Consumers have an impoverished product network; on the average, they restrict product relationships to three or four attributes, or attribute clusters, compared to twice that number among dairy workers. Note that warehouse assemblers – the group, by the way, with the lowest average amount of schooling – have the most diversified ways of associating products.

Carrying the analysis further (Table 24.1, bottom portion), we find that consumer groups relied almost exclusively on the category *kind of product* to organize their recall. In contrast, only 42 percent of office workers' associations, and roughly one fourth of driver and warehouse assemblers' associations, consisted of simple links by product kind. Overwhelmingly, workers' dairy product associations were of a complex nature, involving several dimensions at once, such as quality and kind: *chocolate* homogenized *milk* linked to *chocolate* lowfat *milk;* or size and kind: *gallon* homogenized *milk* linked to *gallon* skim *milk.*

Thus far we have distinguished members of the dairy group from members of society at large. Occupational distinctions within the dairy become clearer in a second study of product knowledge. In this task, we presented people with names of 25 products, using the company descriptors, and asked them to sort these products into groups of items that went together.

Table 24.2. *Sorting organization by product attribute*

	Consumers		Dairy occupations		
	Students	Institute employees	Office	Drivers	Warehouse
Product Attributes*					
Kind	77	91	85	67	36
Size	2	0	11	22	31
Location	0	0	0	0	32
Other**	21	9	4	11	1
TOTAL (percent)	100	100	100	100	100

*The average number of groups into which items were sorted was 5.1 (students), 5.4 (institute employees), 4.6 (office workers), 4.5 (drivers), 4.3 (warehouse).
**This category includes groups organized by place of sale, season of greatest use, and idiosyncratic reasons.

As Table 24.2 indicates, consumers (institute employees and students) relied mainly on kind of product to constitute similarity groups. Dairy office workers resembled them in this respect, but on a small number of occasions they also used size as a defining feature. Workers in the two blue-collar occupations made greater use of size as a grouping principle. Warehouse assemblers were exceptions. One third of the time they sorted by location – an attribute that we had not built explicitly into the product list. Location refers to the area of the warehouse in which various goods are stored – a critical thing to know about dairy products if you spend eight hours every night fetching them.

These results would seem to indicate that different work tasks provide opportunities for people to learn different things about the products. *What* you learn is bound up with what you have to do. This is certainly the case, but it is an incomplete explanation of the findings. Warehouse assemblers are not the only ones to know where products are located. Many of the drivers first started working in the warehouse, and all are familiar with the general layout, yet not one of them used location as a grouping principle. Consider size also. When office workers encounter product names on company forms, they often see them written with the size specified. They have considerable exposure to information about size, but they rarely single it out as a defining feature of product clusters on this task. Only those currently working with size in its physical embodiment employed it as an organizing principle.

What do these findings suggest? Even when we are concerned with a domain of common knowledge in our society, we cannot assume that the richness of such knowledge or the attributes by which it is organized are uniform across population groups. Even within one social subsystem – exemplified here in the dairy – the structuring of a domain of common knowledge takes different forms for groups that are related functionally to that domain in different ways.

Dynamic factors, not merely static structural factors, are at work in the organization of knowledge. What factors influence the selection and organization of knowledge? These studies offer two intriguing clues. One is that the modality in which objects are most frequently encountered – whether in symbolic or material form – makes certain properties more salient than others as organizing principles. The second clue has to do with purpose – what people aim to accomplish in their actions. Certain object attributes may be essential to the performance of a task, just as product location is to a warehouse assembler, whereas others may be peripheral, and essential attributes come into play when people are asked to think about how things go together.

Now let us reverse our perspective and consider the knowledge-action relationship from the point of view of how knowledge guides action. For research illustrations, we go to the dairy warehouse and take a closer look at the product assembly task. Two assemblers typically work as a team. They consult a truck order form that is kept at a centrally located stationary point. Each then initials items to be fetched on a single trip, locates them, and carries them to a common assembly area. This sequence is repeated until all items on a particular order form are assembled and sent out to the loading platform, whereupon the assemblers begin on a new truck order form. In the course of a night's work, a team may go through 50 or 60 order forms and assemble over 1,000 items. Since the warehouse measures 145 by 45 feet, they have a lot of ground to cover. And they are interested, as they explained to us, in organizing their work to save their own backs and feet. Management's motivation is to have the work done as speedily as possible – an interest that overlaps, although only in part, with the workers' interest in saving effort.

How does knowledge enter into the organization of this task? To approach this question, we need to make a distinction between accumulated social knowledge and knowledge in the heads of individual product assemblers. Over generations, the experience of thousands of people in the dairy business has produced an environment and instruments that support intelligent organization of work. Social knowledge is incorporated in the way dairy products are stacked in the warehouse: milk, cheese, and fruit drinks are not distributed at random but are assigned particular locations depending on such considerations as proximity to the area in the plant where the item is packaged, proximity to similar items, and floor space. The warehouse organization from night to night remains constant in certain respects, yet it also changes in response to such factors as size of inventory, amount of production, and other fluctuating conditions.

In addition to being in the physical environment, organized social knowledge is embodied in the load-out order form from which assemblers get their instructions. This form does not list items at random, but tends to group them according to gross divisions (bulk products versus others, for example) and roughly according to kinds. So assemblers work in a partially stabilized environment and with an imperfectly organized order list. To determine how they use this reified social knowledge, we observed one team getting items for 22 truck load orders.

The first thing we noticed is that although assemblers sometimes fetch one item at a time, they frequently sign off to get 2, 3, or 4 items in a single trip. As they rush around the warehouse, this requires them to remember a set of products and the quantities attached to each – to engage in extra mental effort.

Second, we noticed that some of these groups were not composed of successive items on the order form but consisted of items separated from each other by a number of lines. For example, one group started with one item, "16 gallons of sour cream," omitted the next three products, included the next two, omitted two, and then included the last item on the list. We have no reason to think that groupings and reorganizations are haphazard. It seems evident that assemblers organize list items in the service of their overall goal of saving steps. If this is the case, the actual trips they made using their groups of items should represent a savings in travel distance over alternative ways of using the product list.

This proposition was tested by applying the principles of graph theory (Ore 1963) to a scale map of the warehouse.[2] Travel distances were estimated for the two assemblers we observed, under assumptions of different trip organizing principles.

First consider the worst case, the distance the assemblers would have had to travel if they had passively accepted the list as given and gone for one item at a time: 20,016 feet, or roughly four miles. Next, consider the case of a grouping strategy that adheres rigidly to the list item order. Frequencies were computed for groups of various sizes organized by the assemblers in their actual trips. We then assigned randomly the same number of these various-sized groups to the items as they were given on the list, working from top to bottom. In other words, the lists were segmented into the same number of groups of the same sizes, but these groups, unlike the actual ones, were composed of items in sequential order. This procedure gave us a measure of the savings effect of item order on the list. We might consider it to measure the efficiency of the social knowledge embodied in the given organization of product names on the order lists. This sequential grouping procedure was applied to the lists five times, with the following results: the mean travel distance for the five generations of sequential groups was 13,279 feet. (Individual calculations for each generation ranged from 12,632 to 13,942 feet.) When we calculated the distance for the trips the assemblers *actually* took (including all their single items, groups, and reorganizations) it amounted to 10,922 feet. This was a little more than two miles of walking, a savings of approximately 2,500 feet over the random groupings on the socially ordered list.

Assemblers accomplished this feat speedily; they did not linger over the load-out order forms, nor did they engage in discussions with each other as to how

Table 24.3. *Estimated travel distance for different trip organizations*[a]

One item at a time	Successive items in random groups	Assemblers actual groups
20,016	13,279 (average)	10,992

[a]After Scribner, Gauvain, and Fahrmeier (1984).

they were going to divide the list. To work in such a coordinated and efficient manner, each assembler needed to have some internally represented knowledge of the spatial arrangement of the warehouse that could be used flexibly to organize the items on hand. Each also needed some knowledge of the customary sequence of items, and recurring chunks of items, on the load-out order forms. With such knowledge (and, of course, much more) they elegantly mapped one organization on to the other – the symbolic onto the spatial – to meet their own needs and to satisfy externally imposed task requirements. Product assemblers creatively synthesized several domains of knowledge as a means of organizing and regulating their own actions.

This is a small set of empirical observations. Their principal usefulness will be to stimulate new ways of thinking about knowledge and practice that avoid the old entrenched dualisms. What we discovered in the dairy are the complexities of working knowledge – its dependence on forms of action and its regulation of forms of action. In the dairy, social knowledge is differentiated from, but not opposed to, individual knowledge. If social knowledge organizes the dairy – its physical environment and symbolic forms – individuals use this social knowledge creatively to shape work that is better adapted to human needs. We can only regret that our social institutions – industrial workplaces – are so organized as to limit the ways in which the thought and action of individual workers can turn back, enrich, and humanize social knowledge and practice.

Notes

Acknowledgments. Research cited was supported by a grant from the Ford Foundation. My collaborator in these studies was Edward Fahrmeier. All our studies have drawn on an extensive ethnography of the dairy provided by Evelyn Jacob.
1. Studies described here are reported in detail in Scribner (ed.) 1984.
2. Special thanks are due to Mary Gauvain who devised and applied this method of analysis (Scribner, Gauvain, and Fahrmeier 1984).

References

Anderson, J. R. (1976). *Language, memory and thought.* Hillsdale, NJ: Lawrence Erlbaum Associates.

Au, K., & Mason, J. (1981). Social organizational factors in learning to read: The balance of rights hypothesis. *Reading Research Quarterly, 17,* 115–152.

Bartlett, F. (1958). *Thinking: An experimental and social study.* New York: Basic Books.

Brainerd, Charles J. (Ed.). (1982). *Children's logical and mathematical cognition.* New York: Springer-Verlag.

Capon, N., & Kuhn, D. (1979). Logical reasoning in the supermarket: Adult females' use of a proportional reasoning strategy in an everyday context. *Developmental Psychology, 15,* 450–452.

Carpenter, T. P., Moser, J. M., & Romberg, T. A. (Eds.). (1982). *Addition and subtraction: A cognitive perspective.* Hillsdale, NJ: Lawrence Erlbaum Associates.

Carraher, T., Carraher, D., & Schliemann, A. (1982). Na vida dez, na escola, zero: Os contextos culturais da aprendizagem da matematica. [Life ten, school zero: The cultural context of mathematical learning]. Sao Paulo, Brazil: *Caderna da Pesquisa, 42,* 79–86.

Carraher, T., Carraher, D., & Schliemann, A. (1983). *Mathematics in the streets and in schools.* Recife, Brazil: Universidade Federal de Pernambuco.

Carraher, T., & Schliemann, A. (1982). *Computation routines prescribed by schools: Help or hindrance?* Paper presented at NATO Conference on the Acquisition of Symbolic Skills. Keele, England.

Chase, W. G., & Simon, H. A. (1973). Perception in chess. *Cognitive Psychology, 4,* 55–81.

de la Rocha, O. (In preparation). *Common sensibilities: An ethnographic study of arithmetic used by Weight Watchers.* Unpublished doctoral dissertation, University of California, Irvine.

Erickson, F. (1982). Classroom discourse as improvisation: Relationships between academic task structure and social participation structure in lessons. In L. C. Wilkinson (Ed.), *Communicating in the Classroom.* New York: Academic Press.

Gay, J., & Cole, M. (1967). *The new mathematics and an old culture.* New York: Holt, Rinehart and Winston.

Gentner, D., & Stevens, A. L. (1983). *Mental models.* Hillsdale, NJ: Lawrence Erlbaum Associates.

Ginsburg, H. P. (Ed.). (1983). *The development of mathematical thinking.* New York: Academic Press.

Ginsburg, H., Posner, J., & Russell, R. (1981a). The development of knowledge concerning written arithmetic: A cross-cultural study. *International Journal of Psychology, 16,* 13–34.

Ginsburg, H., Posner, J., & Russell, R. (1981b). The development of mental addition as a function of schooling and culture. *Journal of Cross-Cultural Psychology, 12,* 163–178.

Goody, E. (Ed.). (1978). *Questions and politeness: Strategies in social interaction.* New York: Cambridge University Press.

Heath, S. (1982). Questioning at home and at school: A comparative study. In G. Spindler (Ed.), *Doing the ethnography of schooling.* New York: Holt, Rinehart and Winston.

Herndon, J. (1971). *How to survive in your native land.* New York: Simon and Schuster.

Hiebert, J. (1981). Children's thinking. In E. Fennema (Ed.), Mathematics and education research: Implications for the 80s. Alexandria, VA: Association for Supervision and Curriculum Development.

Hutchins, E. (1980). *Culture and inference.* Cambridge, MA: Harvard University Press.

Kleinfeld, J. (1983). First do no harm: A reply to Courtney Cazden. *Anthropology and Education Quarterly, 14,* 282–287.

Lancy, D. F. (1983). *Cross-cultural studies in cognition and mathematics.* New York: Academic Press.

Lancy, D. F. (Ed.). (1978). The indigenous mathematic project. *Papua New Guinea Journal of Education, 14 (special issue).*

Lave, J. (1982). A comparative approach to educational forms and learning processes. *Anthropology and Education Quarterly, 13,* 181–187.

Lave, J. (n.d.). *Tailored learning: Education and cognitive skills among craftsmen in West Africa.* Unpublished manuscript.

Lave, J., Murtaugh, M., & de la Rocha, O. (1984). The dialectic of arithmetic in grocery shopping. In B. Rogoff & J. Lave (Ed.), *Everyday cognition: Its development in social context.* Cambridge, MA: Harvard University Press.

Leontiev, A. N. (1979). The problem of activity in psychology. In J. V. Wertsch (Ed.), *The concept of activity in Soviet psychology.* Armonk, NY: M. E. Sharpe.

McDermott, R., & Gospodinoff, K. (1981). Social contexts for ethnic borders and school failure. In H. T. Trueba, G. Pung Guthrie, & K. Au (Ed.), *Culture and the bilingual classroom.* Rowley, MA: Newbury House Publishers.

Mehan, H. (1982). The structure of classroom events and their consequences for student performance. In P. Gilmore & A. A. Glatthorn (Eds.), Children in and out of school. Washington, DC: Center for Applied Linguistics.

Murtaugh, M. (1985). *A hierarchical decision process model of American grocery shopping.* Unpublished doctoral dissertation, University of California, Irvine.

Ogbu, J. (1982). Cultural discontinuities and schooling. *Anthropology and Education Quarterly, 13,* 290–307.

Ohuche, R. O. (1975). The uses of real numbers in traditional Sierra Leone. *West African Journal of Education, 19,* 329–338.

Ore, O. (1963). *Graphs and their uses.* New York: Random House.

Petitto, A. (1979). Knowledge of arithmetic among schooled and unschooled tailors and cloth merchants. Unpublished doctoral dissertation, Cornell University.

Petitto, A. (1982). Practical arithmetic and transfer: A study among West African tribesmen. *Journal of Cross-Cultural Psychology, 13,* 15–28.

Petitto, A. (n.d.). *Long division of labor: In support of an interactive learning theory.* Unpublished paper, Rochester, NY: University of Rochester.

Philips, S. U. (1983). *The invisible culture.* New York: Longman.

Posner, J. (1978). *The development of mathematical knowledge among Baole and Dioula children in Ivory Coast.* Unpublished doctoral dissertation, Cornell University.

Reddy, R., & Newell, A. (1974). Knowledge and its representation in a speech understanding system. In L. W. Gregg (Ed.), *Knowledge and cognition.* Potomac, MD: Lawrence Erlbaum.

Reed, H. J., & Lave, J. (1979). Arithmetic as a tool for investigating relations between culture and cognition. *American Ethnologist, 6,* 568–582.

Resnick, L. B. (1980). The role of invention in the development of mathematical competence. In R. H. Kluwe & H. Spada (Eds.). *Developmental models of thinking.* New York: Academic Press.

Resnick, L. B., & Ford, W. W. (1981). *The psychology of mathematics for instruction.* Hillsdale, NJ: Lawrence Erlbaum Associates.

Rommetveit, R. (1983). In search of a truly interdisciplinary semantics: A sermon on hopes of salvation from hereditary sins. *Journal of Semantics*.

Rosch, E. (1975). Cognitive representations of semantic categories. *Journal of Experimental Psychology: General, 104*, 192–233.

Sahlins, M. (1981). *Historical metaphors and mythical realities*. Ann Arbor, MI: University of Michigan Press.

Saxe, G. B. (1982). Culture and the development of numerical cognition: Studies among the Oksapmin of Papua New Guinea. In C. J. Brainerd (Ed.), Children's logical and mathematical cognition. New York: Springer-Verlag.

Saxe, G. B., & Posner J. K. (1983). The development of numerical cognition: Cross-cultural perspectives. In H. P. Ginsburg (Ed.), The Development of Mathematical Thinking. New York: Academic Press.

Schank, R., & Abelson, R. P. (1977). *Scripts, plans, goals and understanding*. Hillsdale, NJ: Lawrence Erlbaum Associates.

Schoenfeld, A. H. (1982). Measures of problem-solving performance and of problem-solving instruction. *Journal for Research in Mathematics Education, 13*, 31–49.

Scribner, S. (1984). Studying working intelligence. In B. Rogoff & J. Lave (Eds.), *Everyday cognition: Its development in social context*. Cambridge, MA: Harvard University Press.

Scribner, S. (In press). Vygotsky's uses of history. In J. V. Wertsch (Ed.), *Culture, cognition and communication*. New York: Cambridge University Press.

Scribner, S. (Ed). (1984). Cognitive studies of work. *The Quarterly Newsletter of the Laboratory of Comparative Human Cognition, 6 (special issue)*.

Scribner, S., & Fahrmeier, E. (1982). *Practical and theoretical arithmetic: Some preliminary findings*. Industrial Literacy Project, Working Paper No. 3. Graduate Center, City University of New York.

Scribner, S., Gauvain, M., & Fahrmeier, E. (1984). Use of spatial knowledge in the organization of work. *The Quarterly Newsletter of the Laboratory of Comparative Human Cognition 6*, 32–33.

Sherman, M. B. (1982). Education in Liberia. In A. B. Fafunwa and J. U. Aisku (Eds.), *Education in Africa: A comparative survey*. London: George Allen and Unwin.

Simon, H. A. (1957). *Models of man*. New York: Wiley.

Stein, N., & Glenn, C. (1979). An analysis of story comprehension in elementary school children. In R. Freedle (Ed.), *New directions in discourse processing 2*. Norwood, NJ: Ablex.

25 Thinking in action: Some characteristics of practical thought

> If two and a half decades of AI research has done nothing else, it has given researchers a sense of awe in the face of the ordinary.
>
> Waldrop (1984)

Is practical thinking a "kind" of thinking, and, if so, how does it compare to other "kinds?" Not many years ago, such a question, reflecting preoccupations of the naturalist rather than of the experimentalist, might not have found its way into discussions of human intellect. Yet today an increasing number of cognitive scientists are not only taking the question seriously but answering it in the affirmative. In constituting practical thinking as a kind, some set it up as a contrast class to a form of thinking considered instrumental for performance on intellectual tasks such as those encountered in school, on IQ tests, and in certain psychological experiments. This contrasting mode of thought is variously characterized as "academic," "formal," or, in my own usage (Scribner, 1977; Scribner & Fahrmeier, 1982) "theoretical."

Psychological archives, Neisser (1968) reminds us, are replete with other dichotomous schemes for organizing cognitive phenomena, from Freud's (1900) primary/secondary distinction to Levy-Bruhl's (1910) logical/alogical opposition and Vygotsky's (1962) comparison of spontaneous and scientific concepts. Why add another? As with any simple pair of dichotomous terms, the contrast is likely to be true in some respects (otherwise it would not be advanced as a serious proposition) and false or incomplete in other respects (it would otherwise displace competing categorical schemes and become the sole organizing framework for theory and research).

This essay originally appeared in *Practical Intelligence,* ed. R. J. Sternberg and R. K. Wagner (New York: Cambridge University Press, 1985). Reprinted with the permission of Cambridge University Press.

In spite of these well-remarked limitations of dichotomous schemes, several considerations suggest that a practical/theoretical distinction is a useful framework for thinking about thinking.[1] For one thing, a time-honored philosophical tradition, reaching back to old Aristotle (in McKeon, 1947) commends it as a distinction of substance. Contemporary interest is the outcome, not of faddism, but of sustained and serious efforts to make sense of accumulating evidence that people's intellectual accomplishments vary greatly according to domain, task, and setting. Discrepancies between IQ levels and expertise in everyday affairs (see Chapter 6, this volume; Cole and Traupman, 1981; Wagner & Sternberg, in press) can no longer be ignored. More than a decade of research by anthropologists (Gladwin, 1970; Hutchins, 1980; Lave, 1877; Quinn, 1981) and cross-cultural psychologists (Cole, Gay, Glick & Sharp, 1971; Dube, 1982; Price-Williams, Gordon & Ramirez, 1969; Scribner, 1977) has documented sophisticated memory and reasoning abilities among traditional peoples who perform poorly on standard experimental tasks. In the laboratory, manipulations of task materials and demands (Donaldson, 1978; Hayes & Simon, 1977; Newman, Griffin & Cole, 1984) shift not only levels of performance but qualitative characteristics of the problem-solving process as well. We cannot review here the various theoretical responses to this unanticipated variability, except to note that some take the form of salvage operations designed to maintain unimodal theories of thought, while others abandon theoretical models altogether in favor of situationism and particularism. The construct "kinds of thinking" occupies middle ground between these positions, and, if empirically supported, would provide new possibilities for a coherent structure of explanation. The practical/theoretical distinction is one set of terms for a "kinds" taxonomy with special applicability to problem-solving systems. To proceed as if practical thinking were a natural variety requiring its own account has evident heuristic value.

Perhaps the most compelling argument for considering practical thinking as a definite mode of thought is that we now have on hand a small but growing body of research supporting such a conjecture. Formerly, attempts to claim *sui generis* characteristics for practical thinking foundered on inadequate evidence. Practical thinking was represented in the exchange primarily through anecdote, discursive description, or appeals to "what everyone knows." The imbalance in knowledge, although still great, is not nearly as one sided. In recent years, investigators from various disciplines have succeeded in extracting some specimens of practical thinking from the stream of naturally occurring behavior and studying them microscopically. A number of these specimens has been analyzed under conditions of control customary for laboratory tasks. Accordingly, we can begin to bring schematic ideas and hunches about the nature of practical thinking into confrontation with some acceptable, if still quite limited, evidence. We can ask: Do the specimens on hand exhibit common characteristics that justify us in considering them members of a natural kind rather than an accidental collection of singular tasks? If so, how do these characteristics compare with models of cognition representing formal or theoretical thought? Is practical thinking a "defective" version of "ideal" thought, as represented in these models, or is it qualitatively different but equal? Or – and the possibility should not be overlooked – do the characteristics of practical thought suggest that current cognitive models are defective for representing any mode of thought?

The project of this paper is to tackle only the first of these questions: do exemplars of well-analyzed practical thinking tasks exhibit common characteristics? On the basis of a selected set of studies, I propose to answer the question provisionally in the affirmative and to offer a description of salient characteristics of practical thinking. As will become clear, this descriptive model is based on research covering a limited range of practical activities, and thus it represents a speculative extrapolation from the evidence on hand. Its principal purpose is to open discussion on the characteristics of practical thinking and the usefulness of considering it a kind.

To provide a context for this portrait of practical thinking, I will first comment on the theoretical perspective I bring to the topic and then summarize the observational and experimental studies that constitute the core evidence for the model.

Starting points

My notion of practical thinking can be glossed as "mind in action." I use the term to refer to thinking that is embedded in the larger purposive activities of daily life and that functions to achieve the goals of those activities. Activity goals may involve mental accomplishments (deciding on the best buy in a supermarket) or manual accomplishments (repairing an engine) but, whatever their nature, practical thinking is instrumental to their achievement. So conceived – as embedded and instrumental – practical thinking stands in contrast to the type of thinking involved in performance of isolated mental tasks undertaken as ends in themselves.[2]

This orientation sets some parameters for the enterprise. Because it emphasizes dynamic processes – the functions of thinking – it entails no claims about the underlying abilities of individuals or structures of intelligence. Thus practical thinking in the present usage is not to be assimilated to notions of faculties or of factors of mind. Because this approach links thinking to action, it is also at variance with prevailing cognitive science approaches to thinking. The computer metaphor, dominant today, portrays mind as a system of symbolic representations and operations that can be understood in and of itself, in isolation from other systems of activity. Researchers adopting this metaphor seek either to model mental tasks undertaken for their own sake ("recall a narrative," "solve this arithmetic problem") or to analyze individual mental functions (e.g., inference, imagery) abstracted from tasks and separated from one another. Whatever may be said about the value of this framework and these research approaches (and their accomplishments are recognized), they offer little possibility for probing the nature of practical thought. This endeavor requires an analysis of the role of thought within a system of activity, not cut off from it. To achieve such an analysis, the investigator needs to select as her object of analysis not an isolated mental process or task in itself but an integral action directed toward some specifiable end and accomplished under specifiable circumstances. Actions as units of analysis permit the researcher to tackle the what-for of thinking, to examine how thinking is related to doing, and to identify the factors in the world, as well as the representations in the head, that regulate its functioning.[3]

Consistent with this perspective, the research on practical thinking on which our model is based consists of studies of naturally occurring actions. Because I am most familiar with them, I rely primarily on studies of cognitive aspects of work which I carried out with colleagues in a milk-processing plant (Scribner, 1984a, 1984b; Scribner & Fahrmeier, 1982) and studies my students conducted, respectively, among bartenders (Beach, 1985), sales engineers (Laufer, 1985), and waitresses (Stevens, 1985). These studies take as their units of analysis job tasks ("goal-directed actions") that are a routine part of people's occupational activities. All employ a common methodology combining ethnographic and experimental techniques. This corpus is enlarged by other studies of problem solving at work, including research on tailors (Lave, in preparation), on magistrates (Lawrence, in press), on auto mechanics (McLaughlin, 1979), and on office workers (Suchman, 1985), which similarly take naturally occurring work tasks as their starting point and extend the analysis by simulation or test methods. Anthropological and sociological descriptions of occupational activities (among them, Applebaum, 1984a, 1984b; Chinoy, 1964; Gamst, 1980; Kusterer, 1978; Schrank, 1980; Zimbalist, 1979) contribute supplementary materials. The model of practical thinking we present is thus largely based on the study of well-defined and interdependent work tasks whose goals and conditions of accomplishment are socially determined and often highly structured. However, a crop of studies of quantitative problem solving in nonoccupational settings (de la Rocha, in press; Lave, Murtagh, de la Rocha, 1984; Carraher, Carraher & Schliemann, 1984) displays points of overlap and gives us some grounds for anticipating that the features we have singled out for attention may be attributes of intellectual activity in a wide variety of worldly pursuits.

Selected case studies from the dairy[4]

A modernized milk-processing plant was the scene of my early investigations of problem solving at work. The research program began with an ethnographic study (Jacob, 1979) that familiarized us with the dairy as a production system and social organization and highlighted the intellectual requirements of various jobs. We selected four for intensive study: product assemblers, wholesale delivery drivers, inventory men, and office clerks. After conducting systematic observations of principal work tasks in these occupations, we designed a series of job simulations and experiments to analyze the constituent operations and knowledge which these tasks involved. Participating in simulation studies was a panel of thirty-five workers with representation from each target occupation. Workers in the occupation from which the task was drawn served as experts; those from other occupations were novices. Ninth grade students were included in some studies for comparative purposes. Analyses of performance in both natural and simulated situations focused on modes of solution and features distinguishing the intellectual performance of novices from that of workers with on-the-job experience. Three job studies are summarized here.

Assembling products

Assemblers, classified as unskilled workers, are responsible for locating products stored in the warehouse and sending out to the loading platform the amount of each product ordered by drivers for their daily routes. Assemblers secure information about product orders from a computer-generated form that represents quantities according to a setting-specific system, using a dual metric of case and unit. Dairy products are stored and handled in standard size cases that hold a certain number of containers (units) of a given size (4 gallons, 9 half-gallons, 16 quarts, 32 pints, 48 half-pints). If a particular order involves a quantity not evenly divisible into cases, the order form represents it as a mixed number: x cases plus or minus (according to rule) 4 units. For example: 1–6 on the order form stands for one case minus 6 units. The numerical value of this expression depends on the container size it qualifies: 10 quarts, 26 pints, 4 half-pints. Whenever the assembler encounters a case-and-unit problem, he or she must interpret the symbolic representation on the form to determine the unit quantity needed, map this quantity onto the physical array, and collect as many units as will satisfy the order.

In our recorded observations of two product assemblers filling mixed case and unit orders on the job, we made several discoveries:

1. Assemblers often departed from the literal format of the orders.
2. They filled what looked like the identical order (e.g., 1 case − 6 quarts, or 10 quarts) in a variety of ways, depending on the availability of empty or partially filled cases in the vicinity. Observed solutions on this order included, for example, subtracting 4 from a partial case of 14 quarts and adding 2 quarts to a partial case of 8.
3. On all occasions, the mode of order filling, whether literal or nonliteral, was exactly that procedure that satisfied the order in the fewest

moves – that is, of all alternatives, the solution the assembler selected required the transfer of a minimum number of units from one case to another. Assemblers calculated these least physical effort solutions even when the "saving" in moves amounted to only one unit (in orders that might total 500 units).

4. Mental calculations for these least-effort solutions required the assembler to switch from one base number system to another. The mental effort involved in problem transformations was increased by the fact that assemblers typically went for a group of orders at one time, thus having to keep in mind quantities expressed in different base number systems.

5. Solutions representing least physical effort were accomplished with speed and accuracy; errors were virtually nonexistent.

6. In job simulations, only experienced assemblers consistently employed least physical effort strategies. Novice groups were literal problem solvers, filling orders only as indicated in the representations on the order form (always responding to the order "one case − 6 quarts," for example, by removing 6 quarts from a full case regardless of whether more efficient alternatives were available.

7. Over the course of many encounters with different types of problems in job simulations, novices acquired least physical effort strategies without instruction.

Pricing delivery tickets

Wholesale delivery drivers are responsible for determining the cost of their daily deliveries to customers. For this purpose they use standard delivery tickets, preprinted with the customer's name and products usually purchased. A driver who completes a delivery enters on the ticket the number of units of each product left with the customer (e.g., 24 gallons of homogenized milk; 428 half-pints of chocolate drink) and then computes its cost. For this chore, the driver has available a company price list displaying unit prices for each major product (e.g., price per quart or per half-pint of orange drink). Since the amount of each product is recorded on the ticket in units, and prices are in units, the computation task seems straightforward; that is, multiply number of units by unit price and enter the result in the appropriate column. School-taught multiplication algorithms, if executed properly, would always produce accurate delivery costs.

Recorded observations and interviews with drivers pricing out their tickets disclosed that algorithmic procedures could not account for all modes of solution, as demonstrated by the following instances:

1. Pricing problems with the identical structure (number units × unit price) were solved in a variety of ways, each exquisitely fine-tuned to

the specific number properties of the problem at hand. One old-timer displayed twenty-three different solution procedures on his batch of eight delivery tickets.

2. Departures from the multiplication algorithm simplified the arithmetic required (were least-mental-effort solution procedures); as a result, drivers solved many problems mentally without the use of aids (paper and pencil, calculator, or adding machine).

3. A prominent problem-transformation procedure involved converting the unit amount of a product into an equivalent case amount, and computing cost through the application of case prices. In other words, drivers represented the case – a material object in the dairy – as a quantitative symbol. Since the case is not a fixed number but a variable (depending on the product container size) conversion of unit amounts to case amounts involved the driver's shifting back and forth in different base-number systems.

4. On all occasions, substitution of case for unit price reduced the work load of the arithmetic problem. Case conversion sometimes recast the multiplication problem in simpler form, as in the following example:

Problem on delivery ticket	*Problem reorganized by driver*
32 quarts skim milk @ .68 per quart	2 cases skim milk @ 10.88 per case

In other instances, combinations of case and unit quantities enabled drivers to reorganize multiplication problems into addition or subtraction problems:

17 quarts skim milk @ $.68 per quart	1 case skim milk @ $10.88 plus 1 quart @ .68
31 pints choc. milk @ .42 per pint	1 case choc. milk @ 13.44 minus 1 pint @ .42

5. In simulations in which problem parameters and computational resources were manipulated, drivers modulated their pricing techniques in accordance with the presence or absence of computational aids of a specific kind. Solution operations on the same problems changed under conditions of calculator use, paper-and-pencil arithmetic or mental arithmetic.

6. Computational techniques were dependent on each driver's personal knowledge of case and unit prices for particular products in particular amounts. Thus, solution procedures varied by individual as well as by problem and by calculating device.

7. Novices tended to solve all pricing problems by algorithmic procedures based on either unit prices or case prices.

8. On a paper and pencil arithmetic test such as those administered in school, drivers, whose on-the-job accuracy rate was near perfect, made many errors on decimal multiplication problems similar in format to their pricing problems.

Taking inventory

Taking warehouse inventory involves careful assessment of the quantities of some 100 products and accurate recording of these amounts on the paper forms. Counts for each product are recorded on the inventory form in case units and need to be accurate within a 1% or 2% margin of error. Typically, the entire quantity of one product is massed together in a single location in the form of stacks of dairy cases which are placed with sides touching and stacked six high, volume permitting. Large product arrays may contain as many as 1,000 cases. Because the warehouse is densely packed, inventory men have limited walk room for maneuvering around such arrays and for much of the time are taking counts of arrays containing invisible cases. Although clipboards and scratch paper were available, enumeration was primarily accomplished through mental arithmetic.

To learn the strategies used in counting these large masses of stock, we observed three men taking inventory and later simulated inventory counts in the laboratory with miniature arrays constructed of *lego* blocks. In a logical analysis of the inventory job, it would appear that the case is the countable and the product array is the set of countables. But empirical analyses disclosed that the "case" was rarely employed as a unit of count. Rather,

1. Inventory men had a wide variety of strategies for determining case number.
2. Strategies were closely fitted to properties of arrays. Quantities in large arrays (more than 300 cases) were arrived at by procedures building on multiplication. Men used known dimensions of the storage space (the depth of an area known to hold seventeen cases) and combined these with computed dimensions of the particular array to be enumerated (say, width of eight cases) and then multiplied again by fixed stack height (six cases). Combinatorial procedures, building on known and calculated dimensions and several arithmetic operations, varied with array configurations.
3. In the interest of using multiplication short-cut methods of enumeration, inventory men mentally transformed array configurations to make them amenable to these techniques. When a large array was not a solid rectangle, but had gaps, the men mentally squared off the array by visualizing phantom stacks and counting them. They then multiplied by rectangular dimensions and completed the solution by subtracting

the phantoms from the product. In the instance of "add-ons" (protrusions), they mentally separated out a rectangular central core, multiplied and completed the solution by adding the "odd stuff" to the product.

4. Medium and small arrays were enumerated primarily by counting procedures. The unit of count varied, depending on the size of the array, its regularity and other physical properties. Counting strategies included jump counting by stacks, single counting of stacks, and jump counting by number of cases in each stack. At no time did we observe the single case used as the unit of count, although all counts were expressed on the completed inventory form in terms of case units.

A suggested model of practical thinking

Work tasks studied in the dairy present very simple instances of problem solving. Yet, even here, under the microscope, practical thinking emerges as an intricate and dynamic system organized by both factors in the world and subjective goals and knowledge. Its complexity, the "challenge of the ordinary," arises from this property – that it is simultaneously adaptive to ever-changing conditions in the world and to the purposes, values, and knowledge of the person and the social group.

Here we will consider some of the salient characteristics of skilled practical thinking, extrapolated from the dairy studies and other research. To stimulate thinking about kinds of thought, we will also draw contrasts where appropriate between these observed characteristics of workaday thinking and the properties of formal thinking offered by computer models of mind. We discuss each characteristic individually, but as attributes of a system they are interrelated and implicate each other.

Problem formation

Skilled practical thinking involves problem formation as well as problem solution. Models of formal problem solving suggest that problems are "given" and intellectual work consists of selecting and executing a series of steps that will lead to a solution; the initial problem may be decomposed into subproblems as part of the solution procedure, but its terms are fixed. By contrast, dairy studies suggest that expertise in practical problem solving frequently hinges on an apt formulation or redefinition of the initial problem. In commonplace everyday activities, Lave and associates discovered that problems do not necessarily control actions (Lave, Murtagh, & de la Rocha, 1984). Budget-conscious supermarket shoppers who claimed they were interested in figuring out best buys, rarely undertook the laborious arithmetic involved in unit price comparisons of bulk or packaged products and made their decision on other grounds, shifting the "problem space," as it were. Customers engaged in comparative arithmetic only when circumstances made it possible for them to reach an answer by simple computational or estimation procedures. Lave describes this process as the dialectical constitution of problem and solution.

In the world of work, people have fewer options for shifting problem terrain entirely. It is a peculiarity of occupational activities that many of the problems they pose are preset by social-institutional objectives and technological conditions. But even preset problems may be subjectively reconstituted. On many occasions, problems arise that have a general shape but not a definite formulation. One artful aspect of practical thinking is to construct or redefine a problem that experience or hunch suggests will facilitate a solution or enable the application of a preferred mode of problem solving (see discussion on effort-saving, below). This form of creativity is noticeable and has been well-remarked in professional activities, such as judicial decision-making (Lawrence, in press) and engineering and architecture (Schön, 1983) in which the capacity to devise problems that fit good solutions is highly prized. Dairy studies take us a step further. The dairy is a prototypical industrial system in which many occupational activities involve standardized and repetitive duties performed under highly constrained conditions. It would appear from job specifications that a great many problems are immutable. Yet closer scrutiny reveals that, on all jobs analyzed, experienced workers on some occasions (frequency varying by work task) departed from the literal format of problems and reformulated them in terms of new elements or operations. Drivers recast unit price problems into case price problems; product assemblers converted take-away problems (e.g., $16 - 6 = 10$) into add-to problems ($8 + 2 = 10$), and inventory men mentally squared off irregular areas to transform counting problems into multiplication problems. These examples indicate that if degrees of freedom are available, even in restricted activities, people find ways of redefining preset problems into "subjective" problems.

Flexible modes of solutions

Skilled practical thinking is marked by flexibility – solving the "same problem" now one way, now another, each way finely fitted to the occasion. Formal models of problem solving lead us to expect that repetitive problems or problems of the same logical class will be solved by the same sequence of operations (algorithms) on all occasions of their presentation. Variability sometimes enters the system in the guise of shifts in executive control from one higher-order strategy to another. These strategies, presumably, differ from each other in the modes of solution they regulate, but each generates consistent solutions to all instances of a given problem type.

Such models fail to account for the unexpected variability routinely displayed by dairy experts. Only novices used algorithmic procedures to solve problems. Comparisons of their performance with that of experts suggests that learning how to satisfy the intellectual requirements of a job is not so much a matter of becoming efficient in running off all-purpose algorithms as it is in building up a repertoire of solution modes fitted to properties of specific problems and particular circumstances. The variability experts displayed was exactly that type excluded from formal models: use of different component operations to solve recurring problems of the same kind.

What drives this variability? In the cases we studied, workers' proclivity to "do the same problem differently" on different occasions was unrelated to the objective outcome of performance. On well-practiced tasks of the skill level described, experts made few errors. In any event, available algorithms properly executed would always have yielded the right answer. Changing solution modes reflected experts' concern with the how of performance and were regulated by higher-order worker-evolved strategies for accomplishing the task in the least effortful ways (see description below). Here is an interesting example of a higher-order strategy generating inconsistency in modes of solution.

Flexibility in meeting changing conditions and ingenuity in devising "short cuts" are well-documented aspects of practical intellect across a broad spectrum of occupations. Schön (1983) considers "informal improvisation" the hallmark of professional expertise. Kusterer's (1978) exceptionally detailed studies of bank tellers and machine operators demonstrated that a good part of their working knowledge consisted of knowing how to handle conditions the "standard operating plan" did not cover. Suchman (1985) provides a striking example of the discrepancy between such plans and office-workers problem-solving procedures on the job. Secretaries learning how to use a new copying machine did not follow written instructions but collaboratively constructed effective methods for overcoming problem situations the instructions failed to anticipate. Suchman claims that these ad hoc procedures are unavoidable because they reflect the essence of how people use each other and their circumstances to "achieve intelligent action."

Incorporating the environment into the problem-solving system

Skilled practical thinking incorporates features of the task environment (people, things, information) into the problem-solving system. It is as valid to describe the environment as part of the problem-solving system as it is to observe that problem solving occurs "in" the environment.

This notion of the constitutive role of the environment in practical intellectual activities contrasts with prevailing conceptions of cognition-world relationships. In cognitive theories built on the computer metaphor, the world is a stage on which actors execute the outcomes of their mental operations. For others with a contextualist world view, the environment is a context, an external "envelope," as it were, affecting cognitive processes largely through interpretive procedures; the task in this view remains a unit (see Newman, Griffin & Cole, 1984, for a critique of the position that a "task" can be moved from "context" to "context" while remaining the "same" task). The characteristic we claim for practical thinking goes beyond the contextualist position. It emphasizes the inextricability of task from environment, and the continual interplay between internal representations and operations and external reality throughout the course of the problem-solving process – an interplay expressed in activity theory (Leont'ev, 1981) as the mutual constitution of subject and object. The thrust of the position has been captured by Neisser (1976, p. 183), who has argued that perception and action occur in continuous dependence on the environment and therefore cannot be understood without an understanding of the environment. We are extending this observation to the higher cognitive processes involved in practical problem-solving tasks, with a further critical elaboration. In problem solving, properties of the environment do not enter the problem-solving process deterministically or automatically; they assume a functional role only through the initiative and constructive activities of the problem solver.

Exploitation of the environment takes many forms. On some tasks in the dairy material objects in the environment functioned as terms in symbolic problems. Consider order filling on product assembly. A formal analysis would suggest that this task consisted of a written problem (the product order) that the assembler solved and later executed at the product array. On the job, however, an experienced worker interpreted the written order, not as "the problem" but as input to an, as yet, unspecified problem. On arriving at the array, he used information from the physical configuration of containers in a case, in conjunction with symbolic information stored in memory, to define the form of the problem (addition or subtraction). A partial case functioned as one term in the equation and the assembler determined the number that needed to be combined with it to satisfy the order. Inventory provided a somewhat different example of experts' use of environmental properties to achieve an initial representation of the problem to be solved. Dimensions and configurations of product arrays were primary determinants of how the inventory person represented the generic problem of enumeration on different occasions, each time constructing a problem whose form best fitted properties of the object to be enumerated.

Skilled workers exploited the environment for problem-solution as well as problem formulation. The specific operations used to solve problems reflected the peculiar capacities and constraints of objects which social convention classifies as tools or aids for mental work. Recall how dairy drivers changed their arithmetic operations as they moved from paper and pencil to calculator arithmetic. Current research on computers, literacy, and culture-specific artifacts such as the abacus amply support the principle (Vygotsky, 1978) that modes of solution come into being around means of solution. But what is most revealing in current studies is the extent to which people, through cultural or individual invention, make mental "tools" of things in the environment the conventional functions of which are wholly unrelated to intellectual work. Lave (1977) draws attention to the ubiquity of specialized "environmental calculating devices": a piece of sheetrock is a metric unit for carpenters (Perin, undated) and a stack of dairy cases a unit of count for an inventory man; a cup is a canonical measure for a Liberian rice farmer (Gay & Cole, 1976), and the hull of a canoe establishes a scale for master boat builders in the Pulawat Islands (Gladwin, 1970). Nor is the role of objects in problem solving restricted to their quantitative properties. Bartenders learn to manage the memory load of their jobs by using glass shape and position as memory cues (Beach, 1985) and waitresses organize to-be-remembered customer orders by the location of food stations (Stevens, 1985). Most interestingly, things in settings may come to function as symbols, entirely separated from their material forms. An elegant example from the dairy is the drivers' use of "case" as a quantitative variable in arithmetic problems; what was initially a physical object takes on an instrumental role in problem solving in a purely symbolic mode.

These examples serve as accessible illustrations of the functional role of the environment in practical problem solving. They make the point, but do not limit it. The concept of the environment germane to practical problem solving is not a physicalist notion. Here "environment" includes all social, symbolic and material resources outside the head of the individual problem solver. In this sense, activities such as seeking information from other people, "putting heads together" to come to collaborative solutions, or searching documents and looking things up in files, may be understood as extended and complex procedures for intellectual use of the environment. Individual differences in abilities to use the environment in these ways may make a crucial difference to effective cognitive performance. In the dairy, experts displayed greater resourcefulness than novices in using things on hand in an effort to simplify and improve the accuracy of their solution procedures. Beach's (1985) experiments with bartenders also demonstrated that experience makes for greater rather than less reliance on environmental sources of information: Advanced bartending students used external memory cues to remember drink orders and recipes whereas beginners resorted more often to information retrieval from memory. If experts in a domain use the environment more (or more effectively) than novices, two implications follow: becoming skilled in a practical domain may move in a direction opposite to that posed by classic psychological learning theory, namely, from the abstract to the concrete. A second implication is that models of thinking that can only deal with the world as represented in the head may find analysis of many practical thinking problems quite intractable.

Effort saving as a higher-order solution strategy

Skilled practical thinking often seeks those modes of solution that are the most economical or that require the least effort. We have remarked that flexibility appears to be a defining characteristic of practical problem solving. Yet the kind of flexibility documented by the research implies more than random variation or variation for "its own sake" (although we certainly do not preclude these possibilities). As a hallmark of practical skill, flexibility requires that variation serve the purpose of "fitting means precisely to their occasions of use" (Welford, 1976). What is "fittingness" or "fine tuning to the occasion"? Analyses of dairy tasks suggested that fittingness was often indexed by a least-effort criterion: Workers chose just that mode of solution on a particular occasion that accomplished the required end with the fewest steps or the least complex procedures. Product assemblers reformulated "order problems" to save physical moves; inventory staff constructed mental representations for arrays that enabled substitution of short-cutting arithmetic procedures for lengthy processes of enumeration; drivers used case units to simplify multiplication problems on their delivery tickets. As these examples indicate, effort saving here is unrelated to an engineering concept of "efficiency" but refers rather to the psychological reorganization of practical tasks in the interests of economy or simplicity. Evidence on hand from other work settings (see Kusterer, 1978) indicates that effort-saving strategies are widespread and appear in clerical and technical occupations as well as those with manual components. And studies on everyday arithmetic (Lave et al., 1984; de la Rocha, 1985) indicate as well that procedures for simplifying and shortening solutions are common across a range of settings.

The principle of simplicity has been advanced as a criterion for good solutions in certain formal problem-solving domains. Although the concept is vague, Polya (1957) proposed that shortness of solution be considered one characteristic of what constitutes a good solution in mathematics. Empirical research indicates that math problem solvers often move spontaneously toward shorter solutions, even at a tender age (see Resnick & Ford, 1981). If these findings are subsumed under the rubric of effort saving, it would appear that the presence or absence of this higher-order strategy does not in itself set practical thinking apart from theoretical. But deeper probing suggests that certain regulative characteristics of the strategy may be quite different in the two domains. In practical tasks, least-effort strategies are commonly the basis for adoption of different solution modes for identical problems – a form of flexibility not yet documented, to my knowledge, for formal domains. What comes to the fore in this distinction is that practical problem solving tends to occur in task environments that have variable aspects. In a changing task environment, problems are often formally but not functionally the same. Thus, an understanding of least-effort strategies in practical thinking requires taking into account the environment and its conditions. Moreover, the analysis needs to be extended to the values and goals of the problem solver. Objective conditions in the task environment represent potential resources for problem solving, but people need to discover and take advantage of them. Numerous strands of evidence pointed to the fact that least-effort strategies in the dairy were the outcome of processes operating on a conscious level – workers wanted to make their jobs easier or otherwise more compatible with their needs. If least-effort strategies represent conscious constructions, their investigation requires going beyond the formal requirements of problems and the objective conditions of the environment to the larger institutional and cultural contexts in which individual tasks and purposes take shape.

Dependency on setting-specific knowledge

Practical thinking involves the acquisition and use of specific knowledge that is functionally important to the larger activities in which problem solving is embedded. In recent years the centrality of knowledge to intelligent performance has been widely recognized in cognitive theory. From earlier assumptions that problem solving can be understood in terms of "pure process," a consensus has arisen that problem-solving procedures are bound up with amount and organization of subject matter knowledge. Practical problem-solving research reinforces this view by disclosing the diverse forms of knowledge-strategy interactions and the complexity of the knowledge involved in even the simplest tasks. It also contributes some new insights into the specificity of practical knowledge and conditions influencing its acquisition, and our comments will concentrate on these.

The crucial role of setting and task-specific knowledge is well documented in practical problem-solving. The hallmark of expert problem solving in the dairy lay in the fact that experienced workers were able to use specific job-related knowledge to generate flexible and economic solution procedures. In every job examined, these procedures were constructed around, and relied on knowledge specific to the setting and relevant to the task at hand – case equivalencies, storage dimensions, numerical representation systems. What emerges unexpectedly from the research is the degree of specificity of the knowledge involved. From an analyst's bird's-eye point of view, the amount of even so-called specific knowledge required for task performance often appears vast and unbounded. But from the problem solver's point of view, what needs to be known may have quite definite boundaries, drawn in terms of the functional requirements of the task. A trivial example makes the point. Price knowledge was important to delivery drivers; it saved them time (pricing out was faster if they did not have to consult the company price list), and it reduced their risk of error. Yet drivers knew prices primarily for products they handled on their own routes – not prices in general as represented on the price list. Some were explicit about the functional bases of their knowledge. When questioned about prices in our interviews, they rarely said they did not *know* a price, but replied that they *did not handle* the product in question. A typical comment: "Gallons of chocolate drink, I don't even sell that. I don't even put that in my memory bank." Standard interviews conducted to assess workers' knowledge of a record-keeping form used by several occupations disclosed that members of a given occupation were able to explain only those portions of the form which they themselves had to read or fill in and were unfamiliar with the meaning of label headings to the right or left of the columns they used. Kusterer (1978), who conducted one of the most thorough studies of knowledge on the job, reaches similar conclusions about the extraordinary selectivity of some areas of working knowledge. More importantly, he suggests an underlying principle accounting for this selectivity – namely, that people acquire knowledge in the problem-solving mode: "unstudied phenomena remain unknown because they do not normally have any practical consequences affecting the worker's ability to carry out his assigned tasks" (1978, p. 131). Kusterer pointed out that knowledge acquisition varies greatly among individuals (some people have more or less intellectual curiousity) but general functional principles apply. Whether any individual's store of working knowledge is large or small is related to the diversity of functions she carries out and their degree of routinization. Less routinized activities pose more "problems" and thus require the acquisition of more information for overcoming problems. A group of machine operators in his study had to pack products as well as tend machine, but packing was a more routinized function. Kusterer found that, although most of the operators' physical activity involved the packing function, most of their working knowledge involved the machine-tending function.

Another possible functional factor is the saliency of knowledge for accomplishment of the activity goals. Dairy workers were found to organize their knowledge into hierarchical structures constructed along dimensions salient for their job functions. Thus, warehouse workers who had to locate products (the goal of their task) tended to use "location of the product in the warehouse" as a superordinate classification attribute, whereas office workers relied on "kind of dairy product" as the main taxonomic principle.

Knowledge-strategy relationships are so complex and so little explored in practical problem-solving research that generalizations are limited. What we know thus far, however, indicates that functional requirements have an important role in structuring these relationships.

Concluding remarks

The narrow evidentiary base of our description makes it likely that some characteristics selected for discussion may turn out to be particular to one or more practical pursuits rather than candidates for features of a general "kind." It is likely, too, that other aspects of practical thinking basic to its "kindness" have been overlooked. But whatever the limitations of the descriptive enterprise, studies of practical thinking under actual conditions clearly press against the restrictions of laboratory models. Unlike formal problem solving, practical problem solving cannot be understood solely in terms of problem structures and mental representations. Practical problem solving is an open system that includes components lying outside the formal problem – objects and information in the environment and goals and interests of the problem solver. Expertise in practical thinking involves the accomplishment of a fitting relationship among these elements, an accomplishment aptly characterized as functionally adaptive. Beneath the surface of adaptation, however, lie continuing acts of creativity – the invention of new ways of handling old and new problems. Since creativity is a term ordinarily reserved for exceptional individuals and extraordinary accomplishments, recognizing it in the practical problem-solving activities of ordinary people introduces a new perspective from which to grasp the challenge of the ordinary.

Notes

1. As we use the terms here, practical and theoretical thinking both refer to problem-solving activities; the scheme is not proposed as exclusive.
2. The classical antecedents of these distinctions are well-known. Compare Aristotle's descriptions of practical and theoretical thinking, which attributed a principal source of their qualitative differences to differences in their ends or purposes. He claimed that all practical processes of thinking go on for the sake of something outside the process, some end or good to be attained. Theoretical thinking, on the other hand, proceeds for its own sake; it is noninstrumental and "complete in itself." Accordingly, practical sciences have performance of actions as their end, while theoretical sciences are directed to the acquisition of knowledge.
3. Psychologists from several philosophical schools have advanced proposals for a psychology based on the analysis of action. Principles guiding our work are derived from Soviet activity theory; for a brief exposition, see Leont'ev (1979).
4. This research was supported by a grant from the Ford Foundation.
5. An earlier description of some of these characteristics may be found in Scribner (1984b).

References

Aristotle. (1947). *De anima* and *Introduction to metaphysics*. In R. McKeon (Ed.), *Introduction to Aristotle*. New York: Random House.

Beach, K. (1985, March). *Learning to become a bartender: The role of external memory cues at work*. Paper presented at Eastern Psychological Association, Boston, MA.

Carraher, T. N., Carraher, D. W., & Schliemann, A. D. (1985). Mathematics in the streets and in the schools. *British Journal of Developmental Psychology, 3*, 21–30.

Cole, M., Gay, J., Glick, J., & Sharp, D. W. (1971). *The cultural context of learning and thinking*. New York: Basic.

Cole, M., & Traupmann, K. (1981). comparative cognitive research: Learning from a learning disabled child. In A. D. Pick (Ed.), *Minnesota/Symposia on child psychology* (Vol. 14). Hillsdale, NJ: Erlbaum.

de la Rocha, O. (1985). The reorganization of arithmetic practice in the kitchen. *Anthropology and Education Quarterly, 16*, 193–198.

Donaldson, M. (1978). *Children's minds*. New York: Norton.

Dube, E. F. (1982). Literacy, cultural familiarity, and "intelligence" as determinants of story recall. In U. Neisser (Ed.), *Memory observed* (pp. 274–292). San Francisco: Freeman.

Gay, J., & Cole, M. (1967). *The new mathematics and an old culture.* New York: Holt, Rinehart & Winston.

Gladwin, T. (1970). *East is a big bird.* Cambridge, MA: Harvard University Press.

Hayes, J. R., & Simon, H. A. (1977). Psychological differences among problem isomorphs. In N. J. Castellan, D. B. Pisoni, & G. R. Potts (Eds.), *Cognitive theory* (Vol. 2). Hillsdale, NJ: Erlbaum.

Hutchins, E. (1980). *Culture and inference.* Cambridge, MA: Harvard University Press.

Kusterer, K. C. (1978). *Know-how on the job: The important working knowledge of "unskilled" workers.* Boulder, CO: Westview.

Laufer, E. (1985, March). *Domain specific knowledge and memory performance in the work place.* Paper presented at Eastern Psychological Association, Boston, MA.

Lave, J. (1977). Cognitive consequences of traditional apprenticeship training in West Africa. *Anthropology and Education Quarterly, 8*(3), 177–180.

Lave, J. (1985). *Tailored learning: Education and cognitive skills among tribal craftsmen in West Africa.*

Lawrence, J. A. (1985). Expertise on the bench: Modelling magistrates' judicial decision-making. In M. T. H. Chi, R. Glaser, & M. Farr (Eds.), *The nature of expertise.* Hillsdale, N.J.: Erlbaum.

Leont'ev, A. N. (1979). The problem of activity in psychology. In J. V. Wertsch (Ed.), *The concept of activity in Soviet psychology* (pp. 37–71). White Plains, NY: Sharpe.

Levy-Bruhl, L. (1966). *How natives think* (Trans.). New York: Washington Square Press. (original work published 1910).

Murtagh, M. (1985). The practice of arithmetic by American grocery shoppers. *Anthropology and Education Quarterly, 16,* 186–192.

Neisser, U. (1968). The multiplicity of thought. In P. C. Wason & P. N. Johnson-Laird (Eds.), *Thinking and reasoning* (pp. 307–323). Baltimore: Penguin.

Newman, D., Griffin, P., & Cole, M. (1984). Social constraints in laboratory and classroom tasks. In B. Rogoff & J. Lave (Eds.), *Everyday cognition: Its development in social context.* Cambridge, MA: Harvard University Press.

Perin, D. (undated). Transcript of a carpenter at work. (Mimeo).

Quinn, N. (1981). A natural system used in Mfantse litigation settlement. In R. W. Casson (Ed.), *Language, culture and cognition* (pp. 413–436). New York: Macmillan.

Reckman, B. (1979). Carpentry: The craft and the trade. In A. Zimbalist (Ed.), *Case studies on the labor process* (pp. 73–102). New York: Monthly Review.

Resnick, L. B., & Ford, W. A. (1981). *The psychology of mathematics for instruction.* Hillsdale, NJ: Erlbaum.

Schön, D. A. (1983). *The reflective practitioner.* New York: Basic.

Scribner, S. (1977). Modes of thinking and ways of speaking. In P. N. Johnson-Laird & J. C. Wason (Eds.), *Thinking.* Cambridge: Cambridge University Press.

Scribner, S., & Fahrmeier, E. (1982). *Practical and theoretical arithmetic: Some preliminary findings*. Industrial Literary Project Working Paper No. 3. New York: The Graduate School and University Center, City University of New York.

Scribner, S. (1984a). Studying working intelligence. In B. Rogoff & Lave, J. (Eds.), *Everyday cognition*. Cambridge, MA: Harvard University Press.

Scribner, S. (1984b). Cognitive aspects of work. *Quarterly Newsletter of Laboratory of Comparative Human Cognition*. Univ. of Calif., San Diego.

Stevens, J. (1985, March). *An observational study of skilled memory in waitresses*. Paper presented at Eastern Psychological Association, Boston, MA.

Suchman, L. A. (1985). *Plans and situated actions: The problem of human-machine communication*. Palo Alto, CA: Xerox Corporation.

Vygotsky, L. S. (1962). *Thought and language*. Cambridge, MA: MIT Press.

Vygotsky, L. S. (1978). *Mind in society*. Cambridge, MA: Harvard University Press.

Wagner, R. K., & Sternberg, R. J. (1985). Practical intelligence in real-world pursuits: The role of tacit knowledge. *Journal of Personality and Social Psychology*.

Waldrop, M. W. (1984). Artificial intelligence (I): Into the world. *Science, 233*, 802–807.

Welford, A. T. (1976). *Skilled performance: Perceptual and motor skills*. Glenview, IL: Scott, Foresman.

Zimbalist, A. (Ed.). (1979). *Case studies in the labor process*. New York: Monthly Review.

26   Studying working intelligence

In the Western philosophical tradition, theoretical and practical thinking have often been opposed to each other as two distinct forms of thought. Aristotle (1963) considered theoretical thinking characteristic of philosophers and those who pursue the why of things; practical thinking is characteristic of artisans and others whose social task is to get things done. He believed theoretical thought to be the superior of the two, the fount of wisdom and the true object of metaphysics. Practical thinking simply fell outside his sphere of interest.

Modern psychologists, though far from Aristotle's world view, still share his philosophical preoccupation with modes of thought central to theoretical inquiry – with logical operations (Piaget, 1950), scientific concepts (Vygotsky, 1962), and problem solving in symbolic domains (Newell & Simon, 1972). Most appear, too, to maintain Aristotle's high esteem for theoretical thought and disregard for the practical.

The studies described here shift this focus. They are concerned with practical knowledge and thought for action. They were carried out among workers in an industrial milk-processing plant, referred to as a dairy, and were undertaken for two related purposes: to contribute to a functional theory of practical thinking and to test a research strategy appropriate to its investigation. The concept of practical thinking guiding this research, unlike Aristotle's, entails no presuppositions about its relationship to theoretical thinking, nor does it imply a dichotomy between the intellectual and manual spheres of human action. As used here, "practical thinking" refers to all thinking that is embedded in larger activities and that functions to carry out the goals of those activities. Goals may involve mental accomplishments (e.g., computing the cost of a milk delivery) as

This essay originally appeared in *Everyday Cognition: Its Development in Social Context*, ed. J. Lave and B. Rogoff (Cambridge, Mass.: Harvard University Press, 1984), pp. 9–40. Reprinted with the permission of Harvard University Press.

well as manual accomplishments (e.g., loading a truck). The phrase "working intelligence" thus has two senses: it refers both to the intellect at work in whatever contexts and activities those may be and, more narrowly, to the particular context of the dairy studies – the workplace.

A practice framework of cognition

The theoretical approach to these studies of practical thinking has its roots in earlier efforts to understand the formative role of culture in cognitive development. Research and concepts developed in this field seem to have implications for a general functional account of thinking (Cole & Scribner, 1974). In particular, cross-cultural research highlights the dependencies of particular thinking skills on the socially organized experiences that mark the lives of people in different cultures.

Considered in an atheoretical sense, the role of experience has long been accorded its due in psychology; it did not await discovery in other cultures. But as William James (1890, 619) warned in the founding of the science, "the first thing to make sure of is that when we talk of 'experience,' we attach a definite meaning to that word." Attaching "a definite meaning" and specifying the links between concrete forms of experience and selective functional aspects of cognition have proved even more difficult than James's warning portended. Within any given society, significant experiences tend to co-occur in patterned ways. For example, in the United States, the increasing independence of children from parents parallels their progress through school.

It is difficult to go beyond observations of cognitive change that are associated with such patterned configurations to uncover specific mechanisms at work. Here cross-cultural research has proved helpful. In spite of the many ambiguities in this field (Cole & Scribner, 1974; Dasen, 1977), investigators have taken advantage of changing co-occurrences of events in different cultures to make some headway in identifying formative "prior experiences." Most prominent in this line of work is the well-demonstrated association between Western-style schooling and features of performance on cognitive tasks and tests (Rogoff, 1981; Scribner & Cole, 1973). School-related cognitive skills have been demonstrated among many cultural groups and through a variety of research techniques, including survey interviews (Inkeles & Smith, 1974); clinical interviews (Ginsburg, Posner & Russell, 1981); ethnographic observations combined with paper-and-pencil tests (Lave, 1977); and, commonly, psychological experiments (Greenfield, 1966; Scribner, 1974; Laurendeau-Bendavid, 1977; Stevenson, Parker, Wilkinson, Bonnevaux & Gonzalez, 1978; Wagner, 1978; Sharp, Cole, & Lave, 1979).

While many interpretations are offered as to the nature of these skills and their theoretical significance (Brown & French, 1979; Cole, 1979), the evidence to date makes a persuasive case that school effects are just that –

outcomes of certain experiences that individuals encounter in this distinctive institution called school. Accounts of how school "makes a difference," however, remain speculative. Little is known about the nature of critical learning experiences in school that might underlie aspects of performance on cognitive tasks. Active research is now underway on possible causal mechanisms, such as learning to read text (Olson & Nickerson, 1978), participating in certain forms of classroom discourse (Mehan, 1979), and acquiring meta-cognitive skills (Brown, 1977).

In one such attempt to untangle experiences occurring in school, Michael Cole and I conducted a series of comparative studies examining whether literacy – knowledge and use of a written language – constitutes a crucial set of skills (Scribner & Cole, 1981).

We carried out this research among the Vai people of West Africa, who practice literacy in three scripts: English, acquired in government-sponsored schools; the indigenous Vai script, learned from tutors; and Arabic or Qur'anic literacy, typically acquired through group study with a teacher but without actual schooling.

We began with experimental tests of speculative propositions about the intellectual operations that literacy presumably either generates or fosters. Many of these propositions involve assumptions about the dependency of general abilities, such as abstract thinking (Havelock, 1963; Greenfield, 1972) or logical reasoning (Olson, 1977), on mastery of a written language. In the Vai setting, we failed to confirm such speculations. Moreover, we found that literacy without schooling (Vai script, Qur'anic) was not associated with the same cognitive skills as literacy with schooling.

The second phase of the research succeeded in identifying linguistic and cognitive skills related to the two nonschooled literacies. With the exception of some common encoding and decoding skills, these skills were specific to one or the other literacy. Interpretation of literacy effects in these studies was not as troublesome as the interpretation of school effects because the skills displayed on our contrived tasks were clearly implicated in reading and writing activities normally carried on in Vai villages. We did not have to "hypothesize" formative experiences; we could, at least on some occasions, point to them. We were able to make these links because we derived our experimental tasks in the first place from informal observations of literacy in operation. For example, while watching young boys memorize the Qur'an, we noticed that beginners were often taught to learn a verse by an incremental chaining technique: learning the first three words, then the next three, then putting all six together, and so on. When this technique was modeled in an experimental memory task, men with experience in Qur'anic study recalled more material in accurate order than inexperienced comparison groups, both nonliterate and those literate in other scripts. This positive result was buttressed by negative outcomes on other memory tasks (e.g., repeat a story, freely recall a list of words) in which

Qur'anic students displayed no superiority over others. Through similar procedures, certain communication skills on experimental tasks were found to be related to prior experience with letter writing in the Vai script, and language comprehension skills were related to reading proficiency in the script.

In Vai society, links between well-practiced activities, such as memorizing the Qur'an or writing letters, and specific cognitive skills were especially visible because the three literacies are put to specialized uses and are based on different orthographies. The pattern of skills found across literacies closely paralleled these uses and the distinctive features of each script. This outcome suggested the need to rethink the nature of literacy within a functional framework. Instead of conceiving of literacy as involvement with written language that is the same everywhere at all times and therefore likely to implicate some fixed inventory of skills ("reading is reading, writing is writing"), we began to think of literacy as a term applying to a varied and open set of activities with written language. These activities might range from simple record-keeping to the composition of historical chronicles (Goody, 1968, 1977). The functional skills that literacy fosters beyond some possible common set might then be expected to vary with the nature of the activities with written language that particular cultures develop and individuals within cultures undertake.

This view attaches one definite, if not exhaustive, meaning to the ambiguous concept of experience. It particularizes experience as the active engagement of an individual in some pursuit involving socially organized domains of knowledge and technologies, including symbol systems. It conceives of functionality in the instrumental sense of supporting accomplishment of some goal-directed action. Writing a letter to secure repayment of a debt is a goal-directed action that is common among Vai script literates. Letter writing involves knowledge of the script and conventions of composition as well as topics discussed; it requires ability to use the implements that the culture makes available for producing written messages. Letter writing is related to other goal-directed actions that share certain of these knowledge and skill components and manipulate the same object, the Vai script; together these actions constitute "literacy."

We offered this account of our work at the conclusion of the Vai research, calling it a practice account of literacy. We used the term "practice" to highlight the culturally organized nature of significant literacy activities and their conceptual kinship to other culturally organized activities involving different technologies and symbol systems. Just as in the Vai research on literacy, other investigators have found particular mental representations and cognitive skills involved in culture-specific practices: navigation in Puluwat (Hutchins, 1979), weaving in Zinacanteco (Childs & Greenfield, 1980), and tailoring in Liberia (Lave, 1977; Reed & Lave, 1979). Lave's studies of tailoring, in particular, were carried to a level of specification which linked features of tailors' performance on a pure arithmetic paper-and-pencil task to the quantitative operations they used every day in sewing trousers for a living.

In these cross-cultural investigations, we have the skeletal outlines of one functional approach to cognition. The general construct of practice offers a possibility for integrating social-cultural and psychological levels of analysis and achieving explanatory accounts of how basic mental processes and structures become specialized and diversified through experience.

Methodological implications

A functional approach to cognition implies a methodological principle. If cognitive skill systems are closely tied to the intellectual requirements of the practices in which they are embedded, one way to determine their characteristics is to study them as they function in these practices. Put somewhat differently, the practices themselves need to become objects of cognitive analysis. What intellectual tasks do these practices pose? What knowledge do the various tasks require, and what intellectual operations are involved in their accomplishment?

With this set of questions, a practice approach to cognition makes common cause with other efforts to develop techniques for studying thinking in context. Difficulties in this enterprise (Cole, Hood & McDermott, 1978; Bronfenbrenner, 1979) involve both conceptual and technical issues. A well-known conceptual difficulty is determining useful units of analysis. How does one locate cognitive phenomena that can be classified as similar in kind and that are sufficiently bounded to be amenable to analysis? The constructs of practice and task, (here an alternative term for goal-directed action), offer one potential approach to these dilemmas. If a particular practice is selected for study, it should in principle be possible to increase the power of decision rules for determining which of the multiple tasks that people carry on in certain settings are relevant to a cognitive analysis. Lave, for example, was concerned with how tailors measure cloth, a task essential to the practice of tailoring, not how tailors play cards, although both activities might be carried out in the tailor shop or its vicinity. There is also a basis for assuming that tasks within a practice will share some common intellectual requirements, such as, in tailoring, the need to use measuring operations in taking the customer's size and in laying out a pattern. The dairy studies attempted to test the problems involved in operationalizing these notions and using tasks-within-practices as basic units of analysis.

A claim has been made (Bronfenbrenner, 1979) that in the present state of the art, studies of everyday cognition involve a trade-off between the relevance that naturalistic settings provide and the rigor that laboratory settings make possible. The rigor-relevance controversy is often posed as an opposition between explanatory (usually equated with experimental) and descriptive (observational) methods of study. A cognitive analysis of actual practices, however, requires the two approaches. Observational methods are needed to determine what tasks are involved in certain practices, to describe their characteristics, and to discover the constraints the setting imposes. Experimental methods are needed to refine these descriptions and to analyze the component knowledge and cognitive processes involved in task accomplishment. In a rudimentary way, we attempted to carry out this progression from observation to experiment in the Vai literacy research, but were hampered by conditions of work in an unfamiliar culture. The dairy studies had as one of their aims a deliberate test of method: can we derive models of cognitive tasks empirically from a study of ongoing activities that will help us understand the characteristics of practical thinking?

Industry as a research setting

Our first research decision was to define the target cognitive activities as those occurring in the course of work-related tasks. Three considerations motivated this decision: significance, strategy, and social concern.

The significance of these activities is apparent. Just as schooling represents a dominant activity for children, work is a principal activity for adults. Work offers many occasions for the development of expertise in tasks involving complex intellectual skills. The labor market provides incentives, both positive and negative, for acquiring such expertise.

Considerations of research strategy pointed in the same direction, leading us to concentrate on a single industrial plant. In developing methods for studying intellectual activities in context, researchers can benefit from an environment that imposes tight constraints on these activities. An industrial plant commends itself as such a constrained environment. The functional requirements of the production system shape work activities in both their technical and their social aspects. A plant can be viewed for some purposes as analogous to a "culture." Occupational activities are socially organized for socially defined objectives and make use of "culture-specific" knowledge domains and technologies. An industrial plant has the added feature, useful for research purposes, of making required tasks and norms of performance explicit, often in the form of official job descriptions. Work tasks are repetitive and tend to recur under conditions of practice whose range of variation is known and can also be made explicit. Under these conditions, the research does not have to begin with the problematic exercise of defining discrete units of behavior or determining which qualify as the "same" or "different." Initially, the investigator can accept the social system's definition of a work task as a unit of behavior and allow the evolving research to test its adequacy.

Most important, in factory work, cognitive activity is often embedded in larger manual activities which have observable behavioral outcomes. Thought is related to action in ways that facilitate psychological reconstruction of the knowledge and operations brought to bear in the accomplishment of a task. If we can achieve some rigorous analysis of tasks involving external operations, it might then be possible to consider how such analyses might function as models for understanding cognitive tasks whose operations are primarily internal.

Social concerns also motivated selection of factory work for study. Class-related differences in educational achievement are well known. Children from families on the lower rungs of the economic ladder tend not to do as well in school as the offspring of professional and middle-class families. Yet many working-class children go on to learn jobs requiring technical knowledge and skills and to perform them competently. Some psychologists (e.g., Neisser, 1976) have attempted to take account of these differences in performance by making a distinction between academic and general intelligence. The usefulness of this distinction for instructional purposes is limited, however, by lack of knowledge of the nature of general intelligence or practical thinking. If researchers can achieve a fine-grained specification of how certain job-related tasks – say tasks involving reading or arithmetic – are accomplished in the workplace, there will be a better basis for comparing cognitive requirements that young people encounter in the two settings. Educational implications might follow.

With these considerations in mind, we selected a medium-sized milk-processing plant in a large urban city as the research site. This plant, employing some three hundred people, has a representative array of blue-collar and white-collar jobs, including machine production, warehouse, distribution, clerical, and computer operations.

The research began with a descriptive case study (ethnography) of the dairy as a whole, detailing the way it carries on its business and the role of various occupations in the enterprise. The ethnography included a general picture of literacy, math, and other cognitive skill requirements in various occupations. On the basis of this background knowledge, four common blue-collar tasks were selected as candidates for cognitive analysis. All tasks were essential to job performance, and all involved operations with written symbols and numbers: product assembly (performed by preloaders), counting product arrays (inventory people), pricing delivery tickets, and using a computer form to represent numbers (wholesale drivers; Table 26.1).

The research objective was to describe skilled performance on each task and identify its systematic characteristics. As a first step, we conducted naturalistic observations of task performance under normal working conditions. These observations resulted in a first-level description of the major strategies workers employed on the task and their variability across individuals and occasions. On the basis of this description, we generated hypotheses or, more accurately, "hunches" about factors that might regulate variability. To explore these hunches, we introduced modifications in the task and observed performance under more constrained conditions than those occurring in the ordinary work environment. These modifications took the form of job simulations, which were administered, along with other experimental tasks, to employees in the occupations of interest. As we proceeded with job simulations and experimental tasks,

Table 26.1. *Comparative experimental design (all groups received all tasks).*

Groups[a]	Tasks
Preloaders ($n = 5$)[b]	Product assembly
Inventory ($n = 4$)[b]	Counting the product
Wholesale drivers ($n = 10$)	Pricing delivery tickets
Clerks ($n = 11$)	Representing product quantities on computer form (Comparison group only)
Students ($n = 30$)	Paper-and-pencil math test

[a]Either exhaustive or random selection methods were used, depending on the number of individuals employed in each occupational group. Students were a random stratified sample of all math ability groups in the ninth grade of a junior high school in the same neighborhood as the dairy.
[b]Preloaders and inventory people, both of whom work in the icebox, are occasionally referred to here collectively as icebox workers.

we occasionally returned for more narrowly focused on-the-job observations to resolve particular questions.

For greater analytic power, a novice/expert contrast was built into the experimental design. All job simulations were given to all occupations; each occupation served as expert on its own task and novice on the others. For example, preloaders were experts on product assembly and were novices on delivery tickets, whereas the situation was reversed for wholesale drivers. Inclusion of office clerks provided the most marked novice-expert contrast. Their work does not involve them in manipulating physical products, a common task component for preloaders; inventory people, and drivers, while at the same time they share a common "cultural knowledge" of dairy products and operations and are familiar with the products in their symbolic representations (written names and abbreviations). A school math–work math comparison was also incorporated into the study by inclusion of a stratified sample of ninth graders in a nearby junior high school. Students received a small set of simulated dairy tasks and a paper-and-pencil math test which represented their own well-practiced activity; the test was also given to dairy workers. Average schooling for preloaders and inventory people was tenth grade; for drivers, eleventh grade; and for billing clerks, twelfth grade. Two tasks, product assembly and pricing delivery tickets, represent the more successful efforts at cognitive analysis and offer interesting contrasts in the problems they posed for research.

Product assembly

Product assembly is a warehouse job. It is classified as unskilled manual labor and is one of the lowest paying jobs in the dairy. The perishable nature of dairy products requires that warehouse temperature be maintained at 38 degrees Fahrenheit; accordingly, the warehouse is, and is referred to as, an icebox. During the day, thousands of cases of milk products (e.g. skim milk, chocolate milk) and fruit drinks are moved on conveyor belts from the plant filling machines into the icebox, where they are stacked in designated areas along with many other dairy products (e.g., yogurt, cottage cheese). Preloaders arrive at the icebox at 6 P.M. Awaiting them is a sheaf of route delivery orders, called load-out order forms. Each form lists the products and their amounts that a wholesale driver has ordered for his next day's delivery. The preloader's task is to locate each product. Using a long metal "hook," he pulls the required number of cases and partial cases of that product and transports them to a common assembly area near a moving track that circles the icebox. When all the items of a given truck order are assembled, they are pulled onto the track and carried past a check-point out to the loading platform.

Our attention was first drawn to an interesting feature of this job when we studied the load-out form used by preloaders. This form is generated by a computer program which follows a certain rule in expressing quantities. Drivers place their orders for products in terms of the number of units needed (e.g., how many half-pints of chocolate milk are needed, how many quarts of skim milk). Fluid products, however, are not handled by unit within the plant. Gallons, quarts, pints, and other containers are packed in plastic cases as they move off the filling-machine production line. These are stacked in cases in the icebox and loaded in cases on the drivers' trucks. Cases are a standard size, and therefore the number of units they hold varies with the type of container (one case equals 4 gallons, 9 half-gallons, 16 quarts, 32 pints, or 48 half-pints).

When load-out order forms are produced, the computer "cases out" the driver's orders by converting units into case equivalencies. If the required number of units does not amount to an even number of cases, the leftover amount is expressed in units. Consequently, the load-out order form represents some orders as mixed case-and-unit quantities. If the leftover amount equals half a case or less, it is expressed as the number of cases plus the number of units; if the leftover amount is more than half a case, it is expressed as the number of cases minus the number of units. Consider quarts, which come 16 to a case. Orders for 17 to 24 quarts are expressed as 1 case + 1 unit up to 1 case + 8 units. For example, 1 case + 3 units equals 19 quarts. Orders for 25 to 31 quarts are expressed as 2 cases − 7 units up to 2 cases − 1 unit. For example, 2 cases − 5 units equals 27 quarts. The terms *case* and *unit* are not expressed on the load-out order form: "1 case + 3 units" is written simply "1 + 3."

How do preloaders handle these mixed numbers? Do negative numbers pose a special problem? Do preloaders always fill the orders as written; that is, do they always add units to an empty case when the order calls for a case plus units (e.g., 1 + 6) or remove units from a full case when the order calls for that (e.g., 1 − 6)? Informal observations suggested at the start that preloaders had worked out interpretive procedures for the number representations and often departed from literal instructions.

We prepared for a night of organized observation to obtain more systematic information. Logistics were not simple. The icebox is tightly packed. Preloaders run over slippery floors through aisles between stacks of cases. We could not follow them without interfering with their work or risking accident. We needed a stationary point of observation, but which location would be advantageous? Since we were especially interested in mixed orders and partial cases, we wanted to be in a position to watch as many of these orders as possible. Our access to the plant afforded a solution: we were able to obtain the complete set of load-out order forms for that night prior to the beginning of the shift. We counted the frequency with which mixed and partial orders occurred for different types of products. Having previously made a map of the locations of various products in the icebox, we knew which products were stored in adjacent areas. In this way, we were able to select a suitable lookout point across the track from products (quarts of buttermilk, chocolate milk, skim milk) which had the greatest number of partial-case orders.

Two researchers worked as a team for this aspect of the observation. One drew a diagram of the physical array that the preloader would find on arrival, noting the empty or partially filled cases that were available for use; the other described into a tape recorder how many quarts the preloader moved from one case to another to fill the order and what cases were taken away. On several orders, we intervened in the situation by creating mini-experiments. Before the preloader arrived, we added to or subtracted from the number of units in a partly filled case to test hunches about factors regulating choice of case and method of assembly. These changes were made without the knowledge of the preloaders who were working this location. They had no disruptive consequences. Preloaders customarily read off orders for several products at one time and need to keep these quantities in working memory until all are assembled. They said that they could not process other information at the same time and made no effort to remember how many units they were leaving in partial cases.

Using the diagrams and transcriptions from the observations, we were able to reconstruct for each order the initial state of the array, the preloader's moves, and the final state of the array. With these classes of evidence on hand, we could analyze the product assembly task as an example of problem solving within the tradition of laboratory-based research (Newell & Simon, 1972; Simon, 1975; Simon & Reed, 1976; Klahr & Robinson, 1981).

The first thing learned from these systematic observations is that preloaders have a large repertoire of solution strategies. Consider the set of strategies recorded on a particular order which recurred six times during the observation in the icebox: 1 − 6 quarts. On two occasions this order received a literal solution, with the preloader removing six quarts from a full case. But on four occasions the order was rewritten behaviorally. Two of these solutions took advantage of partially full cases to reduce the number of units that had to be moved to satisfy the order: 4 quarts were removed from a case of 14, 1 from a case of 11. In the two more interesting solutions, the take-away problem was transformed to an add-to problem: 2 units added to 8 and 4 units added to 6.

These forms of solution were not product-specific. They occurred for quarts of buttermilk as well as for chocolate. Nor were they restricted to particular quantities. Orders such as $1 + 6$ or $1 - 4$, for example, were also assembled in variable ways.

Nonliteral solutions such as these require that the assembler transform the original information into some representation that can be mapped onto quantitative properties of different arrays. We may infer that such solutions involve mental processing or, broadly speaking, mental work over and above retention in short-term memory of the quantity given on the load-out order sheet, which literal solutions also require. When does a preloader elect to engage in such additional mental work? Are nonliteral solutions haphazard or rule governed? We postulated a "law of mental effort": "In product assembly, mental work will be expended to save physical work."

We tested this possibility against the observational records. These records provided a precise metric for scaling physical effort: the number of units an assembler moved in completing an order. By comparing various modes of solution in terms of the number of moves they required, we could determine which strategy represented a "least-physical-effort solution" under a given set of circumstances. For example, if an order is $1 - 6$ (10) quarts and a preloader has the option of using a full case and removing 6 quarts (the literal strategy) or using a case with 2 quarts already in it and adding 8, the literal strategy is optimal from the point of view of physical effort: it saves 2 moves. If the partial case, however, has 8 quarts and only 2 quarts must be added, filling the order as $8 + 2$ is the least-physical-effort solution (the saving is 4 quarts).

According to this test, preloaders during the observations used literal strategies 30 times, and 25 of these times were also least-physical-effort solutions. Nonliteral strategies were adopted 23 times; on every occasion, such strategies represented a least-physical-effort solution. In view of the fact that in the course of a night's work preloaders must engage in some housekeeping operations (e.g., consolidating partial cases) that might run counter to least-physical-effort solutions on particular problems. The evidence overwhelmingly favors the postulated relationship between mental and manual operations on this task.

At this point, we moved to task simulation to further our analysis. On the simplest level, we wanted to determine whether preloaders would continue to apply optimizing strategies to the task when it had to be performed out of context and for study reasons only. In other words, would solution strategies transfer? We wanted to examine the effects of job experience through a comparison of preloaders with such novice groups as office workers and students. Audio and video records of performance were needed to support a microanalysis of solution processes. Finally, the simulation was designed to increase understanding of the hypothesized mental effort – physical effort trade-off by the systematic manipulation of levels of mental and physical difficulty in the problems.

These objectives reflect factors that have traditionally motivated psychologists to set up contrived situations (experiments) to help answer questions about complex phenomena which either cannot or can only with great inefficiency be answered on the basis of naturalistic observations. One example of the class of unanswerable questions is, "How do student strategies compare with those of expert preloaders?" Psychologists are unlikely to find students either working in a dairy icebox or doing product assembly in school. It would be inefficient to study interactions between problem type and solution mode by waiting until a sufficient number of each kind of problem had turned up on load-out order sheets to support systematic analysis.

The simulation was devised in such a way as to make sense to participants, retain veridicality, and at the same time satisfy experimental requirements for standardized conditions. We prepared facsimiles of load-out order sheets with orders prelisted on them. To simplify matters, only orders of less than a case were used, and these were restricted to two container sizes, quarts and pints – all empties. After reading the order, the individual proceeded to an assembly area containing an array of milk cases. The array always consisted of a full case, an empty case, and a partial case, but the number of units in the partial case varied from trial to trial to fulfill the parameters of the problem list. Interviewees represented the four dairy occupations and the junior high school students.

First, consider the use of least-physical-effort strategies, or optimal solutions, by the various groups (Table 26.2). To what extent did members of these groups employ an optimal (least-physical-effort) solution when it involved carrying out a literal instruction (least mental work), and to what extent did they adopt this strategy when it involved the greater mental effort of producing equivalents to the presented problem? When optimal and literal strategies coincided, all occupational and student groups were optimizers virtually all of the time. But when the optimal strategy required some transformation of the problem, major group differences appeared. Preloaders, as expected, made the greatest use of nonliteral optimizing strategies, using them 70% of the time. This outcome is evidence for transfer of solution strategies from a natural to an arbitrary performance context. It is also important validation of the job simulation technique as a device for cognitive analysis of "real-life" activities.

As might be suspected from other problem-solving research, group rankings confirm that expertise is a function of experience. Inventory people and drivers were not far behind the preloaders. As it turned out, all but one of the inventory people either worked at preloading occasionally or were formerly preloaders; and wholesale drivers, on occasion, made up orders for themselves. But consider the distant groups. Clerks showed little tendency to adapt strategies to the

Table 26.2. *Product assembly simulation (quarts).*

Population group	Solution strategy, percent problems ($N = 16$ per person)[a]	
	Literal strategy selected when it is optimal (LPE = LME)[b]	Nonliteral strategy selected when it is optimal (LPE ≠ LME)[b]
Preloaders	100	72
Inventory people and drivers	92	65
Clerks	92	47
Students[c]	94	25

[a]All solutions could be classified according to this twofold classification except for 15 idiosyncratic solutions, 3 among clerks and 12 among students. These were excluded from the analysis.
[b]LPE = least physical effort; LME = least mental effort.
[c]The method of sampling students resulted in an interview population evenly distributed across the full range of math abilities as determined by performance on a national math achievement test. Twelve students were at or above grade level (highest grade equivalency score was 12.9), and eighteen students were below grade level (lowest grade equivalency was 3.5). Supplementary analyses show the below-grade group hardly ever gave nonliteral solutions (15%), while even the upper group used them on only 42% of applicable problems.

properties of the problem at hand, using nonliteral solutions in less than half of the instances in which they were strategies of choice. Students by and large were single algorithm problem-solvers; they were overwhelmingly literal.

Group disparities are highlighted in a supplementary analysis spanning two rounds of this task, which measured the extra physical effort each population group expended through failure to adopt the optimal solution on all occasions. Scores for students, who received only one round of this task, were extrapolated from their first session. Overexpenditures of physical effort by population group were: 26 units for preloaders, 37 units for inventory people and drivers, 95 for clerks, and 139 for students.

Novices are thus clearly distinguishable from experts in thinking out optimal solutions to these mundane problems. Does this mean that they have difficulty with the necessary mental arithmetic? A second set of simulated problems administered some weeks after the first included a set of problems which forced the use of nonliteral solutions. For example, if the order called for $1 - 6$ quarts, the problem solver was not presented with a full case but was given a choice of two partial cases, one holding 11 quarts and one 14. Clerks and most students (the novice groups) filled these orders accurately, indicating that the mental work involved was not beyond them. But their use of optimal strategies contin-

PRODUCT ASSEMBLY SIMULATION
EXAMPLES OF POOR SOLUTIONS

Example 1

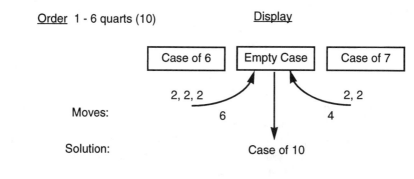

Example 2

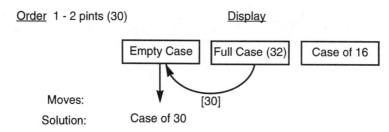

Figure 26.1. Poor solutions in product assembly simulation.

ued to be dependent on the nature of the problem and the type of conversion required.

Comparison of skilled and unskilled performance in terms of best solution is only part of the story. Strategies may be optimal, or adequate (as when an assembler follows literal instructions even if these involve extra effort), or patently poor. A student's protocol furnishes one example of a poor solution; a billing clerk's another (Fig. 26.1). All idiosyncratic performances of this kind were restricted to these two groups; preloaders and drivers may have failed to use optimal strategies on some occasions, but they never resorted to such inefficient assemblies.

Following Wertheimer's (1959) lead, we are tempted to refer to these solutions as "blind" solutions. Such an evaluation, however, unlike Wertheimer's judgment, does not require imposition of a standard that psychologists developed in laboratory research. We have available a standard that expressed empirical regularities observed in the work performance of individuals whom all would acknowledge to be skilled. This is one of the advantages of taking actual occurrences of practical thinking as a starting point for cognitive analysis. They make it possible to say what "intelligent" practical thinking actually is in a particular setting, not merely what, according to existing theories, it ought to be. In product assembly, we have a suggestion as to one possible defining characteristic of practical thinking which might warrant the use of the qualifier "intelligent," that is, the extent to which thinking serves to organize and make more economical the operational components of tasks.

Even when novices selected an optimal strategy, they tended to carry it out quite differently from preloaders and drivers. Audio and video records indicate that office workers relied heavily on numerical solutions and counting operations, especially on early trials. In the following example, where the order is 1 − 6 (1 case less 6 quarts), the clerk begins to fill the order while saying: "I'm going to remove six quarts and put them in an empty case. Oh, that won't . . . oh, no, that's wrong. (*Starts over again and returns units that she removed from the full case.*) It was one case minus six, so there's two, four, six, eight, ten, sixteen. (*Verifies that the case is full again by counting, pointing a finger as she counts.*) So there should be ten in here. Two, four, six, eight, ten. (*Counts her moves as she makes them, keeping track.*) One case minus six would be ten."

In contrast, preloaders often appeared to shortcut the arithmetic and work "directly" from the visual display. A preloader discussed how he filled an order for 1 − 8 (half a case):

Preloader: I walked over and I visualized. I knew the case I was looking at had ten out of it, and I only wanted eight, so I just added two to it. (*Later, in an exchange with the interviewer on another order.*) I was throwing myself off, counting the units. I don't never count when I'm making the order. I do it visual, a visual thing, you know.

Interviewer: OK, well, do it the way that you would do it, I mean, as far as that's concerned.

Preloader: If I did it that way, you wouldn't understand it. See, that's why . . . this is what's throwing me off, doing it so slow.

Videotapes of five preloaders and four white-collar workers (all billing clerks) provided more systematic evidence that different processes of comparison and solution characterize expert and novice assemblies. A particularly crucial phase of the assembly is the premovement period, the interval between a person's arrival at the array and execution of the first movement. During this time, the assembler has to evaluate the partial case and adopt a solution strategy. A tally of the frequency of overt counting operations (verbal and/or gestural) in this premovement phase showed that all clerks, on some occasions, counted out loud with or without pointing gestures. There was a total absence of overt counting among preloaders. Using a second-sweep watch, we measured the duration of this period for all 89 problems in the two administrations of this task for which there was an optimal solution. Preloaders averaged 1.4 seconds processing time; clerks averaged 3.2 seconds. This differential in planning time supports indications in the protocols that preloaders used perceptual information from the array to determine quantity in the cases, while clerks used slower, enumerative techniques.

These analyses suggest that becoming a skilled product assembler involves learning the value of various configurations of containers (e.g. one layer of half-pints is 16; two rows of quarts is 8). Visual inspection then provides the quantitative information necessary to fill the order with little or no recoding into the number system. Some psychologists (deGroot, 1966; Chase & Simon, 1973) believe that master chess players are distinguished from lesser competitors by their vocabulary of perceptual units (configurations of pieces), which enable them to "see" move possibilities rapidly and without recourse to verbal analysis (Olson & Bialystok, 1980). Skill in as simple a task as product assembly may follow a similar course of acquisition from the primarily linguistic to the primarily perceptual. Follow-up training studies could be designed with this question in mind.

The last question pursued in these simulations concerned the postulated mental effort – physical effort trade-off. While we had a precise scale for measuring physical effort, no general methodology for assessing mental effort is available. We used an intuitive scheme for classifying types of problems by "mental difficulty" for which we secured partial confirmation. The analysis of preloader skill leaned heavily on the notion that nonliteral solutions (transformations of problems) require more mental work than the simple execution of literal solutions. If the time required to adopt a solution strategy (the premovement period) is provisionally considered to be an index of the difficulty of a problem, the distribution of average processing time falls into place. Preloaders required a second (1.0) to get started on problems in which literal solutions represented the optimal, least-physical-effort strategies, as compared to 1.4 seconds for problems in which the optimal solutions involved departures from the literal. The corresponding averages for billing clerks were 1.4 and 3.6 seconds.

Pricing delivery tickets

The second example of cognitive analysis of a work task involves wholesale drivers, a group whose earnings, including commissions, are among the highest in the dairy. In contrast to product assembly, wholesale delivery is regarded as an occupation with demanding intellectual and personality skills. Many a company executive today, we were told, began worklife as a milk driver.

Among their other daily chores, wholesale milk drivers must compute the total dollar value of their deliveries. For this purpose, they use computer-generated delivery tickets, which come to them preprinted with the customer's name and the products to be delivered that day. Quantities are left blank, but after a delivery is completed, drivers enter the amount of each item at that stop. This amount is always expressed in units. At that time, or after they have returned to the dairy to settle accounts, drivers are required to "extend the ticket" – find the total price for each line item and then the dollar value of the entire delivery. Accuracy counts. Drivers are responsible for the exact value of the products they take out of the dairy, and delivery tickets are also the basis of the company's billing system. To help drivers price out, the company provides a mimeographed wholesale price list, which gives prices for the various kinds of milk products. All prices are expressed in units on this list, as on all lists, because the price structure consists wholly of unit prices. Since the size of each product order is recorded on the delivery ticket in units and since prices are in units, the computation task seems straightforward: take the unit price from the price list or from memory, multiply it by the number of units recorded on the delivery ticket, and enter the result in the appropriate column; proceed in this fashion down the list; total the entries.

Informal observations revealed that drivers, no less than preloaders, frequently depart from this literal format. The most interesting departure involved importing into the problem information about the number of containers of different sizes that fit into a case. A driver who was accompanied on his route provided one of the first instances of this computational strategy. He read the item, "32 quarts homo milk" (dairy abbreviation for homogenized milk), found a price on a crib sheet in his pocket, doubled it, and entered the resultant product on his delivery ticket. His crib sheet, personally prepared, was an organized arrangement of tables listing prices by the case for products he frequently handled and prices by case multiples (8-case prices, 12-case prices) for high-volume items.

The milk case played an instrumental role in the product assembly task both in its physical aspects as a container and in its symbolic aspects as a variable that could take certain number values. Pricing out is an activity occurring wholly in the symbolic mode; as a material object, the case is without significance for this activity, yet it appears here, too, as a variable in arithmetic operations. Unremarkable as this may first appear, one can think of the case price as a prototype of human sign-creating activities that play such an important role in theories of higher mental functions. An object which first possesses instrumental value in physical activity begins to serve a sign function and becomes incorporated in mental operations (Vygotsky, 1978).

How widespread among the drivers was the case-price technique? And what specific functions did it serve? Again, we turned to task simulation to pursue the analysis.

As with product assembly, we planned to model simulations on the task as performed under normal working conditions. But unlike product assembly, where the operator's overt behavior is informative as to strategies of solution, a driver's use of a calculator or entry on a delivery ticket is mute with respect to the path of problem solution. We therefore transferred our observations from the dairy settlement room to an office in the basement where we recorded drivers talking out loud as they went through some of the day's delivery tickets. An observer noted which numbers the driver marked on scratch paper or entered into his calculator, and whether he consulted a price list. These converging lines of evidence permitted reconstruction of the driver's representation of the problem and method of solution (Table 26.3).

Drivers differed in the range and type of their solution strategies, but with the one exception of a relief driver who was not handling his own route, all used a case-price strategy on at least one occasion. Most commonly, the case price appeared on quantities convertible to an even number of cases. Older drivers, however, especially those without calculators, used the strategy flexibly and in many forms. Some devised combinations of case and unit prices, reminiscent of the mixed orders on the load-out order form, which permitted them to solve these multiplication problems through addition and subtraction:

Order	Solution strategy
17 quarts	Driver took the case price and added a unit price.
31 pints	Driver took the case price and subtracted a unit price.
48 gallons	Driver took ten times the case price and added two case prices.
98 half-pints	Driver took two times the case price and added two times the unit price.

A problem-by-problem analysis of strategies suggested that the case-price technique functioned as an effort saver in a manner analogous to the nonliteral optimal solutions in the product assembly task. Effort saved in pricing delivery tickets, however, is mental rather than physical. Use of a case price either eliminates computation altogether or simplifies it. Such effort saving would appear to be dependent on whether an individual driver has access to the case price, either in memory or on paper through a crib sheet or his own modification of the dairy's unit price list.

The task simulation examined how knowledge of case prices affected pricing strategies. In separate interviews we had elicited each drivers' knowledge of case and unit prices for all products carried on wholesale routes. We were, therefore, in a position to test the knowledge-strategy interaction against an individual driver's recall record and pricing protocol. Standardized delivery tickets were prepared, composed of items for which most drivers knew the case prices and including many orders whose quantities were convertible to an even number of cases. As before, drivers who used calculators normally were allowed to use them on this task if they desired.

Results support an effort-saving hypothesis as well as highlighting the important role of knowledge in the choice of solution strategy. When drivers knew the applicable case prices on orders equivalent to single cases, they handled 77% of these orders by plugging the case prices into the cost column, bypassing computation altogether. All orders solved by the use of unit prices involved some

Table 26.3. Pricing delivery tickets (example of data for analysis from one driver).

Ticket item (reproduced from driver's ticket)	Unit price (reproduced from dairy wholesale price list)	Driver's computation (reproduced from scratch sheet or driver's ticket)[a]	Ticket entry (reproduced from driver's ticket)	Protocol (driver talking out loud; transcribed from audio tape)
120 gal. homo D	$2.33	932 30 — 27960	279.60	All right, so it's nine thirty-two a case and we have four into a hundred and twenty is thirty cases. So, I'll take thirty times nine thirty-two. I'll figure that's the easiest way to do it. Two seventy-nine sixty. See, in other words, it's two thirty-three a gallon, there's four gallons to a case, that's how you get nine thirty-two.
16 qt. homo VD	.74	11.84 74 16 — 11.84	11.84	Sixteen quarts of white is seventy-four. Now that's eleven eighty-four. We know it from memory, 'cause we use it over and over. So you take seventy-four times sixteen, you get eleven eighty-four. Yeah, it's eleven eighty-four a case. Seventy-four cents a quart.
12 gal. punch	.84	840 168 — 1008	10.08	All right, you got twelve, now it's eighty-four a gallon, so ten gallons would be eight forty. So I take the eight forty and two gallons would be one sixty-eight. That's two times eighty-four. So it's ten and two is twelve. Ten-o-eight.

[a]Observer's record also available. For drivers who used calculators, the observer's record of numbers entered on calculator was used. Note the variable use of decimal point on the scratch sheet (items 1 and 3 have no decimals).

recourse to paper and pencil or calculator to determine cost. Reduction in effort is apparent here.

Some orders presented quantities equivalent to two, three, and four cases; others to five and ten cases. Use of case prices on these problem classes dropped off to 59% and 38%, respectively. In all instances, case prices were used on orders for which the driver knew the price for a single case; the case price was never computed as a step to the solution of a problem involving multiple cases. Although multiple-case-price knowledge had not been assessed in the elicitation interview, some drivers spontaneously remarked that they knew or did not know how much N cases of X was because they did or did not handle this particular product in that volume. If a driver did not know the multiple-case price, the use of case-price strategy on these problems met an effort-saving criterion only in the sense of simplifying, rather than eliminating, computation. Analysis of case price solutions provided ample evidence of simplified arithmetic: two-thirds of the time drivers either entered the total price, giving no overt indication of computation, or did mental arithmetic (e.g. "That's $15.40 a case and there's two of them, so that would be $30.80"). Mental arithmetic did not suffice for unit-price solutions; these always involved some paper-and-pencil or calculator operations.

In addition to knowledge, the technological means drivers used in delivery ticket settlement affected their solution strategies. Except for three senior drivers who did paper-and-pencil arithmetic, other drivers owned and used calculators. The calculator encouraged greater reliance on the repetitive and literal solution strategy (number of units times unit price). Nonetheless, drivers with calculators also shifted to a case-price strategy on even-case orders in the simulation, providing additional evidence of an effort-saving hypothesis. In a subsequent study, drivers with calculators were required to price out the same set of facsimile tickets in different ways on two occasions; in the first session, in their customary manner; in the second session, without their calculators. The presence or absence of a calculator did not affect the incidence of case-price use on single-case orders, which was high under both conditions. But on more complex problems, either involving multiple-case orders or allowing solution by mixed case-and-unit price strategies, the removal of calculators resulted in a marked jump in case-price shortcutting strategies.

To explore the versatility of pricing-out techniques and compare novices with experts, we equalized all groups for ignorance. We prepared tickets exhibiting orders for products that were not handled by the dairy but represented sensible additions (e.g. iced coffee, 1% low-fat milk). Pseudo-price lists displaying both unit and case prices for these products were made available to informants, along with charts showing how many containers of various sizes fit into cases. In this group comparison, only students were unfamiliar with the case system and true novices. Preloaders and inventory men knew the case system but not the price system and had never before worked delivery tickets. White-collar workers were familiar with the price system, and one subgroup (billing clerks) worked on wholesale delivery tickets daily, checking and posting totals.

We devised orders to represent an array of efficient solution strategies, including case-price strategies. Special care was taken to include problems that would be diagnostic of versatility as negative instances; that is, they could be solved more easily by unit than by case prices (e.g. 10 quarts). We expected that skill related to experience would be demonstrated by a flexible use of case- and unit-price strategies on problems where each was appropriate.

Quite aside from the great variety of techniques that skilled people used to optimize solutions, individuals could be readily classified in terms of whether or not they were flexible or inflexible (single algorithm) problem-solvers. All drivers except one were flexible problem-solvers; most of them used optimal strategies as well. Approximately one-third of the white-collar and icebox workers were flexible. Without exception the students were inflexible problem-solvers. Most of them tended to use the literal unit-price strategy throughout. The small number who took up on the case-price technique applied it indiscriminately to all problems, regardless of their numerical properties, including an order for 101 quarts which involved working with long division to find the number of cases and ending up with a fraction of a case.

We set up these group comparisons not so much to characterize novice performance as to increase understanding of the characteristics of skilled cognitive activity. We are not implying that some special ability is involved in the use of a case-price technique. Obviously the situation could have been structured in such a way that everyone used case prices or, alternatively, everyone used unit prices, simply by being told to do so. But knowing to do something does not necessarily make for skilled performance. Skill requires knowing how to, sometimes referred to as procedural knowledge. In the pricing task, domain-specific subject knowledge (information about cases and prices) combined with procedural knowledge to produce flexible least-effort strategies. These could be raised to the level of a virtuoso performance, as shown by an experienced driver's repertoire of pricing strategies on our tasks (Table 26.4). In addition to straightforward multiplication using either unit price or case price, this driver converted many problems to subtraction and addition, factored some problems, and used combinations of case and unit prices to simplify others.

Conclusions

Let me now try to reestablish ties with the broader questions that motivated these studies of working intelligence. One motivation was a test of method. We wanted to determine if we could bring some rigor to the study of thinking as it functions in the world of purposeful activities in which people customarily engage. We are not prepared at this stage to offer a full assessment, but several observations about method seem warranted. Several bear on the

Table 26.4. *Expert pricing strategies used by a veteran wholesale driver on his own and experimental delivery tickets.* [a]

Solutions using unit price	Solutions using case price	Solutions using mixed case and unit prices
Multiples without overt multiplication	Single case	
2 UP	CP	CP + UP
3 UP	Multiples without overt	CP + 2 UP
4 UP	multiplication	2 CP + 2 UP
5 UP	CP × C	
10 UP	$\dfrac{U}{U/C} = C; CP \times C$	CP − UP
100 UP		2 CP − UP
	$UP \times U/C = CP; CP \times C$	10 CP − UP
Multiplication	Factoring & addition	
U × UP	10 CP + CP	
UP × U		
Factoring & addition		
10 UP + 2 UP		
100 UP + 2 UP		
Factoring & multiplication		
Factored UP; $UP_1 \times U$; $UP_2 \times U$		
Factored U; $UP \times U_1$; $UP \times U_2$		

[a] UP = unit price; U = number of units; CP = case price; C = number of cases; U/C = number of units per case.

technical problems of conducting basic cognitive research in a nonresearch setting; others have to do with broader methodological issues.

On the technical level these studies have demonstrated the usefulness of an industrial environment as a setting for research on practical thinking. At the present state of theorizing, categories such as "practice" and "goal-directed action" are insufficiently specified to guide research in many settings. In the industrial environment, these constructs could be translated into "occupation" and "task," naturalistic categories defined by the environment, which facilitated the selection of appropriate phenomena for study. Working within a single plant also proved advantageous. In both the product assembly and delivery ticket analyses, our access to materials and information was instrumental in minimizing random variation in both observational and experimental situations. Recall that we were able to determine the most frequent partial-case product assemblies from the complete set of load-out order forms, thus avoiding the problem of dealing with atypical or less familiar orders in the search for systematicity.

Access to the company's price lists allowed assessment of each driver's knowledge of wholesale prices, a control lessening the risk of working with a small sample. The factory as a research site substituted in some respects for the school, an institution that for years has been exploited for experimental studies. However, in one important respect the factory does not substitute for a school: its population is not captive for purposes of research. While in these particular studies selection-biasing factors were held to a tolerable level, they could not be avoided. Some individuals drawn at random declined to participate; others were discharged and lost motivation for participating; two dropped out, finding the sessions difficult. This experience indicates that studies of adult practical thinking are likely to benefit from methods which maximize the interpretability of individual performance and draw on, but do not rest on, statistical comparison between groups.

The research strategy in these studies combined laboratory methods such as task analysis with observational methods characteristic of field work. In bringing task analysis to the field, we reversed the typical laboratory paradigm. Most investigators begin with a formal or rational decomposition of the task of interest and then go on to refine their model by empiric or computer simulation studies (Siegler, 1980; Resnick, 1976, is an exception). The dairy research began with empirical observations, which were used to generate a description of the task-in-context. We then refined this description by considering it against laboratory models, such as models of problem solving. The description was useful when it guided us to significant knowledge and strategy components of the task and suggested parameters to investigate in task simulations.

We have made some progress in analyzing skills involved in performance of certain work tasks. To the extent these analyses support the laboratory models, they increase the range and power of these models. To the extent these analyses uncover characteristics not represented or inadequately represented in the models they contribute to the advancement of laboratory as well as naturalistic studies of thinking.

We were concerned to carry out these studies in such a way as to achieve an account of the processes and knowledge underlying task performance. However, limitations in time and level of specificity of the data did not always support microanalysis. Laboratory examples of well-analyzed cognitive tasks have built on years of accumulated experience with particular tasks and paradigms (e.g., number series problems, conservation problems). As yet, there is no such heritage of model tasks for the study of practical thinking. Well-analyzed tasks require many interrelated studies spanning a long time period. To determine, for example, whether mental representations of product arrays change with increasing experience, specially designed studies are necessary, and these may well benefit from the use of recording devices that are suitable in a laboratory-like setting. It is questionable whether process models of practical problem-solving can be developed without reiterative cycles of both laboratory- and nonlaboratory-based studies.

What general problems arise with respect to the interpretation of these studies? Simon (1976) raised this question with respect to laboratory-based task analysis and specified key questions that a process-theory model must satisfy. These include the validity and uniqueness of the task description, generalizability, and usefulness for studies of transfer and learning. The problem of generalizability is especially important, and it has two aspects. The first is task generalizability: to what extent does the task selected for study share at least some characteristics with other tasks involving problem solving? Only the assumption of cross-task commonality of process can justify studies of performance on arbitrarily selected laboratory tasks. Similarly, laboratory investigations must assume some interindividual commonalities in strategy in order to make statements about "human problem-solving" on the basis of the small number of individuals whose performances are observed and analyzed. Recognition of these problems requires a long-range strategy of development and test of various problem-solving models.

Field-based cognitive analysis, such as that reported here, also encounters problems of validity and generalizability, but as the foregoing assessment makes clear, these problems do not reflect special liabilities inherent in field settings. Laboratory studies have no intrinsic methodological advantage. The advantage of relevance, however, remains on the side of field-based studies. In occupational or school settings, the researcher works with tasks whose requirements and conditions of performance reflect the demands that our society poses for intelligent performance.

Leaving aside questions of method, these naturalistic studies of problem solving lend support to a practice framework of cognition. We began with a functional theoretical orientation holding that cognitive skills take shape in the course of individual participation in socially organized practices. The dairy studies examined practices that involve neither esoteric bodies of knowledge nor highly technical skills. Yet the evidence suggests the fruitfulness of a practice-based approach.

In spite of the small number of people involved in the comparisons, the job-related nature of skilled performance is readily discernible. It is most evident in contrasts between dairy employees as a group and students. Although on some tasks employees and students achieved similar levels of accuracy, their strategies differed markedly. Students tended to treat problems according to their literal format and to handle the quantitative aspects of manual tasks, such as product assembly, by applying rules of procedure appropriate to paper-and-pencil arithmetic. These findings justify the continued exploration of the contrasting characteristics of academic and practical problem-solving (Scribner & Fahrmeier, 1982).

Differential patterns of skills appeared as well on an occupational basis. In each case, the occupation providing on-the-job experience also provided the greatest number of experts on the simulated tasks. While this finding may appear trivial, it goes beyond the common-sense observation that practice makes perfect. The issue is not accuracy or error but rather modes of solution. Strategy analysis demonstrated that experience makes for different ways of solving problems or, to put it another way, that the problem-solving process is restructured by the knowledge and strategy repertoire available to the expert in comparison to the novice. Other studies have amply demonstrated these effects of experience in pursuits such as chess and music (Bamberger & Schon, 1976), which require mastery of symbol and rule systems not encountered in everyday activities. The present studies suggest that a pattern of development from novice to expert performance may not be restricted to such specialized activities but may represent the course of adult skill acquisition in commonplace tasks as well.

The pattern of occupation-skill relations, while present, is mixed, and it would be an oversimplification to imply that the skills found in these studies are tied to particular jobs in any deterministic way. In each comparison, one or more individuals who apparently lacked on-the-job experience with the task showed the same fluency in optimizing solution strategies as practitioners. Conversely, in every case, one or more individuals from the occupation in question did not turn in a skilled performance. The probabilistic nature of experience-based skills poses problems that a functional approach to thinking must meet.

Although only a handful of tasks has been studied in depth, they reveal common features which offer interesting suggestions for a general theory of practical thinking. Variability was an outstanding characteristic of skilled performance on all tasks examined. Product assembly and pricing-out appear on first inspection as prototypical examples of repetitive industrial work. They both present the worker with recurring problems of the same kind, often problems of an identical kind. A rational task analysis might not have revealed the diversity of operations hidden under these same-problem formats. In some approaches to problem solving, an individual's inconsistency in strategy and performance is troublesome to the model. Yet increasingly investigators are turning up such "inconsistencies." In almost every area of cognitive development, psychologists have discovered that subtle differences in task demands may lead to widely varied performance (Klahr, 1979). Controversies are keen. Why do versions A and B of task X lead to such wide differences in performance? Why do problem isomorphs – that is, problems designed to have an identical structure of solution moves – often fail to operate as isomorphs (Hayes & Simon, 1977)? Explanatory concepts are advanced, but many attempts to take account of situational changes in performance have the status of appendages to the theoretical machinery rather than of components integrated within it.

Bartlett's (1958) classic studies of thinking avoided this dilemma. He considered that problem solving has the same characteristics as skilled performance in other modalities and that a defining attribute of skill is variability. Moreover, he held that variability is rule-governed: "all forms of skill expertly carried out possess an outstanding characteristic of rapid adaptation . . . so what is called the same operation is done now in one way and now in another, but each way is, as we say, 'fitted to the occasion'" (p. 14). This is a fitting description of the kind of thinking we have seen in action at the dairy. The variability we observed was neither random nor arbitrary. It was sufficiently systematic to appear in analyses without benefit of statistical tests. Following Bartlett, we might consider these regularities as forms of adaptation. We can then put to future studies this proposition: skilled practical thinking is goal-directed and varies adaptively with the changing properties of problems and changing conditions in the task environment. In this respect, practical thinking contrasts with the kind of academic thinking exemplified in the use of a single algorithm to solve all problems of a given type.

The concept of adaptive thinking need not be left on an analogical level. The dairy research raises one line of speculation that would be intriguing to pursue: practical thinking becomes adaptive when it serves the interests of economy of effort. Product assembly provided a vivid example of thinking saving manual effort; pricing-out provided a parallel demonstration of thinking saving mental effort. Effort-saving functioned as a criterion distinguishing skilled from amateur performance, not only for the researchers but for dairy employees evaluating their own or others' work. We do not know how general a characteristic of working intelligence such effort-saving might be. It may be peculiar to the special environment of the industrial workplace, or it may be specific to Western culture with its emphasis on efficiency and time- and labor-saving devices. Alternatively effort-saving may be a general characteristic of practical thinking, conferring "elegance" on solutions to problems in mathematical theory as well as to those confronted on the shop floor. These speculations suggest possible common questions for future functional studies of thinking, wherever they take place.

References

Aristotle. 1963. Book I, Metaphysics. In R. Bambrough, ed. *The philosophy of Aristotle.* New York: Mentor.
Bamberger, J., & D. A. Schon. 1976. The figural formal transaction: a parable of generative metaphor. Mimeo. Cambridge: Division for Study and Research in Education, MIT.
Bartlett, F. 1958. *Thinking.* New York: Basic Books.
Bronfenbrenner, U. 1979. *The ecology of human development.* Cambridge: Harvard University Press.
Brown, A. L. 1977. Development, schooling and the acquisition of knowledge about

364   *Thinking at work*

knowledge. In R. C. Anderson, R. J. Spiro, & W. E. Montague, eds. *Schooling and the acquisition of knowledge.* Hillsdale, N.J.: Erlbaum.

Brown, A. L., & L. A. French. 1979. Commentary. In D. W. Sharp, M. Cole, & C. Lave, eds. Education and cognitive development: the evidence from experimental research. *Monographs of the Society for Research in Child Development* 44(1–2, no. 178):101–108.

Chase, W. G., & H. A. Simon. 1973. Perception in chess. *Cognitive Psychology* 4:55–81.

Childs, C. P., & P. M. Greenfield. 1980. Informal modes of learning and teaching: the case of Zinacanteco weaving. In N. Warren, ed. *Advances in cross-cultural psychology,* vol. 2. London: Academic Press.

Cole, M. 1979. Reply. In D. W. Sharp, M. Cole, & C. Lave, eds. Education and cognitive development: the evidence from experimental research. *Monographs of the Society for Research in Child Development* 44(1–2, no. 178):109–112.

Cole, M., L. Hood, & R. McDermott. 1978. Ecological niche picking: ecological invalidity as an axiom of experimental cognitive psychology. Univ. of Cal., San Diego, and The Rockefeller University.

Cole, M., & S. Scribner. 1974. *Culture and thought.* New York: Wiley.

Dasen, P. R. 1977. Introduction. In P. R. Dasen, ed. *Piagetian psychology: cross-cultural contributions.* New York: Gardner Press.

deGroot, A. D. 1966. Perception and memory versus thought: some old ideas and recent findings. In B. Kleinmuntz, ed. *Problem-solving: research, method and theory.* New York: Wiley.

Ginsburg, H. P., J. K. Posner, & R. L. Russell. 1981. The development of knowledge concerning written arithmetic: a cross-cultural study. *International Journal of Psychology* 16:13–34.

Goody, J., ed. 1968. *Literacy in traditional societies.* New York: Cambridge University Press.

———. 1977. *The domestication of the savage mind.* New York: Cambridge University Press.

Greenfield, P. M. 1972. Oral and written languages: the consequences for cognitive development in Africa, the United States, and England. *Language and Speech* 15:169–178.

———. 1966. On culture and equivalence. In J. S. Bruner, R. R. Olver, P. M. Greenfield, et al., eds. *Studies in cognitive growth.* New York: Wiley.

Havelock, E. A. 1963. *Preface to Plato.* Cambridge: Harvard University Press.

Hayes, J. R., & H. A. Simon. 1977. Psychological differences among problem isomorphs. In N. J. Castellan, D. B. Pisoni, & G. R. Potts, eds. *Cognitive theory,* vol. 2. Hillsdale, N.J.: Erlbaum.

Hutchins, E. 1979. Conceptual structures in pre-literate Pacific navigation. Paper presented at Social Science Research Council, San Diego, Cal.

Inkeles, A., & D. H. Smith. 1974. *Becoming modern.* Cambridge: Harvard University Press.

James, W. 1950. *The principles of psychology,* vol. 2. New York: Dover. Originally published 1890.

Klahr, D. 1979. Self-modifying production systems as models of cognitive development. Paper presented at Biennial Meeting of Society for Research in Child Development, San Francisco.

Klahr, D., & M. Robinson. 1981. Formal assessment of problem-solving and planning processes in preschool children. *Cognitive Psychology* 13:1–36.

Laboratory of Comparative Human Cognition. 1979. Cross-cultural psychology's challenges to our ideas of children and development. *American Psychologist* 34:827–833.

Laurendeau-Bendavid, M. 1977. Culture, schooling and cognitive development: a comparative study of children in French Canada and Rwanda. In P. Dasen, ed. *Piagetian psychology: cross-cultural contributions.* New York: Gardner Press.

Lave, J. 1977. Cognitive consequences of traditional apprenticeship training in West Africa. *Anthropology and Education Quarterly* 8:177–180.

Mehan, H. 1979. *Learning lessons.* Cambridge: Harvard University Press.

Neisser, U. 1976. General, academic, and artifical intelligence. In L. B. Resnick, ed. *The nature of intelligence.* Hillsdale, N.J.: Erlbaum.

Newell, A., & H. A. Simon. 1972. *Human problem-solving.* Englewood Cliffs, N.J.: Prentice-Hall.

Olson, D. R. 1977. From utterance to text: the bias of language in speech and writing. *Harvard Educational Review* 47:257–281.

Olson, D. R., & E. Bialystok. 1980. Mental representations of space: the representation of objects and the representation of form. In B. de Gelder, ed. *Knowledge and representation.* London: Routledge and Kegan Paul.

Olson, D. R., & N. Nickerson. 1978. Language development through the school years: learning to confine interpretation to the information conventionalized in the text. In K. E. Nelson, ed. *Children's language,* vol. 1. New York: Gardner Press.

Piaget, J. 1950. *The psychology of intelligence.* London: Routledge and Kegan Paul.

Reed, H. J., & J. Lave. 1979. Arithmetic as a tool for investigating relations between culture and cognition. *American Ethnologist* 6:568–582.

Resnick, L. B. 1976. Task analysis in instructional design: some cases from mathematics. In D. Klahr, ed. *Cognition and instruction.* Hillsdale, N.J.: Erlbaum.

Rogoff, B. 1981. Schooling and the development of cognitive skills. In H. C. Triandis & A. Heron, Eds. *Handbook of cross-cultural psychology,* vol. 4. Boston: Allyn and Bacon.

Scribner, S. 1974. Developmental aspects of categorized recall in a West African society. *Cognitive Psychology* 6:475–494.

———. 1977. Literacy as a cultural practice. Paper presented at American Anthropological Association Annual Meeting, Houston.

———. 1978. The concept of practice in research on culture and thought. Paper presented at Soviet-American Conference on the Psychological Theory of Activity, Institute of Psychology, Moscow.

Scribner, S., & M. Cole. 1973. Cognitive consequences of formal and informal education. *Science* 182:553–559.

Scribner, S., & M. Cole. 1981. *The psychology of literacy.* Cambridge: Harvard University Press.

Scribner, S., & E. Fahrmeier. 1982. *Practical and theoretical arithmetic.* Working Paper 3, Industrial Literacy Project. New York: The Graduate School and University Center, CUNY.

Sharp, D. W., M. Cole, & C. Lave. 1979. Education and cognitive development: the evidence from experimental research. *Monographs of the Society for Research in Child Development* 44(1–2, no. 178).

366   *Thinking at work*

Siegler, R. S. 1980. Recent trends in the study of cognitive development: variations on a task-analytic theme. *Human Development* 23:278–285.

Simon, H. A. 1975. The functional equivalence of problem-solving skills. *Cognitive Psychology* 7:268–288.

———. 1976. Identifying basic abilities underlying intelligent performance of complex tasks. In L. Resnick, ed. *The nature of intelligence*. Hillsdale, N.J.: Erlbaum.

Simon, H. A., & S. K. Reed. 1976. Modelling strategy shifts in a problem-solving task. *Cognitive Psychology* 8:86–97.

Stevenson, H. W., T. Parker, A. Wilkinson, B. Bonnevaux, & M. Gonzalez. 1978. Schooling, environment, and cognitive development: a cross-cultural study. *Monographs of the Society for Research in Child Development* 43(3, no. 175).

Vygotsky, L. S. 1962. *Thought and language*. Cambridge: M.I.T. Press.

———. 1978. *Mind in society*. Cambridge: Harvard University Press.

Wagner, D. A. 1978. Memories of Morocco: the influence of age, schooling and environment on memory. *Cognitive Psychology* 10.1–28.

Wertheimer, M. 1959. *Productive thinking*. Ed. Michael Wertheimer. New York: Harper.

27 Mental and manual work: An activity theory orientation

One of the central contributions activity theory offers cognitive psychology is a new conceptualization of the relationship between mind and behavior.

Cognitive science in the United States, in spite of its youth, remains loyal to Descartes' division of the world into the mental and physical, the thought and the act. As against this way of carving up reality, activity theory offers another set of distinctions. Leontiev (1978) describes the two positions clearly.

The Cartesian world is divided, on the one hand, into the "external world of space to which external physical activity also belongs, and, on the other hand, the world of internal phenomena and processes of consciousness." This distinction gives way in activity theory to a split between what Leontiev calls "objective reality in both outer and idealized forms," and the activity of the subject, which includes both external and internal processes (1978, p. 61).

The implication of this reorganization for problems in psychology is profound. Analysis of human activity cannot proceed merely by splitting activity into two parts or sides as if they belonged to two different spheres of reality, with cognitive psychology taking one sphere and a psychology of action the other. Rather, if external and internal processes belong to the same sphere – that of motivated and mediated activity – psychology confronts a new problem: investigating the relationships between these forms in particular activities and mapping the transitions from one to another that occur with experience over time.

Studies I will report here attempt such an analysis for several tasks arising in work activities. Like other research in our laboratory, these studies are motivated by an interest in elaborating an approach to the study of thinking that

This paper was presented at the First International Congress on Activity Theory, Berlin, 1986, and printed in Proceedings of the Congress (1988). Reprinted with permission of Dr. Georg Rueckriem.

CARTESIAN VIEW

EXTERNAL WORLD	INTERNAL WORLD
Material Objects	Ideal Objects
External Processes	Internal Processes

ACTIVITY THEORY

OBJECT WORLD	ACTIVITY WORLD
Material Objects	External Processes
Ideal Objects	Internal Processes

Figure 27.1

draws on Vygotsky's (1986, 1978) concept of cultural mediational systems as well as the basic categories of activity theory (Scribner, 1984).

We chose work activities as the object of investigation for reasons of both research strategy and concern for social usefulness. In our analytic scheme, various occupations represent motivated activities, and specific work tasks represent goal-directed actions undertaken within these activities. (For a fuller exposition, see Scribner, 1984). Our research efforts begin with systematic observations of a targetted activity in the actual workplace. We then select one or more tasks for which we devise experimental simulations, treating these tasks as model systems for investigating certain aspects of goal-directed actions. We have thus far concentrated on production and service tasks in which the worker has certain options to select among alternative operations and mediational devices. Constructive tasks of this kind furnish the richest opportunity to study transitions between inner and outer processes, and to identify the personal, as well as external, factors regulating them.

Our guiding concept is that these goal-directed work actions take the form, not of fixed hierarchical structures (as described, for example, by Volpert, 1982) but of dynamic functional systems, hierarchically organized. In his classic description of a functional system, Luria (1973) singled out as distinguishing characteristics its complex organization and the variability of its components. A basic feature of a functional system is the presence of an invariant task and an invariant end result which can be reached by different means. Luria first elaborated this concept with respect to physiological functions, but it has since been extended to perceptual-motor and cognitive functions, and, in Zinchenko's research (Zinchenko and Gordon, 1981) to microanalysis of such functions in work tasks. In proposing a functional system analysis of action, I have in mind a further extension – namely that the system be conceptualized as the action unit as a whole, including not only its inner and outer operations but the objects to which these are directed. In a functional system model of action, attention is directed to such questions as the following: what are the qualitatively different ways in which the same end result can be achieved? Are there conditions under which external and internal operations are functionally equivalent? What is the role of different mediational objects in establishing functional equivalence among inner and outer operations?

Our notions of a functional action system have not yet been formalized and can best be conveyed through illustrative research material. I will describe one line of research in our laboratory concentrating on analysis of the mental and manual components of a warehouse assembly job in a modern milk-processing plant (dairy).

Mental and manual transitions in a workplace task

In the plant selected for study, warehouse assemblers use a computer-generated order form to get information on the kinds and amounts of products needed on different delivery routes. This form expresses quantities in a metric system specific to the dairy, one composed of cases and units. Dairy products are stored and handled in cases of a standard size which hold a certain number of unit containers of milk. The number of units in a case varies with the size of the container. For example, a case holds 9 half-gallons, 16 quarts and so on. If a particular order involves a quantity that is not evenly divisible into cases, the order form represents it as a mixed number: x cases *plus* y units, or x cases *minus* y units. For example, 1–6 on the order form stands for one case minus six units. (The *plus* or *minus* form is determined by rule).

When we observed assemblers at work, we found they had many different ways of filling these mixed orders. On some occasions, they filled them as written: they filled *plus* orders by adding the specified number of units to an empty case and *minus* orders by removing the specified number of units from a full case. Their operations – adding or taking away – and the number of units moved were isomorphic to the symbolic expression of the order. I will refer to these procedures as literal solutions. Assemblers, however, frequently departed from these literal interpretations. For example, an assembler filled an order for 1 case *minus* 6 quarts by removing 4 quarts from a partially full case of fourteen that was located nearby. On another occasion, he filled the same order by adding 2 quarts to a partially full case of 8. In this latter instance, the assembler not only changed the number of units to be moved but converted a take-away operation into an add-to operation. I call these nonliteral solutions.

Consider these nonliteral solutions. They require mental work over and beyond those required by literal solutions. In addition to retaining information in the order – a general requirement – an assembler engaging in a nonliteral solution must transform this information into some representation that can be mapped onto quantitative properties of the different case arrays he may encounter on the floor. A nonliteral solution to the order, 1 case *minus* 6 quarts, for example, requires the assembler to search the product array for a partially full case, make a mental comparison of the distance between the number in this case and the desired end result, and determine how many units to move. Such a comparison can be made by mental calculation (subtracting 6 quarts from sixteen to obtain ten and comparing ten with the number in the partial). Alternatively, it may involve matching a template of the order (a case with 6 quarts out of it) to the configuration in the partial (say, a case with 2 quarts out of it) and computing or estimating what moves are needed. Many different ensembles of subprocesses may be involved in a particular solution.

Our research initially addressed the question of the conditions under which assemblers adopted either literal or nonliteral solution modes. We conducted systematic observations of a number of assemblers under normal working conditions, recording for each order the cases available to be used, the cases the assembler actually used and the number of containers he moved from one case to another. We found that 80% of literal solutions and 100% of nonliteral solutions were those which satisfied the order in the fewest number of physical moves in the given circumstances. That is, of all the modes of solution possible in a given array of milk cases, the assembler selected just that solution which required him to transfer the fewest units from one case to another.

If we consider "filling an order" to be an action, and an action to be a functional system organized for achieving a goal, we can make the following statements about this task as it is carried out under typical working conditions.

1. The objective, externally imposed goal is completion of the order with accuracy and speed. The subjective goals is to satisfy this requirement with the least physical effort. It is concerned with the *how* of performance rather than the *what* of the task. This goal remains invariant under changing circumstances.

2. With changing circumstances, different means are brought to bear in the service of the invariant goal. Variation in constituent operations involves, among

other things, displacement of some external motor operations (moving milk cartons) by visual search and inner computational or estimation procedures.

3. These inner processes are not interiorized, abbreviated forms of the outer operations theyy replace. Assemblers do not imagine they are picking cartons out of a case. Inner operations involve use of a socially constructed symbol system of arithmetic. More exactly, they involve the use of *two* systems of arithmetic – the decimal system used in the culture at large and the case-unit metric system elaborated by generations of dairy workers.

4. The different functional organizations underlying literal and nonliteral solutions are available as selective options to assemblers. Each solution is closely fitted to the particular quantitative properties of a particular order and case array. It might be said, then, that the functional action system underlying product assembly is constructed on each occasion of use in the service of the goal of least physical effort. This does not imply, of course, that each construction occurs *de novo* or that functional systems do not undergo abbreviation and stereotyping over time. What the present analysis emphasizes is the conscious, nonautomatic aspect of solution variability.

Mental and manual transitions in an experimental task

Thus far, I have provided a synchronic analysis of functional organizations of the assembly task which characterize skilled performance in the actual work environment. In experimental simulations with one hundred fifty secondary school students, we examined the course of development of these functional systems and some of the objective and subjective factors regulating this development.

First, we established the fact that with extended practice many learners who begin with a literal functional organization adopt nonliteral modes of solution spontaneously and without instruction. The course of change is from literal to nonliteral solutions. Mental operations come to substitute for physical operations, not the other way around.

Secondly, we learned that construction of nonliteral solutions is not an all-or-none affair but takes the form of a learning curve. A major factor regulating this acquisition is the nature of the mental effort-physical effort tradeoff involved in particular problem types. The more difficult the particular transformation required for a nonliteral optimal solution – the greater the mental effort involved – the longer it takes the learner to shift to a nonliteral solution. Evidence for this proposition is consistent and striking, and I will cite only one class. A logical analysis suggests that *minus* orders (e.g. 1 case *minus* 6 quarts) require more mental work than *plus* orders since their surface form does not contain information about the actual number of units required in the final order. The assembler must compute a mental representation of that number.

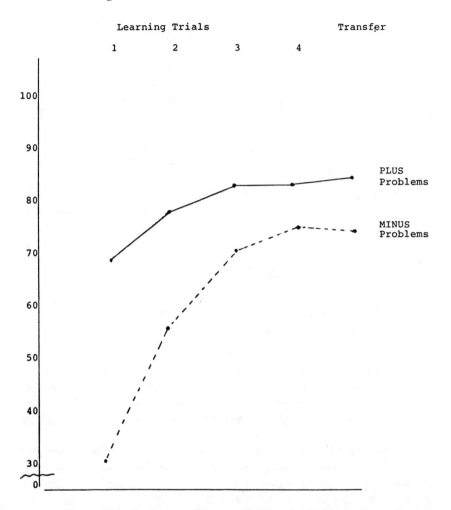

Figure 27.2. Optimal solutions on *PLUS* and *MINUS* problems, Product Assembly Learning Task (in percent)

Figure 27.2 shows acquisition of nonliteral optimal solutions in one of our learning studies. On Trial 1, only half as many *minus* problems received non-literal solutions as *plus* problems and acquisition on *minus* problems continued to lag over trials. In a subsequent study, we conducted within-subject analyses of solutions to *plus* and *minus* forms of the same problem types. There were 523 occasions in which an individual learner solved one form of the problem pair nonliterally and the other literally. Of these, 479 instances – 92% of all mixed pairs – consisted of a nonliteral, least physical effort solution to the *plus* form and a literal, greater physical effort solution to the *minus* form. These findings provide compelling support for our interpretation that, among learners (though not necessarily experts), a calculated tradeoff is involved between mental effort and physical effort in this task.

So much for objective factors. Subjective factors also regulated adoption of least physical effort strategies in the experimental situation. A majority of participants adopted a least physical effort strategy at the outset or acquired it in the course of assembly experience, but some remained literal throughout the learning session. In interviews after experimental sessions, however, members of both groups justified their strategies in exactly the same terms. They said, "The way I did it was easier." One group maintained literal solutions were easier because they did not involve work with numbers. The other group claimed nonliteral solutions were easier because they saved physical work. Herein lies a dilemma. Researchers such as Hacker (1982) have noted that workers in many occupations consciously try to organize their operations to get the job done with least effort. Hacker refers to this standard as an optimization criterion. Determining what this criterion is for certain jobs may appear to be a straightforward matter, but our results indicate that on some tasks, appearances may be deceptive. If we interpret the term "easier" to mean "less effortful," all participants in the experimental learning sessions were striving to meet an optimization criterion. However, the optimization criterion was applied to physical effort by some and to mental effort by others. We could not tell from the outside – from a logical or engineering analysis of the task alone – what mode of solution would be least effortful for a given individual.

Variability in subjective goals in the experimental situation contrasts with the commonality of workers' subjective goals in the actual work situation. In the workplace, the optimization criterion was always interpreted in physical effort terms. This difference between the experimental and work situations is helpful in drawing our attention to factors outside of the technical aspects of a particular task that may be especially important sources for norms of "effort." These factors include other characteristics of the work activity such as rhythm of the day, diversity of tasks, and accumulated load of physical and mental work over time. Of special significance to an activity analysis is the role of social factors in establishing a common interpretation of a preferred mode of task organization. We need a greater understanding of the ways in which the institutional setting, norms and values of the work group and, more broadly, cultural understandings of labor contribute to the reorganization of work tasks in a given community. Unfortunately, these factors are rarely investigated in cognitive research. The concepts of "subjective goal" and "goal formation" are singularly difficult to examine experimentally. Laboratory methods are peculiarly unsuited to them and we need to shift to a social level of analysis and other methods of research to advance our knowledge of their role in regulating mental and manual transitions.

Concluding comments

These observations on the dynamic changes in work action systems remain descriptive, but we hope they suggest the fruitfulness for cognitive research of pursuing questions concerning the functional equivalence of mental and manual operations.

Although the questions I addressed arise within activity theory, the findings might be expressed in other theoretical frameworks. The fit between activity theory and data is not a close one. Activity theory provides a metatheory for psychology but, in my opinion, the work of developing theories in various sub-branches, including cognition, that are consistent with its basic categories remains to be done. In this enterprise, the concept of a functional action system may prove especially useful. A functional system view of actions brings the investigator into confrontation with the range of possibilities available for reaching goals – even those which, as in work activities, may be preset by institutional requirements. Such a confrontation should not only enhance psychological theory but contribute to a deeper understanding of the creative processes involved in work, and the need to encourage that creativity through the social reorganization of mental and manual labor.

References

Hacker, W. (1982). Objective and subjective organization of work activities. In M. von Cranach & R. Harre (Eds.), *The analysis of action.* New York: Cambridge University Press.

Leontiev, A. N. (1978). *Activity, consciousness and personality.* Englewood Cliffs, N.J.: Prentice-Hall, Inc.

Luria, A. R. (1973). *The working brain.* New York: Basic Books, Inc.

Scribner, S. (1984). Cognitive aspects of work. Special Issue. *Quarterly newsletter of Laboratory of Comparative Human Cognition.* La Jolla, California: University of California, San Diego.

Scribner, S. (1986). Thinking in action: some characteristics of practical thought. In R. J. Sternberg & R. C. Wagner (Eds.), *Practical intelligence.* New York: Cambridge University Press.

Volpert, W. (1982). The model of the hierarchical sequential organization of action. In W. Hacker, W. Volpert & M. von Cranach (Eds.), *Cognitive and motivational aspects of action.* Amsterdam: North-Holland Publishing Co.

Vygotsky, L. S. (1978). *Mind in society.* M. Cole, V. John-Steiner, S. Scribner & E. Souberman (Eds.) Cambridge, Mass.: Harvard University Press.

Vygotsky, L. S. (1986). *Problems of general psychology. Volume 1. Thinking and speech.* New York: Plenum Publishers.

Zinchenko, V. P. & Gordon, V. M. (1981). Methodological problems in analyzing activity. In J. V. Wertsch (Ed.), *The concept of activity in Soviet psychology.* New York: M. E. Sharpe, Inc.

28   Toward a model of practical thinking at work

One purpose of research in the dairy was to increase our understanding of the nature of thinking embedded in naturally-occurring work activities. Descriptions and task analyses generated in this research have been thick with particularities and job-specific content, ranging from the details of case conversion arithmetic to facts about the location of products in a warehouse. The question arises: does the research approach pursued here allow us to move toward the identification of general features of thinking at work, or does it lock cognitive science into an ever-increasing collection of task analyses of specific jobs?

This question is readily recognized as one version of a general theoretical problem confronting functional approaches to cognition. The problem of moving from specifics to the general is not peculiar to research in naturalistic settings, but arises as well in laboratory research when investigators attempt to base general statements about "human problem-solving" on process analysis of specific tasks (Simon, 1976).

We would like to advance the claim that the empirical analyses presented here have general implications for a theory of practical thinking. This claim rests on the finding that expert performance on all tasks, differing as they did in many basic properties (predominance of manual versus mental operations, for example), had certain characteristics in common. The appearance of common attributes of skilled performance suggests a route to generalization. We need not, for the time being, query whether the particular operational components of these tasks are bound to the tasks or are "general" – that is, are constituents of many other tasks (a form of the question, "does the particular generalize?"). Rather, we can treat the common characteristics of expert intellectual performance on these tasks as candidates for general features of thinking at work.

This essay originally appeared in a special issue of the *LCHC Newsletter* 6, nos. 1–2 (1984). Reprinted with the permission of Dr. Michael Cole.

Future research can determine whether these features characterize cognition in a wide range of work settings and across tasks varying in their social organization, technical means and intellectual demands. At the same time, we can use these features to examine the limits of current theoretical approaches and to elaborate new constructs for understanding thinking. We might characterize this approach as an attempt to discover the general *in* the particular – an enterprise that calls for reciprocal development of theory and research.

In this article we will briefly summarize common attributes we have identified. For exposition purposes, we will first consider these attributes individually and then we will move up a level of generality to integrate them around several core constructs in the psychology of thinking. In this analysis, we are extrapolating from dairy jobs to other work tasks, and in a concluding section we will describe the type of work activities to which the model we are developing best applies. By this activity-specific approach, we do not preclude the possibility that some of the characteristics of skilled thinking at work, now described in a circumscribed way, may in the future qualify as fundamental properties of goal-directed thinking in many different domains of activity.

Flexibility: Variation in modes of solution

Expert performance on problem-solving tasks was marked by diversity of solution modes.

Flexibility most clearly distinguished experts from beginners. Novices tended to rely on algorithms which produced correct solutions through repeated application of a single solution procedure; with increasing experience, they replaced all-purpose algorithms with a repertoire of solution modes fitted to properties of specific problems in changing task environments.

What is outstanding about the variability documented here is that it represents the use of different component operations to solve problems that on formal analysis are problems of the same kind. Jobs such as product assembly and pricing-out are prototypical examples of repetitive industrial work. It might have been supposed that, to carry out the recurring intellectual chores these jobs demanded, workers would engage in standardized, repetitive mental operations. Instead they brought different mental operations to bear on repeated problems, reaching the same end result now one way, now another. This pattern of change has nothing in common with trial-and-error modes of problem-solving which involve experimentation with many solution procedures until the correct procedure is found. In the dairy tasks, all modes of solution used by experts yielded results meeting conventional accuracy requirements. Solution variability was therefore unrelated to the objective *outcomes* of performance, and related entirely to the *how* of performance.

Though central to skilled performance on dairy tasks, flexibility in the how-to of problem-solving is a neglected aspect of laboratory-based approaches to thinking. Investigators concerned with rules and strategies of thinking make the simplifying assumption that these higher-level regulating principles generate consistent solutions to problems of the same kind or the same logical class. Whether or not this assumption holds for the problem genres investigated in the laboratory, models based on such an assumption would be inadequate to account for intellectual performance on problem-solving tasks in the dairy.

Fine-tuning to the environment

Skilled problem-solving in the dairy was finely-tuned to the properties of the external, material environment and to changing conditions within it.

The ability to exploit (that is, effectively utilize) resources in the environment for problem-solving purposes distinguished experts from novices and often provided the basis for their solution versatility. The term "exploitation" is used here to emphasize that the physical environment did not determine the problem-solving process but that it was drawn into the process through worker initiative. Task analysis illustrates a variety of ways in which things and settings in the environment were pressed into a functional role. On some tasks, the environment provided the terms of the problem-to-be-solved. Consider order filling on product assembly. A formal analysis would suggest that this task consisted of a written problem (the product order) which the assembler solved and later executed at the product array. On the job, however, an experienced worker interpreted the written order, not as "the problem," but as input to an, as yet unspecified, problem. On arriving at the array, he used information from the physical configuration of containers in a case, in conjunction with symbolic information stored in memory, to define the form of the problem (addition or subtraction). A partial case functioned as one term in the equation and the assembler determined the number that needed to be combined with it to satisfy the order.

Inventory provides a somewhat different example of experts' use of environmental properties to achieve an initial representation of the problem-to-be-solved. Dimensions and configurations of product arrays were primary determinants of how the inventory man represented the generic problem of enumeration on different occasions – sometimes setting it up as a multiplication problem, sometimes as a jump-counting task, but each time constructing a problem whose form best fitted properties of the object-to-be-enumerated.

Skilled workers drew things in the environment not only into problem formulation, but into solution procedures as well. In inventory, properties of the given product array functioned as selection devices for the micro-steps constituting a given solution procedure. Counting routines were precisely adapted to the shape of the things to be counted: stacks five-cases high prompted counting by fives; six cases high, counting by sixes. Another aspect of fine-tuning was experts' adjustment of solution procedures to the various material means or devices available to their intellectual work. On the "purely mental" task of pricing-out, experienced drivers modified both their problem constructions and their arithmetic operations in conformance with the particular facilitating powers provided, on the one hand by calculators, on the other by paper and pencil. Modes of solution came into being around means of solution.

As these examples suggest, on many dairy tasks the environment was more than an external "context" in which problem-solving occurred; it was an integral component of the intellectual activity itself. Neisser (1976, p. 183) has argued that, because perception and action occur in continuous dependence on the environment "they cannot be understood without an understanding of the environment itself." In the dairy setting, this observation can properly be extended to the higher cognitive processes involved in many problem-solving tasks.

Economy: Effort-saving
as an optimal solution strategy

Skilled thinking on dairy tasks was regulated by a "least effort strategy."

In the context of this discussion, "effort-saving" refers to the *psychological* reorganization of work tasks to reduce the number of physical or mental steps required for their accomplishment and/or to simplify steps that cannot be eliminated; it has nothing to do with efficiency of movement or other industrial engineering concepts. Product assembly provided two examples of least-effort strategies in which mental operations were reorganized to save physical effort; pricing-out and inventory provided examples of the organization of mental procedures to save mental effort.

The least-effort strategy commends itself as a basic organizing principle of thinking-at-work because of its ubiquity and because other characteristics may be derived from it. Flexibility in solution procedures, and sensitivity to resources in the environment, for example, follow from the consistent employment of a least-effort strategy under changing circumstances.

An outstanding characteristic of least-effort strategies is that they were the outcome of processes operating on a conscious level. Various classes of evidence point to this fact. In the dairy community at large, least-effort strategies were widely acknowledged as "cultural norms" for intelligent ways of working. Individual workers reported making a conscious effort to devise such strategies, often explicitly describing their active search for short cuts or easier ways to do a job. Once adopted, effective use of such strategies depended on processes requiring active attention and awareness – processes involved in problem analysis, solution choice, and executive monitoring. Thus, the acquisition of skill on these intellectual tasks, insofar as it implicates a move toward least-effort strategies, cannot be accounted for solely in terms of automatization of procedures as a result of experience.

If least-effort strategies represent conscious constructions, their investigation requires going beyond the formal requirements of problems to a consideration of individual ideals and purposes, and of the larger institutional and cultural contexts in which these take shape. Only by such extension of the theoretical framework will we be able to determine whether adoption of least-effort strategies in the workplace rests on a particular configuration of institutional and personal goals or on more fundamental "norms of thought" held by people in many cultures and expressed in a wide range of mental and manual activities.

Dependency on setting-specific knowledge

Skilled problem-solving strategies in the dairy were dependent on specific knowledge about the things and activities in the workplace itself.

Most dairy tasks required a fund of "general knowledge" – background information of a worldly or academic kind, and some level of basic skills (numeracy, literacy). But the hallmark of expert problem-solving lay in the fact that the experienced worker was able to use specific dairy and job-related knowledge to generate flexible and economical solution procedures. Expert problem-solving procedures were content-infused, not content-free.

The relationship between job-related knowledge and expert solution performance cannot be encompassed in one general description. Analyses of dairy tasks disclose that critical job knowledge involved many classes of information and took many forms and, consequently, that knowledge-strategy interactions were diverse and complex. In some tasks, critical knowledge took the form of specific factual information: an inventory man drew on his knowledge of the dimensions of a storage area to construct an efficient procedure for counting a particular product array. Some forms of critical knowledge can be conceptualized as mental representations: product assemblers drew upon their spatial knowledge of the warehouse to organize their product-fetching trips in the most efficient manner.

Symbolic forms of knowledge were central to a range of jobs. As a social and cultural system, the dairy over generations had evolved system-specific alphabetic and numerical symbol systems adapted from those prevailing in the society at large but taking a form peculiar to this setting. Mastery of these institutionalized symbol systems was a necessary condition for minimal performance on most jobs. But, in addition, experienced workers invented and/or mastered the use of individual symbols which made possible a level of performance satisfying the "optimal strategy" criterion. Various material objects in the dairy were converted into symbols which workers used to achieve short-cut solutions in problem-solving. The principal, though not the only, example in this research was drivers' symbolization of the dairy case, which provided the basis for efficient solutions to many pricing problems.

Not only was setting-specific knowledge central to the psychological reorganization of work, but, we have some evidence to indicate, that goals and conditions of work activity in turn influenced the specific knowledge that workers acquired and the saliency of such knowledge for conceptual organization in non-job contexts. These findings suggest dynamic and complex interactions among particular working activities, specific knowledge, and expert problem-solving strategies, interactions which have scarcely begun to be explored.

Problem-solving at work:
A summary description

We have described a set of attributes characterizing problem-solving activities in the dairy – flexibility and economy of procedures, effective utilization of knowledge, fine-tuning to the environment. These attributes, of course, were interdependent and jointly defined skilled practical thinking. We might summarize their interrelationships in this way: Thinking in the dairy was goal-directed and regulated by a principle of economy which, operating under changing conditions and on the basis of knowledge and information in the environment, generated flexible solution procedures adapted to particular occasions of use.

The picture that emerges is of a dynamic, interactive cognitive system that departs in significant respects from the models of problem-solving proposed by information-processing theorists. In these models, problem-solving is linear and one-way, proceeding from a defined problem through a sequence of steps to a solution. In the dynamic system of problem-solving observed in the dairy, the movement of thought is two-way. In addition to going from problem to solution, thinking proceeds from "anticipated solution" to "construction of problem." Steps to solution are variable and modified in kind and in order by fine-tuning to the environment; they do not invariably follow a fixed or "one-best" sequence for a given class of problems.

These studies of how problem-solving occurs under actual working conditions thus are helpful in indicating the boundary conditions of laboratory models and in presenting new schemes for an enlarged psychology of thinking. They pose challenges, too, to certain well-established concepts in psychology. Two such challenges especially interest me – one having to do with the course of learning and the other with the nature of "ordinary" or practical thought, and I will make a few observations about each.

Mastery of the concrete

On the basis of our specification of the nature of skilled problem-solving at work, we can generate a speculative model of the course of acquisition of work-related cognitive skills. The conventional psychological model of learning assumes a progression from the particular and concrete to the general and abstract, from "context-bound" to "context-free" intellectual activities (see, for example, discussion in Brown et al., 1983). This progression undoubtedly represents one aspect of the course of change in individual learners as they increase their mastery in a particular domain of activity. But an opposite process may be occurring simultaneously and it is this process which is highlighted by the present studies: skill acquisition at work moves in the direction of mastery of the concrete. The novice enters the workplace with a stock of knowledge, some school-based and some experience-based, and with certain general problem-solving skills (e.g., mental rehearsal, means-end analysis). An important aspect of learning at work involves adapting this prior knowledge and these general skills to the accomplishment of the task at hand. Such adaptation proceeds by the individual's assimilation of specific knowledge about the objects and symbols the setting affords, and the actions (including cognitive actions) that work tasks require. Domain-specific knowledge reveals relationships that can be used to shortcut those stipulated in all-purpose algorithms; with domain-specific knowledge, workers have greater opportunity to free themselves from algorithms and to invent flexible solution procedures. What emerges through this process is a qualitatively different organization of problem-solving procedures from that initially brought to the job. Problem-solving skill in this model implies not only knowledge and know-how but creativity – an attribute of the work group as a social entity if not of each individual within it.

Mastery of the concrete, of course, does not imply the absence of a reciprocal process of abstraction. We have drawn attention to the various forms of symbolization and mental representation involved in dairy tasks, and the present research also offers one candidate for a general rule that might be acquired in a variety of work activities – the least-effort strategy. (McLaughlin, 1979, offers a detailed description of specific skills and general concepts acquired in the auto mechanic trade.) Without minimizing the abstract processes involved, it seems appropriate to describe the primary course of attainment of problem-solving skills at work as a process of "concretization." Because of the relative neglect of this process in theory and research, and its educational implications, it warrants emphasis here.[1]

Creativity at work

Thinking at work is fitted to the functional requirements and resources of particular tasks, and seems aptly characterized as adaptive. Because adaptation is a concept that emphasizes the fit of human thought and behavior to an existing environment, describing thinking at work as adaptive would seem to preclude its characterization as creative. The notion of creativity stresses the human production of something new. Yet thinking in the dairy was *both* adaptive *and* creative. Adaptation of thought to its functional requirements had an active, not passive, character, and it proceeded on the basis of worker invention of new solutions and strategies. Invention is a hallmark of creativity and it played a major role in all the occupations studied in the dairy community. One might say that cognitive adaptation in the dairy occurred, not as a result of processes happening to the employees, but as a result of their continual creativity.

Since creativity is a term ordinarily reserved for exceptional individuals and extraordinary accomplishments, recognizing it in the problem-solving activities of ordinary people at work introduces a new perspective from which to evaluate working intelligence.

Boundaries of the analysis

Although we have referred to target activities as work activities, the analysis presented here is limited to a subset of such activities. For one thing, tasks studied were components of blue-collar jobs; whether or not all the characteristics we have specified apply to clerical and other white-collar jobs is a speculative, but empirically testable, matter. The jobs we considered were individually executed, and analyses, accordingly, do not inform us of the social organization of intellectual operations when work responsibilities are distributed among two or more people.

Most important for the general significance of the psychological analysis is the fact that all tasks included in these studies permitted the worker one or more "degrees of freedom." Conditions of work allowed the individual employee some latitude in determining task parameters: a worker might select her own means for getting the job done (e.g., use a hand calculator or paper and pencil) or might reorganize the task sequence (e.g., regroup products on the order list) or change the specified operations (e.g., satisfy a minus order by adding containers to a case). Such latitude stands in sharp contrast to the restrictive conditions of work on routinized, mechanized and automatically paced jobs such as those symbolized by the automobile assembly line (Chinoy, 1964) and widespread throughout manufacturing. Detailed studies of the labor process on certain factory jobs (Lamphere, 1979; Shapiro-Perl, 1979) indicate increasing management efforts to bring all operations under automatic control and to hold to a minimum worker-introduced variation in the way the job is carried out. The intent of such efforts, spelled out at the turn of the century by Taylor (1911), is to increase worker output and profit, and to reduce the cost of labor.[2] To the extent such conditions are established, it will be increasingly difficult for workers to display the flexibility and ingenuity we have documented. Whether or not flexibility can be entirely eliminated, however, short of robotization, is an open question.

If individual latitude on the jobs studied here may limit the application of the analysis to some, not all, work activities, it opens up the possibility of extending the model to thinking embedded in other practical activities in which individuals have control over their own actions. Research and analyses by Lave and her colleagues (1984) suggest such possibilities. Their studies reveal that problem-solving in the mundane pursuits of shopping, cooking and tailoring share certain family resemblances with problem-solving in the dairy. These congruences give us some warrant for assuming that practical thinking is orderly, that it exhibits certain common characteristics in a wide variety of purposeful life activities, and that it is amenable to scientific understanding.

Notes

1. Anzai and Simon, 1969, have also described the attainment of problem-solving skills on a task as the transformation of weak general strategies into more powerful task-specific strategies.
2. The difference in interests between employer and employee is not considered in the present studies. What is being addressed is the ingenuity workers bring to the accomplishment of their jobs under conditions that allow them to exercise such creativity.

References

Brown, A. L., Bransford, J. D., Ferrara, R. A., & Campione, J. C. (1983). Learning, remembering and understanding. In J. H. Flavell & E. M. Markman (Eds.), *Handbook of child psychology* (4th ed.). New York: John Wiley & Sons.
Chinoy, E. (1964). Manning the machines – the assembly line worker. In P. L. Berger (Ed.), *The human shape of work*. South Bend, Ind.: Gateway Editions.
Lamphere, L. (1979). Fighting the piece-rate system: New dimensions of an old struggle in the apparel industry. In A. Zimbalist (Ed.), *Case studies on the labor process*. New York: Monthly Review Press.
Lave, J., Murtagh, M., & de la Rocha, O. (1984). The dialectical constitution of arithmetic practice. In B. Rogoff & J. Lave (Eds.), *Everyday cognition: Its development in social context*. Cambridge, Mass.: Harvard University Press.
McLaughlin, S. D. (1979). *The wayside mechanic: An analysis of skill acquisition in Ghana*. Amherst, Mass.: Center for International Education, University of Massachusetts.
Neisser, U. (1976). *Cognition and reality*. San Francisco: W. H. Freeman.
Shapiro-Perl, N. (1979). The piece rate: Class struggle on the shop floor. Evidence from the costume jewelry industry in Providence, R.I. In A. Zimbalist (Ed.), *Case studies on the labor process*. New York: Monthly Review Press.
Simon, H. A. (1976). Identifying basic abilities underlying intelligence performance of complex tasks. In L. Resnick (Ed.), *The nature of intelligence*. Hillsdale, N.J.: Erlbaum Associates.
Taylor, F. W. (1911). *The principles of scientific management*. New York: Harper & Brothers.

29   Head and hand:
An action approach to thinking

In introducing my talk, I will ask you to imagine the following scenes: a warehouseman is moving quarts of milk from one dairy case to another; an expediter is tracing the whereabouts of a stock item; a bartender fills mixed drinks from memory.

Although this may sound like a list of random observations, they all have something in common. They are tasks which my students and I have been studying as instances of "mind in action." I use this term to index an approach to the study of cognitive processes which views them as embedded in human action in the world. My research aims at analyzing the characteristics of memory and thought as they function in the larger, purposive activities which cultures organize and in which individuals engage. In earlier research I studied cognitive aspects of literacy activities in a West African society. Recently, I have been investigating cognitive aspects of practical activities occurring in the world of work. To acquaint you with this research, and to exemplify it, I will describe in some detail a series of studies which examined how thinking and doing – head and hand – are integrated in an industrial work task.

Hence my title. I am using the expression "head and hand" in a double sense: literally, to refer to the use of both instrumentalities in practical action, and metaphorically, to indicate a theoretical approach that links thinking to action in the world.

It is evident that this position contrasts with dominant approaches to cognition today. The prevailing perspective views mind as a system of symbolic representations and operations that can be understood in and of itself, in isolation from other systems of activity. Researchers adopting this perspective

This paper was originally presented at the Eastern Psychological Association meeting, Arlington, Virginia, April 11, 1987. It was published as Occasional Paper no. 3, of the Laboratory for Cognitive Studies of Work by the National Center on Education and Employment. Teachers College, Columbia University.

typically study cognitive processes by analyzing performance on isolated mental tasks. If we study memory, we ask people to recall some information or event under conditions which we design. If we study problem-solving, we ask people to do calculations or talk aloud while they try to answer the questions we have set before them. In these tasks, remembering and problem-solving are goals in themselves; they are the ends to which all operations are directed. When research is well-developed, it is sometimes possible to specify the component operations in these tasks with sufficient precision to program them on a computer – a computer which sits in a room having no transactions with the external environment, a computer that is, so to speak, lost in thought.

This approach to cognition has important achievements. Without minimizing them, it is fair to say that the metaphor "mind as computer" fails to capture significant aspects of human mental functioning. We all know that memory and thinking in daily life are not separate from, but are part of, doing. We undertake cognitive tasks not merely as ends in themselves but as means for achieving larger objectives and goals, and we carry out those tasks in constant interaction with social and material resources and constraints. What are the characteristics of remembering and thinking as they occur in such activities? Can we discover them by means of theories and models which begin by treating them as isolated processes to be understood in themselves?

In these questions, we hear echoes of the great debate that has haunted psychology since Ebbinghaus' day. How can the tools available to our science be brought to bear on an understanding of the complex phenomena of everyday life? This debate is often couched in terms of methodological choices. But I do not think that we can make great progress in a contest that pits laboratory against field, psychology against anthropology, or, for that matter, computer against person. The relationship of models to the phenomena they purport to represent is determined in the first place, not by method, but by theoretical conceptions of the phenomena. The practice of studying thinking in isolation from doing is consistent with a Cartesian view of the world that orders these two sets of processes – mental and behavioral – to two different spheres of reality. So long as we adhere to that metaphysical position, we cannot rely on finding a clever method that will put the two halves together again.

I have adopted a theoretical framework which stems from a different philosophical tradition, one that I believe affords the prospect of an integrated account of mind in action. This framework, known as activity theory, has its origins in the works of the Soviet psychologists L. S. Vygotsky and A. N. Leontiev. It has been elaborated over the years by their successors in psychology and philosophy, initially in the USSR but increasingly among psychologists in Europe, and to some extent the United States. I cannot, of course, exposit this theory here. But since it informs my research, I will offer a few schematic propositions as an orienting framework, and then I will rely on my case history to put some meat on these bare bones.

Activity theory perspective

Activity theory holds that neither mind as such nor behavior as such can be taken as the principal category of analysis in psychology. The starting point and primary object of analysis is the actual process of interaction in which humans engage the world and each other. Such interaction represents a synthesis of mental and behavioral processes. Sequences organized around specific motives constitute activities. We can roughly grasp this concept if we note that play, school, and work have been proposed as classes of activities of special importance to intellectual development. Activities – whether carried out by one person or many – are always part of a system of social life: people strive to satisfy purposes that have meaning within their community, and, in their activities, they use tools, symbols and modes of action that are culturally developed and transmitted. For this reason, the concrete content of activities and the motives they satisfy are historically changing. And so too are the modes of thinking incorporated in these activities.

One other set of constructs is important to the analysis I will be making. Activities may be analyzed psychologically on a number of levels: on the molar level of activity as such, or in terms of the goal-directed actions which comprise them, or the specific operations by which actions are carried out. As we will see, action goals are changeable; and equally important, even when goals are invariant, the operations used to achieve them may vary with circumstance and time.

A methodological principle is implicit in this approach. If thinking is an aspect of concrete activities, and we want to understand its genesis and forms, we need to begin with an analysis of the activities and actions in which it is embedded. We need at least a two-way street, one in which we move from the world to the construction of models, as well as the other way around.

Research objectives

These constructs shape my research, which has three objectives. On the most ambitious level, I would like it to serve as a vehicle for elaborating the very general constructs of activity theory. I want to develop and test a method that integrates observational studies of naturally occurring phenomena with experimentation on model tasks. And most concretely, I want to discover something about the characteristics of practical thinking in everyday life.

What activities might be suitable for investigating practical thinking? I chose to study work activities for reasons of both significance and strategy. Significance is apparent. In all societies, work is basic to human existence; in most it consumes the greater part of waking time, and, in many – certainly our own – it is a principal source of self-definition. Although we are not wholly defined through our participation in productive activities, the circumstances under which we work and what we do when we work have deep implications for intellectual and personal development.

Considerations of research strategy also commended work as an object of study and led me to concentrate initially on industrial and service occupations and crafts. Many of these occupations are highly structured and involve tasks whose outcomes are predetermined. They are thus more amenable to analysis than activities in other domains and offer favorable opportunities for devising and testing research methods. An important advantage is that work activities, especially those carried out in institutional settings, are socially defined and organized *as* activities. We can start with classifications already existing in the workplace and allow the evolving research to test their adequacy. That is the course I took. In my analytic scheme, occupations such as assembler, waitress, or bookkeeper represent motivated activities and particular work tasks represent goal-directed actions.

Our studies begin with systematic observations of people carrying out their responsibilities under normal working conditions. These result in a first-level description of cognitive aspects of a particular job. On the basis of this description, we devise a job simulation that allows us to observe performance under more constrained conditions than those occurring in the ordinary work environment. Simulations function as model systems for investigating specific hypotheses about the factors regulating variability on a task and the characteristics that distinguish expert from novice performance. (See Figure 29.1.) From time to time, we set up special experiments using established laboratory techniques to probe questions on a more specific level of analysis than simulation studies make possible.

Now let me turn to an illustrative line of research. For this purpose I will take you to a milk-processing plant that was the site of our first work studies. The occupational activity we will be examining is that of product assembly, and I will present a case history of our cognitive analysis of the assemblers' principal work task. The manual components of this task could be grasped by eye but its intellectual intricacies required some time to ferret out.

Thinking at work: A job description

Assemblers are responsible for locating and sending out to a loading platform the milk products ordered by wholesale drivers for their next day's deliveries. Accuracy counts – each man is responsible for his errors; and so does speed – the work shift does not end until all orders are loaded.

Assemblers use a computer-generated order form to get information on the kinds and amounts of products needed on different delivery routes. This form expresses quantities in a metric system specific to the dairy, one composed of cases and units. Dairy products are stored and handled in cases of a standard size which hold a certain number of unit containers of milk. The number of

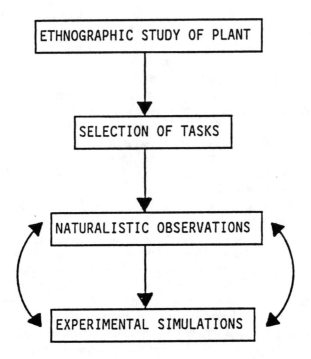

Figure 29.1. Research Strategy for Cognitive Analysis of Work

units in a case varies with the size of the container. One case holds four gallons, nine half-gallons, 16 quarts, and so on. If a particular order involves a quantity that is not evenly divisible into cases, the order form represents it as a mixed number: "x cases *plus* y units" or "x cases *minus* y units." For example, 1–6 on the order form stands for "1 case *minus* 6 units" – the exact number of units required for the completed order depending on the type of container specified. After the assembler reads the order (in actuality he handles several at a time), he proceeds to the area in the warehouse where the product is stored and uses a long metal hook to pull out from the array as many cases and units as required.

Product assembly is classified at the lowest skill level in the plant, and the job I have just described is in many ways prototypical of repetitive manual work. Yet it has a number of interesting features which recommend it for analysis of practical thinking. For one thing, filling an order requires processing of quantitative information from both symbolic expressions – the orders as printed on the computer form – and from physical configurations – milk containers in cases. It is neither wholly a symbolic task nor wholly a material task. For another thing, filling an order can be considered a form of problem-solving. It has a number of formal features: it proceeds within a rule-regulated number system in a determinate universe of admissible problems for which there are fixed criteria for solution. It thus shares some of the characteristics of formal problem-solving tasks well-studied in laboratory experiments. Yet the job differs in crucial ways. Product assembly problem-solving takes place in continuous interaction with an environment that is socially organized and is in constant flux. Locations of products and numbers of full, empty, and partially full cases of milk change from night to night and momentarily during the course of the work shift. Moreover, while this job is performed individually, there is a common culture in the warehouse which shapes patterns of work activity.

We concentrated on the procedures that assemblers use to fill the mixed case and unit orders I have described. Informal observations revealed they had many different ways of going about it. On some occasions, they filled orders as written: they filled *plus* orders by adding the specified number of units to an empty case and *minus* orders by removing the specified number of units from a full case. Their operations – adding or taking away, and the number of units moved – were isomorphic to the symbolic expression of the order. I will refer to these procedures as literal solutions.

Assemblers frequently departed from these literal interpretations, however. Take the order, "1 *minus* 6 quarts." Remember that there are 16 quarts in a case, so that 10 are needed. On one occasion, an assembler filled this order by removing four quarts from a partially full case of 14 that was located nearby. On another occasion, he filled the same order by adding two quarts to a partially full case of eight. In this latter instance, he not only changed the number of units to be moved but converted a take-away operation into an add-to operation. I will call these nonliteral solutions. (See Figure 29.2.)

Solution variability to identical problems commands interest for at least two reasons. First, it is not necessary for satisfying task requirements. In all instances, assemblers could produce correct solutions (cases with the correct number of containers) by following literal instructions. Second, recourse to nonliteral solutions would appear to increase the mental difficulty of the task. One aspect of mental difficulty involves memory requirements: the assembler must keep in mind the quantity specified in the order while walking through the warehouse to locate the product. Literal and nonliteral solution modes impose comparable memory demands of this nature. But, beyond these, nonliteral solutions require some additional mental manipulation of the numerical information in the order so that it can be mapped onto quantitative properties of different physical arrays. (See Figure 29.3.)

A nonliteral solution to the order, "1 case *minus* 6 quarts," for example, requires the assembler to search the product array for a partially full case, make a mental comparison of the distance between the number in this case and the desired end result, and determine how many units to move. Many subprocesses

ORDER: 1 Case - 6 Quarts (or, in unit terms, 16 - 6)

OBSERVED SOLUTIONS

LITERAL SOLUTIONS   NONLITERAL SOLUTIONS

16 - 6 (take away from full case   14 - 4 (take away from partial)
       as instructed)

                                     11 - 1 (take away from partial)

                                     8 + 2 (add to partial)

                                     6 + 4 (add to partial)

Figure 29.2. Example of Variability in Solutions To a Product Assembly Order

LITERAL   NONLITERAL (OPTIMAL)

1. No computations required   1. Computations required

2. Identical orders receive   2. Identical orders receive
    identical solutions   different solutions in
                                         different contexts

3. Solution plan can be   3. Solution plan needs to be
    formulated a priori   constructed from information
                                         in the problem

Figure 29.3. Features of Literal and Nonliteral (Optimal) Solutions on Product Assembly Task

may be involved in such solutions, but all require search, comparison, and quantity judgments not required in literal solutions.

Interrelationship of mental and physical operations

Why did product assemblers choose to engage in such extra mental work? What regulated their choice of solution mode for a particular problem?

We put forward two hypotheses concerning solution variability: 1) choice of solution mode is regulated by a criterion of least physical effort; and 2) extra mental effort may be expended to satisfy this criterion. We were postulating a trade-off between mental and physical effort.

To test the first hypothesis we conducted systematic observations of assemblers filling mixed case and unit orders on the job.

As a measure of physical effort we used the number of containers the assembler moved from one case to another to arrive at the final order. Applying this measure, 80% of all literal solutions and 100% of nonliteral solutions – everyone – satisfied the least physical effort hypothesis. That is, of all the possible ways of filling an order, the assembler chose just that mode of solution which required him to transfer the fewest containers from one case to another under the given set of circumstances.

We turned to the laboratory to test the second hypothesis about a mental effort-physical effort tradeoff, and to map the acquisition of such a strategy. For this purpose, we devised a task simulation, using dairy cases and empty milk containers and tested it with experienced product assemblers and novice groups of other workers and students. Although the simulation removed the task from its actual work context and involved little physical strain, assemblers continued to fill the orders with nonliteral, least physical effort strategies. Novice groups, and especially the students, tended to proceed algorithmically, carrying out literal instructions.

Since assemblers' simulation performance was consistent with their actual job performance, we had some confidence that our task captured and preserved essential characteristics of the job. We had the possibility then of using the simulation as a model system for experimental studies on the acquisition of least physical effort solution strategies.

Approximately 200 students, most in secondary school, assumed the role of novice assemblers in a series of learning studies conducted in our laboratory and in the schools.

Our first question was whether novices would acquire nonliteral least physical effort strategies simply through doing – filling orders of various kinds – without instruction. Over the course of a number of studies, the answer is that the majority did. As they gained experience, many students adopted nonliteral modes of solution spontaneously, and some reached the same level of optimal performance as experienced assemblers on the job. In all cases, the course of change in mode of solution was from predominantly literal to predominantly nonliteral. In the terms in which we have been analyzing this transformation, mental operations came to substitute for physical operations: the head replaced the hand, not the other way around (Figure 29.4 illustrates one such transformation.)

We also learned that construction of nonliteral solutions is not an all-or-none affair but on a group basis takes the form of a learning curve. In line with our

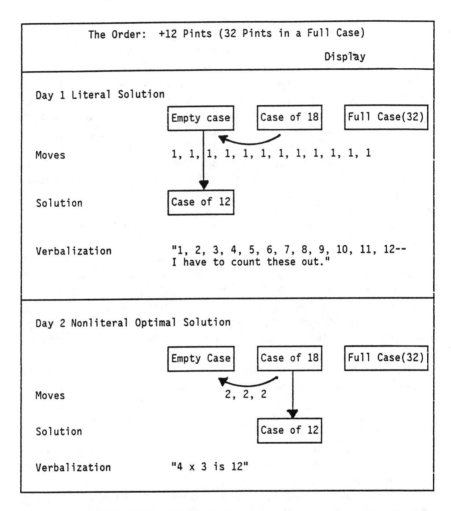

Figure 29.4. Product Assembly Simulation Learning Study Example of a Student's Change in Solution Mode

hypothesis that moving from literal to nonliteral solutions involves a tradeoff of mental effort for physical effort, it seemed sensible to suppose that the rate of appearance of nonliteral solutions would be regulated by terms of this exchange. In some studies we varied the number of physical moves that could be saved by nonliteral solutions, holding the problem structure constant. Amount of physical savings ranged from one unit to six. Counter-intuitively, this manipulation had no effect on rate of acquisition or level of nonliteral solutions. When a nonliteral solution saved a move of only one milk container it appeared as early as a nonliteral solution that saved six.

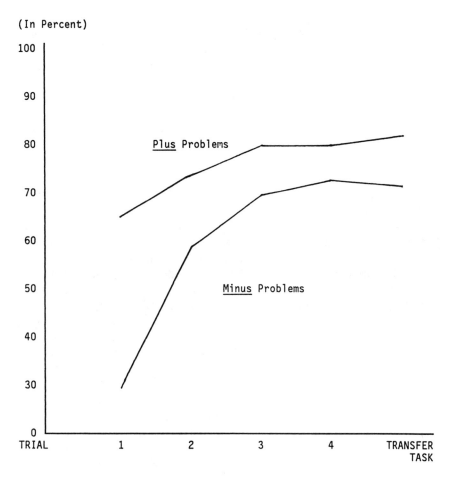

Figure 29.5. Acquisition of Nonliteral (Optimal) Solutions on Product Assembly Learning Task

The situation is entirely different with respect to mental effort. Some transformations from literal to nonliteral optimal solutions are more difficult than
others, and the evidence is unequivocal that it takes the learner longer to shift to
nonliteral solutions for the more intellectually difficult problems. Several
classes of evidence support this proposition.

A logical analysis suggests that *minus* orders (e.g., "1 case *minus* 6 quarts")
require more mental work than *plus* orders since their surface form does not
contain information about the actual number of units required in the final
order. The assembler must compute a mental representation of that number.

Figure 29.5 shows acquisition of nonliteral optimal solutions in one of our learning studies. On Trial 1, only half as many *minus* problems received non-literal solutions as did the *plus* problems, and acquisition on *minus* problems continued to lag over all the trials. These are averaged group data. In a subsequent large-scale study, however, we conducted *within-subject* analyses of solutions to *plus* and *minus* forms of the same problem types. There were 520 occasions in which an *individual learner* solved one form of the problem pair nonliterally and the other literally. Of these, 480 instances – 92% of all mixed pairs – consisted of a nonliteral, least physical effort solution to the *plus* form and a literal, greater physical effort solution to the *minus* form.

The third class of evidence is most compelling. We undertook to reduce mental difficulty by extracting one known mental operation from the task and providing practice on it. Beginning assemblers must learn to interpret the numerical expressions on the printed orders regardless of what solution mode they employ. But use of nonliteral solutions requires in addition that the assembler attend to a partially full case and make a quick judgment of how many units are in the case. We set up a numerosity judgment task, using a T-scope to display the printed order, followed by a photographic slide of a partially full milk case. The informant was to judge whether the number in the case was the same or different from the number called for in the symbolic expression of the order. Students participating in this judgment task prior to experience with actual assembly gave significantly more nonliteral least physical effort solutions on their first learning trial than did a comparison group without that training. This suggests that when judgments of quantity in the partial case were easier to make, students were more inclined to use that case to save physical moves.

So much for objective factors. Subjective factors also regulated solution shifts in the experimental learning situation. Here individual variations are informative. In all studies, some student participants defied the law of averages. They began as literal problem solvers and over many trials continued to fill orders algorithmically, never adopting a least physical effort strategy.

But, in interviews after the sessions, these literal problem solvers justified their solution choices in exactly the same terms as nonliteral problem solvers. Members of both groups said: "The way I did it was easier." Most students claimed they found nonliteral solutions easier because they did not have to move as many milk cartons; others said literal solutions were easier because they did not involve numbers. From a rational point of view, both explanations are sensible. Selection of a strategy that is intellectually easier seems no less appropriate than selection of a strategy that is physically easier – if, as here, both lead to the same acceptable outcomes. In evaluating product assemblers' performance on the job. We are inclined to accept their adoption of a least-physical effort strategy as so appropriate that it needs no explanation. Yet when we encounter variability in the experimental situation, especially different interpretations of "easiness," the obvious becomes problematic and prompts us to reexamine product assemblers' performance which we initially took for granted.

There were individual differences among assemblers. They differed in educational background and job history and in the extent to which they consistently followed a least physical effort strategy. But all followed a least physical effort strategy most of the time, and *not one relied on a literal problem-solving algorithm.* In the plant there was a clear consensus that trading head for hand was the better way to do the job. To account for this common aspiration, we have to move away from constructs such as personal preference or individual difference to consider the structure of the work activity in its broader institutional contexts. Our experimental analysis thus returns us to a new ethnographic enterprise, one which aims at identifying the social processes which give use to preferred modes of solution among members of a given work community. But that is beyond the scope of our present inquiry.

Concluding observations

My description has been thick with particularities. Let me summarize the product assembly studies in terms of the constructs with which we started. From the work activity known as product assembly, we extracted the job of filling an order to analyze as an instance of a goal-directed action. The aim of the analysis was to understand how manual and mental operations are coordinated in this action and how they changed with changing conditions and expertise.

The first finding was that goal is a multi-sided concept. It cannot be entirely specified from a task analytic perspective since it has its subjective as well as objective aspects. In product assembly the objective externally imposed goal is completion of the order with speed and accuracy. Assemblers' personal goal is to satisfy this requirement with the least physical effort. To a remarkable extent, given the conditions of work, they were able to maintain this goal as invariant under continually changing circumstances. To do this, they had to draw flexibly on a wide repertoire of constituent operations, organizing them into a smooth action system on each occasion of order filling. Others who have studied action systems – I think of Miller, Galanter and Pribram's classic book – have shown the essential role of mental representations and regulatory processes in manual actions. Such analyses emphasize the role of the mind in constructing a plan for action and monitoring its execution – the mind directs, the body does. Our analysis goes further in demonstrating, for one particular action system, that execution has its mental as well as manual components, and that mental and motor processes may substitute for each other. We might say that, in certain circumstances, operations of the head and of the hand are functionally equivalent.

Our learning studies suggest that such functional equivalence comes about through practice – the head takes over for the hand, first for the simpler problems, then for the more complex. What is achieved through practical thinking is intelligent organization of action, finely fitted to task demands and resources and to the intentions of the actor.

It is tempting initially to place the burden of explanation for this reorganization of the task on the demands of the assembly job per se; it is physically strenuous and monotonous. But the kind of reorganization we have described turns out to be one instance of a large class of instances that are not tied to physical features of work. In the two years we were in the plant, we analyzed six or seven key jobs in blue collar and office occupations. Some of these jobs were wholly symbolic in nature – pricing out customer deliveries, for example, or preparing bills; others were physically undemanding. Nonetheless, across all jobs, wherever working conditions allowed for optional modes of action, experienced workers displayed flexible forms of problem-solving that served to save effort. The effort saved on symbolic jobs, of course, was mental, not physical. In the factory community at large, least-effort strategies were widely acknowledged as cultural norms for intelligent ways of working. Individual workers reported making a conscious effort to devise such strategies, often explicitly describing their active search for mental or physical shortcuts. Researchers in labor psychology laboratories in Paris, Dresden, and elsewhere report similar phenomena and refer to a least-effort "optimizing criterion" as a basic principle of workers' subjective organization of work.

In laboratory research on problem-solving, we tend to interpret goals solely in terms of the objective outcomes set by the experimenter, taking no account of the ends the problem solver has in mind. Laboratory conditions appear singularly unsuitable for yielding knowledge about personal values and understandings. Experimental records disclose differences in goals but give us little insight into conditions of their origin. To examine this aspect of human functioning we need to shift to a social level of analysis and a study of the larger institutional and cultural contexts in which individual ideals and purposes take shape.

I have given an interpretation of product assembly research within an activity theory framework. And this brings me back to the broader question that motivated these studies of practical thinking at work.

One purpose was to try to concretize and elaborate activity theory constructs. I may have made some small progress here. But it is obvious that the fit between theory and research evidence is not a close one. I could have presented the studies and their findings in other theoretical terms – there are action theories from other traditions – and much of what I have discussed can be translated into the more familiar conceptual frameworks we find in psychology journals. Activity theory is not in itself a theory of cognition. It seems appropriate to consider it, rather, as a metatheory, offering certain basic categories and principles for theory construction in the various fields of psychology. These categories direct us to new questions, and, in the field of cognition, give us the possibility of enriching theories of thinking. I hope many will find these questions and this perspective worthwhile.

A second motivation for our research was a test of method. I wanted to see if we could bring sufficient rigor to the study of thinking in naturally-occurring activities to produce experimental models which preserve essential characteristics. Since the initial studies of five occupations in the milk-processing plant, my students and I have extended the framework and methodology to other occupations – sales engineers, carpenters, waitresses, bartenders. We are currently analyzing the impact of the introduction of integrated computer systems on the intellectual demands of jobs in material design and control. For some jobs, we have achieved fine-grained specification of the knowledge and skills required; for others we remain at the level of first description. I cannot offer a full assessment of how far we may travel with our approach, but the methodology does travel and can be given away. I have gained some confidence in the analyzability of practical thinking. As we go along, certain old dichotomies that have impeded an action-oriented approach to thought become increasingly irrelevant. Observation is not opposed to experiment, but may be the forerunner of it. Description is not opposed to explanation but may function as a first approximation to it.

Finally, what have we learned about practical thinking at work? I remember the first occasions on which I presented some of the dairy studies. "Very interesting, Sylvia," some said. "But what can we learn of these job analyses that is useful to cognitive theory? Does product assembly generalize?"

I see no reason to think that the specific operations involved in product assembly – or any other job – will transfer to or be identical with constituent operations in other tasks. But that is beside the point. We are interested, not in whether *particulars* about practical tasks generalize, but whether we can find *general* characteristics across a wide range of *particular* tasks. Our research offers some candidates for such characteristics, a number of them already exemplified in my description of product assembly. Common to expert performance in all jobs we have analyzed to date are a set of interrelated attributes: flexibility in modes of solution to formally identical problems, creative shortcuts to simplify and economize on mental and physical effort, fine-tuning to the environment, and effective utilization of setting-specific knowledge.

Future research can test the range and variation of these features. One limitation to generalizations about thinking at work, however, needs to be pointed out here. All jobs we studied permitted the worker one or more degrees of freedom in organizing the task. This measure of latitude stands in sharp contrast to the restrictive conditions of work on routinized, mechanized, and automatically paced jobs epitomized in the assembly line. On such jobs, I assume it would be difficult for workers to display the flexibility and ingenuity we have documented. Whether or not flexibility in practical thinking at work can be entirely eliminated short of robotization, however, remains an open question.

If individual latitude on the jobs studied here limits application of the analysis to only some work activities, it opens up the possibility of extending the model to thinking embedded in other practical activities in which individuals have control over their own actions. A flock of recent studies reveals that problem-solving in shopping, cooking, and other mundane pursuits shares certain family resemblances with the modes of problem-solving we have found in certain work occupations. These congruences give us some warrant for assuming that practical thinking is orderly, that it exhibits certain common characteristics in a variety of purposive life activities, and that it is amenable to scientific understanding.

Chronology

September 22, 1923	born in New Bedford, Massachusetts; daughter of Harry and Gussie Cohen
1929?–35?	attended Mount Pleasant Grammar School
1932–33	poetry published in *New Bedford Standard Times;* winner of Blue Ribbon for poem, "Be a Man"
1935?–39	attended New Bedford High School
late 1930s	summer employment in lace factory
1939	HITLER INVADES POLAND; WORLD WAR II STARTS
	high school class valedictorian
1940–43	attended Smith College on full scholarship (William Allan Nielson scholar)
	studied with Dr. Dorothy W. Douglas, labor economist
1941	UNITED STATES DECLARES WAR ON JAPAN AND GERMANY
	awarded Arthur Ellis Hamm Scholarship Prize for academic achievement
	Vice President of American Student Union chapter
1942–43	FBI INVESTIGATION OF STUDENT POLITICAL ACTIVITIES: ASU OFFICERS NAMED
1942	became Chairman of Interrace Commission; spoke at Interrace Commission Conference, pointing out importance of eliminating Jim Crow in the armed

399

forces while United States was fighting war against
fascism

1943 · B.A. summa cum laude, elected to Phi Beta Kappa,
class valedictorian

1944–54 · Research Director and Organizer: United Electrical, Radio, and Machine Workers of America (UE)

involved in issues of: minorities, women in industry, equal pay for work of comparable value, improved working conditions

UE was first international union to organize a conference on ending discrimination against women

led union's negotiations with a large electrical manufacturing plant in New Jersey; one issue was
"comparable worth" principle
(see Duffy, June, Women's Rights Law Reporter,
Rutgers-The State University of New Jersey, vol. 8,
nos. 1–2 at 107, Winter 1984)

met David Scribner, attorney for UE

1947 · PRESIDENT TRUMAN VETOES, AND CON-
GRESS PASSES, TAFT–HARTLEY ACT

1950 · JOSEPH MCCARTHY CONDUCTS CONGRES-
SIONAL HEARINGS ON "COMMUNISTS" IN
GOVERNMENT, THE ENTERTAINMENT IN-
DUSTRY, AND PUBLIC LIFE

David defends people who refuse to answer questions before House Un-American Affairs Committee

1951 · TRIAL OF JULIUS AND ETHEL ROSENBERG
ON CHARGES OF SPYING FOR THE SOVIET
UNION

1953 · arrested for demonstrating against Rosenberg execution sentence

1954–58 · Research Director and Organizer: International
United Electrical, Radio, and Machine Workers of
America

1954 · SUPREME COURT OVERRULES DOCTRINE
OF "SEPARATE BUT EQUAL" IN CASE OF
BROWN v. BOARD OF EDUCATION

son, Oliver, is born

1956	MARTIN LUTHER KING JR. LEADS SANITA-TION WORKERS' STRIKE
1958–62	Assistant to Director and Operational Research Analyst: Jewish Board of Guardians, New York City
1958	daughter, Aggie, is born
1961	enrolled in graduate program in psychology at the New School for Social Research
	organized brown bag lunches with Howard E. Gruber at the New School where students and faculty discussed social responsibilities of psychologists and opportunities for social action
1962	UNITED STATES ESTABLISHES MILITARY COUNCIL IN VIETNAM
1963–65	Associate Director, Mental Health Program: National Institute of Labor Education, New York
	participated in developing national policy for programs to meet mental health needs of labor; helped organize multidisciplinary teams to design and implement research proposals
1963	presents paper at the American Orthopsychiatric Association Meeting
	"Issues in the Development of a Labor Mental Health Program"
	TWO HUNDRED THOUSAND "FREEDOM MARCHERS" DEMONSTRATE IN WASHINGTON; MARTIN LUTHER KING JR. DELIVERS "I HAVE A DREAM" SPEECH
	PRESIDENT KENNEDY ASSASSINATED
	THE FEMININE MYSTIQUE, BY BETTY FRIEDAN PUBLISHED
1964–65	Research Director, Mental Health Program: Sidney Hillman Health Center, New York
1965–66	Research Consultant, Mental Health Program: Sidney Hillman Health Center, Garment Industry, New York
1966	presents paper at the Mental Health Seminar of trade union health and welfare administrators
	"Insurance Coverage for Mental Illness"

M.A. in psychology from the New School for Social Research

recipient of Dorothy Kelgor Prize in Psychology

1966–67   full-time doctoral studies

studied levels of integration and dialectical materialism with Eleanor Leacock and Ethel Tobach; became interested in Vygotsky

1967–73   Assistant Clinical Professor: Albert Einstein Medical College, Department of Psychiatry

worked to develop material for postdoctoral training in community psychology; conducted research on concepts of mental disorders in various cultures

"Cognitive Consequences of Literacy" (1968)*

1967–68   Teaching Assistant: New School for Social Research

lectured on memory and thinking

1967   FIFTY THOUSAND PERSONS DEMONSTRATE AGAINST VIETNAM WAR IN WASHINGTON

1968   MARTIN LUTHER KING JR. AND ROBERT KENNEDY ASSASSINATED

PUBLICATION OF ARTHUR JENSEN'S PAPERS, "SOCIAL CLASS, RACE, AND GENETICS: IMPLICATIONS FOR EDUCATION" AND "ABILITY AND SOCIO-ECONOMIC STATUS"

POLICE BRUTALITY AT DEMOCRATIC NATIONAL CONVENTION IN CHICAGO

APA VOTES TO CHANGE VENUE OF CONVENTION FROM CHICAGO TO WASHINGTON IN PROTEST AGAINST CHICAGO POLICE ACTION, AS PROPOSED BY GROUP LATER TO FORM PSYCHOLOGISTS FOR SOCIAL ACTION

PROFESSIONAL PSYCHOLOGY AFFECTED BY MOVEMENTS FOR PATIENT AUTONOMY; DISCUSSION IN PSYCHOLOGICAL PROFESSION OF HOW TO DEFINE MENTAL HEALTH AND ILLNESS

1969	helped found Psychologists for Social Action
	presented paper at the American Psychological Association symposium on community development, Washington, D.C.
	"Research as Social Process"*
1970	Ph.D., New School for Social Research, under the sponsorship of Mary Henle. The committee members were Solomon Miller and Bernard Weitzman. Thesis title: "A Cross-Cultural Study of Perceptions of Mental Disorder."
	corresponded with Michael Cole
1970–78	Senior Research Scientist: Michael Cole's laboratory of comparative human cognition, Rockefeller University
	research in culture and thought, reasoning, memory, children's narratives, and intelligence testing
1971	PUBLICATION OF WILLIAM SHOCKLEY'S PRESS RELEASE, "DYSGENICS – A SOCIAL PROBLEM: REALITY EVADED BY THE ILLUSION OF INFINITE PLASTICITY OF HUMAN INTELLIGENCE," BASED ON TALK AT APA CONVENTION
	Review of *Psychology and the Problems of Society*, by Korten, Cook, and Lacey*
1972	traveled to Liberia, where she conducted cross-cultural research with the Kpelle
1973–78	traveled to Liberia on three occasions, where she engaged in research with the Vai
	Scribner and Cole: "Cognitive Consequences of Formal and Informal Education" (1973)
1974	Visiting Professor: Ferkauf Graduate School of Arts and Sciences of Yeshiva University
	Cole and Scribner: *Culture and Thought: A Psychological Introduction*
1975	PUBLICATION OF ARTHUR JENSEN'S *A THEORETICAL NOTE ON SEX LINKAGE AND RACE DIFFERENCES IN SPATIAL VISUALIZATION ABILITY*

presented paper at Seminar on Merit and Equality in a Just Society at MIT

"Psychologists, Process, and Performance"*

1978–79   Associate Director, Teaching and Learning Program: National Institute of Education, Washington, D.C.

sought to institute broader conceptions of learning to include learning by adults and in the workplace; with the APA, promoted a program with minority researchers; initiated discussion of technology and learning

"Modes of Thinking and Ways of Speaking" (1978)*

Cole, John-Steiner, Scribner and Souberman: *L. S. Vygotsky: Mind in Society* (1978)

1979–81   Research Scientist: Center for Applied Linguistics, Baltimore, Md.

began research program on thinking at work at dairy distribution plant in Baltimore

invited research presentation, Bellagio IV workshop on Literacy Research in Developing Countries, Italy

member of U.S. Department of Education Delegation on Educational Research to the People's Republic of China

"Observations on Literacy Education in China" (1982)*

invited research presentation, NIE Conference on Basic Skills for Productivity and Participation

"Studying Literacy at Work: Bringing the Laboratory to the Field" (1980)

invited presentation, American-Soviet Conference on Psychological Problems of Activity, Moscow, 1980 (under joint auspices of the American Council of Learned Societies and the Soviet Academy of Science Institute of Psychology)

"The Concept of Practice in Research on Culture and Thought" (1980)

Fellow: New York Academy of Sciences

editorial board member: *Journal of Cross-Cultural Psychology, Ethos*

1981–91   Professor of Developmental Psychology: City University of New York, Graduate School and University Center

taught graduate seminars; attracted and trained graduate students

> Scribner, S., Cole, M.: *The Psychology of Literacy* (1981)

1981   received grant from Ford Foundation to continue the study of "industrial literacy" that was begun with the dairy project in Baltimore and moved to New York

member, research planning task force: National Council on Educational Research of the NIE

Chair, panel on cross-cultural and ecological research: Society for Research in Child Development, 1981 biennial program

organized demonstration of academics to protest berthing of nuclear submarines near Staten Island

The Psychology of Literacy is reviewed in the *New York Times Book Review*, December 13

Fellow: American Association for the Advancement of Science

editorial board member: *Journal of Applied Psychology*, Human Development, Plenum Series of Collected Works of L. S. Vygotsky

1982   founded Laboratory for the Cognitive Study of Work at The City University of New York

1982–83   received a grant from the National Science Foundation to study practical problem-solving skills in a laboratory setting

1982   Melville J. Herskovits Award of the African Studies Association is awarded to Scribner and Cole for *The Psychology of Literacy*

invited presentation, Conference of Psychological and Linguistic Approaches to Literacy, New York Academy of Sciences, May

1984   paper prepared for presentation at the 23rd International Congress of Psychology, Acapulco, Mexico

"Does Ontogeny Recapitulate History: An Examination of Vygotsky's Sociohistorical Theory"

1985–89   Principal Investigator on a five-year research program awarded from the National Center for Education and Employment based at Columbia Teachers College. The study analyzed learning as it took place in the stockroom of an electronics manufacturing plant

1985   invited presentation, First International Conference on Activity Theory, Berlin

"Mental and Manual Work: An Activity Theory Orientation"*

invited presentation, Conference on the Future of Literacy in a Changing World, University of Pennsylvania

"Literacy and Human Development"

organized and chaired a session for student presentations at the Eastern Psychological Association meeting in Boston

1986   received a grant from the Ford Foundation to study children's writing

member: Board of Directors of International Society for Cultural Research and Activity Theory

June 2, 1987   grandson, Alex, born

invited presentation, Eastern Psychological Association annual meeting at Arlington, Va.

"Head and Hand: An Action Approach to Thinking" (1988)*

1989–91   Principal Investigator on a three-year grant from the National Research on Vocational Education at the University of California–Berkeley

received a grant from the Spencer Foundation to study on-the-job learning in the context of the introduction of computerized production and inventory systems on a jobsite

1990 a report by Scribner and Sachs summarizing the stockroom project is featured in a *Business Week* magazine column, September 24

"On the Job Training: A Case Study"

presents material to the Secretary's Commission on Achieving Necessary Skills: hearings sponsored by the U.S. Department of Labor

UNITED STATES GOES TO WAR AGAINST IRAQ OVER ITS INVASION OF KUWAIT

1991 helped organize meeting at the graduate school of City University to protest Persian Gulf War

Martin, L. M. W., Scribner, S., and Beach, K.: "Hand to Symbol: Studying the Transformation of Machining Activity" (1990)

participated with City University faculty and students in protest against racism and sexism

March 10, 1991 grandson, Scott, is born

March 15, 1991 diagnosed with cancer

April 10, 1991 David dies

July 20, 1991 dies at sixty-seven

Bibliography

Notes: This bibliography includes published works and unpublished documents found in Sylvia Scribner's files. The original documents, and her correspondence, will be deposited in the Archives of the History of American Psychology at the University of Akron. They are part of her estate, and her heirs have been most gracious in making them available to the editors.

The editors, with the assistance of Malka Grinkorn, attempted to identify the settings for the talks and manuscripts not subsequently published. However, in order to make Scribner's work available to the scientific community in a reasonable period of time, the more difficult questions about the origin of the documents had to remain unanswered.

*Indicates the paper is included in this volume.

Part I: Books

Cole, M.; Scribner, S. (1974): *Culture and Thought: A Psychological Introduction.* John Wiley & Sons, New York.

Cole, M.; John-Steiner, V.; Scribner, S.; Souberman, E. (1978): *L. S. Vygotsky: Mind in Society.* Harvard University Press, Cambridge, Mass.

Scribner, S.; Cole, M. (1981): *The Psychology of Literacy.* Harvard University Press, Cambridge, Mass.

Scribner, S. (Ed.) (1984): *Cognitive Studies of Work.* Special issue of the quarterly newsletter of the Laboratory of Comparative Human Cognition (LCHC), 6, nos. 1–2. (See below for the individual papers contained in this issue.)

Part II: Articles

Scribner, S.; Reiff, R. (1964): Issues in the new national mental health programs relating to labor and low income groups. In: *Mental Health of the Poor.* (Ed.: Riessman, F.) The Free Press, New York, 443–56.

409

Scribner, S.; Riessman, F. (1965): Underutilization of mental health services by workers and low income groups: causes and cures. *American Journal of Psychiatry* 121, 798–801; abstracted *Modern Medicine*, June 7, 1965, 178.

Scribner, S. (1970): Advocacy: strategy or solution? A shorter version, Which arena for advocacy? was published in *Social Policy* 1, 40 (1970).*

Scribner, S.; Reiff, R. (1970): Rehabilitation and community mental health: employability and disability issues. *Journal of Rehabilitation* 36, 11–15.

Scribner, S. (1970): What is community psychology made of? In: *Introductory Readings In Community Mental Health.* (Ed.: Cook, P. E.) Holden-Day, Merrifield, Va. 13–21.*

Scribner, S. (1971): Review of *Psychology and the Problems of Society* by F. R. Korten, S. W. Cook, and J. I. Lacey (Eds.). *Social Action* 4, 3.*

Scribner, S.; Cole, M. (1972): Effects of constrained recall training on children's performance in a verbal memory task. *Child Development* 43, 845–57.

Scribner, S.; Cole, M. (1973): Cognitive consequences of formal and informal education. *Science* 182, 553–59.

Scribner, S. (1974): Review of *The Biopsychology of Development* by E. Tobach, L. R. Aronson, and E. Shaw (Eds.). *Brain* 9, 80.

Scribner, S. (1974): Developmental aspects of categorized recall in a West African society. *Cognitive Psychology* 6, 475–94.

Scribner, S. (1974): Psychology and anthropology: getting it together. Review of *Psychological Anthropology* by F. L. K. Hsu (Ed.). *Contemporary Psychology* 19, 42–43.

Scribner, S.; Cole, M. (1974): Review of *Class, Codes, and Control*, vol. 1, *Theoretical Studies towards a Sociology of Language*, and vol. 2, *Applied Studies . . .* by B. Bernstein. Reviews in *Anthropology* 1, 387–95.

Scribner, S. (1975): Review of *Culture and Cognition: Readings in Cross-Cultural Psychology* by J. Berry and P. Dasen (Eds.). *Journal of Cross-Cultural Psychology* 6, 122–26.*

Scribner, S. (1975): Recall of classical syllogisms: a cross-cultural investigation of error on logical problems. In: *Reasoning: Representation and Process.* (Ed.: Falmagne, R. J.) Lawrence Erlbaum Associates, Hillsdale, N.J., 153–73.*

Cole, M.; Scribner, S. (1975): Theorizing about socialization of cognition. *Ethos* 3, 249–67.

Scribner, S. (1976): Situating the experiment in cross-cultural research. In: *The Developing Individual in a Changing World*, vol. 1, *Historical and Cultural Issues.* (Eds.: Riegel, K. F.; Meacham, J. A.) Mouton & Co., The Hague, 310–21.*

Scribner, S. (1976): Review of *Societal Structures of the Mind*, by U. G. Foa and B. Edna. *American Anthropologist* 78, 655.*

Cassallas, M.; Cole, M.; Hall, W. S.; Meissner, J.; Scribner, S.; Traupmann, K. (1976): Memory span for nouns, verbs and function words in low SES children: a replication and critique of Schutz and Keislar. *Journal of Verbal Learning and Verbal Behavior* 15, 431–35.

Cole, M.; Scribner, S. (1977): Cross-cultural studies of memory and cognition. In: *Perspectives on the Development of Memory and Cognition.* (Eds.: Kail, R. V., Jr.; Hagen, J. W.) Lawrence Erlbaum Associates, Hillsdale, N.J., 239–71.

Cole, M.; Scribner, S. (1977): Developmental theories applied to cross-cultural cognitive research. *Annals of the New York Academy of Sciences* 285, "Issues in cross-cultural research" (Ed.: Adler, L. L.) 366–73. Reprinted in L. L. Adler (Ed.), *Cross Cultural Research at Issue*, New York, Academic Press, 1982.

Scribner, S.; Goody, J.; Cole, M. (1977): Writing and formal operations: a case study among the Vai. *Africa* 47, 289–304.

Pratt, M.; Scribner, S.; Cole, M. (1977): Children as teachers: developmental studies of instructional communications. *Child Development* 48, 1475–81.

Scribner, S. (1977): Modes of thinking and ways of speaking. In: *Thinking: Readings in Cognitive Science* (Eds.: Johnson-Laird, P. W. and Wason, P. C.) Cambridge University Press. Reprinted in R. O. Freedle, *Discourse Production and Comprehension*, vol. 2. Hillsdale, N.J., Lawrence Erlbaum Associates, 1978.

Scribner, S.; Cole, M. (1978): Introduction. In: *L. S. Vygotsky: Mind in Society*. (Eds.: Cole, M.; John-Steiner, V.; Scribner, S.; Suberman, E.) Harvard University Press, Cambridge, Mass., 1–14.

Scribner, S.; Cole, M. (1978): Literacy without schooling: testing for intellectual effects. *Harvard Educational Review* 48, 448–61.

Scribner, S.; Cole, M. (1978): Unpackaging literacy. *Social Science Information* 1, 17, 19–40. Reprinted in J. Dominic, M. Whiteman, C. Fredericksen (Eds.), *Writing: The Nature, Development and Teaching of Written Communication*, vol. 1, 71–87. Lawrence Erlbaum Associates, Hillsdale, N.J., 1981, 71–87. (This paper has been translated into Russian.)

Scribner, S.; with members of the Laboratory of Comparative Human Cognition (1978): Cognition as a residual category in anthropology. In: *Annual Review of Anthropology* 7, 51–69.

Orasanu, J.; Lee, C.; Scribner, S. (1979): The development of category organization and free recall: ethnic and economic group comparisons. *Child Development* 50, 1100–9. Reprinted in S. Chess and A. Thomas (Eds.), *Annual Progress in Child Psychiatry and Child Development* (1980).

Scribner, S. (1980): Review of adult illiteracy in the United States, by C. St. John Hunter and D. Harman. *Journal of Reading* 24, 176–78.

Mandler, J. M.; Scribner, S.; Cole, M.; Deforest, M. (1980): Cross-cultural invariance in story recall. *Child Development* 51, 19–26.

Scribner, S. (1981): Cultures and textbooks. In: *The Textbook in American Society*. (Eds.: Cole, J. Y.; Sticht, T. G.) Library of Congress, Washington, D.C., 6–8. From a longer paper, "Textbooks in Cross-Cultural Perspective," presented at the conference, "The Textbook in American Education," held at the Library of Congress, Washington, D.C., May 1979.

Bartlett, E. J.; Scribner, S. (1981): Text and context: an investigation of referential organization in children's written narratives. In: *Writing: The Nature, Development and Teaching of Written Communication*, vol. 2. (Eds.: Dominic, J.; Whiteman, M.; Fredericksen, C.) Lawrence Erlbaum Associates, Hillsdale, N.J., 153–67.

Scribner, S. (1982): Observations on literacy education in China. *The Linguistic Reporter* 25, 1–4.*

Orasanu, J.; Scribner, S. (1982): The development of verbal reasoning: pragmatic, schematic and operational aspects. In: *Linguistics and Literacy*. (Ed.: Frawley, W.) Plenum, New York, 285–313.

Scribner, S. (1984): Literacy in three metaphors. *American Journal of Education* 95, 1, 6–21. Originally given as a talk at Planning Conference on Library and Information Service, The White House, Washington, D.C., April 1979. Reprinted in N. L. Stein (Ed.), *Literacy in American Schools*. Chicago, University of Chicago Press, 1986.*

Scribner, S. (1984): The practice of literacy: where mind and society meet. *Annals of the New York Academy of Sciences* 433, volume edited by S. J. White and V. Teller, *Discourses in Reading and Linguistics*, 5–19.*

Scribner, S. (1984): Organizing knowledge at work. Quarterly newsletter of the Laboratory for Comparative Human cognition (LCHC) 6, (1&2), 26–32, special issue: S. Scribner (Ed.), *Cognitive Studies of Work*, 26–32.

Scribner, S. (1984): Practical problem-solving on the job. Quarterly newsletter of LCHC 6, (1&2), 5–6, special issue: S. Scribner (Ed.), *Cognitive Studies of Work*.

Scribner, S. (1984): Pricing delivery tickets: "school arithmetic" in a practical setting. Quarterly newsletter of LCHC 6 (1&2), special issue: S. Scribner (Ed.), *Cognitive Studies of Work*, 19–25.

Scribner, S. (1984): Product assembly: optimizing strategies and their acquisition. Quarterly newsletter of LCHC 6 (1&2), special issue: S. Scribner (Ed.), *Cognitive Studies of Work*, 11–19.

Scribner, S. (1984): Technical note: frequency effect on retrieval of job-related knowledge. Quarterly newsletter of LCHC 6 (1&2), 34–37, special issue: S. Scribner (Ed.), *Cognitive Studies of Work*, 34–37.

Scribner, S. (1984): Toward a model of practical thinking at work. Quarterly newsletter of LCHC 6 (1&2), special issue: S. Scribner (Ed.), *Cognitive Studies of Work*, 37–41.*

Scribner, S. (1984): Use of spatial knowledge in the organization of work. Quarterly newsletter of LCHC 6 (1&2), special issue: S. Scribner (Ed.), *Cognitive Studies of Work*, 32–34.

Scribner, S. (1984): Studying working intelligence. In: *Everyday Cognition: Its Development in Social Context*. (Eds.: Lave, J.; Rogoff, B.) Harvard University Press, Cambridge, Mass., 9–40.*

Hawkins, J.; Pea, R. D.; Glick, J.; Scribner, S. (1984): Evidence for deductive reasoning by preschoolers. *Developmental Psychology* 20, 4, 584–94.

Scribner, S. (1985): Knowledge at work. *Anthropological Education Quarterly* 16, 3, 199–206. Special issue: J. Lave (Ed.) Originally presented at symposium on the social organization of knowledge, American Anthropological Association annual meeting, 1983.*

Scribner, S. (1985): Thinking in action: some characteristics of practical thought. In: *Practical Intelligence*. (Eds.: Sternberg, R. J.; Wagner, R. K.) Cambridge University Press, New York, 13–30.*

Scribner, S. (1985): Vygotsky's uses of history. In: *Culture, Communication and Cognition*. (Ed.: Wertsch, J. V.) Cambridge University Press, New York, 119–45.*

Scribner, S. (1987): Introduction to Part B. In: *The Future of Literacy in a Changing World*. (Ed.: Wagner, D. A.) Pergamon Press, New York, 19–24.*

Scribner, S. (1987): Head and hand: An action approach to thinking. *Teachers College Record* 92, 582–602.

Scribner, S. (1988): Mental and manual work: an activity theory orientation. In: Proceedings of the First International Congress on Activity Theory. (Eds.: Hildenbrand-Nilshon, M. and Reuckriem, G.) Drack und Verlag System Drack, Berlin, 221-230.*

Stephens, J.; Scribner, S. (1989): Experimental studies on the relationship of school math and work math. *NCEE Technical Paper* no. 4.

Scribner, S.; Sachs, P. (1990): On the job training: a case study. NCEE Brief no. 9, August 1990. Condensed version of report by Scribner and Sachs (1989–90).

Scribner, S. (1990): A sociocultural approach to the study of mind. In G. Greenberg and E. Tobach (Eds.): *Theories of the Evolution of Knowing.* Lawrence Erlbaum Associates, Hillsdale, N.J., 107–20.*

Scribner, S.; Martin, L. M. W. (1991): Laboratory for cognitive studies of work: a case study of the intellectual implications of a new technology. *Teachers College Record* 92, 4, 582–602.

Scribner, S.; Sachs, P. (1991): Knowledge acquisition at work. IEE Brief no. 2, December 1991. Condensed version of report by Scribner, Sachs, DiBello, & Kindred (1991).

Scribner, S.; Beach, K. (1993): An activity theory approach to memory. *Applied Cognitive Psychology,* 7, 185–90.

Part III: Invited presentations

Scribner, S. (1963): Issues in the development of a labor mental health program. Paper presented at the American Orthopsychiatric Association Meeting.*

Scribner, S. (1966): Insurance coverage for mental illness. Paper presented at mental health seminar of trade union health and welfare administrators, New York.

Scribner, S.; Adler, D. (1968 or 1969): Effect of written verbal stimulus materials on grouping performance in a free-sort test. Lecture.

Scribner, S. (1969): Research as social process. Paper presented at the American Psychological Association symposium on community development, Washington, D.C., September 3.*

Scribner, S. (1974): Description of research program on Vai literacy and its cognitive consequences. Rockefeller University lecture.

Scribner, S. (1975): Psychologists, process, and performance. Paper presented at seminar on merit and equality in a just society of the Technology and Culture Seminar, Massachusetts Institute of Technology, Cambridge, Mass. Proceedings were printed and distributed in plastic ring binders; see pp. 84–87.*

Scribner, S. (1976): Studying cognitive consequences of literacy. Paper presented at the 21st International Congress of Psychology, Paris.

Scribner, S.; Cole, M. (1976): Studies of subcultural variations in semantic memory: implications of cross-cultural research. Paper presented at Symposium on Race and Sex Differences in Ability, American Psychological Association annual meeting. A longer version, in French, was published in Bulletin de Psychologie, special annual for 1976, titled "La memoire semantique," Paris.

Bartlett, E. J.; Scribner, S. (1977): In reference to writing: some analyses of texts produced by children. Paper presented at NIE Conference on Writing, June 13–15.

Scribner, S. (1979): Invited presentation. Bellagio IV Workshop on Literacy, Italy.

Scribner, S. (1980): The concept of practice in research on culture and thought. Lecture.

Scribner, S. (1980): Studying literacy at work: bringing the laboratory to the field. Paper presented at NIE Conference on Basic Skills for Productivity and Participation, Washington, D.C., May.*

Scribner, S. (1981): Psychology and education in China. Paper presented at the Center for Applied Linguistics, January 19.

Scribner, S. (1983/1992): Mind in action: a functional approach to thinking. Paper presented at the Society for Research in Child Development biennial meeting, April 24, 1983. Posthumously printed in quarterly newsletter of the Laboratory of Comparative Human Cognition, 14, 4, 103–10, 1992.*

Scribner, S. (1984): Does ontogeny recapitulate history?: An examination of Vygotsky's sociohistorical theory. Paper prepared for presentation at the 23rd International Congress of Psychology, Acapulco, Mexico, September 2–7.

Scribner, S. (1985?): Externalizing mind. Paper possibly presented at American Anthropological Association Meeting at symposium on Soviet psychology and the social construction of cognition.

Scribner, S. (1985): Introductory remarks and discussion from session, "Literacy and Human Development," in which Scribner was a discussant, at the Conference on the Future of Literacy in a Changing World, University of Pennsylvania.

Scribner, S. (1985): Three developmental paradigms. Paper presented at symposium, "Soviet Psychology and the Social Construction of Cognition," American Anthropological Association annual meeting, Washington, D.C.*

Scribner, S. (1987): Literacy as a social activity. Paper presented at the Center for the Study of Writing and Literacy, School of Education, State University of New York at Albany.

Scribner, S.; Sachs, P. (1987): Cognitive studies of work. Paper presented at the annual meeting of the American Anthropological Association, Chicago, November 27.

Sachs, P.; Scribner, S. (1989): Technology and production ideology. Paper presented at American Anthropological Association, Washington, D.C.

Martin, L. M. W.; Scribner, S.; Beach, K. (1990): Hand to symbol: studying the transformation of machining activity by the introduction of computer control. Paper presented at the Second International Standing Conference for Research on Activity Theory, Helsinki, Finland.

Sachs, P.; Scribner, S. (1990): Work practices, knowledge and culture: organization confusion. Lecture.

Part IV: Reports

Scribner, S. (1964): Notes on insurance coverage of mental illness (excerpts from a report of the National Institute of Labor Education).

Scribner, S. (1966): Mental health and labor organizations. Final report by National Institute of Labor Education (NILE) to National Institute of Mental Health.

Scribner, S. (1974): Cross-cultural studies of cognitive skills among an adult blue-collar population. Prospectus submitted to NIE.

Bartlett, E. J.; Scribner, S. (1977): A study of referring expressions in children's written narratives. Report to the Ford Foundation.

Scribner, S. (1982): Acquisition of practical problem-solving skills. Proposal submitted to National Science Foundation.

Scribner, S. (1982): Learning studies of practical problem-solving. Proposal submitted to National Institute of Education, later withdrawn.

Scribner, S. (1983): Acquisition of practical problem-solving skills. Narrative report reviewing the first year of the project, submitted to National Science Foundation. (See proposal by same title, 1982.)

Scribner, S. (1985): Cognitive skill acquisition at work. Proposal to National Center on Education and Employment (NCEE) through Institute on Education and the Economy (IEE), Teachers College, Columbia University. (See progress reports, 1987 and 1988.)

Harman, D.; McDermott, R. P.; Scribner, S. (1986): Literacy and the workplace: interdisciplinary perspectives and recommendations for a troubled area of educational practice. Proposal by the Institute on Education and Economy (IEE), Teachers College, Columbia University.

Harman, D.; McDermott, R. P.; Scribner, S. (1986): Illiteracy: conceptualizing it and solving it. Preproposal submitted to Rockefeller Foundation by IEE, Teachers College, Columbia University.

Scribner, S. (1987): Cognitive skill acquisition at work. Progress report to National Center on Education and Employment (NCEE). (See proposal, 1985, and progress report, 1988.)

Scribner, S. (1988): Cognitive skill acquisition at work. Progress report to National Center on Education and Employment (NCEE). (See proposal, 1985, and progress report, 1987.)

Scribner, S. (1988): Technical and symbolic knowledge in CNC machining. Proposal to National Center for Research in Vocational Education (NCRVE) through IEE (Institute on Education and the Economy), Teachers College, Columbia University.

Scribner, S. (1989): Analysis and synthesis of cognitive studies of work. Proposal to National Center for Research in Vocational Education (NCRVE).

Scribner, S.; Sachs, P. (1987–90): A study of on-the-job training. Final report to National Center on Education and Employment, later issued as *NCEE Technical Paper* no. 13.

Scribner, S. (1990): Learning in the workplace. Narrative report to Spencer Foundation.

Scribner, S.; Sachs, P.; with DiBello, L.; Kindred, J. (1991): Knowledge acquisition at work. Final report to National Center on Education and Employment. Later issues as *NCEE Technical Paper* no. 22.

Beach, K.; Scribner, S.; Zazanis, E. (1992): Counting by weighing in a stockroom: the transformation of ratio in technological artifacts and practice. Report to Spencer Foundation.

Part V: Other unpublished works

Scribner, S. (1966): Comparison study of Amalgamated Clothing Workers [Health] Insurance Fund Claimants. Part I: Characteristics of claimants with chronic nonmental conditions. Part II: Psychiatric claimants.

Scribner, S. (1966): Some observations on the influence of task requirements on the recall process.

Scribner, S. (1968/1992): Cognitive consequences of literacy. Albert Einstein College of Medicine, New York. Posthumously printed in the quarterly newsletter of LCHC (1992) 14, 4, 84–102.*

Scribner, S. (1970): A cross-cultural study of perceptions of mental disorder. Dissertation submitted to the Faculty of Political and Social Science of the New School for Social Research, New York.

Scribner, S. (1976): Critical review of *Social Class and Mental Illness,* by August B. Hollingshead and Frederick C. Redlich, New York, 1958.*

Scribner, S. (1977): Intelligence tests: a comparative perspective. Working paper no. 1, Institute for Comparative Human Development and Laboratory of Comparative Human Cognition (LCHC), Rockefeller University, New York.*

Crandall, J.; Jacob, E.; Scribner, S. (1979): Looking at literacy. To have been published in *North East Training News.*

Scribner, S.; Fahrmeier, E. (1983): Practical and theoretical arithmetic. Working Paper no. 3. Industrial Literacy Project. City University of New York.

Scribner, S.; Schafft, G. (1983): Literacy in unions: an interview account. Working Paper no. 2. Industrial Literacy Project. City University of New York.

Scribner, S.; Orasanu, J. (1987): Investigations of syllogism schema development in cross-cultural perspective.

Name Index

Subject index

activity theory, 231–3, 237, 239, 241–3, 258–62, 296–307, 309, 319–35, 367–74, 375–83, 385
  in the workplace, 367–74, 386
  See also sociohistorical theory, and cognitive psychology
Ad Hoc Committee of Psychologists for Social Responsibility. *See* Psychologists for Social Action
advocacy, 3–4, 15, 28–30
American Psychological Association (APA), 16, 402, 404
American Student Union (ASU), xxi, 399
anthropology, 95–6. *See also* cross-cultural studies

bias
  cultural, 96–7
  empirical, 108, 121, 140
    examples of, 132–5
    task-dependent, 137–9

child–primitive comparisons, 241–2, 247–53
  counting, 248
  memory, 248
  writing, 248
China
  extent of literacy in, 216–17
  literacy education programs, 218–21
  measures of literacy, 217–18
cognition
  as culturally mediated, 268–9
  mode of development, 270–1
  purposive activity and, 269–70
  See also culture, cognition and
cognitive development, 237–9, 241–62, 266–78, 281–7
  See also ontogeny; phylogeny; recapitulation theory
"cognitive revolution," 3
community psychology, representatives of
  "new clinical" psychologists, 35–6
  "social action" psychologists, 33–5
  social engineers, 36–7
  social movement psychologists, 32–3
concepts, formation of, 180–2

creativity, 381–2
cross-cultural studies, 90–3
  the experimental method and, 94–104
  on verbal reasoning, 126–9
  See also Kpelle research; Vai research
culture
  cognition and, 72–3, 90–3
  logic and, 125–43
  oral versus literate, 172–80

developmental paradigms
  individualist, 281–2
  social interactionist, 282–7

explanations
  empirical, 131–2, 135–7
  population differences and, 131–2, 134–5
  theoretical, 131–2, 135–7
  for wrong answers, 135–7

genres, logical, 140–3. *See also* performances; schemas
Group Health Insurance study/pilot program, 20, 22

Hunts Point Multiservice Mental Health Center, 60–3

infallibility–fallibility myth, 56
integrative levels concept, 178–80, 230–1
  higher psychological functions, 253–8
intelligence
  tests
    categories of, 148–9
    comparative use of, 91–2
    historical background, 150–2
    medical tests, compared, 146–8
    nonspecificity of, 149–50
    social selection function, 152–3
  at work. *See* work
International Symposium for Literacy, 209
Interrace Commission (Smith College), xxi, 399–400

Learning in doing: Social, cognitive, and computational perspectives

GENERAL EDITORS: ROY PEA
JOHN SEELY BROWN

The construction zone: Working for cognitive change in school
Dennis Newman, Peg Griffin, and Michael Cole
Plans and situated actions: The problem of human–machine interaction
Lucy Suchman
Situated learning: Legitimate peripheral participation
Jean Lave and Etienne Wenger
Street mathematics and school mathematics
Terezinha Nunes, Analucia Dias Schliemann, and David William Carraher
Distributed cognitions: Psychological and educational considerations
Gavriel Salomon (editor)
Understanding practice: Perspectives on activity and context
Seth Chaiklin and Jean Lave (editors)
Sociocultural studies of mind
James V. Wertsch, Pablo del Río, and Amelia Alvarez (editors)
Sociocultural psychology: Theory and practice of doing and knowing
Laura Martin, Katherine Nelson, and Ethel Tobach (editors)